Broadcasting Baseball

MW00339350

Broadcasting Baseball

A History of the National Pastime on Radio and Television

Eldon L. Ham

McFarland & Company, Inc., Publishers
Jefferson, North Carolina, and London

All photographs herein are from the Library of Congress
unless otherwise credited

LIBRARY OF CONGRESS CATALOGUING-IN-PUBLICATION DATA

Ham, Eldon L., 1952–
Broadcasting baseball : a history of the national pastime
on radio and television / Eldon L. Ham.
p.   cm.
Includes bibliographical references and index.

ISBN 978-0-7864-4644-5
softcover : 50# alkaline paper ∞

1. Baseball announcers — History.   2. Radio and baseball —
History.   3. Radio sports events — History.
4. Television and baseball — History.
5. Televised baseball games — History.   I. Title.
GV742.3.H36   2011
070.4' 49796357 — dc23   2011020120

BRITISH LIBRARY CATALOGUING DATA ARE AVAILABLE

©2011 Eldon L. Ham. All rights reserved

*No part of this book may be reproduced or transmitted in any form
or by any means, electronic or mechanical, including photocopying
or recording, or by any information storage and retrieval system,
without permission in writing from the publisher.*

Front cover: Graham McNamee of W.E.A.E. broadcasting
a game of the World Series, October 5, 1924 (Library of Congress);
background © 2011 Shutterstock

Manufactured in the United States of America

*McFarland & Company, Inc., Publishers
Box 611, Jefferson, North Carolina 28640
www.mcfarlandpub.com*

If the medium is the message, then baseball is more,
It is not just a game, it is history and legend and American lore.
So no gratitude is done nor any dedication true,
Unless it is thus: for friends and family — and posterity, too.

Acknowledgments

Many thanks are owed to those who made this book possible, including friends and family, especially my wife Nan and children Carla and Brandon for their continuing support; Chicago-Kent College of Law for its belief in a promising student long ago; a cadre of teachers who made a difference throughout the years as well as my parents who did more of the same; my assistant, researcher, and critic Meghan Malooly; a parade of icons on the field from Ruth and Gehrig to Robinson, Mays, Mantle, Maris, and all the rest; and the treasure trove of announcers, technicians, and visionaries who molded baseball with their words, insight, and love for the game, including these who offered their personal time and insight: broadcast legend and Ford Frick winner Milo Hamilton, Mitch Rosen from WSCR Sports Radio Chicago, CBS Radio executive Rod Zimmerman, and radio host and baseball aficionado Mike Murphy.

Contents

Acknowledgments vi
Preface 1
Introduction 5

1. Watching Radio 9
2. The Talking Box 20
3. Little Cat Feet 32
4. Going, Going — Gone! 44
5. Murderers, Monkeys, and Radio Men 58
6. Radio Wars 72
7. A Game of Infamy 84
8. The Game of Our Fathers 98
9. The Quantum Leap: Television 115
10. The Game of the Week 126
11. The Great Home Run Chase 139
12. Holy Cow 154
13. Seashells, Balloons, and Walk-Off Home Runs 168
14. All's Fair in Love and Baseball 184
15. A Word from Our Sponsor 200
16. Wagging the Dog 213
17. The Prodigal Game 233

Chapter Notes 241
Bibliography 256
Index 265

Preface

There are legions of books on baseball history, several of which specifically address baseball either on television or on the radio. This book, *Broadcasting Baseball: A History of the National Pastime on Radio and Television*, combines all such elements by studying the evolution of baseball broadcasting from the rather crude game-time reports telegraphed to neighborhood bars in the late nineteenth century to the New Millennium and the Internet. By the 1920s the game would be influenced greatly by the commercialization of radio, and later the development of transistors, television, color television, satellite transmission, sophisticated visual graphics like the Fox K-Zone, instant replay, and now, of course, the Internet.

There are also many other books on the great baseball broadcasters, some recounting the top announcers as a group, some taking on one broadcaster at a time in detailed biographies. This book necessarily includes many of the most influential broadcasters from radio and television, but it is not intended solely as an anthology of the game's great broadcasters. Rather, this is a study of baseball broadcasting as a much broader product of technology, business, entertainment, baseball history, and even fate. Nonetheless, there certainly is a significant role that continues to be played by the game's announcers, many of whom became almost a family friend to their loyal listeners. Accordingly, this book devotes particular attention to 18 of baseball broadcasting's prestigious Ford Frick Award winners including Mel Allen ("Going, going — gone!"), Harry Caray ("Holy cow"), Jack Buck, Milo Hamilton, Harry Kalas, Jack Brickhouse, and Vin Scully; several other key broadcasters like Chip Caray, Joe Buck, and Tim McCarver; and a host of early announcers such as Harold Arlin, Grantland Rice, and later Dizzy Dean and even Ronald Reagan.

Since there is a paucity of books that address the entire amalgam of baseball broadcasting from the telegraph to the HD-TV and the Internet, this book partly fills that gap — yet I have tried to offer still more by taking the relationship between broadcasting and baseball much further, recognizing both the impact of baseball on broadcasting as well as the inverse: the profound influence of broadcasting on the game itself. As it happens, the deliberate pace of baseball was perfect for radio, a medium that relies upon the creation of images through descriptive word pictures painted by skilled announcers who discovered that radio may by the most visual of all the electronic media. Moreover, it so

1

happens that baseball home runs and scoring took a quantum leap forward with Ruth, Gehrig, and the New York Yankees of the 1920s just as radio was being commercialized. Since all these factors converged at once, radio contributed to the rapid ascension of baseball as our national game, propelling baseball beyond even professional boxing as the premier sport in America. If the game had not done so already, when Ruth dethroned Jack Dempsey as our premier sports icon, baseball certainly solidified itself as the undisputed national pastime.

This book recognizes the inescapable relationship between the game itself and the transmission of the game over the airwaves—the medium, to a large extent, becoming the message, *à la* Marshall McLuhan. The story of baseball broadcasting is told mostly in chronological order, for each step in the necessary evolution of such broadcasting has influenced the next steps, one building on another, some aided by happenstance and fate, like Harold Arlin wandering into the fledgling KDKA in Pittsburgh solely out of curiosity, then emerging as the first genuine baseball announcer on radio. The book tracks the technological innovations that made game transmissions possible and, unlike most other baseball books, also recognizes the impact of other sports, like the NFL's *Monday Night Football*, a prime-time sports experiment with multiple announcers in the booth, and NCAA basketball, which contributed the colorful Al McGuire who reinvented the role of the side-kick color announcer with his magically entertaining vocabulary and observations ("If the waitress has dirty ankles, the chili should be good."). Although necessarily nostalgic, this book is not simply sentimental, for the development of baseball broadcasting was also a cold-blooded chronology of cutthroat business, recalcitrant owners, antitrust cartels, legal wrangling, capitalism, power, and money.

No treatise can thoroughly tell the whole combined history of baseball broadcasting in one volume, of course; regrettably, a number of solid contributors to baseball broadcasting have been left out, but that should not diminish the value of their respective contributions to the continuum of baseball and broadcasting. Still, *Broadcasting Baseball* does paint the comprehensive evolution of baseball, broadcasting, entertainment, and inevitable sentiment as a composite account, one that embraces the on-air talent, the contributions of big business like AT&T, RCA, NBC, and later ESPN and Fox, the entertainment value of the game, and ultimately the impact of broadcasting on the game itself.

Baseball broadcasting is a dynamic marriage of sports and entertainment. Nothing in history, business, entertainment, or sports happens in a vacuum — indeed, all the pieces are interrelated in a cause-and-effect progression best described by Darwin, for the collective impact of such otherwise independent pieces as Babe Ruth, Vin Scully, the radio transistor, satellites, and instant replay is the true essence of the history of baseball broadcasting. Perhaps cartoonist Chic Young recognized as much when his American "everyman" character, Dagwood Bumstead, distilled the essence of baseball even as he exaggerated the game's literal impact: "Baseball, my son, is the cornerstone of civilization."

This book was extensively researched with observations and sources copiously noted over 700 times. It is unique in that it is the product of many web-based sources that would have been impossible to search, compile, and utilize as little as a decade ago. Even so, I attempted to use what appear to be credible sources rather than individual blogs, random personal sites, or even the ubiquitous Wikipedia, although the latter was helpful in establishing timelines and points of interest that I could then verify elsewhere. I have retained a hard copy of each page that was utilized regardless of its origin, including the Internet, an invaluable resource which, by its nature, can be mercurial. Sources include newspaper articles, magazine articles, numerous websites, published books and treatises, and even published legal cases.

All sources were important, but much information came from a few distinct resources: early editions of the *Chicago Daily Tribune* and *New York Times*; websites base balllibrary.com, baseball-reference.com, baseballchronology.com, and baseballalma nac.com; an early edition of Burt Solomon's extensive study *The Baseball Timeline* (from 1997); Curt Smith's *Voices of Summer*; *The Cultural History of Baseball* by Jonathan Frasier Light; John Helyar's *Lords of the Realm*; *Center Field Shot* by James Walker and Robert V. Bellamy, Jr.; and *Baseball's Greatest Quotations* by Paul Dickson. A few personal interviews were included, but the book does not rely extensively on interviews and personal recollections. It does offer, however, a mix of vital anecdotal history, statistics, treatises, and other studies and reports, as well as a number of conclusions and relationships drawn by the author.

In summary, *Broadcasting Baseball* is not just about the chronology of baseball broadcasting, it embraces how it all came to be through a wide variety of print and electronic sources from the early 1900s to the present.

Introduction

Of all the dramatic media, radio is the most visual.
— JOHN REEVES[1]

"All I remember about my wedding day in 1967 is that the Cubs lost a double-header," lamented George Will, national columnist, political pundit, and unabashed Cubs fan.[2] The history of baseball broadcasting is not something that suddenly sprang from a gritty infield. It did not begin; it evolved. Perhaps it began with telegraph reports of games in progress during the late nineteenth century. If there indeed is a starting point for baseball broadcasting, as that term is presently understood, it may have occurred during the frigid North Atlantic darkness of April 15, 1912, when a new wireless communication system provided its mettle as a sinking *Titanic* sent emergency SOS messages that were received by the rescue ship *Carpathia*.[3] The device was not yet called radio and it delivered no audible words, just signals. But nine years later this new technology would find itself inside a talking box that would transport a major league baseball game over the stadium walls to a handful of awestruck listeners in Pittsburgh. From there the evolution of baseball broadcasting would parallel, and to a degree cause, the transformation of a mere game into a metaphor for America itself.

On December 24, 1906, in the dark stillness of Christmas Eve, the radio operators of a ship floating in the frigid Atlantic waters off the coast of New England went about their routine sending and receiving the usual dot-and-dash messages. Suddenly, to their great wonder and astonishment, a human voice penetrated the tranquil darkness and replaced the stark Morse code messaging with words from the Gospel of Luke read over the sound of a violin that serenely played "Silent Night." The mystery voice wished them all a merry Christmas and then disappeared. That threshold event has been described as a near religious experience for those who heard this sweet sounding voice from what seemed like Heaven.

Other ship operators that night shared the same epiphany. But those historic words did not come from God — unless God was 40-year-old Reginald Fessenden, an engineer and hobbyist who had been tinkering with radio voice experiments for years.[4] These first crude efforts were cutting edge, and by 1907 a new radio tube called the Audion was

5

invented to increase clarity and power, thus enhancing the ability of radio to transmit voices in addition to the simple rhythmic tapping of Morse code. Ty Cobb did not know it, nor did the great Honus Wagner or a promising 11-year-old youngster named George Herman Ruth, but that fateful night, somewhere over the blackened, frosty North Atlantic, the history of baseball broadcasting was set into motion.

Perhaps we are a nation of George Wills, for baseball's indelible grip on America reaches nearly every region and fabric of our culture from farmers as they work their fields, auto repair bays, hospital beds, political columnists, and even presidents: Barack Obama is often seen with his White Sox baseball cap, and his predecessor George W. Bush actually owned the Texas Rangers. Some of us may simply be drawn to, if not sadly afflicted by, lost causes and baseball futility, so by whatever confluence of fate, reason, and fiat that may have been at work, baseball did indeed become our national game. Baseball's exalted status is hardly a revelation, however, for its "national pastime" standing has long been a worn cliché of yesterday's news. Yet the more compelling follow-up question is seldom asked: "*Why?*"

Why baseball? Broadcasting is a major reason. Baseball is a deliberately paced game that provided the perfect intervals for early radio announcers to bring colorful tales of baseball lore into America's living rooms. Baseball is a unique game with no clock and irregular outfields that provides explosive slices of drama because, after all, it is really a one-on-one sports confrontation disguised as a team sport. In 1920 a young slugger with a heavy bat and chip on his shoulder found himself on the New York stage just as radio was finding itself. As radio, Babe Ruth, baseball, and the twentieth century all matured together, baseball became the game of our fathers and mothers and grandparents. So part of the *why baseball?* answer lurks within the wistful sentimentality of the game itself, as personified, for example, by the compelling prose of W.P. Kinsella in the quintessential baseball yarn *Shoeless Joe*, the basis for the visually haunting *Field of Dreams* motion picture:

> It is the same game that Moonlight Graham played in 1905. It is a living part of history, like calico dresses, stone crockery, and threshing crews eating at outdoor tables. It continually reminds us of what was, like an Indian-head penny in a handful of new coins.[5]

Moonlight Graham was a real ballplayer who played just a half inning for the New York Giants on June 29, 1905. Archibald Wright Graham had performed in the minor leagues for three years before landing on the Giants roster in May 1905 where he warmed the bench until his chance finally arrived. Graham was sent into a game against Brooklyn (the Brooklyn "Superbas") in the bottom of the eighth inning to play right field, replacing George Browne. In the bottom of the ninth, Graham was on deck when teammate Claude Elliott flied out, ending the game. Graham never batted, and never got another big league chance.[6] His plight has been much fodder for fact and fiction, for Graham personifies the "so close yet so far" whims of fortuity. For Graham, however, it was not all bad; while playing in the minors another three years he managed to get his medical degree from the University of Maryland, then became a small town doctor and practiced for half a century in Chisholm, Minnesota, where the Graham Scholarship Fund still aids two graduating Chisholm students each year.

Author Kinsella had been intrigued by Graham's fleeting glimpse of the majors, making note of his nickname and short career, then later molding him into a character for his book.[7] "The only thing I regret about my baseball career," said this fictional version of Graham, "is not having the chance to stare down a big league pitcher, to give him a wink just to throw him off."[8] The real Graham died in 1965, but his emotional story lives on. In a bid to become governor of New Jersey, candidate Douglas R. Forrester cited Moonlight Graham's hopes and unrealized dreams in an interview run by the *New York Times* on November 3, 2005, four full decades after Graham's death.

Archibald "Moonlight" Graham's fateful 1905 was also the first year that pitchers were allowed to throw the spitball in major league games—an irony that goes beyond Moonlight's missed opportunity, for the spitball still contributes to the wistful legends and mischievous lore of big league baseball. Graham's career and Kinsella's words both paint a visual and nostalgic image for posterity, treating the longevity of baseball as an enduring American romance, one that pays homage to a great pastime without peeling the next layer, an inquiry of cause and effect that suggests the fundamental reason that explains how baseball penetrated our national gut: fate.

The root of all baseball, as with history itself, is the fortuitous force of man and nature that is behind all that has occurred from the dawn of time, and from observation to motivation. A form of sociological evolution placed baseball into the heart of a nation because, in the end, neither posterity nor baseball had a real choice. In the early twentieth century, baseball was pulled forward by an auspicious chain of coincidental forces that converged during one threshold decade, a phenomenon that would forever assure baseball's status as our national game: the prosperous Roaring Twenties, the emergence of Ruth, key rule changes like banning the spitball to boost baseball offense — and radio.

1

Watching Radio

Best-selling author Malcolm Gladwell, a noted observer of cause and effect in life and fortuity, studies the phenomenon we call fate by noting the convergence of numerous apparent coincidences overlaying, and contributing to, such fundamental ingredients as talent, knowledge, insight, and determination. Gladwell argues that although billionaire Microsoft founder Bill Gates was himself the product of intelligence and ambition, he also benefited from a timely string of coincidences. Gates was born at precisely the right moment, within a critical 1950s window of just a few years, a key time that placed him at the beginning of the computer era in, as it happens, the exact right place — Seattle. Just at the cultural precipice of the computer revolution, Gates had been born into a family wealthy enough to send him to a private school where there just happened to be a computer club and unlimited access to a time-sharing terminal that had a direct link to a mainframe in downtown Seattle in 1968 when Gates was emerging as an eager teenager. So Bill Gates found himself doing real-time computer programming in the eighth grade, years and even decades before most people would have such an extraordinary opportunity.[1]

So what about baseball? Those four fateful events — Ruth, radio, rule changes, and the Roaring Twenties — all converged in the same decade partly by coincidence, although some of them were likely manipulated. In any event, whether by fiat or manipulation, had baseball not hit stride during the prosperous 1920s and the early days of radio, the game may never have become what it once was — and what it may largely still be, even in the go-go world of relentless action and video-game speed of football, hockey and basketball. Perhaps baseball's role could, at some point, have been filled by football or basketball or maybe boxing — after all, heavyweight boxing was the king of sports during those days of Jack Dempsey and Gene Tunney. Championship boxing enjoyed many days in the sun, but it could never fully supplant a team sport like baseball since boxers can only fight occasionally while baseball has long enjoyed a prolific season of 154 games or more. Boxing made other good runs after Dempsey, of course, especially during the days of Max Baer and Joe Louis, and again during the last great era of modern boxing defined by the charismatic Muhammad Ali, but its traction began to slip long before the arrival of the New Millennium.

The Advent of Radio

What about baseball, a slower, even deliberate sport known for its cerebral approach? After all, today's NBA provides an entertaining team sport predicated on speed, action, skill, and endurance, yet it is hard to imagine a nation transfixed by nostalgic musings over slam dunks. But such sentimentality is precisely what comes from strikeouts, untimely errors, spitballs, the magical promised land of marquee home runs, and the wistful imagery of such diverse living figures as Moonlight Graham and Babe Ruth. So any distinction based on success, failure, fame, or frenetic speed, though helpful, still only begs the real question.

The answer begins with radio. Like the ingredients of a prize-winning stew or a world-changing potion hinged on the mystical formula of Coca-Cola, it is not just the individual pieces that are important, but also how and when they are stirred together. In the case of baseball, each of Ruth, radio and the Roaring Twenties collided with history at the same fateful time, together giving baseball a bigger-than-life image at precisely the moment it was able to reach beyond the ballpark all the way into pool halls, machine shops, hospitals, parlors, and living rooms. In that very same era, Red Grange exploded onto the football universe with epic touchdowns against Michigan, and soon thereafter Grange helped legitimize the National Football League when he was snatched from the University of Illinois by NFL founder George S. Halas in the midst of those same Roaring Twenties. So why Ruth and not Grange? Even non-sports fans still remember Babe Ruth, but all but the most astute football fans have largely forgotten Grange.

As it happens, professional football would not flourish until the 1950s and 1960s, while baseball had soared to a new level many decades before. Radio, a medium perfectly suited for the deliberate pace of baseball, came first, then television, a visual electronic wonder that capitalized on the speed and imagery of football, proliferated in the 1960s along with football itself. Today, although modern football generally enjoys better television ratings than baseball, and the popular Super Bowl has even spawned a secular national holiday, more fans still attend baseball games in person. After all, there are only eight NFL home games during each team's regular season while baseball packs them in for 81 games in each park, more than 10 times the rate for football, an overwhelming advantage even considering that football stadiums hold more fans than most baseball parks. So for myriad reasons, football never really gripped the soul of America the way baseball did, with the biggest difference traced to a diminutive but profound talking box first referred to as the "wireless" before it was eventually called by the name it is known as today: radio.

"I watch a lot of baseball on radio," confessed former president Gerald Ford in 1978, probably not intending the profound insight that renders his irony all the more interesting.[2] (Even more ironic, Ford himself had been a star football player, leading the University of Michigan to national titles in 1932 and 1933 playing center and linebacker.) Intentional or not, Ford's comment offers an insightful explanation about the symbiotic relationship of radio and baseball, for the visual imagery of radio provided the perfect platform for a thoughtful team game built on timing, careful strategy, and essential intervals. Intervals are not to be overlooked; they are necessary to speech, music, dance, and indeed the cadence of sports in general but baseball in particular. Without intervals, the notes comprising music would just be random noise; without its deliberate interval moments punc-

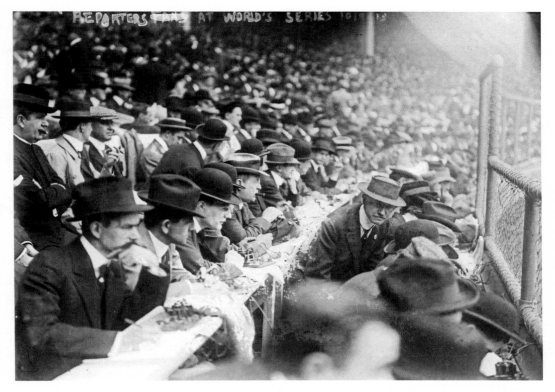

Reporters at New York's Polo Grounds during the 1913 World Series before Babe Ruth, home runs, and radio began to influence major league baseball. Print journalism was still king, with only live games and occasional game-time telegraph reports competing for the baseball entertainment dollar.

tuated by individual effort and team play, baseball could never have been right for radio. But baseball *did* provide a thoughtful, deliberate pace uncontaminated by the relentless time clock that partially drives, but also gets in the way of, other competing diversions. Baseball, without knowing it, was built for radio. The advent of radio necessarily exploited that quality at exactly the right time, propelling both the game and the talking box to new heights of national entertainment by painting dramatic word pictures directly from the ballparks of America.

Another contributing ingredient to the evolution of baseball is summertime, which, of course, is also the product of fate. Baseball began to provide, then became identified with, the wistful sounds of summer, the voices of the game connecting us to open summer windows, the zestful barking of neighborhood dogs, the joyous laughter of children at play, and the singular crack of big league thunder and the ensuing roar of the crowd. Together, these disparate ingredients comprised a fateful American hodgepodge we call baseball, a game of summer that long ago transcended the airwaves to reach the homes, barbershops, and filling stations of America at a time when many of us were at work or play outdoors, or maybe relaxing on the front porch or dozing in the backyard hammock. Wherever Americans could be found, radio was often nearby. And in the spring and summer months, that meant baseball was there, too.

As a result, our language remains laced with baseball references from strikeouts to curveballs and screwballs, left field, touching base, playing hardball, and swinging for the fences—clear evidence of the game's exalted place in the American psyche. For example, one can throw a "home run" in football, but nothing that occurs in baseball is ever referred to as a touchdown. A major reason is that professional football already had at least two strikes against it—pun intended—as the 1920s unfolded. At the time, baseball had already established itself as a national presence even before Ruth with such stars as Honus Wagner, Ty Cobb, Tris Speaker, and Cy Young, while football was still finding itself when radio took hold. But football also lacked the deliberate rhythm of baseball, forever dooming it until television gained traction forty years later. By then it was too late, for baseball was already embedded in our national gut.

With its measured cadence, cerebral approach, and near mythical stars, especially Ruth, baseball was poised for radio, a game to be "seen" through the ears of millions via the resonant broadcast imagery of Red Barber, Grantland Rice, Damon Runyon, Dizzy Dean, Mel Allen and others—not to mention the modest play-by-play beginnings of one future president in Ronald Reagan.

Radio broadcasts were not always easy or even especially entertaining, however, as the new medium worked to find itself. Initially, baseball games produced a lot of dead air from live announcers. The first time a radio voice announced a big league baseball game was August 5, 1921, when the Pirates beat Philadelphia, 8–5, at Pittsburgh's Forbes Field. Harold Arlin was at the game, announcing over Pittsburgh's KDKA from a ground-level box where he plopped a telephone on a wooden plank across his seat. It was a first for radio and baseball, but it was anything but artistic since it produced a sea silence called "dead air," for it had not occurred to Arlin and other early announcers to talk between plays. Baseball on the radio with no dialogue or color proved a great bore, yet the experiment would still profoundly impact baseball history—although not right away.

KDKA was duly licensed as a radio station only one year before, and at the time there were only a few hundred radio receivers within range. Compounding the issue was the baseball owner who not only failed to embrace the new medium, but actually *feared* radio. In fact, the owners would have killed it if they could, thinking that baseball on the radio would keep fans away from the gate. The exact opposite would happen, of course, although the owners were slow to recognize it.

The Arrival of Ruth

With radio firmly on board, baseball also found itself with a built-in source of marquee headlines. In 1920, the same year that KDKA was born, a baseball superstar in the making was shipped from Boston to the grandest stage of the early twentieth century: New York City. Babe Ruth was a promising young pitcher, but he had already shown signs of another unique talent: home runs. In 1918, Ruth the pitcher clubbed 11 long balls, followed by 29 more in 1919, both totals leading the league—not just for pitchers, but all players. Ruth was already making his mark on the game, changing it from a punch-and-Judy singles and doubles exercise to a long ball spectacle that brought a greater sense of awe, excitement, and drama to the game.

Before Ruth, the league leaders often hit only 8 to 10 home runs per year, and one such slugger was so prodigious that "home run" became part of his name — yet Frank "Home Run" Baker banged out just nine long balls in 1914. The last player to lead the league outright prior to Ruth's run was another player stung by fate, the inimitable Wally Pipp, who managed nine homers to top the league in 1917. Pipp, as it happens, contributed to the romance of baseball not with his homers, but simply by getting sick. Pipp, who led the league in homers for two straight seasons, is best known in baseball lore for his famous headache that opened the first base slot to Lou Gehrig in 1925. The headache was real, but the importance of Pipp's role in the arrival of Gehrig is overstated, offering more of a colorful legend than a genuine catalyst. Parenthetically, Pipp was not a hapless loser as legend suggests, but rather was a quality player in his own right who lasted in the league 15 years, including a dozen with the Yankees.

Rule Changes

Another subtle but influential change to the game also occurred in 1920: the spitball was banned. The spitter had only recently been discovered in 1902, making its way to the big leagues in the form of a surprise pitch hurled by Brooklyn's Elmer Stricklett in 1905. Meanwhile the prodigious Ruth was already altering the way baseball would be played, and home run power was suddenly king. Seeing the lure of offense in general and the long ball in particular, the owners took the spitball advantage away from the pitchers— although they did grandfather in the existing spitballers well into the 1930s, 17 such pitchers in all. Veteran Burleigh Grimes threw the last legal spitball in 1934 just before retiring. With Ruth in New York, the spitter banned, and the prosperity of the Roaring Twenties driving both team attendance and technological advances that accelerated radio engineering and also quickly turned the talking box into an affordable consumer product, radio was ready to propel baseball to previously unknown heights.

The owners, though, remained afraid to take the final, full plunge into radio. They were comfortable broadcasting the World Series on the radio, for who would stay home from the Series, they reasoned, radio broadcasts or not? In 1921, Ruth's second year in New York, the Yankees met the Giants in the first "subway" World Series ever played. John McGraw's Giants won 94 games that year, led by Frank Frisch who hit a stellar .341 on the season, and George Kelly, who led the National League with 23 homers. Not only did Ruth smash a quantum leap 59 home runs with a .378 average and 171 RBIs during the regular season, his teammate Bob Meusel clubbed 24 such jacks. Those two sluggers revealed a long ball preview of the coming murderers' row juggernaut that would hit its full stride in 1927.

Interestingly, the "subway" depiction of the 1921 Series may have been colorful as well as legendary, but technically it was not correct. Yankee Stadium would not open until 1923, so at the time both teams played their games at the fabled Polo Grounds and, therefore, no travel at all was involved — not even on the subway. Game One was played on October 5, 1921, resulting in a Yankee shutout, 3–0. But radio and baseball continued to make history, as that first game was broadcast over the airwaves both on WJZ in New Jersey, where wireless bulletins were relayed and read over the air, and also the pioneering KDKA which carried a direct feed announced over the phone wires by sportswriting icon Grantland Rice.[3]

A New York City crowd gathered to "watch" baseball publicly depicted during the 1911 World Series by means of a billboard-type "play-o-graph." Also shown is supporting information displayed to the crowd, while a large graphic of a baseball diamond (which was placed on the adjacent wall, to the right, outside this photo shoot) showed the position of players on the field arranged according to game-time telegraph reports. (David Sarnoff Library, Princeton, New Jersey)

One year later, the Giants and Yankees met once again in the Series following a 1922 regular season that was marred by controversy. After the 1921 season, newly installed Commissioner Kenesaw Landis suspended three Yankees, including Ruth and Meusel, for playing in a post-season barnstorming tour in violation of major league rules. The suspension was for six weeks and was invoked at the very beginning of 1922. As a result, Ruth launched only 35 home runs in just 110 games played, but with fewer spitballs in play, three other players hit over .400 in 1922: the Brown's George Sisler batted .420 while Ty Cobb and Rogers Hornsby managed .401 each.

But the Yankees pushed on, eking out yet another pennant by one game over a very strong St. Louis Browns team. Once again radio provided a post-season first as Game One of the 1922 Series was broadcast in real time, the first time a World Series game was done play-by-play over the live air waves. Grantland Rice did the announcing once again, but this time Bill McGeehan contributed the play-by-play, while the game was carried by WJZ, WGY from Schenectady, and WBZ of Springfield, Massachusetts. Both baseball and radio were still searching for the right formula, though. Sometimes the early announcers were called "radiologists," a remarkably uninspired description that sounds much more medical than baseball. Still, in the early days, those radiologist broadcasters had not yet discovered the art of baseball gab — hence the mostly dead air between pitches, even for the World Series. But with radio receivers proliferating during the prosperous 1920s, this time a mass audience of an estimated five million heard the first game of the 1922 Series — indeed they "saw" the game — on radio.

Numbers that large were certainly capable of making an impact, but the team owners remained skeptical, fearing the power of radio even more. Although Harold Arlin's modest experiment for KDKA in August 1921 had been successful, it did not inspire teams to carry the games live, especially during the regular season. That would soon change, but not without considerable dissension.

Chicago's WMAQ pressed William Wrigley, the chewing gum magnate who had recently acquired the Cubs, to experiment with live Cubs broadcasts. In 1925, Wrigley did just that, but for reasons not fully explained the job of airing the first such game was given to Chicago's WGN radio and not WMAQ.[4] There was little doubt, though, that WGN could do the job.

On May 12, 1923, Zenith Electronics launched WJAZ and began broadcasting from Chicago's acclaimed Edgewater Beach Hotel situated on the city's north lakeshore region. Those broadcasts attracted the attention of Col. Robert R. McCormick, the publisher of the powerful *Chicago Daily Tribune*, and by early 1924 the *Tribune* had conducted a survey and determined there were over 100,000 radio receivers in the Chicago metropolitan area. McCormick tested the waters by leasing substantial blocks of time on Zenith's WJAZ, and at the same time reserved the call letters W-G-N, which stood for the "world's greatest newspaper." McCormick assumed control of WJAZ's broadcasting and gave it the WGN call letters. Meanwhile, the Drake Hotel founded the competing WDAP and so the *Tribune* jumped ship, abandoning its lease deal with WJAZ and eventually taking over WDAP altogether, changing its moniker to WGN in the process. The public announcement of the transition was made during another first, a WGN live broadcast of the Indianapolis 500 auto race on May 31, 1924.

The transition was formally completed the next day when WGN was officially launched. WGN Radio is still broadcasting today, and is one of the most powerful stations in America, reaching 38 states over the air and streaming worldwide via the Internet. By August 1924, the *Tribune* was taking its new subsidiary very seriously, transferring *Tribune* editor Quin Ryan to oversee the development of WGN Radio. In September, WGN again engineered one of many firsts by airing the live courtroom proceedings of the infamous Leopold-Loeb thrill-kill murder case, as famed attorney Clarence Darrow dramatically focused his whole defense on a compelling argument against the death penalty designed to spare the lives of his youthful clients.[5] Thereafter, on October 1, WGN experimented with another innovation when it broadcast an exhibition baseball game between the cross-town rival Cubs and White Sox, setting the stage for a major broadcasting breakthrough later in 1925. But first, WGN traveled to Champaign, Illinois, to broadcast a heavyweight football clash between the University of Illinois, led by "The Galloping Ghost" Red Grange, and the powerful University of Michigan. Quin Ryan broadcast the game from the roof of newly dedicated Memorial Stadium. This was the game that found Grange scoring four touchdowns in the first twelve minutes, anointing the contest as one of the all-time classics in college football history. WGN was there honing its live broadcasting capabilities, especially for marquee sporting events.

The Roaring Twenties

One such marquee event took place on a chilly April day in Chicago where spring is often late due to the cold Lake Michigan breezes that often linger beyond winter. It was Opening Day of the 1925 season for the Chicago Cubs, who took on the Pittsburgh Pirates behind Chicago's strong pitching of Grover Cleveland Alexander. The city eagerly anticipated another baseball season, and the *Tribune* itself looked forward to the day's event, its April 14 issue containing this quaint observation: "That the north side park — newly painted and looking as neat as a Dutch bakery — will be jammed today is a certainty." The paper was right, for over 38,000 people squeezed into what is now called Wrigley Field to witness a Cubs beating of the Pirates, 8–2.[6] Just as it had done for the historic Illinois-Michigan football game, WGN climbed to the rooftop with its field equipment, set up a temporary broadcast facility, and proceeded to air the entire game live, again courtesy of the station's fast-rising announcer Quin Ryan. Instinctively sensing the potential for the commercial application of radio, Wrigley was intrigued by the broadcasting idea, and since WGN was concurrently experimenting in sports broadcasting, the two eventually collaborated to air that Cubs' Opening Day contest.

The year 1925 fell directly in the heart of the Roaring Twenties decade of prosperity and economic growth, as America was brimming with disposable income not only to spend on sporting events, but also to splurge on new inventions like radio. The era was especially prolific for the fields of manufacturing, literature, law and radio: in 1925 alone, the Chrysler automobile company was founded, F. Scott Fitzgerald published *The Great Gatsby*, the landmark Scopes trial became a nationally followed extravaganza from Dayton, Tennessee, with WGN radio on hand, and regular season baseball broadcasts took hold.

Baseball, of course, did its part *on* the field of play, too. When Yankee Stadium opened in 1923, it featured a short right-field porch of just 294 feet, noticeably shallow even by 1920s standards. It likely was installed to enhance — and thus to a degree manipulate — the left-handed home run power of the team's new star (after all, it was called the "House That Ruth Built"), not to mention all the succeeding lefty home run hitters through the ages including Roger Maris and the switch-hitting Mickey Mantle. The field dimensions at the new Yankee Stadium are the same as they were in the original facility prior to closing: 318 feet to the left-field fences, 399 feet to left-center field, 408 feet to center field, 385 feet to right-center field, and 314 to right field. Although right field had been subtly extended over the years, it remains a very inviting target for left-handed pull hitters. The fence at the right-field foul pole is just eight feet tall, tantalizing power hitters.[7]

By 1925, another subtle but important rule change likely influenced the development of baseball on the field: balls with cushioned cork centers were introduced. It was a compelling time in baseball and sports history: the home run was king, Ruth was on the Big Apple stage of Yankee Stadium, the spitter had already been eliminated, the balls were duly juiced, and radio was ready to capture the dawn of a new baseball era.

When the Cubs beat the Pirates on Opening Day in 1925, WGN brought the game alive for a multitude of fans unable to attend the game in person. "Yesterday," reported the *Tribune*, "in the midst of a setting of 40,000 folks — 38,000 paid — he [Grover Cleveland Alexander] swung that good right arm and that trusty bat and when the last ball had been lifted into space for the final putout a howling mob of enthusiasts poured out of the north side park to spread the news."[8]

But stadium attendance concerns would remain an issue for years to come. The American League officially banned radio broadcasts for the 1926 season, but was forced to reconsider when the 1926 World Series, a classic seven-game battle won by the Cardinals over the Yankees, proved wildly popular on radio. Throughout the 1920s, the Cubs and Pirates continued to experiment with radio broadcasts, and in 1927 the first broadcast of St. Louis games was authorized — although unofficial "pirated" broadcasting from neighboring rooftops had already been underway for some time.

Billboarding Baseball

Although the attendance debate lingered, from 1925 through 1931 teams that featured no radio broadcasting experienced aggregate attendance increases of 27 percent while the Cubs, a team that had been increasing its radio exposure throughout the period, saw its own attendance skyrocket by 117 percent, more than four times the average increase for teams without radio.[9] In the early days such results seemed counter-intuitive: why go to the game if the game comes to you? But the real phenomenon at work is called "billboarding." Baseball was promoting itself over the airwaves, for radio was everywhere and, thus, so were the Cubs. As a direct result, the public became more and more hooked on baseball. Wrigley was elated, because this bill boarding effect of radio was *not* reducing attendance, rather it was *increasing* the gate by quantum leaps.

With radio spreading baseball throughout the city and beyond, more fans could follow the team and, more importantly, more non-fans could be reached who were able to follow the Cubs and develop an interest. Even fans in cars could be reached, for radio receivers were being installed in automobiles as early as 1923. Better yet, the geographic reach of the team had been expanded. Listeners in Iowa, Wisconsin, Indiana, and downstate Illinois were able to follow the Cubs, extending the fan base to many states and creating a huge Midwest following for the team. Well into the New Millennium, the Cubs still own a strong fan base in those rural areas, and every summer home game finds thousands of fans from charter buses descending on Wrigley from Des Moines to Peoria and South Bend.

Following its successful baseball debut in April 1925, WGN continued to establish itself as a sports broadcasting powerhouse. In May Quin Ryan broadcast the 51st Kentucky Derby, and in October Graham McNamee and Quin Ryan jointly broadcast the World Series between the Pirates and the Senators. In 1927 WGN was there for the Jack Dempsey vs. Gene Tunney heavyweight bout that filled Chicago's Soldier Field with 104,000 onlookers who witnessed one of the most famous sporting miscues in history: the Dempsey-Tunney long count that gave Gene Tunney at least 14 seconds (some reports suggest much more) to get off the canvas to retain his world title.[10]

What was happening? Some called it the "nowness" of radio. The talking box provided a substantial leap in real-time reporting that rapidly expanded much like the Internet explosion has advanced communication and marketing in more recent years. But in the early days, what was there to report? Radio searched far and wide for programming: political events, concerts, classic recordings, live talk, and of course sports. The same April week when the Cubs debuted on WGN radio in 1925, the following radio programming was offered across the country:

WHN–New York: Dolores Acquerina, soprano
KYW–Chicago: Uncle Bob's bedtime story
WCX–Detroit: Detroit symphony trio
WPG–Atlantic City: Hotel Traymore dinner music
WBAP–Ft. Worth: Classical music
WRZ–New England: Lecture on chief English writers of our day
KDKA–Pittsburgh: Great English storytellers
WGN–Chicago: Rocking chair time — readings from the *Chicago Tribune*
WBCN–Chicago: Police bulletins[11]

Some of those offerings seem excruciating by today's standards, like readings from the *Tribune* newspaper aired by WGN or, perhaps worse, the Hotel Traymore dinner music. But other shows, though still very crude, were ahead of their time. Perhaps a precursor to *Cops* and other law enforcement reality shows, those old police bulletins provided excitement and thus became popular radio offerings. At one point in 1929, WGN even began interrupting regular programming to actually send police bulletins to officers in their squad cars as a public service, an experiment that eventually led to the installation of the first police radios and influenced the war on Al Capone and organized crime during the 1930s.

Sports in general, and baseball in particular, also provided a healthy dose of exciting programming that was easy to produce. The game was there already and needed no script, rehearsal, or choreography. Decades later, Ted Turner recognized the value of sports programming when he purchased the Atlanta Braves to augment programming for his developing TV superstation; then he repeated the process with a purchase of the Atlanta Hawks NBA franchise. The Braves acquisition, in particular, did much to launch WTBS as a cable superstation when Ted Turner decided to send the signal nationally to other stations, creating a virtual cable superstation that gave traction to the expanding cable industry in the 1980s.

The Roar of Summer

Baseball was particularly good for radio because there was a prolific 154-game season played by each team each year (expanded to 162 games in 1961), the games were in the summer, baseball was already more popular than pro football, and the pace of baseball was tailor-made for the visual imagery that radio could muster through the colorful word pictures painted by its early broadcasters. Largely because of radio, there soon was a time when the unmistakable crack of big league bats was followed by a thunderous roar that punctuated the supreme sounds of summer in every backyard, beach, park, barbershop and gas station in America — strains that linger amidst the down-home imagery of storytellers like Bob Elson, Jack Buck, Vin Scully, Dizzy Dean, and Harry Caray. Together these men perfected not just the art of sports broadcasting, but virtually invented the baseball sounds and images that our parents and grandparents remember from Ruth and Gehrig to Williams, Mays, and Mantle.

The golden epoch of baseball came from the Roaring Twenties, flourished in the Depression era of the 1930s, rose above the barbershop din of the 1940s and 1950s, and still lingers from our cars, boats, beaches, patios and porches with a soothing cadence of big league bats, homey yarns, and those implacable big league roars of summer — the same sounds our fathers and their fathers savored in eras long gone but still shared by the great American metaphor, baseball.

Evidencing the strong role of fate in the marriage of baseball and radio were the beginnings of two particularly celebrated announcers, Jack Brickhouse and Graham McNamee. Listening to the threshold Quin Ryan broadcast of the 1924 Red Grange thrashing of Michigan was none other than a youngster destined to become a future Hall of Fame baseball broadcaster himself, Jack Brickhouse. Duly inspired by this new phenomenon of sports broadcasting, Brickhouse was drawn to WGN Radio where he later announced the Chicago Cubs for nearly forty years. Likewise, when Grantland Rice and Bill McGeehan announced Game One of the 1922 World Series to an audience of five million, one of the listeners was Graham McNamee, who lived only five miles from the Polo Grounds. Like Brickhouse, he saw himself as a baseball announcer, and two years later McNamee, originally a piano player and singer by trade, walked in cold and won an audition. By October 1923 he was on the radio calling the World Series — with none other than the same Bill McGeehan who had captivated the young McNamee in the first place.

So as the prosperous Roaring Twenties decade unfolded, the symbiotic relationship of baseball and radio was born: baseball provided the programming that would help propel the meteoric growth of radio, and radio launched baseball as the ultimate team sport during the dog days of our own youth and even that of our grandparents before us. It was a time when Ruth was royalty, baseball was America, and the airwaves were alive with the romantic roar of big league summers. Much has seemingly changed since then, like the advent of surround sound and HD-TV, the Internet, and the proliferation of NFL football shown on breathtaking plasma flat screens. But baseball is still the game heard to be seen on the diminutive talking box that changed the world and provided, as fate clearly would have it, the perfect medium for the deliberate pace of our anointed national pastime.

Baseball and radio remain inextricably tied together. Baseball has endured many ups and downs, but the history of baseball broadcasting is hardly confined to radio. With television, satellites, cable TV, superstations, the Internet, and high-definition technology still to come in the 1940s and far beyond, baseball broadcasting was just getting started. So when broadcaster Chris Berman punctuates a big league moon shot with his exuberant "back, back, back" home run call, he harkens a memorable array of announcers who brought baseball to living rooms, bedrooms, beaches, cars, and indeed America. The likes of Berman and other contemporary announcers from Bob Costas to Joe Buck and enduring legends like Milo Hamilton and Vin Scully are a collective link not only to the game of baseball, but sometimes to the wistful bygone days of our own youth.

Sports and television would be forever impacted by the incumbent drama and entertainment of the Maris-Mantle home run shoot out of 1961, an ironic milestone for baseball broadcasting since 1961 was the same year that FCC chairman Newton Minow publicly derided television as a vast wasteland. Along the way, baseball over the airwaves would influence sports programming and even presidents from Taft to Reagan and even Bush and Obama. Most of all, it has left a lasting impression on much of America largely due to the summer sounds of baseball on the radio, on television, and in the soul of a nation.

2

The Talking Box

Baseball games in progress were being reported by telegraph messages to saloons as far back as the 1890s, and the first sale of baseball "broadcast rights" took place in 1897 with each team receiving $300 worth of future telegrams in trade as part of an overall rights deal negotiated by the league.[1]

Soon the advent of a new real-time broadcast medium called radio would change the world, but to do so this talking box needed content. The early days produced a good deal of music and reading out loud: chamber music, police reports, opera — anything that produced intelligible sound. The newness of what hit the early radio airwaves may have been intriguing but it would not remain entertaining for long. Although unnoticed at first, there was a burgeoning source of audio programming that happened to be reinventing itself in plain view just as radio was being widely commercialized: major league baseball.

The magic of radio would help propel baseball, but only if the game could provide more excitement. It did. On Opening Day at the Polo Grounds in New York, April 13, 1921, George Herman Ruth lumbered to the plate and slapped two doubles and three singles for a sterling five-hit day.[2] This was the last Opening Day in the pre-radio era, although it would take radio a number of years to gain wide acceptance among the baseball owners.

Although the baseball lords were slow to catch on, the game of baseball quickly captured the attention of the new radio broadcasters, rendering 1921 a watershed baseball year for myriad reasons on and off the field of play. Ruth remained on an unprecedented tear for the whole year. The Babe slammed a home run shot on May 7 off Hall of Fame pitcher Walter Johnson that was the longest ever hit in Washington, D.C., then on May 25 Ruth hit the longest homer ever smashed at Sportsman's Park in St. Louis.[3] By year's end, Ruth had clubbed a staggering 59 home runs, a new major league record and almost three times the number slugged by the National League leader, George Kelly of the Giants, who hit 23 homers that year.

Baseball was discovering the entertainment value of the long ball almost daily, so much so that many accused the big leagues of secretly inserting a livelier ball. There was justification for such rumors, for in 1910 baseball had openly introduced a corked center for the regulation baseball, and in 1920 had banned the previously legal spitball. The game was clearly looking for more offense. With a corked ball, a phased-out spitter, the emergence of Ruth, and a new premium on the long ball, baseball offense proliferated like never before. Ruth even hit for a lofty average, too, batting a career high .378 in 1921, a staggering level for a free-swinging slugger.

Before the emergence of Ruth in Yankee pinstripes following his exile to New York by Boston owner Harry Frazee in 1920, baseball was mired in what is now called the Dead-ball Era. In 1901 the National League had begun counting all foul balls as strikes, a practice adopted by the fledgling American League in 1903, and baseball created the lowest scoring era in big league history. Team batting averages sank to .254, not especially low by more modern standards, but the dead ball produced a number of singles and suffocated the game with anemic slugging averages and few home runs. The American League leader in 1903 was John "Buck" Freeman of the Boston Americans who clubbed just 13 on the year, which still bested his National League counterpart, Jimmy Sheckard of the Brooklyn Superbas who hit only nine. This was a time when most top home run hitters barely made it to double digits on the season. Harry "Jasper" Davis, for example, led the majors with 10 homers for the Philadelphia Athletics in 1904. But even league leaders often hit fewer than 10, like Davis who topped the American League with only eight in 1907 and Detroit's Sam Crawford who banged out a paltry seven in 1908. Ty Cobb, a fierce spray hitter who batted for high averages, actually led the American League with nine homers in 1909. Perhaps that was by accident — after all, Cobb hit .377 that year with 216 hits, some of which were bound to clear the fences at some point. In 1911, the year after the corked center was introduced, baseball offense showed signs of life as Frank "Wildfire" Schulte clubbed 21 dingers for the Cubs and Ty Cobb batted a mind-numbing .420 for the Tigers.

By 1921, Ruth, Hornsby, Harry Heilmann of Detroit, and the Browns' George Sisler dominated the offensive game, while Walter Johnson (143 strikeouts for the Senators), Yankee Carl Mays (27 wins and seven saves), and Burleigh Grimes (22 wins for Brooklyn) ruled the pitcher's mound. Grimes, as it happens, was still throwing the spitball at the time — but for him it was legal, since the spitter was grandfathered in for pitchers already using it when the ban was implemented in 1920. Grimes would become the last man to throw a legal spitball with his last game of 1934, the year of his retirement following 19 big league seasons.

The electric long ball summer of 1921 changed the game and stirred the collective soul of a growing base of fans who embraced the excitement of this new brand of baseball offense. Unfortunately, there was more to the summer of '21 than baseball magic, an ugly lurking problem that reared its head that very year, rocking not only baseball but all of America. This was the year when the 1919 Black Sox gambling scandal was exposed, when on June 27, 1921, ten gamblers and eight White Sox players including icon Shoeless Joe Jackson went on trial in Chicago for fixing the 1919 World Series. The trial dominated sports headlines for much of the summer. Then, on August 2, 1921, the case went to the hometown Chicago jury — which then deliberated only two hours before acquitting all eight players, after which the players and jury unabashedly celebrated together at a downtown Italian restaurant. The fun was short-lived, however, for two days later Judge Kenesaw Mountain Landis, the recently installed commissioner of baseball appointed in part to rid the game of gamblers, banned all the charged players for life, notwithstanding their ceremonious acquittal.

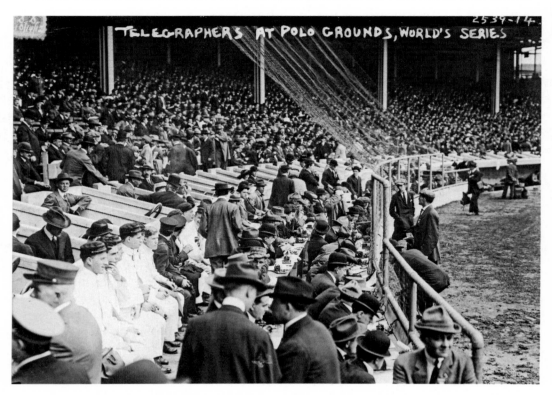

"Broadcasting" by telegraph. Telegraphers in position to send real-time reports of a World Series game from the Polo Grounds in 1912. This was the same year that radio signals were transmitted from the *Titanic* to the rescue ship *Carpathia*, and only nine years before radio would be introduced to major league baseball, again at the World Series, in 1921.

The fallout from the Black Sox suspensions changed baseball forever, but another act of fate would change the game even more — and it happened on the very next day. On August 5, 1921, Pittsburgh's fledgling KDKA radio sent Harold Arlin to announce a major league game from ground level at Forbes Field, a game won by the home team over the Phillies, 8–5.[4] Arlin first visited KDKA as a curious engineer, but he was soon selected to try his hand at baseball announcing. With that, Harold Arlin became the very first full-time radio announcer. KDKA did not broadcast the Pittsburgh Pirates games on a regular basis, though; that would come later. But the KDKA experiment would not only change the course of radio broadcasting, it would change baseball itself.

In those early days all contests were day games, of course, so before radio most fans were forced to wait for the evening newspapers. Aside from the occasional telegraph reports, the only way "real time" scores could be regularly conveyed was through taxi drivers. As the cabbies lined up outside city ballparks waiting for fares, they would either hear the score or get updates from passengers, then that news would creep through the city by word of mouth.

The first widely accepted use of radio waves was not for baseball, or even for entertainment in any form. It was for Morse code communication, particularly for maritime purposes as ships utilized the "wireless" to communicate with each other or with those on shore. The most famous such use, if not the most dramatic, occurred in the very early morning hours of April 15, 1912, when the steamship *Titanic* sent desperate signals of its impending doom through the stark darkness of the cold north Atlantic air. Although most of the 2,227 passengers on board would perish, 705 would indeed survive the ordeal[5] almost entirely due to wireless signals of Morse code messages sent by the ship's two radio officers, John George Phillips and Harold Bride. The *Titanic* sinking, as it happens, was the first time the "SOS" emergency code was used, which the operators sent along with the then standard "CQD" emergency signal.

The wireless room on the *Titanic* utilized the most powerful radio equipment available at the time. The transmitter was a rotary spark design driven by a five kilowatt motor generator that was powered by the ship's lighting circuitry. There was also a battery-powered emergency transmitter and an additional motor generator in the next room. The *Titanic* signals could be detected up to 400 miles away during daylight hours and almost 2,000 miles at night.[6] Just after midnight on April 15, 1912, the White Star Lines equipment was used to send the following plea for help:

12:17 A.M.
15 April 1912
R.M.S. Titanic to Any Ship:
"CQD CQD SOS Titanic Position 41.44 N 50.24 W. Require immediate assistance. Come at once. We struck an iceberg. Sinking."[7]

Two ships initially responded, but the *Frankfurt* was 170 miles away and the *Olympic* even farther. Three minutes later the *Titanic* reached out to the *Carpathia*, the closest ship at just 58 miles to the southeast. After a brief exchange, the *Carpathia* altered her course, headed straight for *Titanic*, and confirmed her objective:

12:32 A.M.
15 April 1912
R.M.S. Carpathia to R.M.S. Titanic:
"Putting about and heading for you."[8]

The wireless transmitter that helped save *Titanic*'s 705 survivors had been invented only 17 years before by Guglielmo Marconi, who was only 21 years old at the time of his discovery. He won the Nobel Prize for his efforts, and certainly altered world communications, if not the world itself, from that point forward.

Radio waves were already known to exist when Marconi began his own experiments in 1894. Heinrich Hertz, a German physicist, demonstrated that radio waves could be produced and detected in a laboratory, but Marconi took the process to a new level by learning how to produce and send those waves over long distances.

Marconi's family lived in Italy near Bologna where his neighbor, a noted physicist, introduced Marconi to electricity and the work already being done by Hertz. Marconi found he could mimic the Hertz experiments in his own attic by producing "Hertzian" waves sparked from one circuit to another. Eventually he managed to transmit those signals for several kilometers across the countryside. He tried to interest the Italian government in his discovery, but government officials were not enthusiastic and rejected Marconi's overtures. Eventually, in 1896, Marconi's cousin introduced him to the chief engineer employed by the British Post Office.[9] Successful demonstrations were conducted in London and on Salisbury Plain, so Marconi was able to obtain a patent. On July 20,

1897, he formed the Wireless Telegraph and Signal Company Limited, which soon opened the first radio factory in history at Chelmsford, England. The company was renamed Marconi's Wireless Telegraph Company in 1900, which changed its name again in 1903 to The Marconi Company and undertook a number of iterations thereafter.

A case could be made that it was Hertz who really invented radio, but it appears that while he discovered the idea Marconi determined how to make it work well enough to be useable outside the lab. Hertz used a crude wire, now recognized as an antenna, to create electromagnetic waves as early as 1886. These are identified as "radio waves," but they originally were called "Hertzian waves" after their discoverer. The Hertz legacy lives on, though, recognized by the measurement of frequencies in Hertz (Hz), which means oscillations per second, and radio frequencies measured in megahertz (MHz).[10]

Hertz himself did not live to see the Marconi expansion and the ultimate validation of his ideas. He died in 1894. Over the ensuing years and decades, Marconi and his company pressed forward and were responsible for some of the most significant advances in radio history. The company conducted transatlantic tests and experimented with high frequency broadcasting, short waves broadcasting, radar (an acronym for "radio detection and ranging"), and even television. More impressively, the company was responsible for the formation of the British Broadcasting Company (BBC) and the Marconi Wireless Telegraph Company of America, later called the Radio Corporation of America or RCA. Much of what once was the Marconi business empire was bought decades later and rolled into the Swedish telecommunications giant Ericsson in early 2006.[11]

Another company with roots traced to a famous inventor soon crossed paths with the developing Marconi empire. General Electric (GE), one of the biggest and most powerful corporate enterprises today, was the 1892 product of two merged competitors, one of which was the Edison General Electric Company founded by the inventor Thomas Edison to exploit his light bulb and numerous other inventions in 1890. On October 17, 1919, GE formed a new company to hold assets that were about to be acquired from American Marconi. The new company was called RCA, and it soon took on two additional ownership partners, Westinghouse and AT&T. In 1926, RCA formed a new company, the National Broadcasting Company (now widely known as NBC), to oversee the operation of the growing radio stations owned by RCA, GE, AT&T, and Westinghouse.[12]

Some of the more productive early Marconi experiments involved marine communications, and the Royal Yacht was soon fitted with a radio device to stay in touch with Queen Victoria at Osborne House. Then, in 1891, technology made it possible for signals to be received virtually across the Atlantic. Soon ships like the *Titanic* were outfitted with radio capabilities. Since these uses had significant military applications, the U.S. government took an active interest in the development of radio in the United States. In fact, when the United States entered World War I in 1917, all American radio development was controlled by the Navy to maintain secrecy and prevent its use by enemies. After the war ended in 1918, the government released its control of all related radio patents, which directly led to the formation of RCA in 1919.[13]

The release of those patents and the relinquishment of control over radio nationwide almost did not happen. As World War I pressed on, the Navy saw both the need and the power of radio, and eventually the Navy tried to confiscate both and to convert the entire industry into a government-controlled monopoly. The Navy even purchased a number of Federal Telegraph Company stations and Marconi stations in the U.S. to further its clandestine objective, but the Navy soon clashed with an unsympathetic Congress that ordered the Navy to give up its attempted stranglehold.

Although Marconi himself developed the ability to transmit radio waves over long distances, it was an early Edison chemist, Reginald A. Fessenden, who later worked for Westinghouse, who first developed the modulation of radio waves known as the "heterodyne principle," all of which made radio transmission feasible as we know it.[14] There is some historical debate over when the actual radio transmission of a human voice may have occurred, however. It could have been as early as the words "Hello Rainey" uttered by one Nathan B. Stubblefield in a test transmission near Murray, Kentucky, or it could have been as late as an experimental program transmitted in 1906 by Reginald Fessenden himself that was picked up by ships located hundreds of miles off the coast. Some might argue that the Budapest Cable Company started the broadcast business when it hired announcers to read the news that was disseminated over the phone lines. Perhaps that was broadcasting of a sort, but it made no use of radio waves since those were not harnessed until the mid–1890s.

Perhaps officially recognized radio broadcasting can be traced to 1915 when human speech was transmitted from New York to San Francisco, and also across the Atlantic to the Eiffel Tower from Naval radio station NAA in Arlington, Virginia. About five years later, on November 2, 1920, KDKA of Pittsburgh, then owned by Westinghouse, broadcast the Harding-Cox presidential election returns and then began a regular schedule of daily programs for the few local listeners with radio receivers.

Early radio station call letters were not "vanity" letters like ABC or KFAN or WGN (a name that harkened its parent *Chicago Tribune* to be the "world's greatest newspaper"). They simply were assigned routine numbers and letters like 6XE or 8XK. KCBS was originally "San Jose Calling," and was assigned the letters FN, then 6XE, 6FX, then KQW. KCBS began transmitting music on Wednesday evenings and claims to be the world's longest continuously broadcasting radio station. WHA, originally assigned the letters 9XM, was constructed by Earle Terry for the University of Wisconsin in Madison which now claims WHA to be the oldest station in the U.S. Along came 8XK, built for Westinghouse in 1916, which soon became KDKA. Regardless of all these other claims, the Department of Commerce began to issue band licenses in 1920. Pittsburgh's predecessor to KDKA was granted the very first "limited commercial" license and thereafter began to broadcast election returns on November 2, 1920. Many stations broadcast those same returns, but KDKA was different because this marked the beginning of its regular broadcasting.[15]

The term "broadcasting" was first officially used by the federal government in printed publications during 1921. On December 1 that year, the government set aside two wavelengths for licensing in the "Limited Commercial" category and described as follows: "Licenses of this class are required for all transmitting stations used for broadcasting news, concerts, lectures, and like matter."[16] The "like matter" catchall may not have been intended for baseball, but baseball entertainment, sort of a cross between news and a concert, certainly fit the general description.

The Federal Radio Commission was established in 1927 to more formally regulate the fledgling industry and serve the public "convenience, interest, or necessity." The broadcast industry proliferated, growing from its first licensed station in 1920 to over 11,000 such stations in the New Millennium.[17] That first entry was KDKA, which officially began at 6:00 P.M. on Tuesday, November 2, 1920, when four men entered a makeshift shack and studio atop the Westinghouse "K" Building in East Pittsburgh and flipped the broadcast switch to begin a succession of continuous broadcasts.

Commercial radio actually began as one man's hobby and made its original mark as part of a personal bet. An assistant engineer at Westinghouse, Dr. Frank Conrad, became interested in the new radio phenomenon as early as 1912. To win a $5 bet, Conrad constructed a makeshift receiver and intercepted the time signals from the Naval Observatory in Arlington, Virginia. Unsatisfied with just receiving signals, the precocious engineer decided to build a transmitter to send signals, which he successfully constructed in his garage and was granted the licensed identification of 8XK in 1916. This little experiment is what became KDKA radio in Pittsburgh. A Westinghouse vice president who already saw radio as a mass communication device for home entertainment soon stumbled across information about Conrad's ad hoc music broadcasts during several evenings each week. Meanwhile, eager listeners buried Conrad in mail, demanding more programming. Conrad played all his own records over the airwaves. When he needed more, he visited the Hamilton Music Store in Wilkinsburg, Pennsylvania, and obtained "free" records to play in an advertising trade-out deal,[18] probably the first of its kind.

Westinghouse then became more aggressive, building and selling amateur wireless "radios" to the general public and applying for its own station license. That license was issued in a matter of days, on October 27, 1920. The letters KDKA were routinely assigned from a master list, and they had no meaning at all beyond sheer random fate. Conrad was not at the fateful shack on the night of the broadcast debut, however. Westinghouse had engaged him and his own makeshift station as a back-up in case anything failed with the main set up, so Conrad was standing by at his own garage in Wilkinsburg. The back-up plan was not used, however; nothing failed that evening, so about 1,000 listeners got an early audible glimpse at the election returns when Warren G. Harding defeated James M. Cox for president.[19]

In January 1921 fate struck again when curiosity drove another engineer, the youthful Harold W. Arlin, to show up and inspect this new radio facility after seeing so much interesting equipment stacked onto the roof. While there, Arlin applied for an opening as full-time announcer and got the job,[20] becoming what most agree to be the first full-time announcer in radio history. With young Harold Arlin, the history of baseball radio broadcasting was soon underway.

On August 5, 1921, Arlin bought a ground-level box seat at Forbes Field, placed a wooden plank across arms of the seat to create a makeshift table, and set about "calling" a Pittsburgh Pirates game against the Phillies by speaking into a telephone with a long cord. Crude as it was, this was the first big league game ever to be broadcast via radio, changing not only radio forever, but baseball, too.

Arlin, born in the small town of LaHarp, Illinois, in December 1896, soon moved with his family to Carthage, Missouri, and later was educated at the University of Kansas. He was still only 24 years old when he announced that first game, if one could call it announcing. The equipment sometimes failed, the crowd was often too loud, and the broadcast was occasionally just dead air. Arlin himself later observed, "No one told me I had to talk between pitches."[21] The idea of endless chatter to fill time between the intermittent action on the field was not intuitive, and of course the color commentator would not be utilized for expert analysis for years to come. Everyone, especially Harold Arlin, was inventing baseball broadcasting on the fly. Hailed as the man who began "play-by-play," Arlin offered both a pleasant yet sometimes thundering voice. He once knocked his own broadcast off the air when he was so loud he broke the modulation meter.

As it happens, the deliberate pace of baseball was perfect for radio, but only when the dead air problem was recognized and solved. The baseball talk between pitches provided intricate word pictures of the events on the field. More significantly, it also made the announcer a good friend of the avid listeners, giving baseball a home-spun feel which graced the game with a consistency over the years that was almost familial in its ability to bind the ensuing generations who not only shared the game and their hometown team, but the familiar voice that called the game and entertained listeners with endless baseball stories.

Arlin had few listeners during his first broadcast from the box seats, for only a few hundred radio receivers

KDKA Radio's Harold W. Arlin in a publicity photograph from the early 1920s. Arlin became the first radio broadcaster of a major league game when he announced a Pirates-Phillies game from Pittsburgh's Forbes Field on August 5, 1921. An engineer by trade, Arlin had wandered into KDKA out of curiosity, then auditioned for the baseball announcing job, which he won. (Courtesy of KDKA Radio/Westinghouse Group)

were in use throughout western Pennsylvania. As radio spread rapidly, baseball's symbiotic relationship to the broadcast airwaves propelled the game's popularity, contributing to the ascent of baseball as our national pastime.

The Pittsburgh Pirates franchise is an old and storied team. According to the Pirates' official website, the team has a long history of great players and a legacy of historic events. Honus Wagner, Roberto Clemente, Willie Stargell, Bill Mazeroski, Dave Parker, and even Barry Bonds were all Pirates for all or portions of their respective careers. On May 6, 1906, the Pirates were the fist team to use a canvas tarp to protect the infield from rain. Interestingly, on May 25, 1935, Babe Ruth hit the final home run of his big league career, homer number 714, at Pittsburgh, a blast that was the first ever to clear the right-field roof at Forbes Field. It is hard to imagine that Ruth's final home run record for the ages was not set as a Yankee. By then he had been dealt to the Boston Braves, thus ending the Bambino's career where it began: Boston. So when Ruth's shot cleared the Forbes roof, Ruth was in Pittsburgh as a Boston Brave.

Home runs are a rich part of the Pirates' tradition. Ralph Kiner led the league in home runs for seven straight seasons, the only player ever to do so, until his string was broken by his own general manager, Branch Rickey, who traded him on June 4, 1953. Before the 1953 season, Rickey told Kiner the slugger would have to take a pay cut. When

Kiner protested, reminding the GM that he had just topped the league in homers once again in 1952 for the last-place Pirates, Rickey responded, "We would have finished last without you."[22] That remark became one of the more enduring lines in major league history. Kiner was soon traded, which was consistent with an oft-quoted Rickey philosophy, "trade a player a year too early rather than a year too late."

Kiner, one of the most prolific power hitters in major league history, had his own take on big league pay: "Cadillacs are down at the end of the bat."[23] High-profile ladies were also a Kiner specialty, for Kiner dated two of the top movie stars of his era, Elizabeth Taylor and Janet Leigh. Kiner himself would one day make a direct mark on baseball broadcasting as the celebrated long-time sportscaster for the New York Mets. He is credited with an oft-quoted line of his own about a Phillies speedy outfielder: "Two-thirds of the earth is covered by water; the other one-third is covered by Garry Maddox."[24] Kiner's no. 4 jersey was retired by the Pirates in 1987.

As a broadcaster, Kiner is credited with many gem comments, though some were memorable only because they were loveably wrong or oxymoronic. "Today is Father's Day," he once began. "So to all you fathers in the audience, happy birthday."[25] Mixed metaphors and other gaffes were a part of Kiner's style and down-to-earth charm, traits that Mets fans adored for decades.[6]

Ralph Kiner was elected to Cooperstown in 1975 as a player, but as a Mets broadcaster he won three Emmy awards and had his Mets television booth officially named for him in 2000. Only the legendary Dodgers' voice Vin Scully was affiliated with one team longer than Kiner's broadcast affiliation with the Mets.

Even though Kiner set records slugging for the Pirates, many know him for his sportscasting, particularly his long running post-game interview show "Kiner's Korner," which is also what Kiner's portion of the infield in Pittsburgh came to be called. As a player, Kiner retired with 369 home runs, far short of the 500-club that normally opens the Hall of Fame door, but he slugged that many in fewer at-bats than anyone except for Ruth himself. Kiner, after all, missed a few years with a military stint in World War II like most of his big league peers, including, among others, Ted Williams and Hank Greenberg.

Among baseball's top all-time sluggers, Kiner had the shortest career. He played only 10 big league seasons, a prolific span when he averaged 37 homers and 101 walks per year. In seven of those 10 seasons, he led the National League in home runs. He led the league in total bases three times, and in 1949 Kiner even made a serious run at Babe Ruth's single-season home run mark, coming up short with "just" 49 that year when he hit for power and high average at .310. Kiner could have done much better, but he was on a weak Pittsburgh team and surrounded by anemic .200 hitters in the lineup — one reason that pitchers walked him over 100 times in six separate seasons.

With all its storied contributions to baseball, though, Pittsburgh may have advanced the game the most when Harold Arlin first spoke at his stopgap announcer's desk from the box seats at Forbes Field in August 1921. Author Curt Smith put it this way in his book *Voices of Summer*: "The most vital first [for Forbes Field]: KDKA, and Arlin, siring baseball on the air."[26]

At the beginning of 1921, another step in a series of broadcast milestones was taken when chewing gum magnate William Wrigley, Jr., took sole ownership of the Chicago Cubs. In 1925, Wrigley would take a profound interest in the possibilities of regular baseball broadcasting, helping Chicago's WGN Radio to accomplish a milestone of its own. But meanwhile, 1921 set the stage on the field leading to a spectacular radio experiment at season's end.

Just two weeks after Harold Arlin called the Pirates game play-by-play, Ty Cobb slapped his 3,000th hit and at age 34 became the youngest major leaguer to reach that vaunted milestone. Ruth remained a one-man wrecking crew, and by September 15 he had slugged is 55th home run, besting his own record of 54 set the previous year, his first in Yankee pinstripes. On September 26, Ruth smashed home runs 57 and 58 in an 8–7 win over the Indians. It is significant that Ruth was on a home run tear at the Polo Grounds in New York, for New York would soon be America's broadcasting mecca, a title that would inch closer with the 1921 World Series.

Meanwhile, on October 2, the Ruth slugfest continued. The Yankees had already clinched the pennant, but in his last game of the year Ruth clubbed yet another long ball, number 59 on the season, which helped the Yankees defeat the Red Sox, 7–6, for their 98th win. It was a headline year for the Babe and the Yankees. Ruth walloped a staggering 59 home runs — more than any other entire *team* in the American League — with a 171 RBIs and a stratospheric slugging percentage of .846 in 1921,[27] captivating the nation and catching the attention of the fledgling New York electronic media.

When the National League pennant was won by the New York Giants, 1921 proved to be a historic World Series for many reasons. It was the first Series for the Yankees, which seems remarkable now given the club's long familiarity with the Fall Classic. It was also a remarkable Series because every single game was played on one site: the fabled Polo Grounds. The Yankees had subleased the Polo Grounds in 1913, which they would continue to do in 1922 as well before heading to the Bronx in their brand new Yankee Stadium — the House That Ruth Built — in 1923. Some have called this the first "subway World Series," but even that description is inadequate, since neither team even had to take the subway to get there because both teams were already "home."

The 1921 Series' most significant contribution to both baseball and broadcasting was, once again, radio. Game One of the World Series was the first to be broadcast over the radio, and KDKA, even though it was in Pittsburgh, was involved in that first transmission.

Two stations were actually broadcasting the game. One was WJZ in Newark, New Jersey, something of a sister station to KDKA since it was also owned by Westinghouse. But WJZ used a relay system whereby game reports were phoned from the Polo Grounds ultimately to WJZ's Tommy Cowan as a relay man who read the reports and virtually recreated the game as it went on. One might say the game was broadcast in "real time," but it was certainly not announced "live" since it took awhile to relay, read, and recreate the reports of the game. Meanwhile, KDKA installed a direct wire from New York and broadcast the play-by-play reports of famed print sportswriter Grantland Rice.

Born in Tennessee and a graduate of Vanderbilt University, class of 1901, Rice worked for several southern newspapers, and even umpired various baseball games between 1907 and 1911 before taking a position with the *New York Evening Mail* in 1911.[28] While at the *Atlanta Journal-Constitution* in 1904 and 1905, Rice pounded away at the typewriter touting a young, largely unknown, southern outfielder by the name of Ty Cobb. In 1908 Rice was actually the baseball coach at Vanderbilt. In 1914 he took a job with the *New York Tribune,* and later the *Herald Tribune* where he earned his reputation as a prolific sportswriter. Some accounts suggest that Rice authored more than 22,000 columns and wrote over 67,000,000 words altogether. One column, "The Sportlight," was the most influential of his day. It was Rice who coined the name "Four Horsemen" for the famous 1924 Notre Dame football backfield, and he is credited with the poetic phrase: "For when the one Great Scorer comes to write against your name, He marks— not that you won or lost— but how you played the game."[29]

Rice himself had been an aspiring athlete. He played on the college football team and was a decent shortstop on the Vanderbilt baseball team. Rice yearned to try his hand at pro baseball, but both his father and grandfather were against the idea. While working at the *Atlanta Journal-Constitution*, Rice met and married Kate Hollis, and the couple eventually moved to New York City where Rice's columns on sports figures like John McGraw, Christy Mathewson, and young Bobby Jones were a hit among readers. Except for a 14-month military tour of duty in World War I, Rice spent the remainder of his journalism career in New York where he befriended such luminaries as Rube Goldberg, Ring Lardner, Heywood Broun, and Damon Runyon. At age 41, at the peak of his sports career, Grantland Rice was a natural choice to "call" the first World Series game on radio.

October 5, 1921. Game One of the first subway series— sans the subway — was about to begin. Grantland Rice settled into his perch at the famed Polo Grounds where he would send accounts of the game over a wire to be broadcast by Pittsburgh's KDKA. At the same time, Sandy Hunt of the *Newark Sunday Call* would telephone reports of the game from the Polo Grounds to relay man Tommy Cowan so that play-by-play accounts could then be broadcast over WJZ in New Jersey.[30]

This was actually the fourth iteration of the Polo Grounds, which was rebuilt in 1911 at a cost of $100,000. In 1921 its capacity was 34,000, and the stadium was jammed for the World Series contest between the Yankees and the Giants. The dimensions of the field were cavernous and oddly shaped. In 1921 left field was extremely short at just 286 feet, but left center swept far away from the plate at 455 feet. Center field was a distant 433, right field a paltry 256, and right center checked in at 440. A typical field in the New Millennium would be around 335 down the lines and about 400 feet to center. Babe Ruth and other left-handed hitters were lured by the short right field of the Polo Grounds where they could pull the ball for home runs.[31]

In 1908 the Polo Grounds was the site of "Bonehead" Fred Merkle's blunder that forced a replay of the last Cubs-Giants game of the year to determine the pennant. Much more history would come from the Polo Grounds over the ensuing years, including Bobby Thomson's "shot heard round the world" that won the pennant for the Giants on October 3, 1951, at 4:11 P.M. local time. One footnote to history, now largely forgotten, occurred at the Polo Grounds in 1901 when a *NY Journal* sports cartoonist could not remember how to spell the word "dachshund" in referring to the "red hot dachshund sausages" served there — so he simply called them "hot dogs" for short.[32] The name stuck.

But the most significant event at the Polo Grounds may have been the Series of 1921 which not only was the first subway series, but also became the first in a stunning string of Yankees World Series appearances, rendering the Yanks the most prolific and storied of all major American sports franchises— and it was all broadcast over the radio airwaves for the first time.

The Yankees won Game One, 3–0, behind the shutout pitching of Carl Mays, even though Frankie Frisch had four hits for the losing Giants. The only run they needed was provided by Ruth, who singled and drove in the first-ever World Series run for the Yankees in the very first inning.

Game Two was also taken by the Yankees, 3–0, with Waite Hoyt firing a two-hitter. The Giants had failed to score in two straight games, but they would hammer the Yankees in Game Three with a 13–5 win driven by a 20-hit attack against four different Yankee pitchers. Ruth launched a home run in Game Four, but it was not enough in a 4–2 loss, even though Carl Mays was pitching again. After Game Four, sportswriter Fred Lieb would report to Yankee ownership that he saw Mays' wife signal the pitcher during the contest. This would launch an investigation by Commissioner Landis, but no evidence was uncovered. The Yankees' manager Miller Huggins believed the fix was in during several games throughout the season, though, and wrote about it in 1928.

The Yankees clawed their way to a Game Five win, 3–1, giving pitcher Waite Hoyt his second victory of the Series. But when Ruth missed Game Six with an infected elbow and various knee and leg injuries, the Giants capitalized, 8–5. Ruth would also miss Game Seven, another loss by pitcher Carl Mays, this time 2–1. With Ruth slowed, the Yankee offense suffered. They could muster no runs at all in the deciding eighth game on October 13, 1921, losing 1–0. Although pitcher Waite Hoyt took the loss in his third start of the Series, Hoyt gave up just six hits and the only run of the game was unearned. Hoyt, in fact, may have been the player of the Series for the Yankees, striking out 18 Giants and allowing no earned runs at all in 27 total innings pitched. Thus, the Giants would capture the world championship in eight games (at a time when the Series could still go nine games).

The Yankees would be back, of course. From 1921 through 1956 there would be 13 subway World Series, and the Mets and Yankees would do it again in 2000. The 1921 Series broke records for attendance (269,976 fans) and gate receipts ($900,233 total).[33] Baseball was making its mark, and with Ruth, and soon Gehrig, together with the expansion of radio, baseball would soon entrench itself as the uncontested national pastime.

It may be the Grantland Rice typewriter that is in the Hall of Fame, but it was his voice that helped launch baseball broadcasting. During that same 1921, KDKA's Harold Arlin would go on to announce the first-ever college football broadcast, a game between Pittsburgh and West Virginia. And some radio pioneers in Chicago began to take note.

3

Little Cat Feet

By 1920, Westinghouse had become one of the biggest manufacturers of the radio box when management got the idea to also produce programming—not primarily to entertain, but to generate more interest so more radio devices could be made and sold. This idea soon led to the advent of Pittsburgh's KDKA and its sister stations, with baseball broadcasting soon to follow when Harold Arlin announced the Pirates game in August 1921.

Arlin did a number of baseball games at KDKA from 1921 to 1924, a time when commercialized radio was growing so fast the industry had to perpetually reinvent itself on the fly. AT&T had an initial strategic advantage due to its control of phone lines across the country, so it utilized WEAF in New York as its flagship, then developed a 26-station mini-network across the entire country. But this was also an era when federal trust busters were flexing their Sherman Act muscle. They fined the Standard Oil behemoth and went after other industrial giants under antitrust powers granted by Congress in 1890, placing integrated big businesses at risk under these new antitrust cases. What implications would these new government policies have for broadcasting?

Worried about its own antitrust exposure, AT&T decided to divest itself of those 26 radio stations, selling them to the new broadcast pioneer RCA in 1926. David Sarnoff, who was chairman of RCA at the time, saw the vast potential of radio and used those stations to create the National Broadcasting Company, now known by its simpler and much more famous moniker, NBC. The first program broadcast over NBC radio was a sporting event, the 1927 Rose Bowl between Stanford and Alabama (the Rose Bowl tradition of pitting Pac-10 teams against Big-10 teams was not yet in place). That game, which ended in a 7–7 tie, was the very first *nationally* broadcast event of *any* kind, not just sports. Soon broadcasters learned the advantage of sports as a broadcast topic; sports not only provide built-in drama and excitement, but they have the magical ability to produce themselves on a moment's notice without the need or expense of scripts, sets, and staging. Moreover, once a dramatic program is produced and played, it cannot be repeated over and over each night—a new one has to be written and produced. But baseball produces a new "script" each night a game is played, virtually writing itself as the excitement on the field unfolds.

32

At the turn of the twentieth century as radio was just finding itself, college football was already hugely popular, a point not lost on the burgeoning radio broadcast industry. In 1921, Harold Arlin did an encore to his Pirates game broadcast by announcing the Pitt–West Virginia football game, a contest widely known as the "backyard brawl," and in 1922, AT&T's WEAF broadcast the Princeton–University of Chicago football game, the latter largely credited as a threshold event in the history of sports on radio.

Just when college football was making its early mark with powerhouse teams east of the Mississippi River, another much different event on the West Coast would soon influence both radio and post-season football. The now famous Rose Bowl would eventually grow out of an 1890 parade organized by the Valley Hunt Club in Pasadena originally to promote mild weather and a colorful image of southern California — particularly Pasadena. Originally it was just a parade with flowers, carnival-like games, and quirky contests like a race between an ostrich and an elephant, but by 1902 the newly formed Tournament of Roses Association had gotten the idea of promoting a big-time sporting event along with the parade. They invited Michigan to play Stanford in the very first post-season college football game ever played. Unfortunately, Michigan was a juggernaut in those days, and after just three periods Stanford was behind 49–0 and gave up. As a result, the Association gave up on football, too, but only for awhile. By 1916 its football games proved so popular that plans were made to build a monstrous Pasadena stadium to rival the great Yale Bowl. The new stadium, soon dubbed the Rose Bowl, was completed in time to host its first New Year's Day game in 1923.[1] By 1927 the Rose Bowl game's vast popularity attracted the attention of RCA's Sarnoff who felt it was the perfect natural draw to test the notion of a national radio broadcast. History would soon prove him right.

KDKA was already proving itself, and within four years of its debut there were 600 commercial radio stations across the country. Because the broadcast equipment proved costly, not to mention the expense of producing all the requisite programming, some stations got the idea to sell advertising. One year after Arlin's Pirates broadcast, the first radio ad, promoting a real estate developer, was aired on August 28, 1922, in New York City over WEAF, later to be called WRCA as the flagship of Sarnoff's RCA network. Most accounts suggest that the first commercial was much longer than a few seconds, and may have resembled what now is described as an "infomercial," during which a Queens businessman urged the listeners to buy shares in a Jackson Heights cooperative apartment building still under construction at the time. Although commercial broadcasting would soon dominate the air waves, it was initially greeted with skepticism, some even viewing it as undignified.[2]

While WEAF and KDKA continued to pioneer radio along with Westinghouse, RCA, and Sarnoff, another media empire in the Midwest was staking its own claim to the airwaves. The *Chicago Tribune*, founded in 1847 with an original run of just 400 papers, was already a communications giant by the time radio began to hit its stride in the early 1920s. Joseph Medill, a politically connected editor of the *Tribune*, acquired part ownership in the growing newspaper enterprise in 1855, then gained full control in 1874 and managed the paper for a quarter century until 1899. In 1911, Medill's two grandsons, Robert R. McCormick and Joseph Medill Patterson, took control.[3] McCormick was an especially colorful entrepreneur with an extraordinary past. He had been a colonel in the First Infantry Division during World War I, a much decorated division that soon became known as "the Big Red One." McCormick also became what has been described as a gentleman farmer, operating *Tribune* experimental fields in the far west suburban countryside of Chicago. And of course he spent 44 years with the *Tribune* where, as publisher and editor, he built it into a giant media organization that would own many newspapers across the country. It was under his stewardship that the *Tribune* empire would also enter the expanding electronic media market of radio. The Robert R. McCormick Charitable Trust, now known as the McCormick Foundation, became one of the nation's largest public charities, doling out over $1 billion in grants and operating Cantigny, a 500-acre park outside Wheaton, Illinois, at the McCormick estate, where one can find three McCormick museums including an elaborate military museum devoted to the exploits of the First Division in World Wars I and II.[4]

The Medill name lives on, too. Northwestern University's world famous Medill School of Journalism is named for the original *Tribune* founder Joseph Medill. Grandson Joseph Medill McCormick spent a brief time running the news giant along with Robert R. McCormick from 1903 to 1907, but he succumbed to depression and alcoholism and actually was treated by Carl Jung in Zurich. A decade later he was elected to Congress from Illinois, then represented Illinois in the U.S. Senate. Medill McCormick eventually lost his battles with depression, taking his own life in 1925 — the year after the mighty *Tribune* threw itself into the radio market.[5]

Chicago's first radio station was KYW, one of the Westinghouse group of stations. In 1921 the *Tribune* agreed to provide news and reports on various markets as content for Westinghouse. Meanwhile, two members of Chicago's social elite, Thorne Donnelley and Elliott Jenkins, developed an interest in radio and formed Midwest Radio Central, Inc. to launch experimental station WDAP which broadcast from the classic white-towered Wrigley Building (the same Wrigley as the Wrigley Field namesake) located on Michigan Avenue just north of the Chicago River. Then a tornado reportedly damaged the broadcast tower at Wrigley, so the broadcast operations were moved to the Drake Hotel. Since the station owned only one microphone, it was placed in the Drake ballroom, so when it was not broadcasting news and other talk, the station offered live dance music in the evenings from the Drake.[6]

In 1923 the Chicago Board of Trade, of all places, bought WDAP and continued to broadcast live music from the Drake, adding additional music from the Blackstone Hotel. At this point, Colonel McCormick developed an interest in radio and even arranged a demonstration of "the little box that picks up sounds from the air" for his influential mother who, of course, was the daughter of the *Tribune* founder. In May of that year, another broadcast pioneer, Zenith, introduced station WJAZ which broadcast from the famed Edgewater Beach Hotel perched near Lake Michigan on Chicago's North Side.[7]

In early 1924, the *Tribune* conducted a survey to help determine the viability of the radio market and determined that there were more than 100,000 receiving sets in the Chicago metropolitan area. Encouraged by these findings, the *Tribune* penetrated the market by leasing large blocks of time from WJAZ, and soon purchased the call letters "WGN," which unabashedly stood for "world's greatest newspaper." Almost immediately the *Tribune* took control of WJAZ, replaced the letters WJAZ, and established the station's new identity as WGN. The station changed its frequency from 670AM, which it had shared with WMAQ Radio, and took over 810AM on the radio dial.[8] Interestingly, 670AM operates today as WSCR sports radio in Chicago, while WGN, the city's most popular

AM station measured by its ratings, is now found at 720AM. Along the way, WGN took part in a complicated flip-flop that began when the Drake Hotel management acquired WDAP from the Board of Trade and then sold it to the *Tribune* which kept the WGN moniker but dumped its relationship with Zenith and WJAZ.[9]

The *Tribune* and WGN immediately understood the value of live programming because it was easy to produce and required no scripts or other complicated preparation. Originally, that meant live music like "zippy jazz tunes by the Oriole Orchestra coached by Ted Fio Rito," but WGN soon discovered the value of big-time sporting events. WGN set up a remote broadcast from the Indianapolis Motor Speedway. On May 31, 1924, it transmitted live from the Memorial Day auto race, calling itself "WDAP, soon to be WGN," which was the first live broadcast of what is now the Indianapolis 500. Announcer A.W. Kaney called the race for more than seven hours during which he spoke with several live guests, one of whom was Henry Ford.

Back in Chicago, WGN settled into its headquarters at the Drake Hotel and officially began over eight decades of broadcasting, and counting. Its original studio was a makeshift sound-resistant room insulated by heavy carpets, canopies, and drapes, but WGN was never wholly confined to its home base. In June and July of 1924, WGN broadcast both the Republican National Convention from Cleveland and the Democratic National Convention in New York.

On August 11, 1924, Quin Ryan was transferred from his job as an editor at the print side of the *Tribune* to a new post as announcer for WGN. It was an historic move. Ryan had been a student actor at Northwestern University and a part-time announcer,[10] so he had experience in speaking and projecting his voice in addition to having a journalist's background and training. It was a natural combination for the *Tribune* and WGN as the media giant continued to explore and perfect the new world of live remotes.

One of the most riveting criminal cases in U.S. history was underway at the same time, the Leopold-Loeb recreational thrill-kill murder of 14-year-old Bobby Franks in Chicago by two wealthy murderers—a case that has inspired many books and even motion pictures, including *The Rope* by Alfred Hitchcock. The drama of the case intensified when legal icon Clarence Darrow was engaged to defend the young killers. When Darrow opted to concede guilt and focus his entire riveting plea to save the boys from the death penalty, America was thoroughly engaged. When criminal courts judge John R. Caverly delivered the sentence—sparing the lives of Leopold and Loeb—WGN broadcast the event live from the courtroom.

A month later, in a tune-up for the broadcast of an official Cubs game the following spring on Opening Day 1925, WGN experimented with baseball broadcasts by transmitting an exhibition series between the Chicago Cubs and White Sox that was announced by Sen Kaney who had come from the Westinghouse station KYW. Kaney set up atop the Wrigley Field grandstand roof next to the press area. At the time, the grandstand was not yet double-decked, so he was not much higher than many current day press boxes. Wrigley Field was not yet called that name, as many still called it Weeghman Park for Charles Weeghman who built the stadium in 1914 to house his Federal League baseball team, the Chicago Whales, which soon folded. Weeghman then bought into the Cubs as part of a 10-investor consortium and moved the team from a park on the West Side to Weeghman Park in 1916. Weeghman sold out to the chewing gum magnate William Wrigley in 1918, and in 1920 the stadium became Cubs Park until it was renamed Wrigley Field in 1926.[11]

Less than three weeks after the Cubs-Sox exhibition in the fall of 1924, WGN was at the dedication of Memorial Stadium in Champaign, Illinois, where a crowd of 67,000 saw football sensation Red Grange explode for four touchdowns in 12 minutes as the University of Illinois upset top-ranked Michigan in one of the most famous college football games ever played. Quin Ryan called the action live for WGN.

It was a chilly spring day on April 14, 1925, when Quin Ryan and WGN again established a remote broadcast facility atop the Wrigley roof. This time it was Opening Day in Chicago, and the *Tribune* reported the day's excitement. "That the north side park — newly painted and looking as neat as a Dutch bakery — will be jammed today is a certainty" wrote reporter Irving Vaughan in the morning paper. Vaughan was right, for the turn-out of 40,000 set a record for National League home openers at the time.[12] The WGN broadcast that day was an important milestone in the history of baseball. Not only was it a first for the Cubs and powerhouse station WGN, it was one of the first wholly live radio broadcasts of a regular season major league game, the success of which helped convince Cubs owner William Wrigley that there was a future in baseball on the air.

Wrigley was one of very few early owners who began to embrace the broadcasting idea for baseball — a point that would be all too obvious as the 1920s and 1930s unfolded. Most owners were terrified of radio, feeling it would keep fans at home and destroy gate receipts at the ballpark. They would be proven grotesquely wrong, of course, but that would take time. Meanwhile, WGN continued to develop its sense for news, sniffing out national stories and captivating listeners with its live broadcast capabilities. The *Tribune* culture for news and Colonel McCormick's entrepreneurial nose for entertainment drove WGN to the forefront of broadcast journalism.

In the summer of 1925, what could have been a diminutive local event in a sleepy Tennessee town captured international attention and would impact America for the better part of a century. WGN was there, again at the forefront of broadcast history. The legendary trial lawyer Clarence Darrow was there, too, as were William Jennings Bryan, a three-time presidential candidate, nationally known orator, and Christian fundamentalist; nationally followed columnist H.L. Menken from the *Baltimore Sun*; and the ACLU from New York, there to defend its first major case. Dayton, Tennessee, was a struggling small town that decided to capitalize on a Tennessee law against the teaching of evolution. The ACLU advertised for a test case defendant, and Dayton town leaders seized upon the opportunity for national fame and found a willing subject in local substitute teacher John Scopes. When William Jennings Bryan made headlines by volunteering to help prosecute, Clarence Darrow could not resist the challenge.[13]

WGN followed Darrow to Dayton in July 1925, placing its microphone in the courtroom where the seating was rearranged to accommodate the broadcasting stand. WGN then paid a whopping $1000 per day for a dedicated phone line to send the live feed back to Chicago where it was broadcast to nearly 40 states through WGN's powerful signal. Quin Ryan, fresh from his baseball and Indy 500 assignments, was on hand to report. The Scopes case may have involved a minor offense with a small fine, but much loftier ideals were at stake, causing many to still call it the trial of the century. Preceding the 1995 O.J. Simpson media circus trial by precisely 70 years, the Scopes case was the first to be broadcast on location.

As radio was exploding across America, the talking box was starved for content. When it was not covering national headline news like Scopes or the Indianapolis 500 or a heavyweight title bout, radio simply offered a great deal of inane talk and endless opera or jazz. The talk shows, though, were often nothing like the engaging conversation of more contemporary offerings. Instead, they frequently featured long-winded speeches like this program listed for WLS radio in Chicago on the same evening as the first Cubs broadcast on April 14, 1925: An inspiring talk by Charles H. Markham, president of the Illinois Central Railway, on "Chicago the Railroad Center."[14]

Even WGN struggled to find programming. Listings from April 20, 1925, included the following: Chicago Board of Trade market reports every half hour (not bad); Lyon & Healy organ recital; luncheon concert at the Drake Hotel; and this riveting piece scheduled for 3:00 P.M.: "Rocking chair time; readings from *Liberty* and *The Tribune*; solos by Vernon Rickard and Drury Lexington."[15] When all else failed, radio simply read aloud from the day's newspaper. The ensuing evening looked better, though, with Quin Ryan's scheduled live interview with movie star Gloria Swanson,[16] but other stations were not so lucky. Chicago's WLS offered a talk on Freudian Theory; WQJ presented a talk by Mrs. Harry Sanger about her European travels; and KYW served up "Uncle Bob's bedtime story." Not to be outdone, WOAW in Omaha offered organ music; KDKA scheduled a talk on English story tellers; and WCB Buffalo broadcast a concert by the Buffalo Girls Glee Club.[17]

Through all of this banality, baseball moved forward — on and off the field, though it occasionally had to take a step back, too. In 1922 Babe Ruth was suspended twice before the end of May, once along with Bob Meusel for playing in an off-season barnstorming tour, and again for throwing dirt into the face of umpire George Hildebrand after being called out at second base.[18] Three weeks later the Bambino was suspended yet again for using "vulgar and vicious language" when he argued a call at second base against the Indians on June 19, 1922.[19] Ruth would actually be suspended five times that year, the last coming after a verbal altercation with umpire Tom Connolly on August 30. Connolly called Ruth out on strikes, and so Ruth was promptly ejected for abusive language again. Then on September 1, Ruth drew a three-game suspension for his behavior. Interestingly, that would be the last time Ruth was ever ejected from a game during his long and storied career.

By September 5, Ruth was back to making history on the field when he clubbed a home run against the Red Sox. It was Ruth's very last four-bagger in the famed Polo Grounds, a home run haven where the 1922 foul lines were just 286 to left and 256 to right. Ruth had hit a lofty 32 homers at the Polo Grounds alone in 1921, a year when he broke the major league record — again — with 59 long ball blasts. Ruth would not lead the league in home runs during 1922, though, mostly due to his multiple suspensions which held the Babe to 35 jacks in just 110 games.[20] The Browns' Ken Williams would have that honor with 39 jacks on the year while Rogers Hornsby topped the National League with 42.

With Ruth out for so many games during the season, the Yankees struggled to win the pennant, which they finally did on September 30 when they beat the Red Sox to clinch, thus outlasting the hot St. Louis Browns that year by one game. Baseball offense was in full swing during 1922, fueling fan interest and setting the stage for an eventual expansion of radio broadcasts in the years to come. The Browns' George Sisler torched pitchers that year for a stunning .420 season average, while teammate Ken Williams not only led the league in homers but also topped the league in RBIs with 155. Wally Pipp hit a sparkling

.329, Frank Snyder .343, Emil Meusel .331—and a youngster named Casey Stengel beat them all with a dazzling .368 in 84 games.[21]

In those days the only games the baseball lords were comfortable broadcasting were those of the World Series, since the owners knew no one would stay home and listen to a World Series game instead of coming to the park. Game One of the 1922 Series was broadcast over New Jersey's WJZ, again featuring sportswriter Grantland Rice.[22] This time, however, Rice called the game in a play-by-play mode, a first for the World Series, rather than the re-creation that Tommy Cowan did based on phone reports from the 1921 Series. It would be a short Series with the Giants besting the Yankees in just five games, but many in the densely populated East Coast would have a chance to hear a slice of the Fall Classic on radio.

League-wide, however, the owners remained both skeptical and fearful. They could have taken comfort from the ranks of heavyweight boxing, but perhaps they viewed those matches as similar to the World Series—rare spectacles that could not be threatened by this new radio phenomenon. Indeed, the broadcasts of games during the 1921 and 1922 World Series came in the wake of an even bigger experiment on July 2, 1921. An article from *The Wireless Age* in July 1921 described the upcoming heavyweight boxing event with great zeal and anticipation:

> Broadcasting by wireless a voice description of the Dempsey-Carpentier championship contest is not only a novelty for the annals of sport, but a development in the field of applied science. The arrangements already made for the radiophone transmission on

World Series crowd for Game One at the Polo Grounds, in 1922. Although radio had been present for the 1921 Series, Game One of the 1922 World Series was the first World Series game to be broadcast play-by-play. Grantland Rice would call the game for WJZ, Newark. Rice, an established print journalist, would broadcast baseball and other sports, coining the term "Four Horsemen" to describe the potent 1924 Notre Dame football backfield.

July 2nd for new and unusual departures in communication engineering. Never before has anyone undertaken the colossal task of simultaneously making available a voice description of each incident in a fight to hundreds of thousands of people. Transmission of the voice by wireless on a large scale is new to the world, and the event has no little historical significance. The plans for its introduction have been carefully made so as to insure a complete success. Due to the fact that French and American causes are to be aided through the exhibitions in various cities, it has been possible to secure apparatus and services that would otherwise be available only at prohibitive cost.[23]

At the time of the fight, Jack Dempsey was a 26-year-old punching machine. He had been fighting since he was 19 years old, first as "Kid Blackie," then under his own new name Jack Dempsey (he had been born William Harrison Dempsey but changed it to Jack 19 years later). Although small by modern heavyweight standards at 6'1" and just 187 pounds, Dempsey was nonetheless a powerful puncher who scored a number of first round knockouts that earned him a shot at the title in 1919 against champion Jess Willard. Dempsey, who was so fierce that famed writer Damon Runyon labeled him the "Manassa Mauler" (after his hometown Manassa, Colorado) took the crown from Willard.[24]

Both Dempsey and his new opponent Georges Carpentier were extremely popular. Carpentier, a French boxer, was world lightweight champion during 1920–22. A string of victories over British fighters made Carpentier a welcome national hero in France, at the time a war-torn country still reeling from the devastation of World War I.[25] Partly because of his success in the ring and his popularity in France, Carpentier was soon matched against Dempsey for a title match in Jersey City, New Jersey, that would make broadcasting history.

The Dempsey-Carpentier match was promoted as "the fight of the century," one of perhaps a half-dozen such fights of the century that would take place over the ensuing decades, and it inspired a mammoth experiment in radio transmission that pre-dated Harold Arlin's Pirates game by just over a month. The transmitter, on loan from RCA, had been built by General Electric at Schenectady, New York, and had to be floated down the Hudson River to be installed at Hoboken, New Jersey, for use in conjunction with a 680-foot antenna tower. The broadcast would have a range exceeding 200 miles in each direction covering over 125,000 square miles, including all of New York City and reaching to the southern tip of Maine, Pittsburgh in the west, and south to Washington, D.C.[26]

The fight signal would not only be picked up by individual receivers, which were very few in number, but it was also sent to mass audiences at a series of theaters and auditoriums in 61 cities, all of which was arranged politically with the help of the American Committee for Devastated France. There were not enough trained technicians in those days, so a plea went out to enlist the aid of hundreds of amateur radio volunteers. It would be the largest broadcast in radio history at that time with over 300,000 total listeners (some accounts report up to 500,000) able to hear the blow-by-blow account, none of which dissuaded the gate receipts paid by a staggering crowd of 80,000 to 100,000 onlookers who squeezed into the massive octagon-shaped stadium that was specially built on a farm outside Jersey City. In marked contrast to the baseball owners of the day, promoter Tex Rickard, who was a Dempsey handler, hyped the fight relentlessly, for he saw a future in radio broadcasting that could elevate the fight game to unprecedented heights beyond just the live gate audience.

As early as 1916, eventual broadcast icon David Sarnoff was promoting the idea of expanding the newly developed "radio music box" into all areas of entertainment. After World War I, Sarnoff wrote a detailed memo on the feasibility of expanding radio to ordinary households. He felt the potential market could be as great as 7 percent of total U.S. families, perhaps generating as much as $75 million annually, a notable sum measured in 1920s dollars.[27] Sarnoff would authorize the funding of the transmitter for use in the Dempsey-Carpentier fight, a move that would help propel RCA as a broadcast power. In April 1921 the idea of broadcasting the fight was tested on promoter Rickard, who instinctively liked the new concept.

Gate receipts blew through the $1 million threshold, reaching over $1.6 million. Present for the fight were scores of dignitaries, including the likes of John D. Rockefeller, Jr., William Vanderbilt, Vincent Astor, and Henry Ford. Perhaps just as important among attendees were highly respected writers H.L. Mencken (who in 1925 would attend the Scopes monkey trial), Damon Runyon, and Ring Lardner.[28] During the fight itself, Carpentier would land some early shots to Dempsey, but in the second round Carpentier broke his own thumb, then got knocked out by Dempsey altogether in the fourth round. No matter that it was a short fight, it made headlines everywhere for its record gate and historic radio transmission in addition to the dramatic Dempsey victory. Five weeks later after KDKA broadcast the Pirates-Phillies baseball game, an eager public was demanding more radio receivers.

By 1922 there were 30 operating radio stations in the U.S., a number that grew geometrically in one year, reaching 550 stations by 1923 when as many as three million Americans had some form of access to radio broadcasts, which soon included stock market reports, weather, music, news, and so on.[29] In 1923, though, things began to change with the very first comedy series debuting on radio (*The Happiness Boys*) as well as radio's first drama, *The Laughing Ladies* featuring the acclaimed actress Ethel Barrymore. Americans found themselves craving entertainment.

During the first two years of experimental transmissions of big league baseball games, notably the World Series, baseball games were treated more like a series of news bulletins—just the events were reported with little concern for the entertainment value of the broadcast itself. That all changed in 1923 when yet another Yankees-Giants World Series was broadcast on radio, this time called by Graham McNamee, who was emerging as one of the first true radio personalities.

The 1923 season was a threshold baseball year, for the Yankees said good-bye to the Polo Grounds and celebrated the opening of the brand new Yankee Stadium in storybook fashion. In the third inning of the home opener on April 18, 1923, the Babe proved why the new park would soon be "The House That Ruth Built" by slamming Yankee Stadium's first homer ever, a three-run shot in the third inning. A mammoth crowd of over 74,000 was on hand with another 25,000 turned away for the inaugural game. It was at the end of that eventful day that an inspired Fred Lieb coined The House That Ruth Built moniker with his subsequent article that appeared in the *Evening Telegram*.[30] By then Lieb was already a sportswriting icon, but that phrase would assure his place in baseball infamy. (Lieb had simply been a clerk working for the Norfolk & Western Railroad years before when he began submitting baseball player bio's to *Baseball Magazine*. Then, in 1911, Lieb moved to New York where he joined the newly formed Baseball Writers' Association holding the prestigious No. 1 card for many years.)[31]

By mid–July of 1923, Boston's owner Harry Frazee, known chiefly for sending Ruth to the Yankees, finally succumbed to a sea of theatrical expenses and baseball fate by selling the Boston Red Sox team for $1.5 million. The Yankees and Giants met for the third World Series in a row, with the 1923 Series broadcast being the first to be wholly originated live at the stadium. Casey Stengel slapped a game-winning inside-the-park home run and lose his shoe running the bases in the top of the ninth for the Giants as Graham McNamee watched from the broadcast booth. McNamee, who would eventually announce twelve straight World Series, is still regarded as one of the game's best announcers.

Young Graham McNamee had thought he would continue through life as a piano player and singer, but his voice training proved worthwhile for a much different vocation. He actually began in the radio business much the way Harold Arlin did around the same time — McNamee stumbled into the local radio station, auditioned during a lunch break while on jury duty, and won a job at WEAF in New York. He warmed up by calling a middleweight boxing match, then was assigned the 1923 World Series where he was to be something of a color man alongside Bill McGeehan who called the action.[32] At first McNamee had little to say, and hardly contributed to the first three games. By Game Four, McNamee could hold himself back no longer, trumping McGeehan's role with his own brand of excited play-by-play announcing as the Yankees thumped the Giants, 8–4, behind a six-run second inning at the Polo Grounds.

Openly calling himself more an entertainer than pure broadcaster, McNamee brought genuine excitement and color to the radio broadcasts. After the Yankees prevailed to win their first World Series in six games over the Giants, WEAF was deluged with 1700 fan letters celebrating McNamee's entertaining approach to the game, a remarkable development given how few radios were in use at the time.[33] Pleased with itself and its new-found star, WEAF pressed McNamee into action everywhere. He called everything from coronations to football and marbles; he was on the scene when Charles Lindbergh landed from Paris after his historic transatlantic flight.

From his first home run on Opening Day to an upper deck

Graham McNamee, who called World Series games from 1923 to 1934, had also performed as a professional singer. Like Harold Arlin, McNamee started his sports broadcasting career by accident, wandering into New York's fledgling WEAF station where his voice was a big hit. Since he could enunciate and project his voice better than most, he was given announcing jobs and immediately became one of the first great professional sportscasters.

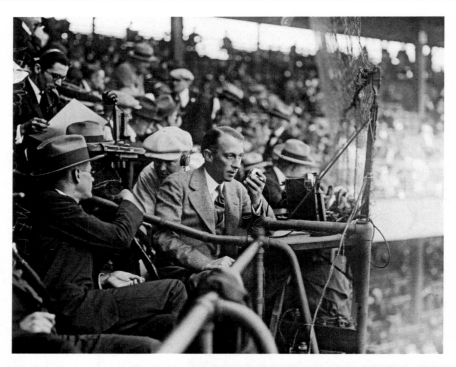

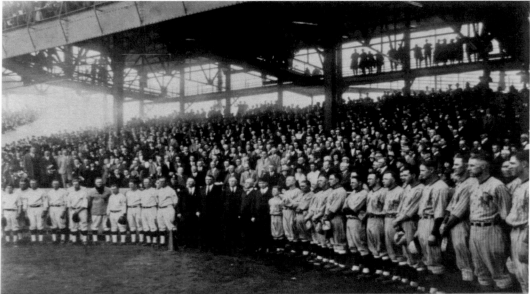

Top: 14. The legendary Graham McNamee broadcasting the World Series for station W.E.A.E. on October 5, 1924. McNamee's sportscasting career was not only boosted by an engaging voice, but by the legendary Ring Lardner, who in 1923 would publicly express confusion over whether to report the game he had just seen, or the same game as announced by the entertaining McNamee. *Bottom:* Players of the Giants and Senators just before the last game of the 1924 World Series. Graham McNamee announced the Series for Westinghouse radio.

shot in World Series Game Six on October 15, Ruth was completely "back" in 1923. He was again at the top of the league in homers with 41, batted a whopping .393 with a slugging percentage of .764, and won the American League MVP honors. With the opening of Yankee Stadium, the first of a record number of Series wins, and the advent of true baseball broadcasting as entertainment behind the voice of Graham McNamee, major league baseball would flourish in 1923 and beyond.

In 1924, the silver screen featured such stars as Douglas Fairbanks, Buster Keaton, Mary Astor, and John Barrymore — but the movies were still silent spectacles. Radio offered something different altogether — sound, and plenty of it. Chicago's WGN broadcast from the Leopold-Lobe case in 1924, and carried Quin Ryan's broadcast from the Illinois-Michigan football game on October 18. Although the Yankees did not take the pennant in 1924, it was nonetheless a stellar year for baseball. Rogers Hornsby led all of baseball with a .424 average, Ruth topped the American League hitting .378 with 46 home runs, and Graham McNamee forged ahead broadcasting on WEAF.

As 1925 unfolded, Quin Ryan found himself calling the Tournament of Roses football game between Notre Dame and Stanford — all while Ryan was still in Chicago at the Drake Hotel where he reconstructed the Notre Dame victory from ticker-tape reports. By April 14, Ryan was announcing WGN's first Cubs game from Wrigley Field in Chicago, followed by the Kentucky Derby in May, and the Scopes monkey trial from Tennessee in July and August.

Finally in October, WGN's Quin Ryan and WEAF's Graham McNamee were paired to provide live coverage of the 1925 World Series between the Washington Senators and Pittsburgh Pirates. It had not been a good year for Ruth, who got off to a slow start with intestinal surgery in April and spent much of the year arguing with manager Miller Huggins. Ruth failed to hit .300 and managed only 25 homers in just 98 games. Some even thought Ruth's career was nearly over. Even so, 1925 was a threshold Yankee year, for on July 2, youngster Lou Gehrig got his first start at first base over Wally Pipp, who was hospitalized after taking a shot to the head during batting practice. During the 1925 World Series, McNamee hit full stride. After the Pirates won a rain-soaked Game Seven played in the mud and fog, 50,000 fans wrote in. "The Series was sport," famed broadcaster Jack Buck would say many years later, "and McNamee was the Series."[34]

Thanks to radio, a baseball announcer had finally taken center stage. This was a profound yet almost enigmatic transition. Radio had been taking hold on the front page and through the airwaves for all to see and hear, but its grip over the game and the fans was strengthening even more than most realized. A half-century later, Commissioner Ford Frick — known for his infamous "asterisk" comment to qualify Roger Maris' home run record as a 162-game mark — would acknowledge radio's significant yet subtle impact. "The advent of radio was different," Frick observed. "Like Carl Sandburg's fog, radio sneaked in on 'little cat feet' before baseball owners and fans realized what was going on. Yet radio and its offspring, television, have had greater and more revolutionary impact on baseball than any other development in more than a century of the game's history."[35]

To complete this transformation, however, there remained one significant hurdle — the reluctant baseball owners. But another threshold development was unfolding in Chicago, one that would affect baseball broadcasting as much as the McNamee success.

4

Going, Going — Gone!

Jack Buck, the Cardinals broadcaster who noted Graham McNamee's impact on radio and the game, also nailed the essence of the coming long-term marriage of radio and baseball: "Turn the radio on, and you'll hear a friend.... Turn the radio on in your car, in prison, on the beach, in a nursing home, and you will not be alone, you will not be lonely. Newspapers fold, magazines come and go, television self-destructs. Radio remains the trusted common denominator in this nation."[1]

Not everyone saw the coming epiphany the same way, however. In 1925, the same year that WGN broadcast the Cubs' Opening Day win over the Pirates, *The Sporting News* was openly antagonistic to the broadcasting idea, stating "Broadcasting stories of games as the games go along is the equivalent of a succotash party with neither corn nor beans."[2] *The Sporting News*, a famed print publication even then, may have been skeptical of the new broadcast medium, or perhaps it was wary of radio as potential competition. Regardless of its motives, the original "Bible of Baseball" was no particular friend of radio in the early days.

The Sporting News first went to print in 1886 and proceeded to cover all sports. It was conceived and founded by a baseball man, Alfred H. Spink, who was a director of the St. Louis Browns baseball team (the old Browns, who later would morph into the St. Louis Cardinals). When the paper changed its mission after the turn of the century to focus on baseball, it made its mark on both the history of journalism and baseball. Its editor Joe Flanner, for example, helped arrange peace between the competing American and National Leagues, and the paper once featured the writings of Ring Lardner before he become much more famous for his short stories. By World War I, the paper had outlasted its competition and was the sole remaining national baseball publication; so when *The Sporting News* spoke, the baseball world listened.

The early depiction of announcers as "radiologists" was not only less than colorful, it symbolized the initial approach to calling baseball games: dull. With stark factual reporting and lots of dead air, who in baseball could have feared the advent of radio? Graham McNamee, however, changed all that. Two of the original icons of sports on the radio, in fact, had already been performers, both in practice and in their hearts, McNamee and WGN's Quin Ryan. They understood the art of voice projection, if not live entertainment overall.

Ring Lardner, with a nose for sports traced to his stint at *The Sporting News*, was quick to observe the essence of McNamee's style with this back-handed compliment about radio's broadcast of the 1923 World Series: "They played two World Series games at the Polo Grounds this afternoon — the one I watched and the one broadcast by Graham McNamee."[3] Lardner was referring to McNamee's colorful style which brought the game to life for the radio audience, apparently surpassing the methodical pace of the real game on the field. Lardner had been sitting near McNamee, but the fans in the stadium may have heard McNamee, too, because by 1922 radio and baseball had implemented the idea of piping the radio broadcast over the loud speaker system at the game itself. That must have been distracting, given McNamee's gift for gab beginning with his first Series in 1923. But for the millions of listeners — as many as five million for the 1922 Series — the World Series was beginning to come alive over the airwaves. This is what the owners originally feared. Would baseball on the radio be so good that it could keep paying fans away from the ballparks?

One significant baseball man from Chicago believed radio would not be the enemy. William Wrigley, Jr., the multi-millionaire chewing gum magnate, became part owner of the Chicago Cubs in 1916, then took full control of the team by 1921.[4] As the 1920s unfolded, Wrigley the opportunist saw the value of radio and its impending role in baseball broadcasting if not the history of baseball itself. This was no accident, indeed it was an important step in a long series of events that began with the inception of the Cubs and extended through the Wrigley years, for Wrigley himself was both a visionary and a born entrepreneur.

Wrigley's father had been a soap maker who manufactured and sold Wrigley's Scouring Soap beginning in 1870 with the formation of the Wrigley Manufacturing Company in Philadelphia. Interestingly, that very same year a fledgling baseball team called the Chicago White Stockings played its first game ever, a 47–1 blow-out of a team from St. Louis. This was *not* the early Chicago White Sox, a team that would not be formed until the advent of the American League in 1900; rather, this group was the forerunner to the Chicago Cubs which began play as the White Stockings, then became the Chicago Colts in the mid–1890s before officially becoming the Cubs in 1906. The Cubs would eventually capture the attention of the younger Wrigley, who had developed into a baseball fan in Philadelphia. The Cubs mystique is well known in modern times — partly a product of the television superstation phenomenon of the 1980s and 1990s — but they were a large draw in the early days, too, attracting big name players and the rising entrepreneurs of the day with the team's growing legends and lore.

Those original White Stockings played in Chicago until they were shut down in 1871 by the Great Chicago Fire that destroyed not only their stadium but equipment and uniforms as well. The team found ways to reinvent itself and to start playing again. After 1875 they acquired pitcher Al Spalding who started 60 games and won a staggering 47 games his first year in Chicago (1876), which turned out to be his only meaningful season of a very short on-field career.[5] They also began to play at their new West Side Park near the Chicago medical center complex that still occupies the West Side, and the team promptly won the National League pennant in 1876. Al Spalding retired early from the game to pursue a promising little side venture called Spalding Sporting Goods, but when the Cubs' owner died in 1882, Spalding the entrepreneur came back to acquire ownership. By this time the Cubs' star player was Cap Anson, an icon in the making who would play

27 seasons.[6] Anson would be the first ballplayer to achieve the 3,000-hit plateau; he knocked in so many runs that the *Chicago Daily Tribune* was inspired to invent a new baseball stat in 1880: runs batted in.[7] It was during Anson's tenure that the team acquired its name Colts, and soon took on the public moniker "Anson's Colts." This model for player dominance and hubris would later be matched by superstar second baseman Nap Lajoie, who bolted from the National League to the upstart American League franchise in Cleveland which promptly became the Cleveland Naps during Lajoie's tenure — then changed to the Indians after his departure.

History largely credits Anson with perpetuating baseball's now infamous "no Negroes" rule, and in 1883 Anson refused to take the same field with the black players, particularly Moses Fleetwood Walker of the Toledo Mud Hens. In those days when Anson spoke, baseball listened. Later, when Anson left, the team went through some official and unofficial name chances before gradually adopting the "Cubs" handle. In 1902, the Cubs debuted perhaps the most famous infield in baseball history: Joe Tinker, Johnny Evers, and Frank Chance, who helped take the pennant with a very lofty 116 wins. That team still holds the modern-era record for winning percentage at .763 and inspired the Franklin P. Adams poem about "Tinker to Evers to Chance." Over the ensuing years, though, the team got older and eventually the Cubs lost their edge and sank into mediocrity for most of the rest of the century.

Charles Phelps Taft, the half-brother to President William Howard Taft, along with minority investors including advertising man Albert Lasker acquired control of the Cubs in 1914, but then sold a controlling interest to Charles Weeghman in 1916 who moved the team to the new Weeghman Park at Clark and Addison. Weeghman had just built the park for his own but short-lived Whales of the competing Federal League — the league that sued the National League for antitrust violations, thus leading to the Federal Baseball case antitrust exemption for major league baseball in 1922. (Although Oliver Wendell Holmes, Jr., wrote that opinion, William Howard Taft, a huge baseball fan in every sense of the word, was Chief Justice at the time.) Lasker, meanwhile, did two things to change baseball forever. First, he helped install Chicago federal judge Kenesaw Landis as baseball commissioner — especially significant since Landis was the original trial judge in the Federal League antitrust case. Then Lasker contacted a special friend about acquiring the Cubs outright, someone with money, marketing savvy, and influence.

William Wrigley had worked in his father's soap manufacturing business for 20 years when youth and ambition brought him to Chicago in 1891. Still young at just 29 years, Wrigley originally thought he would sell soap for his father in this new territory, then got the idea of adding baking powder as a purchase premium to generate interest in the soap products. The customers, though, soon preferred the premium to the actual product and began demanding more and more baking powder. Wrigley, who was nothing if not nimble, soon complied. But now he needed another premium item to offer along with the baking powder — something fun but cheap. He chose a new phenomenon called chewing gum, then fate struck again: the public preferred the gum to the baking powder. So Wrigley went with the flow, this time responding with two chewing gum products. He soon hit the mother lode in 1893 and 1894 with two eternal brands: Juicy Fruit and Wrigley's Spearmint gum.[8]

Wrigley advertised heavily to promote the products, a practice that would drive out competition and bring him close to the advertising business in Chicago, including his friend Albert Lasker who had ties to the Cubs. Knowing Wrigley to be a long-time baseball fan, and especially a devoted fan of the Cubs, Lasker approached Wrigley about buying the team. Riding a wave of worldwide success and drowning in money, Wrigley took a minority interest, then bought all the investors out by 1921. This was the very same year that KDKA had begun to broadcast Pittsburgh baseball, followed by the very first broadcast of the World Series in the fall. Neither event was lost on Wrigley, a natural promoter who loved the idea of this new medium called radio.

Wrigley would make a lasting imprint on Chicago, baseball, architecture, business and radio itself. The Wrigley Building, which still houses the company's worldwide corporate headquarters, was completed in May 1924 when the second of two adjacent tower buildings was completed. Anchoring the south end of the Magnificent Mile and listed on the National Register of Historic Places, the building is a classic structure that features a clock tower modeled after the Giralda Tower in Seville, Spain (Seville and Chicago recognize each other as "sister cities"), and its white terra-cotta façade is brilliantly lit at night by a bank of powerful floodlights that contribute to the Wrigley tower's nickname, "The Jewel of the Mile."[9]

William Wrigley, Jr. The chewing gum magnate understood marketing and promotion. After buying the Chicago Cubs, Wrigley embraced radio by broadcasting Cubs games in 1925, an insightful move that simultaneously brought baseball to more fans and more fans to the game. Cubs attendance soon surged by 117 percent, and Chicago radio became an early leader in baseball broadcasting.

Not to be outdone, the burgeoning *Chicago Tribune* acquired the property immediately across the street on the east side of Michigan Avenue for its new headquarters. McCormick desired a location that spoke both of grandeur and practicality, for the site would need access to the Chicago River waterway to help feed its hungry presses daily with fresh newsprint paper delivered on barges. When the paper offered $100,000 in prize money for a special design contest, the winner was New York City architects John Mead Howells and Raymond M. Hood for their Gothic style entry featuring a classic vertical design with gargoyles and an ornamental crown.[10] Also brightly lit at night, Tribune Tower is a Chicago landmark anchoring Michigan Avenue across from its neighboring Wrigley Building. WGN Radio would one day broadcast from its elaborate studios at the Tribune Tower, maintaining a street-level glassed studio where some radio programming was done for all to see, and piping Cubs games outside for Michigan Avenue strollers and shoppers to enjoy.

These early 1920s were explosive times in Chicago's swashbuckling history that included legions of meatpackers and railroad men plus such varied luminaries as FBI crime fighter Eliot Ness, retailers Marshall Field and Sears and Roebuck, Frank Lloyd Wright, the *Tribune*'s Colonel McCormick, William Wrigley, and of course the ruthless bootlegger Al Capone who was at the peak of his power during the Roaring Twenties prohibition years. A baseball fan, Capone and his brother Ralph "Bottles" Capone could often be seen at the ballparks, sometimes seated next to Judge Landis, also a huge fan of the game in addition to being commissioner. Thanks to Wrigley, it was during these years that Bill Veeck, Sr., was installed as the operating president of the club. Veeck had been a local sportswriter for the now defunct *Chicago American* where he wrote a series of articles on how the Cubs were poorly run. According to *Veeck as in Wreck*, an autobiography by his son Bill Jr. (who is largely remembered for marching midget Eddie Gaedel to the plate for the St. Louis Browns in 1951), Wrigley saw these articles and invited the senior Veeck to dinner. After what must have been a spirited discussion, Wrigley challenged Veeck, "All right, if you're so smart, why don't you come and do it?" Wrigley then installed Bill Veeck, Sr., as the team president in 1917 when the younger Veeck was just three years old; the elder Veeck proceeded to run the team for 16 years.[11]

As an aggressive marketer of Wrigley gum, William Wrigley was keenly aware of advertising and promotion, both of which would exploit the essence of radio's true potential. In fact, the original WDAP that the neighboring *Tribune* eventually acquired was housed in the Wrigley building's first tower in 1922. Later, Wrigley and Veeck were behind the 1925 radio experiment when the Cubs broadcast their home opener in 1925, after which the Cubs would frequently broadcast games on Chicago's WMAQ and sometimes WGN before eventually settling on WGN radio. From 1926 to 1931, the Cubs reported a 117 percent increase in attendance even though the team itself showed no appreciable difference in its success on the field. Teams not utilizing radio broadcasts saw attendance increase in that same period by just 27 percent. Wrigley had discovered the Holy Grail of baseball marketing, but many other owners were still wary of this new medium. They simply did not trust radio.

By sending live baseball games directly into homes, hospitals, service stations, and pool halls, radio was thus "billboarding" the game — which, as previously noted, is an advertising term to describe the widespread exposure baseball received from these broadcasts. This, among other things, is what Wrigley understood so well: as more members of the public became engaged, more developed an interest in the local team, and many more poured through the turnstiles as a result. Radio did not keep fans away, it was creating new fans and drawing more and more listeners to the ballpark. This was a "no-brainer" in today's vernacular, yet there were still plenty of short-sighted baseball owners to go around at the time. In 1926, Ban Johnson, the long-time president of the American League, actually issued an edict *banning* American League baseball from the radio airwaves.[12]

The 1926 season was a threshold year that would see the return of Ruth and Yankee dominance — yet no one heard about these exploits of Ruth on the radio, unless the Yankees were on the road or in the World Series. Ruth served emphatic notice of his re-emergence on June 8, 1926, when he allegedly rocked a pitch 602 feet (probably less, given baseball physics and reality) that flew completely out of the ballpark, symbolically erasing the Babe's dismal 1925 season. The longest regular season blast of Ruth's entire career, the ball reportedly did not stop rolling until it was 800 feet from home plate. Ruth never let up during the year, shredding American League pitchers to lead the entire major

National Baseball Commission, January 1909 — Left to right: Harry Pulliam, August Herr-mann (chairman from 1903 to 1920), Ban Johnson, J.E. Bruce, secretary. With confused team owners fearing the negative effects of radio on gate attendance, Ban Johnson would later issue an edict prohibiting baseball on the radio for American League games during the 1926 regular season.

leagues in slugging (.737), home runs (47), and RBIs (145). Ruth's home runs were more than double those of the National League leader (Hack Wilson, with 21), and he also topped the National League's best in slugging, .737 to .568 (Fred Williams of the Cubs) and in RBIs by a margin of 25.

The Yankees would win the most games that year (91), but Rogers Hornsby's Car-dinals would best the Yankees in seven games to take the Series. But thanks to legend, lore, and Hollywood, the 1926 World Series is largely remembered for something quite different — and radio played a role. All of New York was captivated by the story of one Johnny Sylvester, an 11-year-old kid from Essex Falls, New Jersey, who had fallen ill from what was then reported as blood poisoning. Sylvester claimed to be a third baseman and home run hitter himself; since the doctors allegedly gave young Johnny as little as "30 minutes to live," Sylvester's last wish was for an autographed baseball from Babe Ruth.

The legend, perpetuated by the press and later depicted in the sentimental motion picture called *The Babe Ruth Story* (released in 1948 just before Ruth's death), is that Ruth showed up at Sylvester's hospital room, gave the kid a ball, and then promised to hit a home run in the World Series for him. All of this made Johnny Sylvester an instant photo-op that also attracted football's Red Grange, who sent him a football, and tennis star Bill Tilden, who contributed a racket. In the film, Sylvester is glued to the radio as Ruth slugs not one, but three home runs in Game Four on October 6, 1926, launching the Sylvester legend into posterity and a permanent place in baseball lore. By the next day, Johnny

Sylvester was on the mend as reported by the *New York Times*, strengthening the growing legacy — and incredibility — of Ruth and Sylvester.

While the facts are murkier than the legend, it appears that Ruth never visited Sylvester at all (at least not before the game), although the Yankees did send a ball autographed by the team along with a letter from Ruth. In reality, Sylvester was not in the hospital, he was at home. The press got wind of the letter, though, and somehow managed to embellish the story almost beyond recognition. The whole thing probably would have slid into oblivion had Ruth not hit those three home runs. Remarkably, Johnny Sylvester was apparently ordered by doctors to rest at home and "avoid all excitement," and some accounts even report that the kid was not even allowed to hear Ruth's three-homer game on the radio (although radio had been banned for the regular season, it was allowed for the Series). Since Johnny recovered the next day he probably had not been all that sick in the first place — especially since it appears his parents left him at home and went the game themselves. Hollywood depicted Sylvester hanging on every pitch thanks to the radio.

The October 8, 1926, edition of the *New York Times* carried this story headline: "Boy Regains Health as Ruth Hits Homers." Decades later, when Johnny Sylvester actually did pass away in 1990 at age 74, the *New York Times* revisited the story and updated the truth as best it could determine. Johnny had graduated from Princeton University and became a lieutenant in the Navy, followed by a successful business career, but for 15 proverbial minutes during the 1926 World Series he was the "most famous boy in America." Upon Sylvester's death, the *Times* investigated further and determined that the most likely ailment was not blood poisoning but rather an infection of the forehead, since Johnny had been kicked by a horse after a fall while riding at the family's estate. And Ruth did visit the boy, as it happens, but not until October 11, after the Series was over and the Yankees had ultimately lost.[13]

The legend, though, has acquired the appearance of fact more than fiction over the years. Perhaps the most entertaining footnote to the whole story came the following spring when Johnny's uncle happened to see Ruth and reported that young Johnny Sylvester was doing fine. According to one account, Ruth was perplexed, turned to some nearby reporters, and asked "Who the hell is Johnny Sylvester?"[14]

Radio's role in building the early legend of Ruth may have been overblown fiction, but there was nothing fictional about the commercial explosion of the radio business in the early 1920s. Manufacturers like Westinghouse sought to expand opportunity by getting into the programming business, while radio suppliers looked for ways to exploit the burgeoning new medium. Retail merchants were advised that radio would soon take its place alongside such dependable sellers as the Victrola, Dictaphone, typewriter, and camera — sounding much like the beginning of the personal computer boom during the 1980s and 1990s. The storage battery business saw opportunity to "cash in" by supplying batteries for portable radios, and headphone makers promoted their products for home use. Early radios, in fact, used headsets and not speakers, then speakers were soon installed, making radio a viable living room companion in homes across the country.

As with many innovations, radio gained its popularity from the top down. As early as 1899 London *Electrophone* claimed Queen Victoria as a listener, and in 1922, President Harding had the Navy install a radio receiver for his own use.[15] With radio soon sweeping the nation, the Department of Commerce grew concerned about too many rogue amateur and experimental stations permeating the public airwaves, so the government began to implement regulations by the end of 1921 to promote minimum standards for the new radio broadcasting industry. As a result, the number of private stations dropped to 67 by early 1922, but that was temporary; there was no stopping the free-market expansion of this new and exciting industry. By the end of that year, there were over 500 stations coast to coast that were broadcasting news, music, jazz, opera, and just plain reading of the newspaper. By July 1922, radio stations were operating in 45 of the nation's 48 states.

The new Westinghouse station WJZ recognized children as a potential market, promoting its "radiophone" stories this way: "The radiophone, which is the wireless, has made it possible for the Man in the Moon to talk to you." This shows that overstated hyperbole has been used to reach children for as long as broadcasting has existed. The stories were well received, though, and soon publishers were setting them to print and selling "man in the moon" tales. Soon we not only had music *on* the radio, America began singing *about* radio, like with the playful 1922 tune "I Wish There Was a Wireless to Heaven." As early as 1908, books featuring radio in their plots, or even acting as something of a protagonist, began to appear. By 1922 they could be found on shelves everywhere, including a well-received set called the Radio Boys Books, followed of course by Radio Girls. Some of the books offered great detail about how the radio worked, such as *The Radio Boys' First Wireless*, where the characters built radios with crystal receivers and headphones. In subsequent stories, the "boys" expanded their fictional developments with vacuum tubes, loud speakers, and sophisticated antennas.[16]

A learned protagonist in one such book accurately pontificated, "Radio is yet in its infancy, but one thing is certain. In the lifetime of those who witnessed its birth it will become a giant — but a benevolent giant who, instead of destroying, will re-create our civilization."[17] A bit romantic, but history would prove that the prediction was largely accurate. Such fictional stories were free to speculate outside the box, and some nailed impending developments with a great deal of accuracy, even predicting car radios which, interestingly, began to appear as early as 1923. Meanwhile, the whole country was becoming infested with amateur radio enthusiasts, as books flew off the shelves with such promising titles as *Radio Receiving for Beginners* and *Radio for Everybody*, with an occasional offering that was noticeably less romantic like the sober *A Wireless Warning*.

Some offerings were insightful thought pieces, like this article that appeared in *The Nation* in March 1922: "Radio as a Revolutionist," which openly wondered whether radio would destroy our national solitude and speculated about the fate of Henry David Thoreau had his trip to Walden Pond included a radio receiver, or worse, had a nearby troop of Boy Scouts blasted popular music from radio loudspeakers.[18] Anyone who has endured such distractions from neighbors while attempting a summer backyard snooze would likely agree that too much radio can be intrusive, but such distractions would hardly impede its growth.

With very few exceptions, though, early radio still largely missed the obvious opportunities afforded by baseball. Chicago's WGN crept toward big league broadcasting, but only gradually, offering in 1924 a "radiocast" of baseball results of the day. Baseball scores and summaries were put on the air in the latter part of each evening, both soon these popular recaps were moved earlier as reported by the *Chicago Tribune* on June 29, 1924: "The scores are put on air promptly at 6 o'clock, thus giving the fans a report on the game

Cubs players in the dugout at Wrigley Field before a game during the 1929 World Series. Hal Totten would call the game for CBS, Graham McNamee for NBC. Just 15 days after the Series ended was Black Tuesday, the day of the great stock market crash on October 29, 1929.

before dinner."[19] The public, it appears, had a greater appetite for radio reports of baseball than for dinner, a healthy sign for the future of baseball broadcasting.

In the very early days, Chicago's WMAQ did even better, for it began to broadcast Cubs and White Sox games on a limited basis. In any event, pioneer announcer Hal Totten was involved in those early broadcasts by WMAQ, but he was installed only after William Wrigley first offered the job to former Cub Solly Hoffman, who then did a miserable job and lasted only one day. It was a failed experiment that proved it would take more than on-field baseball experience to become a successful radio broadcaster. Wrigley then settled on Totten, who had been a re-write man at the *Chicago Daily News*. Totten would become a highly accomplished broadcaster doing baseball and other sports, including the Dempsey-Tunney heavyweight fight extravaganza at Chicago's Soldier Field in 1927 (now remembered as the famous "long count" fight).

Baseball was in full swing during the Roaring Twenties, and so was the hand of fate. Not only was Ruth banging out homers on the Big Apple stage just when radio was being widely commercialized, but another new business had rapidly become the largest manufacturing industry in America: building and selling automobiles. Over two million cars were made in the United States in 1920, and production would keep growing to reach an astonishing 5,337,687 in 1929 alone — the very year that ushered in the Great Depression with the cataclysmic stock market collapse in October.[20] Those 1929 auto production levels would not be achieved again for two decades, but they *would* return, for America was clearly in love with its automobiles.

In the early 1920s with assembly line mass production in full scale, a Ford could be bought for as little as $393, a Chevy for $525, and a Dodge for $880 (all expressed in 1920s dollars). The public appetite for cars was pervasive, and the necessary levels of auto production would change the country in many ways—for example, 75 percent of all plate glass made during the 1920s was for use in automobiles. All these cars would directly impact baseball in two major ways. Eventually the automobile and resultant highways would lead to the suburban sprawl, and decades later that sociological change would move big league baseball from its congested inner-city stadiums to more distant ballparks, some in the suburbs—and eventually westward to the vast regions of California. But those changes would materialize in the 1950s, while during the 1920s the automobile impacted the game of baseball in a much different but very direct way: the car radio.

Once radio was established as a viable device, inventors were soon tinkering with the idea of a "portable" radio. The original portable radios were heavy and cumbersome, consisting of one box for the radio itself and another for the speaker and batteries, plus a very long wire antenna. At some point all the components were loaded into one big, heavy box. Awkward or not, once the radio was portable, it was only steps away from appearing in automobiles. The 1904 World Exhibition in St. Louis featured an experimental radio in a very early car, but the car radio industry got a major boost in 1922 by a Chicago high school, Lane High (now Lane Tech High School). George Frost, president of the Lane High School Radio Club, installed a clumsy radio box in his 1922 Ford Model T. At the same time, a "Marconiphone" radio was dropped into a Daimler vehicle across the ocean in England.[21] Once general broadcasting appeared in urban areas, city police forces began experimenting with patrol-car radios, an idea that WGN Radio fostered when it began broadcasting police reports over the air. Once baseball broadcasting took hold, it was a natural to turn the car radio dial to reach the local Cubs, White Sox, Pirates, or other available games.

The first car radios were being offered to the public as early as 1925 (some accounts suggest a 1923 introduction by the Springfield Body Corporation may have been the first), but genuine mass production of automobile radios was not fully geared up until 1927. One of the first was the "Transitone TH-1." Soon Philco became a major player in the market, as did Chicago's Motorola — a company with a name that combines the obvious auto term "motor" with the familiar suffix of another sound-producing device: the Victrola record players.

Meanwhile the overall radio industry was gaining traction at an accelerated pace, with the nation's first "radio world's fair," a massive 1924 trade show held simultaneously at two New York City locations, Madison Square Garden and the 69th Regiment Armory facility. The *Chicago Tribune* called the show "the most successful trade exposition ever staged in America." That lofty description was not just hyperbole, for the trade show was attended by almost twice the number of visitors as any other in history. In one week 175,000 people were admitted, with thousands of others turned away at the door, while 200 exhibitors (180 from the U.S. alone) booked over $3 million in orders (1924 dollars) with four manufacturers selling out their entire stock for the year while three others actually overbooked their capacity.[22]

As portable radios continued to develop, they found another use outside the automobile: sidewalks. In New York sidewalk radios began to proliferate, especially as the 1930s unfolded. Interestingly, although New York would become the broadcast and entertainment center of America for decades, it was not the original radio mecca for baseball broadcasting. With the Giants, Dodgers, and Yankees all playing in New York, and the great radio trade show hosted by New York City, it seems natural that baseball broadcasting would have proliferated in the Big Apple. But if not New York, then where?

Chicago. As the 1920s drew to a close, there was so much baseball on the radio in Chicago, a city with so many radio receivers that one could almost stroll through the neighborhoods and still hear games from the porches and yards. So many local radios would be tuned to the afternoon ballgame, projecting blow-by-blow accounts of the game across the neighborhoods, that the city was alive with baseball — and in many ways, it still is.

One reason for this baseball explosion in Chicago was the sheer number of radio stations that sprang up in the city, many doing baseball games. WMAQ featured Hal Totten; WGN had broadcast icons Quin Ryan and Bob Elson; WJJD offered Johnny O'Hara; Jimmy Dudley and Jack Drees were on WIND; and WENR featured baseball Hall of Famer Tris Speaker, a lifetime .345 hitter throughout a long career that lasted from 1907 to 1928.

There were still more reasons that Chicago was the original baseball broadcasting mecca. One was marketing wizard William Wrigley, of course, who had the vision to exploit the radio medium for his Chicago Cubs. But another was cross-town rival Charles Comiskey, owner of the White Sox and a very powerful baseball man. When American League president Ban Johnson vetoed radio for American League games, Comiskey boldly ignored the edict and continued to broadcast White Sox games anyway. Another reason was that Chicago at that time had also become the original hub of the baseball universe as we know it. As commissioner, Kenesaw Landis wielded unprecedented power, and the Cubs and White Sox were both powerhouse teams in the early days of the twentieth century. Landis is a particularly interesting study, for he operated baseball from his offices at 333 N. Michigan Avenue, just south of the Chicago River and extremely close to its neighbors across the Michigan Avenue drawbridge, the Wrigley Building and Tribune Tower. At first, Landis remained an active federal judge while he was commissioner, but he was eventually forced to give up the concurrent judgeship.

The radio audience for the 1922 World Series reached five million, signaling the power of this new broadcast medium and catching the attention of Wrigley and other business leaders both inside and outside this new industry. By 1925, Chicago's Quin Ryan was paired with New York broadcasting pioneer Graham McNamee to announce the World Series between the Pirates and Senators. This first coast-to-coast live broadcast of baseball was carried by Chicago's WGN radio. WGN would broadcast a number of World Series over the next several years, although not exclusively. In 1926 Ryan and WGN would do each Cubs home game that fell on a Saturday, but when these baseball broadcasts proved extremely popular, more games were added to the schedule.

Even by 1926, radio was unsure how to announce baseball games. Hal Totten called various Cubs games from 1924 to 1944, but also White Sox games during that same span beginning in 1926. Totten had a gentle voice that delivered a dry, unemotional broadcast, the virtual the opposite of the colorful Graham McNamee whose delivery was described at "riveting." Quin Ryan was not as low key as Totten, but even so, WGN sensed that baseball broadcasts needed something more to liven the entertainment value of baseball programming. They turned to two comic actors, Freeman Gosden and Charles Correll, who were already changing the face of radio with their daily WGN comedy series *Sam 'n' Henry*. Placed in the broadcast booth with Quin Ryan, Gosden and Correll offered an energetic, rapid dialogue delivery that was an immediate antidote to dead air.[23]

Most of America would become intimately familiar with the *Sam 'n' Henry* voices, and much of the country still recognizes their friendly energetic exchanges from what soon became the *Amos 'n' Andy* comedy series. WGN was responsible for launching that

This "tomato can" style microphone, shown being donated to the Smithsonian Institution, was the original KDKA Radio device used to broadcast results of the Harding-Cox election on November 2, 1920. The following summer, on August 5, 1921, KDKA, Pittsburgh, became the first station to broadcast a major league baseball game. (DN-0088901, *Chicago Daily News* negatives collection, Chicago History Museum)

historic comedy program, although it failed to fully cash in when the actors bolted for rival WMAQ in 1927 over a contract dispute. They went on to change radio history as *Amos 'n' Andy*, and as a result Freeman Gosden is widely credited with inventing the original situation comedy concept in the same basic form that is commonly utilized even in the New Millennium. Original, funny, and upbeat, the show unfortunately perpetuated a simplistic African American stereotype, although at the same time it did manage to prove the wide acceptance and viability of African American characters—even though the original radio actors were indeed white. (Actual black actors would be used later for the television version of the same show, a program remembered by many Americans who are baby boomers or older).

Featuring the baritone delivery of Amos as "Kingfish" (the name may have been a subtle salute to creator Freeman Fisher Gosden), the *Amos 'n' Andy* radio show became one of the most popular and longest running radio programs of all time The eventual television version ran on CBS only from June 1951 until June 1953, but it was widely syndicated for years thereafter.[24] While still at WGN, these popular characters were leveraged to promote other events on WGN and were featured with Quin Ryan for various early WGN broadcasts of the Kentucky Derby, Indianapolis 500, and eventually baseball games. As it happens, this was a variation of the billboarding concept that was used to promote baseball attendance and would later be perfected during the days of television when various contemporary stars would visit Johnny Carson, David Letterman, and the sports broadcast booth to pitch other network shows. In Ryan's case, the comedic actors in *Sam 'n' Henry* were hardly necessary to make baseball work on the radio, but they did help liven the broadcast until the regular announcers caught on. Quin Ryan became one such announcer, coming to be regarded as an early broadcaster who could describe a game so well that the listening audience could "see" the game through his voice. Another talented young broadcaster was Ronald Reagan, who partially credited Ryan with his own interests in baseball itself and the electronic media in general.

Beginning in 1927, WGN began regular broadcasts of home games for *both* the Cubs and White Sox. Quin Ryan called those games for both, working homestands since the Cubs were almost always on road trips when the Sox were in town. He was soon moved into his own special area, originally called the press "coop," but later known as the press box or booth. This is where the broadcasters would perfect baseball on the radio, honing their skills to the level of an art form that is still evolving today. It was here, in the "press coop," that the stories of the game unfolded, captivating an audience that hung not only on every pitch, but on every carefully crafted word, all of which was soon symbolized by the excitement and allure of the home run call. Such calls would become the audio symbol of all that is baseball on the radio and then later on television, evolving into a unique virtual signature for every baseball man who ever broadcast a game. Some were merely exploitive, of course, with early "product calls" like Mel Allen's "Ballentine blast," while others were simple and succinct such as Vin Scully's "forget it" or the "hey hey" of Jack Brickhouse. Some are still memorable, such as the Harry Caray's cliff-hanging "it could be, it might be, it *is*—a home run." Perhaps the most colorful was Rosey Rowswell's story-like call for the Pittsburgh faithful: "Open the window, Aunt Minnie, here it comes."

Whether colorful, memorable, funny or exploitive, they all were unique in their own way. Ken Harrelson began calling White Sox games in 1990 and developed a distinct signature with "put it on the booooaaaarrrrddd—YES." But there is a singular call that is brief, memorable, and perhaps the one home run phrase that deserves the title "classic." It was originally used by Harry Hartman calling Reds games as early as 1929, but was made famous by one of the all-time great announcers, New York's Mel Allen, who called Yankee games for 25 years during a career that began in 1939 and did not end until a third stint with New York that came to a close in 1985: "It's going, going, *gone.*"[25]

5

Murderers, Monkeys, and Radio Men

Ruth, radio, and the Roaring Twenties conspired with fate to elevate baseball as America's national pastime. It was fortuitous that Ruth began as a pitcher, for that assured the free-swinger fewer at-bats and afforded him lower expectations at the plate. He responded by swinging from the heels, without inhibition, generating home runs like never before. Baseball in those days had never been a game of home runs, primarily due to the ball fields themselves: the original ballparks were in wide open fields of tall grass, lumpy divots, and clumps of dirt, little of which was hemmed in by fences. Deemed "parks" for a very good reason, the originals were often virtual pastures with a batter's box, a diamond, and maybe some makeshift bleachers.

The original old-style ball field is exemplified by a reputed incident involving Charley "Old Hoss" Radbourn, a Hall of Fame pitcher who won a stunning 49 games in 1883 followed in 1884 by 73 complete games, 60 wins, and 678.2 total innings.[1] In 1882, playing for the Providence Grays, Hoss Radbourn found himself at the plate in the 18th inning of a marathon contest against the team from Detroit. Hoss took a mighty swing and launched a ball over the head of left fielder George Wood where it bounced in the tall grass and landed near a farm wagon. A black horse occupying that deep section of left field promptly stood directly on the ball. Wood made a number of efforts to retrieve the ball as the horse kicked, all while Radbourn kept circling the bases, eventually making it all the way home for the first home run of his career. It was a symbolic moment for how the game was originally played, not to mention an ironic one, too, given Radbourn's moniker of "Hoss," a nickname that evolved because he was durable as a horse.

As base ball — the original term was two distinct words, with "base" still an adjective, reflective of an emerging sport that had not yet grown into its own "noun" status — grew in popularity, more urban ballparks were built. These city fields required fences for two reasons: to separate the field from neighboring factories or row houses, and to keep out hoards of non-paying onlookers. The urban parks not only sported fences, typically their fields were smaller: Fenway Park (1912), Wrigley Field (1914), and the original Yankee Stadium, at least in right field (1923).

But old habits die hard, so most ballplayers still preferred the "small ball" approach to the game with singles, doubles, stolen bases, and moving the runners over. Ruth happened to be big, strong, and aggressive, and since he batted less frequently he decided to make the most of it. He not only swung hard, Ruth introduced an entirely new style of swinging the bat, a rotational approach whereby Ruth turned on the ball with a full corkscrew motion instead of the old method where batters stepped into the pitch to slap at the ball, simultaneously shifting their weight to the front foot.

Before 1925, the minimum distance for home run fences was only 235 feet, so when balls began flying over the wall (at least where there *was* a wall), especially at New York's Polo Grounds where the ultra short right-field fence helped boost Ruth to a record-shattering 54 homers in 1920, all of baseball noticed.[2] So did the rest of the world, and soon the owners saw the excitement of those long balls and began to prefer offense over pitching and defense. In 1920 baseball changed the rules to eliminate one of the most potent pitching weapons, the spitball. By 1925, new baseballs with cushioned cork centers were put into use, and throughout the 1920s and 1930s baseball offense was on the rise. The number of home runs tripled, scoring increased by two runs per game, and overall hitting skyrocketed. By 1930, the entire combined National League was batting a mind bending .303.[3]

By 1926, two of the premier hitters in the history of baseball had already made their impact on the game, Babe Ruth and Ty Cobb. Demonstrating the foothold baseball had developed, and reflecting the economic prosperity of the game, Cobb's salary for 1926 had reached $50,000, exceeded only by Ruth's $80,000.[4] In 1926, the average wage for "skilled and semi-skilled male production workers" was $30.60 *per week*, which equaled only about $1500 per year. Only 20,520 tax returns were filed in the whole country by individuals earning between $50,000 and $100,000 in 1926, showing just how lofty those Cobb and Ruth paydays were.[5] (Cobb and Ruth would have paid federal income taxes at 25 percent, the highest marginal rate at the time, due to three tax cuts in the early 1920s that saw rates drop from a whopping 73 percent, probably helping to fuel the decade's economic prosperity.) In current dollars, Ruth's salary would have been in the $3 million to $4 million range, a great paycheck but not that lofty by today's professional sports standards, a difference that would be caused largely by the lucrative advent of one thing: baseball broadcasting (player unions played a role, but the money was there to claim because of broadcasting).

Like the rest of America, baseball would have to endure and then emerge from the Great Depression of the 1930s. By then much of the country would own a radio, which became the source of much very cheap, stay-at-home entertainment, a lucky product of fate that would help propel baseball still further — at least where the owners would allow broadcasting. Not surprisingly, the Depression had been preceded by a decade of explosive economic growth, some sources pegging such growth at 4.2 percent per year from 1920 through 1929. That prosperity, coupled with Prohibition which led to bootleggers, gangsters, and crime-fighting feds, contributed to what is now called the Roaring Twenties. It was an era that indeed roared with automobiles, newfangled talking motion pictures, machine gun bullets, and tape-measure home runs.

Interestingly, there was a one-year economic depression that slipped in during 1920–21, but the country rebounded to full employment by 1923. Even more remarkable, there was a recession in 1927 caused by one man, Henry Ford, who shut down all his Ford automobile factories for six months to retool the assembly lines to switch production from the Model T to the stellar new Model A automobile.[6] In the world of baseball, that year of 1927, the season of Murderers' Row and Ruth's magical 60 homers, might just be the Holy Grail of baseball history. It also would make a significant impact on the new phenomenon of sports broadcasting, but not necessarily because of the wildly popular New York Yankees.

As the country and baseball surged forward during those Roaring Twenties, new technologies in communication were developing rapidly. New electronic amplifiers were invented, which made long distance coast-to-coast telephone calls possible in 1915. During the 1920s, the number of electronic telegrams grew by 60.4 percent, the number of local phone conversations grew by 46.8 percent, and the amount of long distance phone calls skyrocketed by 71.8 percent. Not surprisingly, the American Telephone & Telegraph Company (AT&T) also grew at a rapid pace during this period when the number of U.S. households with telephones reached 42 percent.[7]

Riding this wave of prosperity, and wisely expanding upon its developing savvy about communications, AT&T started its own radio station in New York in 1922, WEAF, which later would become WNBC. At first AT&T thought of radio as an electronic highway, sort of like the long distance phone networks, and envisioned selling time to send messages. As it happened, the most profitable messages turned out to be commercials, but no one would listen to an endless string of commercials without content in between, hence the early days of radio programming from opera to jazz, reading the newspaper aloud, and soon live news and sports, especially baseball and sometimes boxing.

At first the radio stations shunned advertising — they actually thought it commercially offensive and beneath the dignity of this new medium. But by the 1920s AT&T had a lock on the industry with its patented broadcast transmitters, so it began to charge a royalty on all radio broadcasting that violated such patents. Once the stations began paying, they needed new revenue sources, so they turned to that dreaded beast called commercial advertising. Rival RCA saw the same commercial viability of radio, so it entered the radio market through a different network of transmission lines offered by Western Union. AT&T responded by starting its own subsidiary, the National Broadcasting Company, to enhance its focus and ability to compete by creating an elaborate string of stations to form a national "network." With two players in the radio network game, the William Paley family joined the fray with a new entry called the Columbia Broadcasting System, more commonly known today as CBS.

With long distance phone lines and radio networks in place, America became more connected than ever before. As America turned to radio for news and entertainment, radio soon emerged as the prime medium of advertising. By 1930, at the close of the Roaring Twenties and on the eve of the Great Depression, more American homes had a radio than a telephone. In 1927, Congress passed laws creating the Federal Radio Commission, and with that the government began to control the airwaves, issuing licenses to protect the public interest. The 1927 Act was soon replaced by the Federal Communications Act of 1934, but the feds were in the broadcast licensing business to stay. Under the old FRC, the government licensed 24 stations that had as much as 50,000 watts of broadcast power, enough for each station to reach multiple states.[8] No fewer than 21 of those stations soon ended up in one of the emerging radio networks.

Radio was given a quantum-leap boost during the summer of 1925, the same year

T.D. Dutton and J.J. Boone, radio broadcasters of the American Telephone and Telegraph Co., testing the installation for broadcasting the inaugural ceremonies in 1929. AT&T was a pioneer in radio and baseball broadcasting: it demonstrated the first fax transmission in 1924, the first television transmission in 1927, and later was instrumental in the coast to coast broadcast of baseball games by satellite, made possible by Telstar-I in 1962.

that Chicago's WGN broadcast Opening Day from Wrigley Field. Again it was WGN fueling the change, as it utilized the AT&T long distance phone lines to do it in front page, headline fashion: first with monkeys courtesy of a 1925 national controversy over religion and law, and then sports with heavyweight boxing's 1927 "fight of the century" bout between Jack Dempsey and Gene Tunney.

The seeds for the great "monkey trial" planted in 1859 with the publication of *Origin of the Species*, Charles Darwin's famous but controversial scientific essay on the evolution of man, then accelerated with the 1914 publication of the high school textbook Hunter's *Civic Biology* which detailed the evolution theory.[9] The controversy hit the boiling point when several states passed anti-evolution laws like Tennessee's Butler Act that was signed by Governor Austin Peay on March 21, 1925. The law banned the teaching of any theory of man that denied the Biblical version but, interestingly, did not proscribe teaching the theory as it pertained to animals and plant life. More remarkably, up to that point, Hunter's biology textbook had actually been the approved biology text for use in Tennessee classrooms.

Headquartered in New York, the young and idealistic American Civil Liberties Union had set about defending labor causes, although in 1925 it was still searching for its first court victory. When the Tennessee anti-evolution law caught its attention, the ACLU actively advertised for a test case. The community leaders in sleepy Dayton, Tennessee, a shrinking rural town in the central part of the state that was suffering from a difficult local economy, saw this potential confrontation as an opportunity to bring acclaim, if not money, to Dayton. Local substitute teacher John Scopes was recruited, then promptly arrested and charged with violating the law.[10] The ACLU jumped into the fray, volunteering to defend Scopes, which it ultimately proceeded to do. But as the breadth of the Scopes trial swiftly escalated with the force of national headlines, the ACLU soon lost control of the defense. National orator, fundamentalist, and three-time presidential candidate William Jennings Bryan publicly offered help prosecute the cause. With Bryan on board, the nation's most famous defense lawyer, Clarence Darrow of Chicago, could not resist the brewing storm and volunteered to defend the cause in Dayton. Although the ACLU did participate in the defense, it was Darrow who took control of the trial, the issue, and the headlines.

With Darrow and Bryan pitted against each other in the nation's heartland, the "trial of the century" was set into motion. The *Baltimore Sun* sent its famous columnist H.L. Mencken to cover the trial, but Mencken, who had no tolerance for religion let alone the fundamentalist brand, actually helped shape the trial by encouraging Darrow to take the case in the first place. Darrow did, and according to many accounts, it was the only pro bono trial Darrow would ever undertake.

Dayton believed it had struck gold. Newspapers across the globe covered the epic battle, including the New York papers and the powerful International News Service run by William Randolph Hearst. Dayton built a speaker's platform outside the courthouse and constructed a makeshift air strip on the outskirts of town. Western Union sent 22 key operators to type out and to disseminate the news, and the Southern Railway added more passenger service to accommodate the anticipated crowds.

The *Chicago Tribune* took a keen interest in the developing courtroom drama, then actually changed history by sending its own radio station WGN to cover the proceedings. WGN decided not only to cover the trial, but it arranged to set up in the courtroom and broadcast live from the event. It was an unprecedented and bold move that contributed greatly to the evolution of radio, if not the concurrent evolution of live newscasts and, in the end, baseball broadcasting, for it was newsman and baseball broadcaster Quin Ryan who was sent to Dayton for the dramatic festivities.[11]

The Scopes Monkey Trial had little to do with baseball directly — although it is interesting that Jerome Lawrence and Robert Lee, in their play *Inherit the Wind* chose to begin Clarence Darrow's cross examination of his fundamentalist opponent William Jennings Bryan on *The Bible* by announcing "we'll play in your ballpark"— but it had everything to do with the power of broadcasting and fuelling the ravenous hunger for content. Scopes was more than a trial; it was an epiphany for radio in general and WGN in particular — and ultimately one of the greatest forms of reality programming that provided 154 episodes of pure content: baseball.

The *Tribune* itself wrote on the breadth and importance not only of the looming trial, but the significance of the impending broadcast itself. The July 5, 1925, edition of the *Tribune* proclaimed that "the event will be the first of its kind in the history of radio or the American courts of law." The judge himself, Gordon McKenzie, granted the exclusive broadcast rights to WGN, and the *Tribune* crowed about the coming events. "Arrangements have been completed by W-G-N at Dayton for the placing of microphones at points in the court room to assure a clear and distinct transmission of every word spoken." The worldwide circus atmosphere was further described in that July 5 edition of the paper:

> The speeches of William Jennings Bryan for the prosecution, of Clarence Darrow, Bainbridge Colby and Dudley Field Malone for the defense and, indeed, every word spoken in the room during the important days of the trial will be telephoned to the W-G-N studio and put on the air. The service of W-G-N to the public will be even further, in placing of twenty Atlas loud speakers on the court house lawn in Dayton, in the Dayton grammar school, the high school, the American Legion hall and the tabernacle for the great crowds that are expected to flow into the town to hear the proceedings.[12]

Just before the opening of the trial, the *Tribune* wrote that the prosecution would begin by talking "...not only to a judge and jury, but to the greatest audience in the history of American courts." It was not an inexpensive undertaking. Those AT&T phone lines cost the station $1000 per day over the course of the trial, not to mention the expense of maintaining the legions of broadcasters, writers, and support staff on location in Dayton.[13] The courtroom itself happened to be the second largest in the state of Tennessee, accommodating vast crowds of onlookers. Some of the proceedings, though, were conducted outside on the lawn partly due to the summer heat and partly to avoid the floor caving in from the mass of humanity on hand to observe.

The trial preliminaries began on Friday, July 10, at 9:00 A.M. Newspaper reporters were seated along three sides of a surrounding rail, while feature writers and magazine contributors took the first three rows of gallery seats. A WGN radio microphone was strategically placed near the front, with some moving of the courtroom furniture and modifying some of the local customs to do so. Although around 500 visitors would stay in Dayton for the trial, about half of which were from various forms of the media, Dayton itself was disappointed by the ultimate turnout.[14] The trial did not prove to be a goldmine for the town, but it did put Dayton forever on the map of cutting-edge jurisprudence, courtroom journalism, and broadcasting history. Maybe the vast number of anticipated visitors stayed away fearing the immense crowds themselves, or perhaps the novelty — and convenience — of the broadcast proceedings kept them away. This latter phenomenon would be the very same concern expressed by baseball owners who were already afraid that fans would stay home rather than attend, and pay for, the live games. But there was a vast difference. Baseball is a recurring entertainment event that thrives upon building customer enthusiasm, is decidedly more fun than most trials, and is prepared for large crowds with its organized stadiums.

Darrow was brilliant in his defense of Scopes, evolution, and the right to think and teach, but he and the ACLU eventually lost the Scopes trial, costing the defendant a $100 fine; but they nonetheless escalated the evolution issue and helped validate the feasibility and drama of live radio reporting. Thereafter, WGN and other stations would be inspired to report live events like the Indianapolis 500 and many others, including more and more live baseball games just as baseball was gaining increased momentum with home runs, star power, and soon the World Series featuring the 1927 Yankees. Fate continued to intervene as well, for just one month before the Scopes trial, the inimitable Wally Pipp was beaned in the head, allowing newcomer Lou Gehrig to start at first base for the team that history would remember as Murderers' Row. Although 1925 itself would not be a spectacular year for Ruth, the Babe (with 25 homers) and the likes of Rogers Hornsby,

Bob Meusel, and others continued the home run parade — so much so that by July 1925 (just as the Scopes trial was underway), baseball was confronted by a "rabbit ball" controversy to determine whether the league had tampered with the baseballs to generate more offense — sounding much like similar ensuring controversies over decades later. Given the balls and hitting of different eras, it is likely that a number of factors were in play from pitching, rule changes (like the no-spitball rule from 1920), the increased use of new balls during the course of a game, and improved stitching on the balls themselves — not to mention another cause: the home run swings of Ruth, Gehrig, Meusel, and Hornsby.[15]

For the first time in five years, the Giants did not win the pennant in 1925, ceding the National League title to the Pittsburgh Pirates who played the Washington Senators in the World Series. But Ruth and radio would take baseball to new heights during the entire 1926 season, beginning with a five-hit Ruthian day against pitching icon Walter Johnson on April 20. Ten days after that, Satchel Paige began a legendary pitching career that began in the Negro Leagues, where Paige would remain until Bill Veeck, Jr., eventually signed the aging Paige for the Indians in 1948. By mid-summer Ruth was launching long balls in record numbers, but then the Yankees would lose the "Johnny Sylvester" World Series in seven games to the Cardinals. Ruth, though, was back on top with 47 homers and a slugging average of .737, setting the stage for the season to end all seasons: 1927.

Some regard 1927 as the greatest of all baseball seasons, a watershed moment among many landmark years like 1928, 1939, 1947, 1951, 1961, 1969, 1975, and 1998, all great years for various reasons. Much of 1927's contribution to baseball history was earned on the field of play, notably at Yankee Stadium in the Bronx, although fate would play a role, too. Most observers regard broadcaster Vin Scully as among the very best baseball broadcasters, if not *the* best. As it happens, Scully was born just after the 1927 World Series — in the Bronx, no less — on November 22, 1927. The 1927 World Series was the first to be broadcast coast-to-coast, a culmination of the watershed broadcast moments of 1923, the WGN remote broadcasting of Scopes in 1925, and the 1927 Rose Bowl.

The "golden age of radio" would extend from the mid–1920s, when radio became widely commercialized, through the end of the 1950s. C.E. Hooper, Inc., monitored radio ratings through much of radio's golden age. A number of sources suggest a study in 1947, during the heart of radio's grandest years, showed that 82 percent of all Americans were radio listeners. No wonder, for radio exploded during the early portion of the 1920s. The very first radio news program was delivered by station 8MK in Detroit in August 1920, at least according to the *Detroit News* itself in 1922.[16] By March 1922 there were 1,000,000 radios deployed in the United States. The public consumed such programming as big band music, news and commentary, farm reports, mysteries, variety shows, and weather. Soon corporate America was sponsoring broadcasts and individual shows, often with the sponsor in the billing itself with shows like the *Champion Spark Plug Hour*, the *Goodrich Zippers*, the *Ingram Shavers*, and *Ipana Troubadors* — the latter evoking distant memories of Ipana toothpaste.

Some of the most familiar names and most memorable programs included the *Bell Telephone Hour, Amos 'n' Andy,* and *Lux Radio Theater,* while one of the most popular was the *National Barn Dance* offered in 1924 by WLS Radio in Chicago. Radio made huge stars of such personalities as Fred Allen, Jack Benny, Groucho Marx, and other comedians and entertainers, perhaps none bigger than those featured by Nashville's *WSM Barn Dance* which was renamed the *Grand Ole Opry* beginning in the year of the Yankees, 1927. As radio discovered baseball, some of those emerging stars included the baseball announcers like Graham McNamee, Harold Arlin, Quin Ryan, and Hal Totten. Ironically, even though New York was a major hub of the radio networks, and the New York Yankees became the premier sports team in America with its Murderers' Row lineup, the New York fans were largely denied the opportunity to regularly hear exploits of the Yankees on the radio until announcing legend Mel Allen first took the microphone in 1939.

Ban Johnson's American League edict quashed radio broadcasts in 1926, and even though it did not last, New York was slow to catch on afterward. All such efforts to manipulate competition from radio would have been — and should have been — violations of United States antitrust laws under the Sherman Act of 1890, except for one thing: baseball's now notorious antitrust exemption that had been wrestled by the owners in 1922. Baseball was free to suppress competition from radio, which the game attempted at several points in the 1920s and 1930s, especially in New York. But the game ultimately shot itself in the foot, for radio was the last piece of a grand puzzle that would soon solidify baseball as the American pastime. Both Ruth and the Roaring Twenties were in full swing — sometimes literally of course — and radio was taking the nation by storm, even though the radio microphones were not always welcome where baseball was concerned.

The baseball antitrust exemption, which still is largely misunderstood, began with a United States Supreme Court opinion penned by Justice Oliver Wendell Holmes, Jr., which was issued on May 29, 1922, in the case of *Federal Base Ball Club v. National League.* The plaintiff was the Baltimore franchise of the new Federal League formed in 1914 to compete with the American and National Leagues for both players and ticket revenues. When the National League responded with defensive measures to freeze out the Federal League, the new league filed an antitrust claim against the National League, alleging a "contract, combination or conspiracy" under the purview of the Sherman Act.[17]

The original lawsuit was filed at Chicago in the United States District Court where Judge Kenesaw Landis presided, no doubt because Landis had become an antitrust expert. Moreover, Landis was also known for his stance against big business — he had already slapped Rockefeller's Standard Oil with a $29 million antitrust fine — so the Federal League believed it had an impartial, if not a perfectly friendly, forum to pursue its claim against major league baseball. Baseball responded with a scorched-earth defense to drive up the legal fees and related costs to the young Federal League, a tactic that largely worked, forcing the league to ultimately accept a settlement that was arm-twisted by Landis himself who had repeatedly delayed the case, perhaps to aid the defendant National League. Landis, as it happens, was a bigger fan of baseball than he was of the antitrust laws. The Federal League had misread Landis and had not counted on his devotion to major league baseball, but neither had baseball expected the tenacity of one of the competing teams, the Federal League club in Baltimore.

The Baltimore franchise rejected the Landis-brokered settlement and continued on its own, eventually winning damages of $80,000, tripled to $240,000 under the terms of the Sherman Act. When the federal Court of Appeals for the Seventh Circuit reversed that decision, however, the case eventually made it to the United States Supreme Court. The threshold issue was whether major league baseball was subject to the Sherman Act antitrust laws in the first place. If it was, the leagues would be severely limited in the control of player movement, salaries, ticket prices, and competition from radio broadcasting.

But how could professional baseball *not* be subject to antitrust laws? Oil, steel, rail-roads—and in ensuing years the National Football League, NBA, NHL, and NCAA—would all be deemed covered by antitrust. If a single baseball team elected not to sign any radio deals, such would be a business decision, but if the whole league collaborates to freeze radio out, then that would seem to be a "contract, combination, or conspiracy" that illegally harms competition. With no radio, baseball felt it would be free to charge more for tickets to fans who would have no viable alternative than to attend the games in person. Ironically, baseball's original premise that broadcasting is bad for business would one day prove wrong, if not absurd, for broadcasting the games would reap two extraordinary benefits. First, the broadcast revenue would grow exponentially, and second, baseball on the radio would prove to be an exciting draw that not only lures fans to the stadium in droves, it also creates new fans by reaching the vast population at large.

The Supreme Court, however, ruled against the plaintiff Baltimore club with a remarkably short two-page opinion, the essence of which can be found in one concise sentence: "The business is giving exhibitions of base ball, which are purely state affairs." Baseball's antitrust exemption is widely thought to mean that somehow the game is not legally deemed a business at all. To the contrary, the court found that baseball is indeed a business, but not one that uses interstate commerce. No doubt sensing the absurdity of such a conclusion, the court inserted a preemptive sentence to address that point. "But the fact that in order to give the exhibitions the Leagues must induce free persons to cross state lines and must arrange and pay for their doing so is not enough to change the character of the business." Instead of making sense of such lampoonery, the court seemed intent on making it worse by highlighting the obvious interstate nature of major league baseball. The court seemed to be saying that just because legions of players are paid to chug from state to state on trains, playing in monolithic stadiums in multiple states to generate vast revenues, it doesn't mean that big league baseball constitutes interstate commerce.

These distinctions are more than purely academic. The premise is so convoluted that either the Supreme Court was delusional, or something else was afoot. As it happens, William Howard Taft, the former president of the United States, was the sitting Chief Justice. Taft had been a baseball player in college, and like Landis was an enormous fan of the game. His half-brother also happened to be an owner of the Cubs in the 1914 to 1916 period, precisely when the team was competing with the Federal League Chicago franchise. Had Landis whispered in the ear of Taft, hoping to insulate his prized major league baseball from the federal trustbusters, who one day might look to break up the game just as they had done to Standard Oil and others? Landis was intimately familiar with the case, having been the original trial judge assigned to it, and he was an antitrust expert with the means to influence the Court, directly or indirectly through the federal judiciary.

Was the antitrust exemption hatched by a conspiracy? Maybe, or perhaps just a subtle public wink was enough to get the Court's attention. But maybe the Supreme Court really felt this way, that the interstate travel was only "incidental" to the business of the game? Aside from the overt fatuity of such double talk, one need only examine other written opinions of the day as well as the most glaring major league baseball issue at the time: gambling.

The *Federal Base Ball* case came on the heals of the Black Sox gambling scandal in the 1919 World Series. Landis had been installed as baseball's first commissioner to save the game from the infestation of gamblers and their power to influence the integrity of the games played on the field. To do so Landis garnered unprecedented independence and centralized power over baseball, its teams, and their owners; he certainly may have feared that such a headline move could attract the attention of federal trust-busting prosecutors, if not a competing league.

For a period of time after becoming commissioner, Landis actually retained his concurrent post as a federal trial judge. While on the bench, Landis had adopted a philosophy of legal realism and judicial activism, suggesting that he was a believer in "the end justifies the means" philosophy. As president, William Howard Taft had invented the tradition of throwing the first honorary pitch of the baseball season. He would later be offered the job of baseball commissioner, but he chose to remain on the Supreme Court, with the baseball lords turning to their next choice in Landis.

A year after the *Federal Base Ball* ruling, Holmes and the Court were confronted with a similar issue concerning interstate commerce. How the court then wriggled through its logic may say much about *Federal Base Ball*, for Holmes authored a subsequent 1923 opinion conceding that a traveling vaudeville enterprise *could* be a business in interstate commerce, suggesting that the movement of performers, scenery, costumes, and animals across state lines could subject these enterprises to federal scrutiny. (In *Hart v. B.F. Keith Vaudeville Exchange*, the Court specifically found that "...in the transportation of vaudeville acts the apparatus sometimes is more important than the performers, and that the defendants' conduct is within the [antitrust] statute...."[18] Consider also that the Court had already ruled in 1911, during Taft's own trust-busting presidency, that *empty* rail cars moving in-state, or even standing idle, were in fact instruments of interstate commerce (*Southern Rail Co. v. U.S.*, 222 U.S. 20 [1911]). Was the Court really saying that empty stationary rail cars *do* affect interstate commerce, but filling them with ballplayers and moving them from state to state to play for money does *not* affect interstate? Whether by hook, crook, conspiracy, or otherwise, the baseball owners had managed to insulate themselves with antitrust protection. They were free to control the fans, the players, and this new and largely misunderstood "enemy" of the game: radio broadcasting.

Even the season to end all seasons, the Murders' Row year of 1927 — the epoch of Ruth's 60 homers, Gehrig's record-breaking 175 RBIs, and the 1927 radio broadcasts of the World Series — could not reverse much of baseball's aversion to radio broadcasting. But something else soon would, a threshold sporting event — one that awakened the entire sports world to the power of the media — with three common connections linking it to baseball: Chicago itself, WGN Radio with Quin Ryan, and WMAQ Radio with baseball announcer Hal Totten.

The City of Chicago was important in 1927 because baseball over the airwaves was already gaining momentum; the city sported two baseball teams, both of which broadcast many of their home games; it featured a highly competitive newspaper business eager to exploit radio; and it was the home of William Wrigley, one of the early visionaries to see radio as a commercially viable, if not lucrative, electronic medium. When the *Chicago Tribune* entered the radio fray with WGN, its fierce competitor, the *Chicago Daily News,* looked to counter the move. The *Daily News* formed a joint venture with the Fair Department Store to launch another radio station, WGU. The *Daily News* hired Judith Waller from the advertising powerhouse J. Walter Thompson to run the new station. She had no radio experience — who did in 1922? — but she did know big-time marketing. Herbert Hoover, then the Secretary of Commerce, changed the call letters to WMAQ, and in 1923 the *Daily News* bought out its department store partner and moved the operation to the LaSalle Hotel, mimicking the *Tribune*'s initial use of the Drake Hotel for WGN.

There is evidence to suggest that marketing guru Judith Waller may have first given Wrigley the idea of broadcasting Cubs games, as WMAQ did broadcast many games before WGN gained momentum. WGN broadcast the Cubs' season opener in 1925, but only five days later WMAQ broadcast a Cubs game that was called by its own baseball pioneer Hal Totten. WMAQ was an early radio force by featuring a number of hot shows including WGN's *Sam 'n' Henry* which jumped to WMAQ and soon became the long running *Amos 'n' Andy*, a stunning success that attracted as many as 40 million listeners across the country — a staggering number given the population of the entire United States in the 1920s was just 120 million (compared to the 2010 tabulation of 308 million).

WMAQ's Hal Totten would call Chicago baseball games from 1924 to 1944, and beginning in 1926 this included games for both the Cubs and the White Sox. Totten also did a dozen different World Series in that span, but early in his career Totten did another event that would put sports broadcasting squarely on the map and demonstrate the sheer power and expanded magnitude that broadcasting could bring to sports.[19]

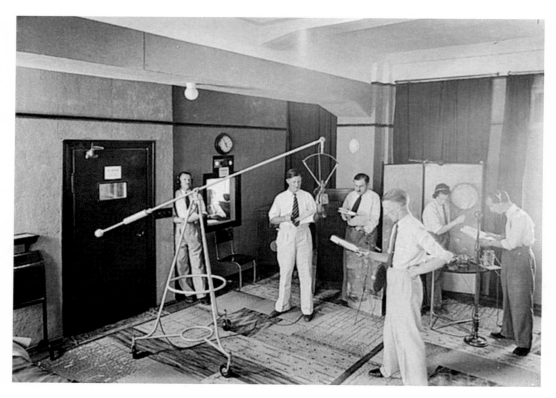

Example of a dramatized news broadcast transmitted from a radio studio, probably between 1934 and 1939. Baseball dramatizations, often called "recreations," were common during the 1930s, although usually with one radio broadcaster manipulating an array of devices to recreate noises of the ball, bat, and the fans.

During the 1920s, one of the biggest sports draws in the country was a name that often rivaled and sometimes was even bigger than Ruth himself. That name belonged to Jack Dempsey, the fierce, relentless puncher called the Manassa Mauler who won fights, titles, and fans worldwide with both his fists and dogged personality. In the fall of 1927, Dempsey even upstaged the Murderers' Row Yankees as he stepped into the ring with Gene Tunney. The heavyweight title bout was considered "the fight of the century" even before the first punch, but after it was over the match would live in infamy as the still famous "long count fight" that cost Dempsey the title.

In those days heavyweight boxing was sports' biggest extravaganza. There was no Super Bowl of course, and the NBA would not even exist for decades to come. Baseball was certainly big, but the World Series was potentially seven games, diluting the drama of any single one of them. Boxing, though, was a one-on-one blood match that did not occur often — there could only be a few heavyweight title fights in a year, sometimes only one. The drama was heightened in 1927 because Dempsey had already lost the crown to Tunney. This 1927 bout was a rematch, a dramatic confrontation fueled by revenge that became perhaps the biggest sporting event of its era, maybe even the whole century until the Muhammad Ali's worldwide 1974 spectacle against George Foreman in Zaire, Africa.

Scheduled for Chicago's Soldier Field, the recently constructed mammoth stadium of classic Greek columns and architecture, the fight drew well over 100,000 fans in person and millions more via radio.[20] No fewer than 50 special trains were deployed to stream fans into Chicago from around the country, including hundreds of posh private cars to deliver dignitaries and captains of industry. Two special trains arrived from Los Angeles, six from New York and Boston, with others from St. Louis, Minneapolis, and other Midwestern cities. Commercial air travel was the almost unknown, but a private Fokker plane carried manufacturing magnate William B. Leeds, Jr., and his wife, the Princess Xenia of Greece, to Chicago for the fight. Other planes brought dignitaries from New York, Denver, and Dallas.

The eventual list of attendees included such diverse names as Walter Chrysler and Ty Cobb; Assistant Secretary of War Hanford MacNider; various mayors, governors, and congressmen; a host of Hollywood names like Jackie Coogan, MGM executives, and movie magnate William Fox; and the presidents of General Motors, General Electric, and Bethlehem Steel, as well as department store magnates Marshall Field and Bernard Gimbel. Also on hand were baseball notables from New York, including Giants manager John McGraw and Yankees owner Jacob Ruppert, both of whom took note of the sheer breadth of this sporting extravaganza.

Most importantly, no fewer than 74 radio stations carried the fight live. The *Chicago Tribune* headline of September 23, 1927, the day after the fight, said it all: "Millions 'See' Fight in Radio Ringside Seats."[21] Indeed they did. Radio, the bourgeoning electronic medium "heard to be seen," exploded onto the sports landscape. The same *Tribune* article reported estimates that 20 million listeners may have heard the fight live, but suggested the number could have been much higher if multiple listeners were counted in the "hotels, clubs, drug stores, barber shops and every manner of store which had a radio set put it in operation...."[22]

Along the Eastern seaboard, especially Washington, D.C., and Boston, huge crowds listened to the fight through public speakers installed by the local newspapers. Seven Chicago radio stations carried the title fight, including powerhouses WGN and WMAQ as well as WLS (which still exists as an ABC affiliate), WEBH, WGES, and WCFL. Moreover, the fledgling National Broadcasting Company linked up 67 different stations, a bold move that solidified the idea — and viability — of a national broadcasting network in general, and for sports in particular.

Not only was the fight a huge draw with all the anticipated drama to be carried coast-to-coast via radio, the fight itself was punctuated by one of the most controversial endings in American sports history. The *Tribune*'s Don Maxwell wrote of the fight the very next day: "Jack [Dempsey] looked savage. He leered. His beard was of several days' growth. There was nothing handsome about him." Tunney, though, was described as handsome yet condescending. The grudge match was on.

Dempsey had been out of boxing when he first met Tunney in the ring during 1926. Dempsey, still rusty from the layoff, was defeated by the superior boxing skills of Tunney. So by 1927, Dempsey was sharp and ready. Then fate took over. A new rule had been implemented about knockdowns: the standing fighter was required to go to a neutral corner during the count. This ran contrary to the Dempsey style, which was to loom over the downed fighter to maul him as soon as he returned to his feet. But there was more. Since Chicago's mob boss Al Capone was at the peak of his power, there were fears that the fight could have been fixed by Capone gamblers. So the referee was replaced at the last minute.

Tunney began by boxing Dempsey and scoring points. But in the seventh round, Dempsey nailed Tunney with a wicked left hook to the chin. Tunney wilted while Dempsey pummeled the champ with three more shots, crumpling Tunney to the mat. But when Dempsey failed to go to the neutral corner, the referee refused to start the mandated 10-count until he did. By the time the referee got Dempsey's attention, four or more seconds had elapsed, giving Tunney extra time to gather himself. Tunney finally rose on the count of nine, but he may have actually had as many as 14 seconds to right himself.[23] Tunney avoided Dempsey for the rest of the round, then continued to outpoint the puncher for the rest of the fight, retaining his heavyweight title.

The Dempsey-Tunney clash of September 22, 1927, was one of the most dramatic sports confrontations of the twentieth century, and it was heard not only across America, but around the globe. The September 24, 1927, edition of the *Chicago Tribune* carried the banner "Fight Fans of World Listen in on Title Battle," and recounted dateline stories about radio audiences from Capetown, London, Vancouver, Melbourne, Shanghai, Tokyo— even U.S. Marines stationed in China, the American Legion in Paris, and ranchers in Australia weighed in. Many of those fans heard the voice of WGN Radio's Quin Ryan, while others heard radio broadcast legend Hal Totten, courtesy of WMAQ. Historian Curt Smith, author of *Voices of Summer* and other baseball works, quotes the workhorse Totten on his event-filled day of September 22, 1927: "My son John was born in the morning, I aired a doubleheader in the afternoon, and covered the [Dempsey-Tunney] fight that night."[24]

The 1927 Murderers' Row World Series was under way just days later on October 5, 1927. Totten aired that, too, along with others. The powerful Yankees swept the Pirates in four games. Ruth batted .400 for the Series with two home runs and seven RBIs. It had been the season of the baseball ages, and perhaps still is. Ruth slugged a lofty .772 and hit the vaunted 60 homer mark while the Yankees' Earl Combs led the league with 231 hits and American League MVP Lou Gehrig bested Ruth's single-season RBI mark with 175 of his own.[25]

The 1927 Yankees, however, were not really the first "murderers' row." The term was originally used in describing the 1918 Yankee sluggers that included Wally Pipp and Frank "Home Run" Baker; the 1927 version eclipsed that earlier team not only with a quantum leap in home run power, but star power as well.[26] The 1927 version was so good that the whole team would become a cliché, as in "Who do you think you are, the 1927 Yankees?" It was the first major league team to lead the standings wire-to-wire for the whole year all the way through the World Series, and it set the American League record for wins (110), wins at home (57), and games ahead of the second-place team (19). The '27 Yankees scored a major league record 975 runs, slugged a record 158 home runs, and was the only team in history to feature the major league's top three home run hitters in one lineup. (The 1961 Yankees would have the top two in Maris and Mantle during another record year.) They powered six grand slam home runs that year, two by Gehrig and two by Ruth; those Yankees were fast, too, as they even slapped six inside-the-park home runs, and stole home six different times, three of them by Gehrig. And they won every single game when those Yankees hit a grand slam or an inside-the-park homer or stole home: 18 wins in 18 games.[27]

Remarkably, although numerous stations broadcast Chicago Cubs games, no New York station broadcast those fabled Yankees during the regular season. Just nine days after the World Series sweep, American League president Ban Johnson resigned moments ahead of getting the boot from the owners at a specially convened meeting. Mostly they were upset with Johnson's previous investigations of wrongdoing by Ty Cobb and Tris Speaker, but with Dempsey-Tunney fight still fresh in the sports headlines and the 1927 Yankees taking their place in history, could those owners have also been concerned over Johnson's edict that had banned the new sports medium called radio from the American League?

6

Radio Wars

They brought me up to the Brooklyn Dodgers, which at that time was in Brooklyn.

— Casey Stengel[1]

The Great Depression was a time when hope was sometimes reduced to the simple aroma of a soup kitchen, when the phrase "brother, can you spare a dime?" was the requiem for a generation. In spite of all that, and perhaps largely because of it, this period may have been the greatest era for baseball, not just for its stars like Hank Greenberg, Gehrig, and a fading Ruth, but for what the game meant to the great age of despair.

Without radio, baseball could never have been the antidote to a national despondency that lingered while the Depression gripped America by its throat for an entire decade. Major league games were played only in large cities beyond the reach of rural Americans, but even among urbanites the ability to attend in person was not always easy and often out of the question during such hard times. Yet still, the singular, unmistakable clunk of a wooden bat punishing a newly corked major league ball evoked cheers, jeers, excitement and, most of all, provided a diversion to millions through the miracle of a talking box. And talk that box did, courtesy of such homespun voices as those of Bob Elson, Red Barber, Rosey Rowswell, and the others who carried radio's torch on the heels of its early pioneers in Hal Totten, Harold Arlin, and Graham McNamee. But for five years from 1934 through 1938 there was no radio in Brooklyn, the Bronx, or anywhere in New York where baseball was concerned, as the New York teams successfully conspired to quash the radio "threat."

Remarkably, the first radio broadcasts, using such term liberally, may have been telegraphed reports of games in progress that were disseminated to taverns and bars. Accordingly, the first sale of broadcast rights may have been as early as an 1897 league-wide deal that provided $300 in free, trade-out telegram rights for each team to transmit real-time play-by-play coverage of games. By 1913 the stakes were raised considerably with Western Union paying the grand sum of $17,000 per year for the rights to distribute game reports.[2]

Hollywood got into the act as early as 1910, paying $500 for the right to film and to

72

distribute newsreel-type footage of the 1910 World Series between the Chicago Cubs and the Philadelphia Athletics, even though there was still no sound and certainly no voices for narration. When those flickering silent highlights proved successful, by 1911 the major league fee for such highlights had expanded to $3,500.[3]

Newsreels didn't mean much without audiences, though, so a means of distribution was required. By 1905, Nickelodeon theaters began emerging in urban areas across the country, and there would be 14,000 such theaters by 1914. In 1910, the heavyweight boxing extravaganza between Jack Johnson and James Jeffries was one of the most popular news films of the day, so popular the Congress passed the Sims Act in 1912 actually making it illegal to distribute fight films across state lines.[4] Whether this was to protect America from the brutality of boxing, which was the pretext, or to control the news of Johnson himself, a flashy, controversial and noticeably black heavyweight champion, is not entirely clear — although it may be helpful to remember that Congress also passed the Mann White-Slave Act in 1910 to control sex with under-age women by means of a law against transporting women across state lines for immoral purposes. Jack Johnson, who had a white girlfriend, was the very first to be prosecuted under the Mann Act, suggesting it was also used to keep Johnson — and other black men — from cavorting with white women. (It is widely believed that that Mann Act had been passed with the flamboyant and so-called "uppity" Johnson in mind in the first place.)

With footage of boxing suddenly unavailable to the newsreels, coverage of other sports expanded, comprising 25 percent of all newsreels by 1940. Although these non-boxing sports would also include the likes of football star Red Grange and horse racing's Seabiscuit, the biggest attraction would be major league baseball.

Europe's Charles Pathé was among the first to enter the newsreel business. By 1914, his company had 37 cameramen in North America and its New Jersey plant alone was producing 15,000 feet of film per week. Several competitors emerged, one the most powerful being the Hearst Newspaper empire. By 1913 Hearst had launched the Hearst News Syndicate and the Hearst News Photo Syndicate. While Kodak and DuPont competed for the rights to produce mass quantities of film stock, Hearst pressed on, first combining with the *Chicago Tribune* to develop the Hearst-Selig News Pictorial, then joining with Pathé to distribute Pathé's extremely popular *Perils of Pauline* serials.[5]

Soon the bloody overseas drama of World War I provided an endless source for compelling footage. By 1919, just after the war, there were 18,000 theaters in the United States craving content; by the mid–1920s, up to 90 percent of those theaters were showing newsreels from one of the six main market competitors at the time, reaching an aggregate weekly audience of 40 million viewers. Newsreels with sound were crudely developed as early as 1924 and became commercially viable by 1926. Movietone News filmed Charles Lindbergh's famed takeoff in 1927, as well as the expansive ceremony in the flier's honor at Washington, D.C., in one of the more significant early uses of the newsreel.

The deliberate, sometimes somber voices of those many newsreels still echo today, one of which belonged to the talented baseball broadcasting pioneer Graham McNamee, who did many throughout the 1930s. On May 6, 1937, one of the most memorable newsreels ever made caught the great explosion of the *Hindenburg* airship as it attempted to land at Lakehurst, New Jersey, which was also broadcast live on radio with the stunned voice of eyewitness broadcaster Herbert Morrison on hand from Chicago's WLS.[6] Morrison's excited voice was filled with emotion yet it was still guided by his reporter instincts as Morrison quickly recounted the fiery disaster that killed 36 of the 91 persons on board when the vast airship exploded in flames. It was a cloudy day that threatened storms when an electrical charge ignited the zeppelin's hydrogen. Morrison's dramatic transmission that day would further propel radio as a viable medium for live news, and his voice can still be heard courtesy of radio archives and occasional televised retrospectives.

Radio thrived in the 1930s with its news reporting, popular comedies and dramas, and baseball. Many team owners had overcome their fears of radio pirating the live gate audience, but as the Depression wore on, baseball did begin to suffer. Baseball on the radio may have inspired a nation of fans looking to escape the economic realities of the day, but those same economic conditions reduced discretionary spending dramatically.

The major league record for total official attendance had been set in 1909 at 7,236,290. Attendance took a quantum leap in 1920, the same year that Ruth debuted in New York just as the spitball was banned and home runs were on the rise, with figures blowing through eight million all the way to 9,120,875 by year-end. Radio had not yet taken hold, but even when it did, fans kept entering the ballparks. Although attendance dipped slightly during the 1921–23 period (there was a short-lived economic depression in 1921), the record was broken again in 1924 at 9,596,083; even though radio was rapidly on the rise, attendance held at well over 9,000,000 for each remaining year of the Roaring Twenties. The first year of the Depression, 1930, broke the record again (10,132,262) as baseball offense peaked just before rule changes concerning the seams and cover of the ball brought team batting averages down to earth.[7] But soon the nation was throttled by economic Armageddon.

It is difficult to determine by statistics alone whether baseball on radio had a depressing effect on live gates, or whether the Depression itself was at fault, but aggregate major league attendance dropped dramatically from 1930 to 1931 (8,467,107), reaching a multi-year low of 6,089,031 in 1933, right during the teeth of the economic downturn. Attendance would slowly climb again, however, averaging nine million in 1938 and 1939.[8] Perhaps the turnstiles would have moderated even more if it were not for low ticket prices and the increasing exposure to the excitement of the game on radio in most venues. Given the dramatic positive impact of broadcasting over the ensuing decades, it is not likely that radio was a greater culprit than the Depression itself in causing gate attendance to wane, a conclusion apparently shared by none other than Commissioner Landis. In 1933, with league attendance at its lowest level since 1918, Landis himself publicly observed, "A man can't go to a baseball game when he doesn't have any money. He can't have any money as long as he doesn't have a job."[9]

Eventually the owners would realize that radio not only was *not* an evil competitor, it could be a vast source of revenue. In the early days, radio broadcasts were just local affairs, arranged on a team-by-team basis. There was an early network of sorts cobbled together by NBC, but the radio network idea would not be fully exploited until the advent of the Liberty Broadcasting System in 1950.[10] The same model would work for television, although the television networks would materialize early in the process, partly due to the media industry's accelerated learning curve that was already enhanced by radio. The NFL's youthful commissioner, Pete Rozelle, would be a major catalyst to establishing the media as a driving force in the sports industry. In 1961 Congress would pass the Sports Broadcasting Act mostly in response to the efforts of Rozelle, who not only saw the lucrative future of sports broadcasting, but who also miraculously persuaded the influential team owners in major media markets to give up their individual television deals and package all the TV rights together for sale to the networks.

The Cubs were the first team to broadcast their games regularly, but even Wrigley had not yet exploited the full potential of radio, for those early broadcast rights were literally given away. He did see the value of billboarding the games to drive live attendance, however, and that worked with striking success. It would still take another 14 years, though, for all the teams to catch on. Ironically, the New York teams were the last to embrace radio, which was strange since New York City had become the hub of the broadcasting industry.

Radio did not invent baseball, although baseball did help invent the radio business with its ready-made content, excitement, and personal touch offered by the game's legendary announcers. As a result, radio did in fact propel baseball to the sports juggernaut we would all come to know and love, the game of our fathers and grandfathers, the great pastime that would capture a nation and never fully let go. But it would take time to evolve.

The early radio sets were more like contraptions than radios as we presently understand the term. They were powered by unwieldy wet/dry batteries, and they had no speakers. The sound was heard only through headphones, which provided decent audio for the solitary listener but did nothing for family excitement or unity. As the 1920s and 1930s moved forward, so did radio technology. Soon these devices morphed into talking boxes that not only featured speakers, but were housed in functional if not attractive wooden cabinets and were driven by AC electric power.

In 1926, RCA combined enough radio stations to operate two separate networks comprising 24 total stations; in 1928, CBS entered the fray with its own 16-station network.[11] The cost of the radio went down as the technology and production capacity improved, making radio the most cost-effective form of entertainment during the Great Depression. Many families could not afford to attend the theater, movies, or baseball games, so they stayed home. Once the radio was purchased, its entertainment value was perpetual, costing the families nothing further. The combination of radio's cost to value and the economic squeeze during the hard times of the Depression caused the broadcasting industry to explode, and that did have a chilling effect on live baseball attendance. But radio did not keep the fans away from the ballpark, economics did. Radio was just there to pick up the pieces.

Three events occurred during the Depression that would help propel radio as the entertainment medium of choice: the collapse of Broadway, the foray of hungry advertising agencies into the broadcast world, and the discovery of baseball as engaging content.[12] Audiences could no longer afford live theater ticket prices, so Broadway and the entire live theater industry was hit hard starting in 1931. Again this kept the population home where the family radio could be found, but it also caused a noticeable void: where would the Broadway talent go? Musical comedy, drama, and vaudeville acts were suddenly out of work and in great supply. What would happen to them? Some found their way into the movie business, but mostly they landed in radio. Edgar Bergen, Jack Benny, George Burns and Gracie Allen, Fred Allen, big band leaders, comedians, and many others gravitated to where the jobs were — in the burgeoning radio broadcasting industry.[13]

With big name talent involved, money was soon to follow. Thanks to the ingenuity of the Madison Avenue advertising houses, corporate America began to recognize radio

Baseball players not only performed for the radio, they sometimes listened, as this team from Oregon did in the summer of 1941 while Chief Justice of the United States Harlan F. Stone gave the "oath of allegiance" over the air. (SDN-069224, *Chicago Daily News* negatives collection, Chicago History Museum)

as an opportunity. Singing sensation Bing Crosby began a long radio career in 1931. Over the ensuing 25 years his shows would be sponsored by Kraft Foods, Philco, General Electric, and Chesterfield cigarettes, among others. *The Lone Ranger* debuted in 1933 and would be tied to Cheerios cereal for many years. The Tommy Dorsey Orchestra began a 12-year run in 1934 that would see sponsorships by Raleigh and Kool cigarettes.[14]

Fibber McGee began a long run in 1935 that would be tied to Johnson's Wax; General Mills and Orange Crush soft drinks would bring the *Green Hornet* drama to the airwaves beginning in 1936; and the Edgar Bergen/Charlie McCarthy act began in 1937 and would be sponsored by the likes of Coca-Cola and Chase & Sanborn coffee. Edgar Bergen would for a time be the most popular radio program, but it was the sponsor that would take top billing when the show was called *The Chase & Sanborn Hour* featuring Edgar Bergen (father of contemporary film and television star Candice Bergen). Ovaltine and Skelly Oil sponsored the popular *Captain Midnight*, which first aired in 1939. But the king of them all scored with Pepsodent, Campbell's Soup, and Rexall Drug Stores: *Amos 'n' Andy*, which began in 1928 and ran for an impressive 32 years until 1960.[15]

The peak of Depression unemployment occurred in 1933 with 16 million Americans out of work, roughly a third of the entire U.S. workforce. Only 75,000 radio sets were sold in 1921, but by the middle 1930s there were 18 million radios in America, and by 1939, the year that all big league baseball was finally on the radio, there were four national radio networks and a total of 1,465 radio stations providing news, sports, and entertainment across the country to an estimated 44 million radio sets.[16] Advertisers increased radio spending to $60 million during those years, a time when newspaper advertising would suffer — sounding something like the New Millennium when the Internet and the 2008 economic downturn would wreak havoc on the newspaper business.

Although the movie industry never faded completely during the 1930s with its numerous musicals and other feel-good offerings, it roared out of the Depression with a monumental collection of films in 1939 alone, a year that many experts peg as Hollywood's single greatest season: *Gone with the Wind*, *The Wizard of Oz*, *Wuthering Heights*, *Stagecoach*, *Mr. Smith Goes to Washington*, and *Goodbye, Mr. Chips*, among others. Those same movie patrons saw countless newsreels while in the theater, much of which was driven by baseball reporting.

At the time, since the breadth and gravity of the Depression itself was news, the nation's woes were followed intently by millions of fearful Americans. On March 12, 1933, President Franklin Roosevelt found himself personally comforting America with the first of his "fireside chats," when a radio audience of 35 million heard him provide personal assurances of the stability of the U.S. banking system.[17] Two years later, an unknown young reporter, Edward R. Murrow, was assigned to the growing tensions in Europe, becoming the European news chief for CBS in 1937. One year later radio itself nearly brought America to its knees as the entire nation shuddered, fearing the ultimate in Armageddon as an attack against Earth by Martian invaders was supposedly reported "live."

Inspired by the H.G. Wells classic story, *The War of the Worlds* radio program that aired on Sunday, October 30, 1938, at 8:00 P.M. Eastern time (Halloween Eve) not only changed radio, it changed America. Orson Welles and his Mercury Theater players decided to tweak America with a realistic news flash "reporting" the alien invasion via the intense newsreel style driven by authoritative baritone voices like that of Orson Welles himself. News bulletins were read intermittently as the drama intensified, when finally the news of the invasion began to break with the following interruption: "It is reported that at 8:50 P.M. a huge, flaming object, believed to be a meteorite, fell on a farm in the neighborhood of Grovers Mill, New Jersey, twenty-two miles from Trenton."[18] When the "news report" turned to a fake Secretary of the Interior addressing the nation from Washington, D.C., the country was in full panic mode:

> Citizens of the nation: I shall not try to conceal the gravity of the situation that confronts the country, nor the concern of your government in protecting the lives and property of its people ... we must continue the performance of our duties each and every one of us, so that we may confront this destructive adversary with a nation united, courageous, and consecrated to the preservation of human supremacy on this earth.[19]

It was then announced that New York City was being evacuated, sending much of the country into a complete state of shock. Welles, though, had announced in the beginning that the program was not real, just a dramatization. So what happened — how did the story spin out of control? Apparently comedian Edgar Bergen was largely responsible. Much of America's radio audience was tuned into the wildly popular *Chase & Sanborn Hour* on Sunday night to enjoy the comedy of Edgar Bergen talking to his dummy Charlie McCarthy. But, as usual, audiences were not so excited about the musical component of the program that always came first. So they turned the channel *en masse*, as they often did, only to discover an authoritative voice describing the end of Earth as we know it. Thousands of terrified listeners called scores of radio stations, newspapers, even the police. Some just fled their homes, period. Deaths, miscarriages, and early births were reported from the mass shock, although not many such events were actually confirmed.

The show of course was fake, perhaps even a put-on, or maybe even an intentional experiment to test the power of radio. Regardless of the intent, the ominous reach of the electronic media had been proven. It was a powerful tool that would find many, many uses from the 1920s and 1930s on into the New Millennium and beyond.

But the *War of the Worlds* debacle was a one-shot event, and even those presidential fireside chats were sporadic and rare. Perhaps even more impressive was the staying power exhibited by radio's most popular show, *Amos 'n' Andy*. Looking back on it, the show's success was bittersweet since much of it was racial stereotyping, especially with the speech patterns of the characters. But white America not only listened, it loved the show, and all of America adored it because so many listeners cared about the characters, their friends, and their families. Remarkably, the show was on six nights a week, for 15 minutes each (until 1943 when it became a half-hour weekly show). That's a lot of writing and programming. It was performed serial style, with events, themes, and characters carrying over from night to night, perfecting the situation comedy as an art form. The show's extensive impact has been revisited, but never quite equaled, with such later phenomena as Milton Berle, the "who shot J.R." episode on *Dallas*, the last *Fugitive* show, and the final *M*A*S*H* episode — all on television. But the stories of Amos and Andy had them all beat. Movie theaters would actually interrupt their films to play *Amos 'n' Andy* over the speakers — otherwise, no one would have attended movies when the show was on. Water usage certifiably dropped six nights every week during the show's 15 minutes, and when Andy was taken to court by his spurned fiancée Madame Queen in 1931 for breach of promise, a story line that had been brewing for a year, 40 million excited listeners tuned in.[20] It was the Depression, Americans felt an emotional affinity for each other, and Amos and Andy were in the same struggling boat as everyone else.

The homespun characters Amos Jones and Andy Brown had come from a Georgia farm to Chicago to make their fortunes. They founded the "Fresh Air Taxi Company," so named because their first car had no roof. The show's creators, Charles Correll and Freeman Gosden, were experienced white actors who did virtually all the voices — and the women characters were meticulously developed by reference and innuendo only, somewhat like the inimitable but never actually seen "Maris" on the long running *Frasier* sitcom decades later. Indeed, the show would influence situation comedies for generations, including such televised offerings as *The Honeymooners*, *All in the Family*, and *Sanford & Son*.

With its longevity, popular story lines, homey style, frequency, and serial-like continuity, what could possibly equal the impact of the *Amos 'n' Andy* approach to programming? Baseball.

The game of baseball provided a 154-episode odyssey comprising an entire season. The listeners developed a vested interest in their home teams and, perhaps most of all, the announcers became part of the extended family of the audience, just as Amos, Andy, and the others had done. By the 1930s baseball had become America's game. With the exploits of Ruth, Gehrig, Murderers' Row, and all the rest, it had achieved a magical infamy just as radio was widely commercialized. It would take many years for all games to be broadcast, especially road games, but baseball quickly proved that it was a game virtually built for radio. As the early announcers and listeners soon discovered, baseball's deliberate pace and sporadic action created much dead air, but that provided the real opportunity. Filling such gaps with homespun tales of the game soon became standard radio fair. It has never waned — even the star-studded ESPN television games of the week during the New Millennium feature great stories of players past and present, laced with color commentary on how the game is played.

With Chicago Cubs' attendance exploding by 117 percent from 1925 to 1931,[21] baseball's impact on broadcasting was clear, even though the owners were slow to catch on. In 1929, the last year of economic prosperity until after World War II, the Cincinnati Reds became the first team to broadcast all their games. During the early 1930s, Chicago's WMAQ covered a "virtual season" by broadcasting *all home* games of both the Cubs and White Sox, 154 games in all.

Radio was poised to carry baseball to new plateaus of success, yet the owners could not resist interfering. The St. Louis Browns, for example, allowed game broadcasts, but prohibited all commentary, allowing just the play-by-play reports when something happened. The result was not only excruciating, it was a waste of both technology and baseball. *The Sporting News*, however, embraced such nonsense: "This should be mutually satisfactory to both the fans and the magnates, for there are some announcers who prove to wander from the actual occurrences on the field."[22] All of baseball *and* broadcasting should be thankful that many announcers did enough "wandering" to transform baseball broadcasting from a dull news report into the lucrative entertainment vehicle it would soon become.

The Browns, though, proved remarkably stubborn, banning all Sunday and holiday broadcasts of their games. The Pirates followed suit. By 1932, as the Depression gripped America in a vice of economic fear and despair, baseball considered eliminating radio altogether as attendance plummeted. Just two years later, in 1934, regular baseball coverage could be found only in three cities: Boston, Cincinnati, and Chicago.[23] But capitalism will find opportunity, and that includes baseball: a year later no fewer than 13 teams had regular broadcast deals in place. Noticeably absent from the list, however, were all three teams from New York: the Giants, Dodgers, and Yankees. Such is ironic, of course, because six decades later the Yankee broadcasting empire would fuel many great Steinbrenner teams with endless flows of media money.

At first New York had actually embraced the idea of baseball broadcasting. By 1931 no fewer than four separate radio stations were broadcasting from Ebbets Field alone, with many of the games being called by icon Graham McNamee as well as a future commissioner, Ford Frick. But the Depression continued to take its toll. By the summer of 1932, major league franchises lost an aggregate of $1,201,000.[24] This sounds small by modern standards, but that was a huge sum in 1932 when even top player salaries were under $50,000. Only four teams made a profit at all that year, two of which were the Cubs and Yankees, who would meet in the 1932 World Series— the one that featured Babe Ruth's alleged "called shot" home run at Wrigley Field.[25] The 1932 Giants drew fewer than 250,000 paid fans for the whole year, and that incited panic among several owners. The Giants clearly needed a boost, so they desperately proposed banning radio in hopes of boosting attendance. The Yankees were still profitable, but they were still nervous enough and did not object.

As a result, all the New York teams not only shunned radio broadcasting, they entered into a cartel expressly to prevent it. All three clubs signed a five-year pact to ban radio transmission of their games from 1934 through 1938, creating a historic void during the peak of the great Gehrig years. Such a cabal would have been impossible but for the baseball antitrust exemption, a striking example of harming both competition and the public itself through the misuse of legal and economic power. In the end, though, these teams may have hurt themselves the most. In 1929, the Chicago Cubs set a single franchise attendance record that would stand for many years with 1,485,166 passing through the turnstiles at the still-new Wrigley Field. With many of their games on the radio for several years beginning in 1925, the Cubs would exceed the one-million attendance threshold for five straight seasons, ending in 1931. By 1932, most of baseball was feeling the squeeze — and that not only included the major leagues, but also the Negro National League which went out of business altogether.

But New York was not the only venue to reject baseball broadcasting in 1934. Joining the New York clubs were the St. Louis Cardinals whose owner, Sam Breadon, also feared radio's impact on attendance. Although St. Louis won the pennant in 1934 behind the pitching of National League MVP Dizzy Dean, season attendance shrank to 334,863. When radio was reintroduced for Cardinals games in 1935, attendance exploded upward by 54.6 percent to 517,805 in just one season.[26] Evidence of radio's positive influence on gate receipts was everywhere, yet the radio phenomenon still ran counterintuitive to most owners. Like the rest of the country in 1935, St. Louis was still mired in the Depression. While the team was still very good and riding the heels of its 1934 pennant winner (it placed second in 1935 to the Cubs), the Cardinals benefited greatly from the broad-based excitement generated by radio.

In the early 1930s, baseball not only struggled with the economic downturn and a tsunami of red ink, the game still managed to shoot itself in the foot two major ways. One was the rejection of radio, the other was to change the baseball itself to combat a surge in scoring, batting, and baseball offense that had been in an upward trend since 1920. With run production up and whole teams hitting over .300 — the entire National League batted .303 in 1930 — the baseball owners reverted to their "purist" roots by tampering with the ball itself. In 1931 the horsehide became thicker and looser, and the seams were raised to give the pitchers a better grip that produced tighter rotation and thus balls that "bit," wicked breaking pitches that depressed batting averages around the leagues. Although the American League did not adopt the thicker ball cover right away, it did raise the seams, so in one season, American League team batting and total runs second per game both dropped noticeably. But the National League had raised the seams *and* changed the cover at the same time with even more dramatic results. In 1931, National League runs were down by 1.2 per game while team batting dropped from .303 to .277.[27]

If the Depression, lower scoring, and an ill-conceived war against radio were not enough, fate also played a major role in the form of weather. The summer of 1930 produced a series of brutal heat waves across the nation's midsection, causing many deaths and noticeably reducing game attendance. This was the same intense heat that contributed to the dust bowl years of the 1930s and ultimately triggered the mass farmer migration from Oklahoma to California made so famous by John Steinbeck's *The Grapes of Wrath*.

Still, one remarkably good development did occur in the 1930s that would benefit both radio broadcasting and, eventually, baseball itself: car radios. With early radios being bulky, awkward, and not even sporting speakers (earphones were used instead), the early advent of car radios would seem unlikely. Motorola founder Paul V. Galvin, however, saw a future in automobile radios and developed a team of engineers to tackle the technical problems. Galvin and his brother started the Galvin Manufacturing Corporation in Chicago in 1928 to make battery eliminators, electronic devices that would allow battery-powered home radios to operate on everyday household electrical currents. The Depression killed demand for the eliminators, though, so when the Galvins found themselves next door to a radio parts company founded by William P. Lear, they began to experiment with the idea of radios suitable for use by one of the country's biggest new industries, the automobile.[28]

Galvan decided to fit his own trusty Studebaker with a newfangled car radio, then proceeded to drive it nearly 900 miles to Atlantic City where the Radio Manufacturers Association Convention was taking place. He had no booth, bookings, or even appointments scheduled for the trade show, but he worked day and night to retrofit a radio into his car. By squeezing some of the components, and hiding others under the car floor, he got the radio working in time. With no official presence at the show, Galvin simply parked his modified Studebaker outside, turned on the radio, boosted the sound with large speakers, and became the hit of the convention. With that, Motorola was reinvented, and soon the Motorola model 5T71 became one of the first commercially successful car radios.[29]

A number of competitors soon appeared, including Advance Electric, Allied Radio Corp., Automobile Radio Corp., Hyatt Electric Corp., and others. Most of those early car radios followed the same basic design with a fairly large tin box that contained a receiver, a speaker, and a power source. Interestingly, those first radios did not feed off a car battery or even the car motor, as they still utilized their own battery power. But when small generators were developed to enhance the process, they interfered with the reception. One of the leaders in the technological development of early car radios was the Delco Radio Corp., which helped transform the car radio from an add-on to a component factory option. By 1938 the car radio was officially offered by General Motors as an option on all Buicks.[30]

There was another crucial development that took place in 1934, the same year that the New York teams overtly shunned radio broadcasts. That new development sat behind the baseball microphone: Red Barber. The modern baseball announcer was thus born. Known later as the voice of the Dodgers, Barber had no chance in New York until the ban on baseball broadcasting was lifted in 1939, so instead he began in one of those few baseball cities that did embrace radio, Cincinnati. Station WSAI hired a very young Walter Barber on April 5, 1934. Barber, who was just 26 years old at the time, proceeded to broadcast the very first baseball game he had ever seen — an anomaly that surely will never be equaled. Three different radio stations broadcast a total of 85 Reds games that year, including a number of away games. For over four decades Barber would live, breathe, and talk baseball until one fateful day in 1966 when the Yankees fired him for telling the truth, after he made the mistake of mentioning that only 413 people were in the stands to watch the last-place Yankees.

In between the Reds and Yankees years, Barber became famous as the voice of the Dodgers during a spectacular career that showcased baseball as a unique "game heard to be seen" on the radio. Those same Reds of 1934 also hired a young kid named Scotty Rustun to perform public relations for the team, but he later would win the Pulitzer Prize writing for the *New York Times* under his real name, James "Scotty" Reston.[31]

The 1934 season proved less than spectacular for the Reds. On Opening Day, the

Reds lost to the Cubs, 2–0, as Barber called the game. Cincinnati finished the season in eighth place in the National League with a record of 52–99, just missing the dubious 100-loss milestone.[32] Barber, no doubt, honed his announcing and story-telling skills during that woeful year, a Reds season that offered little more entertainment than Barber himself.

None of the New York teams won the pennant in 1934, but there was plenty of action on the field with Lou Gehrig leading the American League in all three Triple-Crown categories: batting (.363), home runs (49), and RBIs (165). Giants pitcher Carl Hubbell led the National League in ERA at 2.30; Ripper Collins and Mel Ott topped the Giants and National League in home runs at 35 each; Lefty Gomez won 26 games for the Yankees; and it was the Brooklyn Dodgers who eliminated the Giants from the pennant race with two wins at the Polo Grounds on September 29 and 30.[33] Then on September 30, 1934, Babe Ruth played his very last game in a Yankees uniform, going hitless against the Senators while his teammate Gehrig batted 3-for-4 to sew up the Triple Crown. The New York radio audience heard virtually none of it with local baseball still banned from the airwaves.

In the fall of the following year, boxing and radio were again making history on a national stage. In September 1935, a youthful Joe Louis knocked out Max Baer at Yankee Stadium in a heavyweight bout that topped the $1,000,000 mark in gross receipts. Although most of the revenue still came from the live attendance, the fight did barely surpass $1,000,000 due to the added motion picture rights and a fee from the new medium of radio. According to the *New York Times*, the motion picture rights brought in $25,000 while the radio broadcast rights were sold for a reported $27,500, together bringing the gross receipts from all sources to $1,000,852. That contribution may have been modest at the time, but radio's influence on sports in general and baseball in particular would continue to grow.[34]

The Yankees may have missed the golden opportunity of sports broadcasting during the late 1930s, but they clearly got the one-field part right. With Ruth slowed and soon to be retired, the Babe was replaced by the Iron Horse in Lou Gehrig; but then as Gehrig succumbed to his dreaded bout with ALS, yet another youngster would take the reigns of Yankee stardom, Joe DiMaggio. From 1936 to 1939, the powerful Yankees won four straight World Series titles, none of them with Ruth, and all seasons without the benefit of radio until the 1939 campaign.

In 1939 Larry MacPhail stepped in as general manager of the Brooklyn Dodgers and immediately shook the underpinnings of New York baseball. He not only scrapped the Dodgers' participation in the radio cabal, MacPhail installed lights at Ebbets Field, then brazenly embraced radio. Convinced radio would increase popularity the way it had worked in Chicago and elsewhere, he immediately hedged his bet by hiring Red Barber away from the Reds, who proceeded to call the Dodgers game on April 18, 1939, a 7–3 loss to the crosstown Giants.

Lou Gehrig and Boston's Ted Williams would face each other only one time in their careers, and it took place only two days later on April 20. It was Opening Day at Yankee Stadium, the very first major league game of Williams' career. Gehrig was nearing the end of his famous streak of consecutive games played, and just 10 days later the streak would finally end at 2,130. Gehrig was tired—and sick. At age 35, the Iron Horse was sluggish, worn out, and a step slow. Although he did not yet know it, Gehrig was in the early stages of his famed bout with ALS, the disease that causes spinal paralysis and now carries his name. Parts of his emotional retirement speech would live on from newsreel footage, but there seems to be no complete recorded rendition from either newsreels or radio. Gehrig's "luckiest man" address transcended the game of baseball. Stephen Lucas, a professor at the University of Wisconsin, once surveyed 137 experts to determine the 100 greatest speeches of the twentieth century. King's "I Have a Dream" was number one, and Gehrig made the list at number 73. "It's an iconic moment in American life, not just sports," explained Lucas.[34] Gehrig would be diagnosed with ALS on his 36th birthday. He would never play organized ball again.

On August 22, 1939, while undergoing treatment at the Mayo Clinic, Gehrig agreed to be interviewed by KROC-AM radio in Rochester, Minnesota. Correspondent Dwight Merriam visited with Gehrig at the hospital, where the two of them talked baseball. Gehrig criticized night baseball, saying it was just a way for owners to further line their pockets. He listed the top ballplayers as Ruth, Cobb, and Honus Wagner. They spoke of the All-Star Game, the World Series, and young emerging ballplayers — one of the best youngsters on the horizon, Gehrig felt, was a promising kid playing for the local Minneapolis Millers by the name of Ted Williams.[36]

Surprisingly, that same 1939 also saw the first televised major league game, which took place on August 26. Larry MacPhail was behind that, too. It was a crude two-camera experiment, one at ground level with the other placed in the upper deck. Barber was recruited to call the game and do the commercials, thus finding himself promoting Wheaties as "the breakfast of champions" and pitching co-sponsors Ivory Soap and Mobile Oil.[37] There were two games that day, a Dodgers-Reds doubleheader that Barber called for television station W2XBS as the two teams battled to a split. In those days, however, there were almost no television receivers to be found — so just 400 sets were reportedly tuned in.

But in 1939 radio was king, and in August both radio and baseball made broadcasting history once again when the game inked Gillette Safety Razor Company to a $100,000 exclusive radio rights deal to sponsor the 1939 World Series. Although baseball had received sponsorship money for three previous World Series, this was the first time that *exclusive* rights were sold. The Mutual Broadcasting System was awarded the sole radio rights to the Series, and Gillette would be the exclusive sponsor. Mutual was a radio consortium formed in 1929 with four original stations then known collectively as the Quality Network: WOR, New York; WLS, Chicago; WLW, Cincinnati; and WXYX, Detroit. In 1934 the consortium changed its name to the Mutual Broadcasting System, while adding Chicago's WGN to the core group and dropping WLS. Mutual planned to link 150 radio stations across the country for the Series, including Chicago's powerful WGN, while Canada, Mexico, and Cuba would be reached by radio short-wave transmission. The $100,000 rights fee would be added to the World Series gross receipts, then divided in the usual manner among the league, the teams, and the players.[38]

The 1939 World Series was called by Red Barber and WGN's Bob Elson. The undermanned Reds were swept by the Yankees in winning their fourth Series in a row. The Yankees team took the field without their pride and soul, Lou Gehrig, but they would win nonetheless behind Gehrig's heir apparent, Joe DiMaggio. The Yankee Clipper had debuted in 1936 and had already led the American League in home runs with 46 in 1937. But as 1939 came to a close, the team was truly his.

7

A Game of Infamy

With barely over 100,000 in official population nestled along the Illinois River amidst a sea of farmland and corn, Peoria, Illinois, has a surprising reach throughout the world of commerce, entertainment, and sports. As the international headquarters to one of the world's largest industrial giants, Caterpillar Tractor, it is a strong union town with Caterpillar factories and a plethora of support services together making Peoria the hub of central Illinois. Its surprising national influence extends beyond business to politics, for Peoria is the home town of noted feminist Betty Friedan, one-time House minority leader Bob Michel, and more recently Ray LaHood, Secretary of Transportation in the Obama administration.

A small city that embodies much of what is America, Peoria is a virtual cliché of vaudeville and market research: *Will it play in Peoria?* Along the way it made a substantial impact on our culture when it produced the late comedian and Hollywood star Richard Pryor, one of the most outspoken — and funniest — of the new comedians of social commentary who developed and changed the "funny business" industry of the 1960s and 1970s. Only the 150th largest radio market in the U.S., Peoria also claims a remarkable number of connections to baseball and the airwaves including Jim Thome, one of the most prodigious home run hitters in big league history, Yankees manager Joe Girardi, and two of baseball's all-time top broadcasters, Jack Brickhouse and Bob Elson. Parenthetically, CBS Radio executive Rod Zimmerman grew up in nearby Pekin, Illinois, then found himself at KMOX in St. Louis during the baseball broadcasting heydays of Jack Buck and Harry Caray.

Ranked as the eighth best baseball broadcaster ever by baseball historian and author Curt Smith, Jack Brickhouse was a 40-year broadcaster who called so many Cubs games that his name almost became synonymous with Chicago's North Side team during the decades that preceded Harry Caray.[1] Yet Brickhouse, himself an icon, called Bob Elson "a God of baseball broadcasting." Both were down-home regular people, contributing the "voice next door" approach to baseball on the radio, a style that can be traced to their Midwestern small-town roots. That homespun delivery worked wonders for baseball on radio; it was this country-like charm that won the hearts of the listening public, propelling such engaging radio icons as Wyoming's Curt Gowdy, Dizzy Dean who began life in an Arkansas shack, along with so many others like Brickhouse and Elson.

Elson became one of the pioneers in the art of baseball broadcasting as it is performed today. He was a consummate professional, a bit more journalist than entertainer, and his voice was inextricably tied to baseball for decades. Brickhouse felt that Elson was not only creative, but may have been the most imitated announcer of them all.[2]

Literally a choir boy in his youth, Elson emerged from Peoria to attend both Loyola University of Chicago and Northwestern University. His foray into baseball broadcasting occurred mostly by accident, much like it did for Harold Arlin and so many other radio pioneers. When he was 23 years old, Elson happened to be staying in St. Louis at the Chase Hotel, which housed radio station KWK. Immensely curious, just as engineer Harold Arlin had been in Pittsburgh only a few years earlier, Elson opted to explore the station and found himself in a long line of visitors who were there not for a tour but to audition as an announcer. This was intriguing to Elson so he decided to go along, remaining in line to take his own turn. Reading from an assigned script, Elson did well and actually became a finalist, after which the station listeners voted him the eventual winner.

But Elson did not build his career in St. Louis. Fate intervened when WGN heard of his success and openly wondered why a local Chicagoan should be broadcasting from St. Louis. Elson was hired away to do games for both the Cubs and White Sox, handling chores for both teams from 1929 to 1941. After serving in the Navy during the World War II years, Elson was back for an extended run, announcing Sox games from 1946 to 1970 before finishing his career with a one-year stint at Oakland — owned by Chicago businessman Charlie Finley — in 1971. Becoming a national favorite, he called World Series games from 1930 to 1941 and again in 1943, and also did many All-Star Games, including the very first one in Chicago in 1933, plus a string for the Mutual Broadcasting System from 1935 to 1942. Nicknamed "The Old Commander," Elson was addicted to gin rummy. Known for his emphatic "he's *out*" call on the radio, Elson also introduced the concept of the on-field player interview. Although in the Navy, Elson spent much of World War II stationed at the Navy's Great Lakes Training Center in the northern Chicago suburbs; he still managed to work the World Series in 1943, allegedly at the personal request of baseball fan President Franklin Roosevelt who spirited him from the Navy for a day specifically to do the game.

Baseball would soon find itself embedded in the soul of America in no small part because of its radio broadcasters. FDR was an admirer of baseball and Elson, yet Roosevelt was not the only White House fan of the game and its rich broadcasting history. For many decades baseball has had a profound influence on America's political leaders, and that was a particularly poignant connection during the transcendent years of World War II. Symbolizing the game's poignancy was Dwight Eisenhower, the 34th president who as the leader of the D-Day Invasion on the great "day in infamy" on June 6, 1944, became one of America's greatest war heroes. Eisenhower possessed one of history's greatest résumés, yet he still lamented his first love, baseball.

> When I was a small boy in Kansas, a friend of mine and I went fishing and as we sat there in the warmth of the summer afternoon on a river bank, we talked about what we wanted to do when we grew up. I told him that I wanted to be a real major league baseball player, a genuine professional like Honus Wagner. My friend said that he'd like to be president of the United States. Neither of us got our wish.[3]

Perhaps no president influenced the game of baseball more than the 27th president, William Howard Taft, who served from 1909 to 1913. A pitcher for the Yale University baseball team, the future president had a long affinity for the game, as did a number of members of the powerful Taft family who were strongly rooted in Ohio politics and business. The president's half-brother, Charles Phelps Taft, was not only the owner of the Chicago Cubs from 1914 to 1916, but he was the principal founder of the Taft Broadcasting Company. A media empire that began with the purchase of the *Cincinnati Times-Star* newspaper in 1879, Taft Broadcasting entered the radio business in 1939 when the *Cincinnati Times-Star* purchased the WKRC radio. In the 1950s and 1960s, Taft Broadcasting would acquire numerous media properties, eventually owning 15 various television stations across the country in Phoenix, Miami, Philadelphia, New York, and other major cities, together with a number of radio stations, mostly in the Midwest. In 1967 the company even acquired the Hanna-Barbera cartoon empire from its founders, and during the 1970s it entered the theme park business.

President Taft is widely known for his interest in baseball. He attended three major league games as president in 1909, one each in Washington, D.C., Pittsburgh, and Chicago. Taft attended six more games in 1910, and is best remembered for throwing the first-ever

President and Mrs. William Howard Taft shown at a major league baseball game in 1910, possibly on Opening Day in Washington, D.C. Taft attended six big league games in 1910, including the season opener where he began the tradition of presidents throwing the Opening Day honorary first pitch. Taft was a devoted baseball fan, and later became Chief Justice of the United States, a position he held when the Court ruled in 1922 that baseball is not a business in interstate commerce, effectively exempting major league baseball from federal antitrust laws.

presidential ceremonial pitch to open the 1910 season in Washington, D.C.[4] He is sometimes credited with inventing the tradition of the seventh-inning stretch when the rotund
president (weighing upwards of 330 pounds) stood to stretch his legs in the middle of
the seventh inning, perhaps at that very same game, although many sources dismiss this
tale as more urban legend than truth.

Eight years after his term ended, Taft was appointed to the Supreme Court of the
United States, where he served as chief justice from 1921 to 1931.[5] Taft was chief justice
when Holmes wrote the "baseball is not a business in interstate commerce" opinion in
the landmark *Federal Base Ball* ruling of 1922, effectively exempting major league baseball
from the U.S. antitrust laws. This was an especially ironic if not suspicious ruling since
the Taft presidency was known for its aggressive trust-busting practices with the filing
of no fewer than 67 antitrust actions. Interestingly, Taft himself had been offered the job
of the first commissioner of major league baseball, but turned it down to stay on the
Court, at which point the owners turned to Chicago federal judge Kenesaw Mountain
Landis.

Other presidents have enjoyed an affinity for the game, including John F. Kennedy
and Richard M. Nixon. On July 22, 1969, Nixon told a group of 1969 All-Stars visiting
the White House that if he had it to do all over again, Nixon would have become a sportswriter. Then, just two days later, one day after the game itself, the Apollo 11 astronauts,
including Neal Armstrong, splashed down after returning from their historic first moon
landing. When they were retrieved, Nixon still had baseball on his mind, asking if they
wanted to know how the All-Star Game turned out.[6]

The most direct connection between U.S. presidents and major league baseball was
George W. Bush's ownership of the Texas Rangers baseball team. Coming from a Texas
family with vast political and business interests, Bush seized an opportunity to buy the
club in 1989, then was instrumental in conceiving The Ballpark at Arlington stadium
venture. Bush personally invested a reported $600,000 in the team, took control, spear-
headed the public financing of the new stadium, and then finally sold out less than 10
years later for a profit of about $15 million.[7]

Even President Barack Obama could not abandon his true feelings about the game,
displaying his love for baseball and his hometown Chicago White Sox by wearing his Sox
jacket while throwing the first ceremonial pitch of the 2009 All-Star Game in St. Louis.
When he visited the broadcast booth for a half inning of televised commentary, the left-
handed Obama found himself conceding that had he been able to throw a good curve
ball, he probably would not be president. Obama's advisors, two of whom professed to
be Cubs fans, would have preferred a more neutral stance; major league baseball even
pressed him to wear the game's official All-Star jacket instead. But Obama shunned a
disingenuous political stance in favor of much more: loyalty, integrity, and his genuine
love for the game and his hometown White Sox.

Then there was Ronald Reagan, the 40th president, who lived the fantasy of other
presidents by actually calling baseball games on the radio during his early days as a sports
broadcaster. Reagan grew up in small-town Tampico, Illinois, barely more than an hour's
drive north of Peoria, and in 1932 was hired by WOC Radio in nearby Davenport, Iowa.
Located just across the Mississippi River, WOC happened to be the very first commercial
radio station west of the Mississippi. Reagan's first assignment was to broadcast University
of Iowa football games for $5 a game plus bus fare.[8] Soon, though, he was given the task

Western Union Telegraph Building, New York; the "Switch" General operating department, circa 1875, during a time when telegraph reports of big league games in progress were transmitted to local bars, a practice that extended into the late 1800s. During this same period, however, the telephone was invented (1876) and would soon replace the telegraph as the primary means of electronic communication. But telegraph style ticker reports would still be used by broadcasters (such as Ronald Reagan, Milo Hamilton and others) recreating baseball games on radio well into the twentieth century.

of broadcasting Chicago Cubs games to the local Iowa audience, which he did by recreating the games "live" based upon telegraph reports of each game in progress.

According to popular legend, confirmed as mostly true by many sources including Reagan himself, Reagan's telegraph feed went dead in the ninth inning of a scoreless tie during a Cubs-Cardinals game in 1934. Reagan continued the "play by play" by making up a stream of fabricated pitches that were seemingly fouled off until the telegraph connection reappeared. Reagan's own take on that broadcasting adventure: "There were several other stations broadcasting that game and I knew I'd lose my audience if I told them we'd lost our telegraph connections so I took a chance. I had [Billy] Jurges hit another foul. Then I had him foul one that only missed being a homerun by a foot. I had him foul one back in the stands and took up some time describing the two lads that got in a fight over the ball. I kept on having him hit foul balls until I was setting a record for a ballplayer hitting successive foul balls and I was getting more than a little scared. Just then my [telegraph] operator started typing." Once the transmission was back, Reagan immediately saw that instead of fouling a near-record number of balls, Jurges had actually popped out on the first pitch. Reagan later confessed to a small audible chuckle when he read the truth as it came over the wire.[9]

Milo Hamilton, one of the greatest of all the baseball broadcasters, was born in Iowa and began doing minor league games in 1950 at WOC Radio in Davenport, Iowa, the same station that propelled Ronald Reagan. He moved on to broadcast St. Louis Browns games when Bill Veeck was the owner, when "there were more ushers than people" in the park. Milo found himself in the majors doing Cub games by the mid–1950s, but in those early days he, too, was required to re-create games—notably road games—in the studio. Although eventually they would get the stats from a stock ticker, Milo and others originally received live game data via Morse code, requiring someone to translate. Milo also supplied the sound effects, augmented by actual recordings he and his team made at live games to capture the home crowd sounds of singles, home runs, and so on. If something especially big happened, they simply turned up the volume. He later confessed that doing re-creations makes the announcer a better broadcaster by forcing him to know more about the players, their styles, and their particular pitches.[10] He must be right: Milo Hamilton won the Frick Award in 1992 and in 2010 was still calling Houston Astros games for 26 years and counting.[11]

Ronald Reagan later became one of the country's more popular presidents. Known mostly for pulling the country from an economic malaise of the late 1970s with supply side "Reaganomics," he is also partially credited with the fall of the Berlin Wall and the end of the Cold War. As it happens, baseball broadcasting may have also contributed to Reagan's larger brushes with history, since his early WOC job led Reagan to his first visit of Hollywood in 1937 while touring with the Cubs team in California (one source remembers Reagan's trip as one involving college football). While there, Reagan detoured to Warner Brothers Studios where he took a screen test and soon thereafter inked a seven-year acting deal. He made over 50 films and became politically active with the Screen Actors Guild, becoming president of SAG in 1941. When Reagan hosted television's *Death Valley Days*, he had a speaking/sponsorship deal with General Electric that required Reagan to give hundreds of promotional speeches around the country. Reagan, who had enlisted in the Army Reserve Corps in 1937, was ordered to active duty on April 18, 1942, less than four months after Pearl Harbor. His broadcast and entertainment skills again came into play, for during the war he was assigned to Army Air Force public relations and the related film task force divisions where his unit produced over 400 film shorts. The rest, of course, is history, but without his broadcast stint with WOC and his western trip with the Cubs, how much of Reagan's acting career and subsequent foray into politics would have occurred?[12]

After his fictional game re-creations on radio, Reagan next blended acting and baseball with his 1952 starring role as St. Louis Cardinal Hall of Fame pitcher Grover Cleveland Alexander in a motion picture called *The Winning Team*. The film received warm reviews and not only co-starred Doris Day, it featured a host of real major leaguers including Gene Mauch, Hank Sauer, Peanuts Lowry, and Bob Lemon. Years later during his term as president, Reagan found himself actually playing a little ball during a major league old-timers game, after which he could not contain his joy: "This is really more fun than being president. I really do love baseball and I wish we could do this out on the lawn every day. I wouldn't even complain if a stray ball came through the Oval Office window now and then."[13]

President Reagan proclaimed May 1983 as "National Amateur Baseball Month," and during his two terms he attended four major league games, three of them in Baltimore. He threw the first pitch in 1984, a White Sox victory over the Orioles at Baltimore, then watched the rest of the game from the dugout. On September 30, 1988, Reagan threw two ceremonial pitches in Chicago for a Cubs game, then revisited his media roots by calling an inning and a half from the radio broadcast booth. The following season, Reagan was in the booth again only six months after leaving office when he called a Wade Boggs homer for NBC television during the 1989 All-Star Game.[14]

Neither Reagan nor Obama would likely ever win a Ford Frick Award for their respective broadcasting duties, but their appearances in the booth demonstrate the inexorable ties among baseball, broadcasting, and America. The Frick Award is named for broadcaster and baseball icon Ford C. Frick, the one-time commissioner known for slapping Roger Maris with a qualifying asterisk (even though Maris' home run asterisk never really existed) when he publicly distinguished the 162-game season of Maris as the slugger closed upon the hallowed single season record marked by Ruth's 60 homers in 1927 (when the major league season was just 154 games). The Frick Award has been given annually since 1978 to a broadcaster who has made "major contributions to baseball," and the list of winners is a virtual hall of fame for baseball broadcasters. The first winners of the Frick Award were co-recipients Mel Allen and Red Barber, with Bob Elson winning the following year in 1979. Other recipients have included Russ Hodges, Ernie Harwell, Vin Scully, Jack Brickhouse, Curt Gowdy, Bob Prince, Jack Buck, Harry Caray, and Bob Uecker, among a stellar list of others not the least of whom is Milo Hamilton. Through 2009, the Frick winners included four broadcasters who actually saw playing time in the major leagues, one of whom was Uecker (winning in 2003), the others being Jerry Coleman (2005), Joe Garagiola (1991), and Tony Kubek (2009).

One broadcaster not included on the Frick Award list, at least as of 2009, is the late Ty Tyson, who not only is the namesake of the Ty Tyson Award given annually by the Detroit Sports Broadcasters Association but who also became the first to broadcast an entire season of baseball games according to the *Detroit News* and others. The first report of any major league game on radio was provided, of course, by Harold Arlin for Pittsburgh's KDKA in 1921; Grantland Rice reported the first World Series broadcast in October 1921; and WGN's Quin Ryan did and the Cubs season opener in 1925. But Tyson, who worked for Detroit's WWJ, did call the first regularly scheduled baseball game of a full broadcast season schedule when he took the microphone for a Detroit-Cleveland game on April 19, 1927. His last regular broadcast was in 1940, but he stayed with WWJ for many years as a sports commentator — then jumped to the television booth for the first-ever televised Tigers game in 1947.

In 1934 the Tigers won the pennant, and Tyson was in line to announce the World Series. Baseball, however, feared the appearance of partisanship and removed Tyson from the booth. But 600,000 supportive letters, some less than cordial, strongly objected, so Commissioner Landis allowed him to call the contest for his hometown WWJ. In 1935, when the Tigers were in the Series again to face a strong Chicago Cubs team, baseball remembered those letters and Tyson was allowed to call the games for NBC, which he did again in 1936 for the Yankees-Giants Series along with co-announcers Tom Manning and Red Barber.[15] Tyson's voice can still be heard on many broadcast recordings that have survived the decades, including the oldest major league game audio known to exist, a September 20, 1934, Yankees' win over the Tigers.[16]

Before taking the microphone to call baseball, however, Tyson did what so many players, broadcasters, and others did by serving in the Armed Forces. Tyson served for two years during World War I, including an 11-month tour overseas as a doughboy assigned to the 28th Division. Three years before his death, Tyson returned to Tiger Stadium in 1965 to broadcast one more inning with reigning radio legend Ernie Harwell who had taken the Tiger announcing reins in 1960 and held on for the better part of five decades.[17]

Still feeling the sting of the Great Depression in 1939, a national anguish that was punctuated by John Steinbeck's compelling *The Grapes of Wrath*, America nonetheless invigorated itself with theatrical entertainment (*Gone with the Wind*, *The Wizard of Oz*, *Mr. Smith Goes to Washington*, and others) and, of course, baseball. By year's end, Lou Gehrig had provided baseball a watershed moment with his historic farewell address, and Joe DiMaggio had led the Yankees to a World Series sweep over the Reds. In December, the Yankees and Gehrig completed another first together — when Gehrig's number 4 was retired, the first time any team had ever retired a number for any reason.[18]

In 1940, the last full year before America would fully emerge from the Depression only to then throw itself into the greatest of all wars, Bob Feller made history by hurling baseball's only Opening Day no-hitter. During the 1940 season, teams began to embrace night baseball, and by season's end the Reds were back in the Series, this time for a seven-game victory against the Tigers. DiMaggio, Detroit slugger Hank Greenberg, and Bob Feller dominated the final American League stats for 1940 with DiMaggio winning the batting crown (.352), Greenberg topping the league in home runs (41) and RBIs (150), and Feller leading all pitchers with 27 wins and 261 strikeouts (more than 100 more than the 137 rung up by the National League leader Kirby Higbe for Philadelphia). Poignantly, 1940 also saw the publication of Thomas Wolfe's *You Can't Go Home Again*, a title that not only tweaked the American lexicon forever, but ironically managed to sum up America on the eve of World War II — home would never quite be what it once was, and few Americans would ever be the same again.[19]

With 30 million homes sporting a radio in 1940, America had fully embraced this new broadcast medium. Beginning in the mid–1930s, baseball had begun to experiment with night games, a revolutionary innovation that would help propel both baseball and the broadcast industry. In fact, the very first sports contest ever broadcast by the Mutual Broadcasting System was major league baseball's first official night game ever played, a 2–1 Reds victory over the Phillies witnessed by a then-healthy crowd of 20,422 in attendance in Cincinnati[20] (some accounts suggest at least 25,000 were there[21]). The field was lit by President Roosevelt via a specially installed remote switch that triggered 614 powerful 1500-watt light bulbs dutifully installed by General Electric. Fortunately, there were no errors in the game, for some had questioned the night time visibility and feared the possibility of increased errors.

Professional night baseball can be traced to May 2, 1930, when an experimental minor league game in Des Moines, Iowa, caused attendance to soar by 2000 percent as legions of curious fans watched the first pro game conducted under the lights.[22] Inspired by their own successful nighttime experiment five years later, the Reds continued to play night baseball in 1935, including one game against each of the other seven National League teams. The sub-par Reds finished 17 games under .500 that year, but attendance for those night games more than doubled.

Night baseball attendance not only drew the attention of the owners, it set the stage for a new paradigm in baseball broadcasting. The evening listeners offered a different demographic that would interest future advertisers, while providing a much larger potential audience in "prime time." All teams would soon offer night games, although it would take the Chicago Cubs much longer, until 1988 in fact, to break the Wrigley Field day-game tradition, which the team finally did with a 6–4 win over the Mets on August 9, 1988 (although the first Cubs' night ball actually happened a day earlier against the Phillies, but that game was completely rained out by the third inning).[23]

The Wrigley family saw the potential of night games as soon as anyone, and had actually purchased a number of towers to install lights as early as 1941. Those towers were available for the 1942 season, but Roosevelt's "date which will live in infamy," December 7, 1941, changed everything. After the Pearl Harbor attack and America's entry into World War II, the Wrigley light standards were shipped to the Great Lakes Naval Air Station for government use.[24] Wrigley Field would stay dark for another 46 years.

Night games would still be conducted by some teams during the war years, but the government would periodically stage practice blackouts in the event of a possible air raid. The war was changing everything, of course, putting more than just a chill on night baseball. On January 6, 1942, 23-year-old Bob Feller reported to the Navy, the first of many big leaguers to participate in the Armed Forces during those trying times. Like many to follow, including Ted Williams and scores of others, Feller was in the prime of his career at the time. Feller may have been young, but already he had led the American League in strikeouts three times with 24, 27, and 25 wins over the preceding three seasons.[25] Then came Hitler's invasion of Poland, Pearl Harbor, and all that followed.

There was considerable debate over whether to play baseball at all during World War II, a time of great anguish and perpetual national sacrifice. Many of the game's star players were being sent overseas, brightly lit night games offered potential targets for possible air strikes, and certainly the notion of frolicking in baseball just did not seem right given the scope of the national emergency. President Roosevelt officially left the decision to Commissioner Landis, but the president offered his own personal preference to keep the game going as a source of diversion, continuity, and inner strength for war-torn America, a forceful opinion given Roosevelt's extraordinary national standing and power at the time. In the President's famous "green light letter," which gave baseball his blessings, Roosevelt concluded, "I honestly feel that it would be best for the country to keep baseball going."[26] Baseball took the hint and maintained its normal schedule throughout World War II. If baseball had not become our national game already, it certainly would earn that standing by then as America braced for World War II. A similar poignant point would be made decades later on September 21, 2001, when entertainer Liza Minnelli belted out *New York, New York* in Shea Stadium before a national television audience as America dusted itself off after the 9/11 tragedy. The National Anthem is nothing new to baseball, of course. It was just before the 1942 season that major league baseball opted to play the "Star Spangled Banner" national anthem before every big league game, a tradition carried on ever since and soon spread to all the other major American sporting events.[27]

With baseball in play, all was still right with America — at least that was the sentiment offered by continuing major league ball through the war years. America would be awash in baseball as the public sought diversion if not comfort. Soon there was a plethora of motion pictures performing the same service, especially war pictures, westerns, the classic monster movies that Universal churned out, and certainly motion pictures about baseball itself, not the least of which was 1942's *Pride of the Yankees* featuring Gary Cooper as the inspirational Lou Gehrig.[28]

But while Hollywood flourished and as baseball offered a sense of stability to America, another revolution was already afoot that would dramatically boost the power, credibility, and availability of the radio broadcast medium. When Hitler's German Army invaded Poland, England and France demanded a pullback by precisely 11:00 A.M. on September 3, 1939, to avoid all-out war. The story of that watershed moment was filed by a young CBS correspondent in London who began with a resonant reference to Shakespeare's *Macbeth*: "Stands England where she did."[29] That youthful but promising reporter was none other than the future CBS News icon Edward R. Murrow.

Hitler, as history knows, promptly ignored the England-France ultimatum, so by 11:15 A.M., Prime Minister Neville Chamberlain announced over the BBC that a state of war then existed between Great Britain and Germany. Murrow immediately appeared on the radio during that historic moment, ad-libbing his very first of many watershed broadcasts from London during World War II: "Forty-five minutes ago the prime minister stated that a state of was existed between Britain and Germany. Air-raid instructions were immediately broadcast, and almost directly following that broadcast the air-raid warning sirens screamed though the quiet calm of this Sabbath morning...."[30]

Radio became a national glue holding the nation together during the war years, but radio had already been changing America. When Charles Lindbergh returned from his historical Paris flight in June 1927, a massive parade was held in Washington, D.C., for the returning hero. The Flying Cross medal was delivered to Lindbergh that day by none other than emerging broadcast and baseball icon Graham McNamee in a ceremony that was broadcast on radio.[31] There were about six million radios in use at the time, and historians guess that maybe five people listened in on each set, giving Lindbergh and McNamee an audience of perhaps 30 million. The demand for radio exploded after that. Perhaps it was a coincidence of fate, but that same summer of 1927 is precisely when baseball was reinventing itself with its banner "murderers' row" year.

In September 1927, RCA introduced a new line of radios for the consumer. They were priced between $69.50 and $895.00, even that lesser price representing a healthy sum in those days.[32] But the public craved radio, especially RCA's "Radiola 17" model priced at $157.50, which ran on regular household electricity instead of the cumbersome batteries that had been used before.

By 1928, Herbert Hoover found himself campaigning mostly on radio and through motion picture newsreels, changing the face of politics in America forever. It was then that the attention span of listeners began to shrink, the Hoover campaign finding that the radio audience would no longer suffer long-winded stump speeches, forcing political addresses to become shorter bursts of 10 minutes or less.[33] America was coming together as a single nation more than ever with Americans suddenly able to share great moments together, bonding to each other in the process. Whether a great boxing match, political speech, a historic event like Lindbergh's arrival or Babe Ruth in the World Series, all of America could be there to savor the moment.

The power of radio was proven many different ways, but its emerging economic impact might be summed up by the success of *Amos 'n' Andy* creators Correll and Gosden, who by 1933 were making a staggering $100,000 per year — more than Babe Ruth. Expanding audiences raised the marketing stakes as advertisers flocked to reach the vast audiences of this new medium; Chesterfield cigarettes, Pepsodent toothpaste, Maxwell House coffee, and many other consumer-product manufacturers jumped at the chance to reach millions of consumers in one fell swoop.[34]

By 1933, news and entertainment dominated the airwaves. The familiar voice of Lowell Thomas delivered national and world stories to the listening public, while gossip columnist Walter Winchell's distinctive rapid-fire cadence — made even more famous in the early 1960s as the narrator voice behind *The Untouchables* television series— brought stories of glitz and glamour from the entertainment world. Sporting news was especially popular, with Yankees owner Jacob Ruppert struggling to sign Ruth to a new contract in the $50,000 range.[35] But in those days nothing captured America's attention like politics. It was then, for example, that Huey Long rose to local and national prominence, partly due to the powers of radio, which Long massaged expertly, sometimes using it to multiply his audience as evidenced by the following 1933 address: "Before I begin I want you to do me a favor. I am going to talk along for four or five minutes, just to keep things going. While I'm doing it I want you to go to the telephone and call up five of your friends, and tell them Huey is on the air."[36]

On Christmas night in 1937, the NBC orchestra performed a broadcast concert of a classical Vivaldi piece from its studios from the RCA Building in New York, as radio continued to flourish throughout the 1930s. But 1939 brought more than just news, entertainment, politics, or baseball, it ushered in an era of fear that compelled a different kind of interest by Americans who turned to radio for the latest reports of world events— thus bonding the entire country like never before.

"This is London," began the grave staccato voice of Edward R. Murrow as he broadcast from the London rooftops during the relentless 1940 bombing blitz conducted by Nazi aircraft. As waves of enemy bombers roared over the city, as many as 300 at a time, Murrow broadcast not just the stark facts, but also sought to convey the emotional truths of the Battle of Britain, as the following excerpts suggest. "Tonight, as on every other night, the rooftop watchers are peering out across the fantastic forest of London's chimney pots. The anti-aircraft gunners stand ready.... I have been walking tonight — there is a full moon, and the dirty-gray buildings appear white. The stars, the empty windows, are hidden. It's a beautiful and lonesome city where men and women and children are trying to snatch a few hours sleep underground."[37]

During the course of America's involvement in World War II, over 500 major league ballplayers found themselves in a much different uniform as they performed their duties for the various Armed Forces. There were 35 future Hall of Famers in that group as some of baseball's biggest names went off to war, their headline presence helping to solidify and bond America during its great struggle. They included names like Ted Williams, Joe DiMaggio, Warren Spahn, Hoyt Wilhelm, Bob Feller, who voluntarily enlisted on December 9, 1941, as the ruins of Pearl Harbor still smoldered — and also two lesser names with a very big legacy, Harry O'Neill and Elmore Gedeon, both of whom died while serving.[38]

When Luke Appling was drafted, his wife publicly announced, "It'll be good for him." Feller spent four years in the Navy, one in the U-boat-riddled Atlantic, the rest in the Pacific theater where he saw significant combat — including the invasion of Iwo Jima — while on the USS *Alabama* as an anti-aircraft captain. Williams, nicknamed "The Kid," hit .406 for the Red Sox in 1941, the last major league to top the .400 milestone for a full season. The following year, Williams was in the Navy preparing for air gunnery combat at a training facility in Jacksonville, Florida, where he again was setting records in reflexes, coordination, and visual-reaction time. He was commissioned as a Marine Corps pilot in May 1944, then taught others to fly. Williams spent about four years away from baseball during the war but did not see actual combat until years later in Korea, when he would fly 39 combat missions, some of them as wing man for future astronaut and senator John Glenn.

Not only did the war impact baseball, but baseball influenced the war itself. The game was so embedded in America's soul by then that its lingo spread through and changed military slang. And the soldiers religiously followed the game back home, keeping an eye on box scores as well as enemy targets. Why was baseball so deeply entrenched in our national gut during those war years? Radio. Even a full three-hour baseball game produces under 20 minutes of actual on-field action. There are only three options for the rest of the time: dead air, commercials, and conversation. By contrast, today's NBA game might take about two and a half hours, but its full 48 minutes of clock time will be filled with game action. But baseball is different — we are reminded that the game is virtually built for the talk medium we call radio.

Richie Ashburn was a superstar player for the Philadelphia Phillies just after the war. With two league batting titles, a lifetime .308 average, and more center field speed than even Willie Mays, Ashburn was rewarded by having his number retired by the Phillies in 1979, then was inducted to the Baseball Hall of Fame in 1995. But much of Philadelphia remembered him more as a broadcaster who called Phillies games from 1963 until his death in 1997. When legions of fans streamed to the deceased Ashburn's viewing, grown men engulfed in tears brought not baseballs or gloves to leave behind, but transistor radios. Richie Ashburn was not just a player, he was their friend, the man next door who lived and breathed Philadelphia baseball right alongside each of them, the voice not just of Phillies ball, but of Philadelphia itself.

Harry Kalas called baseball games for four decades, most of it for Philadelphia, and much of that along with Richie Ashburn. When Kalas himself died in 2009, Frank Fitzpatrick of the *Philadelphia Inquirer* wrote, "It's been nearly 88 years since Pittsburgh radio station KDKA first broadcast a ball game, an 8–5 Pirates victory over the Phillies on Aug. 5, 1921, and yet the marriage remains strong, the romance just as enticing."[39] Fitzpatrick explained further, "Even in this summer of 2009, when every game is televised and Webcast, and when fans can watch on cell phones or laptops, radio has its diehard devotees. Many listen even at the ballpark. Others prefer radio for their audio while watching on TV. And nothing enhances a backyard barbecue, a day at the beach, or a long car trip like a ball game on the radio." Curt Smith, author of the *Voices of the Game* study of baseball announcers, adds, "Radio is the perfect medium for baseball. It's active, not passive. It's theater of the imagination. The structure of the game makes it perfect for radio and imperfect for TV."

Throughout World War II, Americans turned to radio for war updates and for the diversion, if not reassuring comfort of baseball. Popular entertainment shows during the war years included *The Shadow, The Lone Ranger*, the *Glenn Miller Show, Adventures of Ellery Queen*, and *The Thin Man*, but none of those shows could offer the friendly voices of radio, the neighbor next door to share a game or an afternoon. Baseball attendance at the ballparks held steady during the war until 1945, the last year of conflict, when it jumped by over 31 percent from an average of 8.26 million to 10,841,123 fans.[40] But that was only a hint of the real explosion to come in 1946, the first full baseball season after World War II. With Feller and Williams and the others back home and donned in full big league garb, over 18 million relieved fans poured into the major league ballparks, a 70 percent at the gate. Baseball was back and America was more than ready.

The war had impacted baseball but not destroyed it, and sometimes that impact reached baseball broadcasting itself. During the war years, for example, the government had prevented baseball broadcasters from providing any information that could be of use to our enemies, like any mention of weather conditions that might facilitate possible bombing missions over the United States. One story about Dizzy Dean has Dean and his St. Louis broadcast partner Johnny O'Hara filling an hour rain delay without ever mentioning the rain.[41] But there still was baseball on the radio, and America listened.

Dizzy Dean may have been the perfect radio voice for the war years. His homespun drawl and country humor were legendary, a trait that severed him in later years as a television broadcaster for NBC's *Game of the Week* telecasts. Dean was very busy behind the microphone during World War II, announcing home games for both the St. Louis Cardinals and the Browns. Born Jerome Hanna Dean in Lucas, Arkansas, Dizzy was a dominant Hall of Fame pitcher for the Cardinals (1930–37), Cubs (1938–41), and even a four-inning stint for the Browns themselves in 1947 when he left the broadcast booth to show how "real pitching" was done. A lanky 6' 2" 182-pounder, Dean won the National League MVP Award in 1934, and four times led the league in strikeouts, victories, and complete games.[42] In 1934 he also won two World Series games for the Cardinals with his younger brother Paul "Daffy" Dean winning the other two, as the siblings pitched St. Louis to a championship. Although Dizzy Dean's official website biography lists sports broadcasting only as his "hobby," Dean was perhaps as good in the booth as he was on the field. Listed by baseball broadcast historian Curt Smith as the ninth best baseball broadcaster of all time, Dean was described by Smith as homey, warm, and "unforgettable."[43]

If the central Illinois announcers like Brickhouse, Elson, and Ronald Reagan brought small-town America to the broadcast booth, Dean brought the "good ol' Arkansas country" to both baseball and radio. He only played six full seasons during a 12-year career in the majors, but Dean performed as a broadcaster for over 20 years. Legend and credible sources differ, but he seems to have been nicknamed "Dizzy" by his own sergeant in the army when Dean practiced pitching by throwing potatoes while on KP duty. Later Dizzy was called up to the majors by St. Louis on the last day of the 1930 season when he responded with a blistering three-hitter, a game where he also bunted a base hit into left field and stole home in the third inning of a 3–1 victory over the Pirates. Egocentric, colorful, and confident to a fault, Dean was nearly the demise of Branch Rickey. "If there were one more like him in all of baseball," Rickey lamented, "just one more, as God is my judge, I'd get out of the game." Dean, though, could deliver. "It ain't braggin' if you can back it up," he said. His official rookie year of 1932 saw Dizzy join the Cardinals and promptly win 18 games, leading the NL in strikeouts. Dean predicted that he and his brother Paul would win 45 games in 1934, but he was wrong. Dean won 30 and Paul 19 for a combined 49 victories.[44] A master of intimidation, Dean often trash talked from the mound, as in, "Son, what kind of pitch would your like to miss?"[45]

The war caused the proliferation of radio, and it literally played a part in the development of radio technology. Indeed, the common term "radar" is a World War II acronym for "radio detection and ranging," which was developed in 1941 on the eve of war by utilizing electromagnetic waves to identify the range, altitude, direction and/or speed of both moving and fixed objects. Ironically, the term has become a staple of modern big league pitching, which utilizes the radar "gun" to measure the speed of virtually every pitch, flashing the result on the stadium scoreboard and often the television screens at home.

The war years saw baseball at work raising money for the Red Cross and the National War Fund, and they also inspired the development of the All-American Girls Baseball League by none other than Philip K. Wrigley, son of the late William Wrigley, an effort later made famous by the 1992 motion picture *A League of Their Own* starring Tom Hanks, Geena Davis, and Madonna. In 1945 the All-Star Game was canceled due to wartime travel restrictions, and it was also 1945, at the close of the war, that Branch Rickey first signed Jackie Robinson to a minor league contract. That same year found the Chicago Cubs in the World Series for the very last time during the twentieth century and beyond, which was partly a fluke of history since the entire league was diluted due to World War II itself.[46]

Dizzy Dean was a rock in the broadcast both during those trying World War II years. He had already done it all from the pitching mound, while his country style both captivated and soothed war-torn America. By the end of World War II, 95 percent of all homes in America had at least one radio, and thereafter baseball would never be far from our parlors, living rooms, porches, and garages. Just after the war, Dean committed the ultimate act of broadcasting heresy, criticizing the players to the point where Browns owner Bill Veeck invited Dean to step down from the booth to pitch again in 1947. Dean had been retired for six years, but said he still could throw better than 90 percent of the team's pitching staff. He then obliged the showman Veeck by pitching the first four innings of the final game of the 1947 season, allowing no runs and slapping a single himself for good measure. Unfortunately, the cocky Dean pulled a hamstring rounding first, sending him back to retirement and the broadcast booth for good.[47]

8

The Game of Our Fathers

The doctors x-rayed my head and found nothing.

— Dizzy Dean[1]

Doris Kearns Goodwin would become a Pulitzer Prize–winning biographer of U.S. presidents. She grew up in Brooklyn not just a baseball fan, but one who was in love with the Dodgers, faithfully listening to her team on the radio. With politics, history, and the Brooklyn Dodgers in her blood, how could she miss?

"My first year as a Dodger fan," writes Goodwin in her acclaimed memoir *Wait Till Next Year* about life, family, and baseball, "ended with a dramatic flourish as the pennant race between the Dodgers and the Cardinals came down to the final week."[2] This was 1949 when Goodwin was six years old. Her beloved Dodgers proceeded to take the season finale in the tenth inning against the Cardinals, winning the pennant and the right to meet the Yankees in the World Series. Both teams had won 97 games that year, but Goodwin's heroes of Don Newcombe, Roy Campanella, Pee Wee Reese, Ralph Branca, Gil Hodges, and National League MVP Jackie Robinson were no match for DiMaggio's Yankees led by their first-year manager Casey Stengel.

In her youth, Goodwin followed the local Little League team, helping to make ice cream sodas for the players at the local soda fountain after games. Her recollections of baseball are ensconced in the memories of her own youth — and of her father, who died of a heart attack in 1972 while watching the Mets on television. She grew up, quite literally, with summer sodas, baseball, and radio — in other words, her childhood was much of what defines America itself:

> On a sultry Friday evening that same summer, after months of listening to games on the radio, I saw my first game at Ebbets Field. As my father and I walked up the cobblestone slope of Bedford Avenue and approached the arched windows of the legendary brick stadium, he explained how, as a boy, he had watched the ballpark being built, since the place where he had been sent to live after his parents died was only two blocks away.[3]

The voice on Doris Kearns Goodwin's radio during that magical Dodgers summer of 1949 was none other than Red Barber, who had already been the voice of the Dodgers for a decade at that point. When the three New York teams ended their radio broadcasting moratorium in 1939, Barber was brought in from Cincinnati where he had been perfecting his announcing craft since 1934. The year immediately following that summer of Dodgers disappointment, 1950, found Vin Scully alongside Barber in the broadcast booth. Scully would later be regarded as one of the best sports announcers of all time — indeed the very top baseball announcer according to many. But it was Scully who admired Barber, often describing the legendary Barber as being "like a father to me."

Evoking fatherhood, as Scully did, should be of no surprise to history, family, or baseball, for baseball is the game of our fathers and their fathers, and frankly our mothers and sometimes daughters, too. When Phillies broadcaster Harry Kalas died in 2009, columnist Frank Fitzpatrick of the *Philadelphia Inquirer* offered: "If you were to ask for the most identifiable sound of an American summer, the answer would almost have to be baseball on the radio. You hear it at the beach, in cars, in backyards, in bars. Radio still matters enormously to the game."[4]

When Red Barber passed away nearly two decades before Kalas, it signaled the inevitable end of a baseball era, one where the radio voice of each team was so distinctive that it *was* that team. Yes, there are good announcers today, many perhaps more polished and more professional than the old-timers, but the announcer meant something different

Baseball broadcast pioneer Red Barber, at the microphone in 1955, eleven years before the Yankees would fire him over a broadcasting dispute. Barber announced major league games from 1934 to 1966, first for the Reds, then the Dodgers from 1939 to 1953, followed by the Yankees until the day he crossed CBS ownership by making note of over 66,000 empty seats.

during those earlier radio days. Mel Allen simply *was* the Yankees; the Red Sox identified themselves by Curt Gowdy's nasal tones; Harry Caray was indeed the Cardinals before he did it again with the White Sox and still again when he became the beloved voice of the Chicago Cubs. All of them, moreover, would become virtual members of each listener's family.

Today the craft has become perhaps too sophisticated almost for its own good. Most of the contemporary announcers are smooth and professional broadcasters with years of training and paying hard-earned dues before landing their big chance. Barber, by contrast, called the very first baseball game he ever saw. It was 1934. He lasted as an announcer until 1966 when the Yankees fired him for openly observing that only 413 people were on hand one day to watch the once-dominant Yankees. Identified largely for his stint with the Dodgers from 1939 to 1953, Barber was a pillar of baseball until his death in 1992, finally laying to rest a career during which Barber personally witnessed Jackie Robinson's debut, Roger Maris' home run number 61, the first night game, and the first-ever televised baseball game. "People tell me you could walk through Brooklyn without a radio and still hear Red describe the game," says network sports icon Bob Costas. "You wouldn't miss a pitch because it would come from an apartment windowsill, from a storefront, from a car radio with its window open."[5] Radio, in other words, filled the summer air with baseball. Frank Fitzpatrick quoted historian Curt Smith on the impact of radio on baseball: "It's active, not passive. It's theater of the imagination. The structure of the game makes it perfect for radio and imperfect for TV."[6]

Baseball does, of course, enjoy its own personal history with television, including some very good years with network television's various "games of the week" as well as the dependable local broadcasts of the hometown teams. But television allowed the visual action of basketball and the breadth and pageantry of football to gain traction, eventually passing baseball as sports best seen on TV. The advent of HD television, though, would help tip the scales back toward baseball as the New Millennium unfolded, for suddenly the widescreen HD format brought the sheer beauty of the baseball parks back to life and allowed the vast angles of the field to come into play in one visual shot. But baseball broadcasting, however, is about much more than just looking good in a theater-wide format.

"Whoever wants to know the heart and mind of America," proclaimed historian Jacques Barzun, "had better learn baseball." This is an often quoted observation from a Barzun piece called *God's Country and Mine: A Declaration of Love Spiced with a Few Harsh Words*, that was published in 1954, the very year of the Supreme Court segregation ruling in *Brown v. Board of Education*. Although his work is well known in history circles, not everyone accepts Barzun's observation without further analysis, if not skepticism.[7]

Weighing in on baseball's exalted status is Gerald L. Early, a foremost American thinker and essayist on matters of African American culture as well as on baseball itself. Early is not only a professor of modern letters and a director of the Center for the Humanities in Arts & Sciences at Washington University in St. Louis, he has been a consultant for several of Ken Burns' acclaimed documentaries, including the film historian's epic work on baseball. "I am not sure in the end why baseball is America's game or why it should say more about our national character, the true subject of the Barzun book, than football, basketball, or boxing," queries Early in an essay published by *American Poetry Review* in 1996. After all, Early suggests, baseball is also played in Cuba, the Dominican Republic, and Japan; so does the game also speak for these other cultures? Is there something political about the game that ties it to an America of more conservative "values"? "Baseball," continues Early, "has the image of stability and conservatism, yet it has been rocked by more labor disputes and unrest than any other popular-culture industry except journalism."[8]

Professor Early views baseball's exalted status as either a myth or even something of a fraud. Early finds few symbolic ties to the larger America when analyzing how the game itself is played; exhibits a level of anger over the game's abject racism for much of the twentieth century; and pokes holes in the breadth, if not exaggerated romance, of Barzun's uniquely sweeping "heart and mind of America" conclusion. All are valid points, and Barzun deserves criticism for begging his own question about baseball's standing in what Early rejects as the "self-evident truth" about baseball. Early is right to question the validity of baseball worship if the game's status is boosted solely by sentimentality. But Professor Early's harsh conclusions are wrong for the wrong reasons, so to speak, for the flaws of the game are much of what actually ties baseball to America itself. That baseball evokes such an unprecedented degree of romance among American sports actually corroborates the original premise: baseball *is* somehow buried deep in America's gut. The real question is *why*.

Baseball grew up with twentieth century America. It endured the Great Depression and survived World War II; it was racist when much of America was racist as well; it has always played loose with its own rules, exhibiting a curious brand of cheating, from spitballs to stealing signs, thus mimicking much of our free-wheeling, tobacco-spitting capitalist society; and, moreover, baseball bonded with America like no other sport could ever do because of the game's deliberate pace and its emergence at precisely the time when radio was making its mark.

The game has always occupied a singular place in American sports history. Baseball became exempt from U.S. antitrust laws with the Supreme Court pronouncement that major league baseball is not a business in interstate commerce, an absurd ruling that nonetheless substantiates the point of baseball's exalted status. The game is largely celebrated for its embrace of Jackie Robinson, but the game should be scolded for making Jackie Robinson necessary in the first place. But baseball still evokes romance, sentimentality, and an ephemeral something that is genuinely American, proving that it remains different from the other sports. Moreover, the game is decidedly unique in how it is played, for baseball is a team sport that relies on a series of individual pitcher-batter confrontations that produce a form of sports drama that is more like boxing than football. It has no imposed time limits and thus no clock, and the fields are irregular. Football's goal posts do not change height from stadium to stadium, and the basketball court does not change shape from city to city. Baseball's infinite irregularities are much more like golf, but they represent something decidedly more symbolic, for these innate differences render baseball much more like life itself.

Baseball's impact on American culture can be found in perhaps its most profound contribution to the American experience, language. The game of baseball dominates American language and therefore impacts its culture, attitude, and personality, all of which evokes the Barzun conclusion about the "heart and mind of America." The language of baseball is the language of America in such deeply embedded ways that it is hard to distinguish it from ourselves, that is, to find the baseball forest among all the trees. This seems true "right off the bat," as they say. No, Barzun was not throwing us a curve, but neither is Early tossing a screwball. Maybe just a little off base, that's all. But neither is his criticism wholly "out of left field," for it does have merit. But ultimately Early strikes out because the standing of baseball in American culture proves its own point. We are a capitalist nation that swings for the fences, a go-for-broke culture that evokes baseball and vice versa. But the debate will continue, as rightfully it should—for as Yogi Berra and history agree, the game "ain't over till it's over."

But why is baseball language such a part of America? Boxing is perhaps a close second in offering sports metaphors such as "knock-out punch," "getting off the canvas," "saved by the bell," "on the ropes," "punched in the gut," and "shadow boxing." It may be no coincidence that boxing is a one-on-one sport, just as baseball essentially is, thus evoking a confrontational brand of drama that translates well to similes and metaphors. But still, how did baseball language get this way? The ultimate answer is likely tied to the advent of radio at precisely the right time in American history, but there are other nuances that contribute to the phenomenon, including the very nature of baseball talk itself.

After all, the language of baseball offers, among other things, a deceptively profound tribute to the obvious. We barely notice its sweeping impact on language and culture, yet baseball talk, quite clearly, has helped mold twentieth century Americana more than any other sport — including boxing. "Who's on First?," the enduring double-talk comedy routine of Abbott and Costello, reminds us of our singular hardball history, a jolting evolution of culture, language, and thought that still influences who we are as a nation. From such patent baseball terms as "screwball" and "curveball" to the game's unparalleled visual metaphors like left field, swinging for the fences, or the circular exercise of discerning who— or "Who"— is on first base, the playful gobbledygook of baseball has become the very fabric of America. The language of baseball, therefore, is an entertaining, often hilarious, and remarkably poignant journey into the American soul.

The breadth of baseball's impact on language, a telling tale of culture in its own right, reveals how the language of the game has so indelibly gripped our country's approach to business, law, politics, humor, and American life. That baseball has contributed so much to the contemporary vernacular is significant in itself, but realizing how universally understood those terms are suggests a Noam Chomsky–like innateness that give us cause to wonder just how embedded baseball may now be in the American soul.

Where did this marriage of baseball and language come from? To a very large and profound degree it is traced to broadcasting — and mostly broadcasting on radio. Red Barber and other baseball broadcasters partly changed who we are by how we speak. The baseball diamond was the "pea patch," an argument was a "rhubarb," a sure-thing win was said to be "tied up in a crocus sack," and the team with a game that was well in-hand was "sitting in the catbird seat."[9] From home run calls like "holy cow" and "open the window here she comes," to baseball stories and lore, the language of the game as delivered by its many announcers was shaping America through radio. Before radio, news of the game was mostly handled by the newspaper media and word of mouth. There were print columnists like Damon Runyon, Ring Lardner, and Grantland Rice hauling in $35,000 per year almost a hundred years ago, while word-of-mouth accounts were much less organized yet almost as effective — and they were free of charge.[10] Indeed, there was a time when news of Doris Goodwin's Dodger games in progress was most reliably conveyed by taxi drivers lined up outside Ebbets Field where they heard scores from exiting fans, then passed along what they knew through the city streets of Brooklyn.

When Damon Runyon first appeared in New York as a young man in 1911, he wanted to write about the characters he had seen and met. He wrote numerous short stories emphasizing uniquely American characters, so many that they almost became their own genre of "Damon Runyon stories." Eventually baseball characters and baseball itself crept into his blood, and as it happens Runyon was there when Yankee Stadium opened in 1923 to usher in what would become one of the greatest ages of baseball, climaxing with the formidable 1927 Yankees. Runyon was stunned by the size and grandeur of the new baseball palace. "Only a veteran dweller of tenth and eleventh floors of apartment houses," he wrote in the *American*, "can sit up there [in the upper deck] without feeling a bit squeamish."[11]

But the impact of the game goes far beyond cathedral stadiums, the cuteness of its words, or the cleverness of its symbols. Those words, phrases, and inherent thoughts defining the game have influenced every meaningful aspect of American life. For example, the law review article cited most often in American judicial opinions is a 1975 *Penn Law Review* piece called "The Common Law Origins of the Infield Fly Rule," a playful but provocative study that suggests much about the game's impact on American law. But the game offers more than just fodder for a clever law review article, it impacts the very substance of American law.

Nowhere was this influence greater than during the history of racism in the United States from the late nineteenth century throughout much of the twentieth century. It may *not* have been merely a coincidence that Barzun's sweeping conclusions were published in 1954, the same year as the Supreme Court' 1954 ruling in *Brown v. Board of Education,* for the *Brown* case came on the heels of Jackie Robinson's entry into, and sweeping impact upon, major league baseball. Commissioner Landis often denied the "no Negroes" rule of major league ball, but the reality of the game's segregated history defies his own words and credibility. Were the best ballplayers of the Negro Leagues—such as Josh Gibson and Satchel Paige—really lesser players than the worst white players in the major leagues? Obviously not. But change did not occur until fate intervened: Landis died on November 25, 1944. Soon thereafter in August 1945, Branch Rickey, Walter O'Malley, and John Smith acquired a controlling interest in the Brooklyn Dodgers. That October, less than one year after the passing of Landis, Rickey found himself signing Robinson to a minor league contract.

Jackie Robinson debuted in the majors on April 15, 1947, at Ebbets Field. Then came Larry Doby, signed by Indians owner Bill Veeck in 1948, and Satchel Paige, also inked by Veeck, followed by Don Newcombe and a stream of black stars. Willie Mays was brought to the majors by the Giants in May 1951, where he graced baseball with an unprecedented combination of speed and power and was promptly named the National League Rookie of the Year.

The very next year, the state of Kansas enacted General Statute 72-1724 validating "separate but equal" facilities for public school children, forcing a black eight-year-old girl in Topeka to travel several miles to school rather than attend a facility in her own neighborhood. Suit was filed on her behalf, and the *Brown* case—her case—clawed its way to a Supreme Court ruling in 1954. "Today ... many Negroes have achieved outstanding success in the arts and sciences as well as in the business and professional world," reasoned Chief Justice Earl Warren, who then struck down the Kansas segregation law.[12]

Warren's opinion did not specifically mention baseball, but it had to have *meant* baseball, at least in part, for the resounding success of African Americans in our sacred national sport was inescapable front-page news—and virtually the only front-page story that dealt with Negroes somewhat evenly with whites. After all, statistics don't lie, and Willie Mays was pretty good both on the field *and* on paper. Baseball gave African Americans a platform that even the mild-mannered Jackie Robinson could not resist. On November 30, 1952, only 10 days after the *Brown v. Board* case was scheduled for argument before the Supreme Court, Jackie Robinson himself appeared on television and ignited a firestorm by accusing the all-white New York Yankees of racism.[13]

On October 8, 1953, Birmingham, Alabama, blocked Robinson's integrated all-star team from playing an exhibition game. This was two months before *Brown v. Board* would be argued for a second time on December 8, 1953, and by that time baseball was already on the Supreme Court front burner — on November 9, 1953, the Court had upheld the game's bizarre antitrust exemption in *Toolson v. New York Yankees* by noting "the high place [baseball] enjoys in the hearts of our people."[14]

The following spring, on May 17, 1954, the *Brown* ruling was finally issued. It followed Hank Aaron's first big league home run by just 24 days. Could the Supreme Court have missed Robinson, Doby, Campanella, Mays, Aaron and the others? Certainly not. Jackie and those who followed may have played on a baseball field, but it was the American landscape they forever altered — all of which helps answer the fundamental questions begged by Jacques Barzun and Gerald Early. Baseball was changing America not just because it was front-page news, for by then it largely *was* America. Maybe Barzun's remarks are cliché; but even that would not change the fact of baseball significance to American history and culture, much of which is traced to language, all which in turn can be attributed to the impact of radio on both baseball and life.

Indeed, the language of baseball routinely spills into life itself. A "moon shot" is a towering home run, but *actually* landing a man on the moon is not called a moon shot at all — while nearly everyone would certainly describe it as a "home run." Adding to the confusion is baseball's oxymoronic contributions to the obvious, courtesy of such diverse luminaries as Bill Veeck, Will Rogers, Franklin Roosevelt, Clarence Darrow, Ernest Hemingway, George Carlin, and a Yankee catcher named Berra who adds, "I didn't really say everything I said."

No one *means* all he says, either, as suggested by historian Henry Adams; thus the use — or misuse — of language fuels some of the most divisive friction in America from politics and business to law, life, and baseball. No wonder truth lives its famously tortured life, leaving little wonder that the words of baseball have become so indelibly American. The use of language is an integral part of any culture, of course, but there is a uniquely American spin that emphasizes sports in a manner that says much of who we are and how we think, and how Americans relate to each other and express our singular Yankee humor, thus forming an unremitting bond that glues us to our collective past — and to each other. "Let's play in *your* ballpark," relented the fictionalized version of Clarence Darrow to William Jennings Bryan, in the 1960 film of the world famous Scopes monkey trial of 1925. "Who do they think they are — the 1927 Yankees?" is a timeless put-down of "uppity" sports opponents from Little League to the big leagues, but it also is commonly used to express contempt for any opposing team not only in other sports, but in business and law as well.

Sports are so entwined with American thought that all of us — even non-sports fans — habitually refer to them without realizing the connection. Although boxing terms were once more prominent — we used to say political "ring" but now it's "arena" — baseball soon came to dominate American lingo and thought, as with the curious phrase "out of left field," a metaphorical land that we all know and refer to regularly but would be hard-pressed to truly define. The origin of the phrase is especially curious, for as all students of the game know, hapless young ballplayers are generally relegated to right field, not left. So where did it come from? As it happens, the phrase indeed came "out of left field" itself, both symbolically and as a point of actual geography.

The "out of left field" wisecrack is sometimes traced to Chicago Cubs lore. Before the Cubs moved to Wrigley Field in 1916 (then called Weeghman Park), they played at

West Side Park just southwest of the Chicago Loop. Then, as now, the area was a medical center with numerous hospitals such as the massive Cook County Hospital (where portions of the popular film *The Fugitive* was filmed and where the fictional television series *ER* took place). In those days a mental hospital was also nearby and loomed over the left-field wall of the baseball stadium. On hot summer days, the story goes, the residents at the neuropsychiatric Institute at the University of Illinois had the habit of leaning out the windows to watch baseball and to stay cool, inspiring the visiting clubs to remark about their peculiar appearance overlooking left field. The local players picked up on it, as did everyone else, and soon any sudden oddity was universally described as "out of left field." Regardless of its true origin, phrase has since become a part of American words and thought.

Although such kitschy sports phrases are plentiful if not very useful, the impact of sports — especially baseball — on our culture runs much deeper than just the use of clichés. Baseball has been the lament of U.S. presidents from Taft to Eisenhower to Nixon and Reagan, and the game permeates our literature, language, and humor so profoundly that it has little choice but to beg *why*.

"I would like to take the great DiMaggio fishing," mused the old man Santiago in Hemingway's novella *The Old Man and the Sea*. The old fisherman is expressing more than just wistful sentiment, he is idolizing perfection. "But I must have confidence and I must be worthy of the great DiMaggio who does all things perfectly...," he adds. Hemingway suggests a symbolic Christ figure in Santiago, whose scarred and bloodied hands make the story's young boy cry, but the author uses the "great" DiMaggio, the Yankee Clipper, as the ideal symbol of fortitude. That might sound blasphemous to some, but to others it simply pays appropriate homage to life's great metaphor, baseball.

"Who's on first?" is a simple query of baseball geography. But when "Who" becomes a proper noun, the question answers itself such that "Who" happens to be the name of the player on first base. In the hands of Abbott and Costello, the simple question invokes ten minutes of hilariously confusing baseball dialogue where all the answers are in fact the questions in a uniquely American twist of language and meaning. The great "Who's on First" routine sends Americans into a fit of laughter yet it might leave the French, Russians, and Chinese bewildered. If "humor is the first to perish in a foreign tongue," as Virginia Woolf once observed, then America's reliance upon inverted sports metaphors must be a complete mystery to the rest of the world.

But those metaphors would not, could not, have become a part of American language and thought if without the capacity to distribute and share such lingo efficiently and over an extended period of time. One of many pieces echoing the sentimental Barzun quote about baseball and America was a 1996 essay by John P. Rossi, published by the Historical Society of Pennsylvania, which specifically corroborates the strong role of radio broadcasting in explaining the position of baseball in America. "The history of baseball," says Rossi, "is also closely linked to the history of mass media."[15] Evoking the works of Ring Lardner, as well as the sentimental contributions of motion pictures from *Pride of the Yankees* to *The Natural*, *Bull Durham*, and *Field of Dreams*, Rossi stresses the impact of the game on literature and pop culture, and he links it directly to the advent of radio.

Rossi specifically quotes Branch Rickey's concern about the advent of television after World War II: "Radio created fans; television satiated them." Rickey, a staunch baseball man who changed the course of baseball history more than once, was nonetheless dead wrong on both points. Only in hindsight was radio seen as a boon to baseball; as stressed repeatedly herein, the owners largely feared radio as an innovation that could keep fans listening at home rather than coming to the ballparks. Television, though, did not precisely satiate the fans either; but it did largely bore them with its slow black-and-white renditions of a game in progress. Baseball on radio was like a member of the family engaged in constant conversation for so long as the game was being played. Radio created word pictures from the artful brushstrokes of colorful words painted by the rhythmic voices of the game's great announcers. Baseball on the radio was in full living color; on television it was a drab black and white.

Even so, perhaps television did not drive baseball away so much as it made other sports more popular, as it did with the faster paced pageantry of football. Football was in black-and-white just like baseball, but it had more action to follow between words. Baseball relies on its own unique narrative, which was largely lost on the early television broadcasts. Television would have its day, of course, courtesy of such gifted television announces as Dizzy Dean, Harry Caray, Jack Brickhouse, and so many others including the quintessential Vin Scully.

Dizzy Dean was a rare talent, a standout on the field and later the broadcast booth. Not many ballplayers are compared to natural wonders, but Dizzy was, according to Red Smith: "As a ballplayer, Dean was a natural phenomenon, like the Grand Canyon or the Great Barrier Reef. Nobody taught him baseball and he never had to learn."[16] Dean, when commenting on himself, was a little more analytical: "The good Lord was good to me. He gave me a strong body, a good right arm and a weak mind." Dean often made a point of weak-minded pitchers, which he regarded as an attribute. "The dumber a pitcher is," Dean insisted, "the better. When he gets smart and tries to experiment with a lot of different pitches, he's in trouble. All I ever had was a fastball, a curve and a change-up, and I did pretty good."[17]

NBC aggressively featured baseball games as television established itself. Dizzy Dean was one of its early — and best — announcers. From 1947 to 1965, NBC would choose the broadcasters for the World Series along with the commissioner and the powerful long-time baseball sponsor Gillette, which had backed baseball since it anted $100,000 to sponsor the Series on radio in 1939.[18]

Major league attendance was 19,874,539 in 1947 and would top 20 million in each of the 1948 and 1949 seasons before slumping for a dozen years, partly due to the growth of television, until the turnstiles finally hit 21 million in 1962 — the year following the great 1961 home run chase of Mantle, Maris, and yes even the long-deceased Ruth, which energized not only baseball, but America. The post-war resurgence of baseball was to be expected, although another cause for renewed interest was not: Jackie Robinson who debuted in 1947, which became "the year that all hell broke lose," as broadcaster Red Barber put it. Not only did Jackie bring his own magical brand of heads-up ball, but he brought audiences, too. A recording of the Game Six broadcast of the 1948 World Series was preserved and still exists, an exciting if not historic 4–3 Cleveland win that was announced by Jim Britt and the great Mel Allen.

In the 1950s, the fair-haired Mickey Mantle brought renewed life to the Yankees if not to all of baseball. Mantle played well on television, and baseball on television played well enough to not only last but to prosper as television itself proliferated in the 1950s and 1960s. Although there would be occasional setbacks, baseball gate attendance would eventually expand as television grew. Attendance exceeded 28 million in 1970, 43 million in 1980, and 54 million in 1990. A stunning 70,257,938 attended major league games in 1993, but then a labor action canceled part of the season and the World Series in 1994 causing attendance to drop approximately 30 percent.

Baseball has long been a litigious national sport, both before and after the 1922 *Federal Base Ball* antitrust exemption case, especially as the players union gained strength in the 1970s and frequently challenged the owners under the stewardship of leader Marvin Miller. But neither strikes nor court rulings could wholly kill the game. Not even the more recent steroid scandal seems to have quashed fan interest, although fans in general became more skeptical, if not jaded. Still, baseball endures, for it is the same game that made columnist George Will remember that the Cubs lost a doubleheader on the day of his wedding, even though he has confessed to forgetting most everything else that day.

When Don Larsen pitched his World Series perfect game in 1956, Dwight Eisenhower was inspired to write Larsen personally. "It is a noteworthy event when anybody achieves perfection in anything," Eisenhower said.[19] Maybe Thomas Wolfe best explained the magical lure of baseball for everyone from laborers to writers to presidents, as in the following excerpt from a letter Wolfe wrote to Arthur Mann: "...one reason I have always loved baseball so much is that it has been not Merely 'the great national game,' but really a part of the whole weather of our lives, of the thing that is our own, of the whole fabric, the million memories of America."[20]

Wolfe wrote further of springtime leaves, the smell of wooden bats and bleachers, and myriad memories of spring that are tied to baseball, which harkens perhaps the one that matters the most: the summer sound of baseball on the radio. *Philadelphia Inquirer* columnist Frank Fitzpatrick once paid tribute to baseball's impact on America through the magical talking box we call radio. "The only reason I still have a radio," one fan was quoted, "is so I can take it to the beach. Phillies baseball and catching some rays. There ain't nothing finer. I only wish these newfangled radios weren't headset only. I miss hearing all the other radios on the beach creating a sound wave that equals the noise of the seagulls or the crashing of the waves."[21]

"My wife and kids think I'm crazy," added another fan, who continued, "but there is nothing like baseball on the radio." He added that for years he had kept a pencil mark on his AM dial to aid in finding the Phillies game — even though he moved to Long Island long ago. Another fan admitted that all his five children went to bed with the Phillies on the radio with the familiar voice of Harry Kalas as their babysitter.[22]

The stories of fathers and sons and sometimes mothers are endless. Phil Heron of Downingtown, Pennsylvania, may have discovered why. "As a kid when I used to ask [my father] why he preferred the radio to sitting with me in front of the tube, he would respond with this succinct gem: 'I can see the game better on the radio.'"[23]

Those voices created the word pictures that made a long impression on the youth of America, most of whom grew up long ago and may now even be grandfathers themselves. President Eisenhower lamented about not making it to the majors; Thomas Wolfe and Doris Kearns Goodwin are among legions of writers who have written about the impact of baseball on their lives. Another was the prize-winning poet Robert Frost: "Nothing flatters me more than to have it assumed that I could write prose — unless it be to have it assumed that I once pitched baseball with distinction."

The golden age of radio was a fluid era largely defined as 1935 to 1950. It coincided with the childhoods of the parents of America's baby boomers, those who would became "the greatest generation" according to news icon and author Tom Brokaw. This was a product of fate, and could not have simply been a mere coincidence. Those fathers and mothers were brought up on the dulcet tones of radio. By 1935, during the teeth of the Great Depression, two-thirds of American homes had at least one radio set. There were twenty regional radio networks and four national networks spewing programming from coast to coast, bringing America together, at once, more than ever before.[24]

By 1936, both national political parties were spending $2 million each on radio advertising, and by 1940 Edward R. Murrow had invented field reporting as it is done today, essentially embedding himself in the bowels of London where his "London After Dark" series evoked the urgent horrors of World War II. Although news on radio was popular, fully half of all radio programming in 1940 was music — big bands, classics, jazz, but not yet the "top 40" mode of later pop and rock music.[25]

The war affected everything, of course, from baseball to the economy, and from radio to movies to politics. There were 13 million radios sold in America in 1941, but due to wartime manufacturing constraints fewer than one million were sold just two years later in 1943. Largely because of the public appetite for wartime information, radio news programming was up to 20 percent of all radio offerings by 1944, and on November 7, 1944, fully half of all the homes with radios were listening to the election results as Roosevelt defeated Dewey for an unprecedented fourth term. The following year *Meet the Press* began on radio and would become the longest continual radio program ever. By 1950, at the end of the official golden era, fully 94 percent of all American households had radio.[26]

Poignantly, if not symbolically, it was that very year — 1950 — that former pitcher Dizzy Dean began announcing NBC's *Game of the Week* for television. The age of radio was not over, but the golden era that provided comfort during the Great Depression, ushered World War II in and then out, and brought baseball to the ears if not hearts of millions, would soon be over.

Dizzy Dean owned perhaps the most down-home drawling voice in the history of the game — at least the game's history from the broadcast booth. In 1941 Dean retired as a big league pitcher at only age 30, then used his voice and his cocky reputation to gain a broadcasting job for the St. Louis Browns. Three years after moving to television, Dizzy Dean was elected to the Baseball Hall of Fame as a player, and he made it ahead of Joe DiMaggio, who was eligible but not admitted that year. It was almost unthinkable to skip over DiMaggio, so perhaps it was Dean's broadcasting visibility and down-home persona that propelled him ahead of one of the all-time great icons of the game. On the field it would take 34 years for another pitcher to win 30 games since Dean last did it in 1930. That pitcher was Denny McLain in 1968 — and no one has done it since.

One of the best baseball broadcasters of all time, Dizzy Dean lasted for 26 years in radio and television, and as the *Game of the Week* star he was a national voice of baseball for many who grew up in the 1950s. It would have driven mothers and teachers wild had they known what their children were listening to, for Dean had his own sub-language within the English genre with words like "slud" for the past tense of slide, or irreverent ad-libs like "they shot the wrong McKinley," which Dean said when umpire William McKinley made what Dizzy the broadcaster thought was a bad call in 1950. Moreover, it was Dean himself who was responsible for his own epitaph: "There'll never be another like me." Indeed.

Perhaps no one was precisely like Dizzy, but there were many who made their own marks on baseball broadcasting. One was Rosey Rowswell who became the "voice of the Pittsburgh Pirates" in 1936.[27] Only in 1955 did Rosey entirely cede to his successor Bob Prince, who had joined the broadcasting team in 1948 and then proceeded to become a Pittsburgh icon in his own right until he was fired in 1975, a move that angered many Pittsburgh listeners. Harold Arlin had been the Pirates' first radio broadcaster, beginning in the old KDKA days in 1921, but the games were not regularly broadcast until Rowswell's tenure. Because Rowswell was an upbeat Pirates fan first, his broadcasts contributed to both Pittsburgh lore and baseball lingo with his descriptions of a base hit as a "doozie marooney" and the strikeout as a "dipsy-doodle." Rowswell also contributed one of the more colorful home run calls of the game, warning the fictional Aunt Minnie to open her window each time, just as his booth partner would drop a tray of nuts, bolts, and other junk to the floor simulating the inevitable crash implying that Aunt Minnie was not quick enough. Rowswell's sound-enhanced home run call may never be surpassed for uniqueness, but it was Jim Woods, Pittsburgh broadcaster from 1958 to 1969, who had one of the funnier Pirates lines: "There are a reported 15,000 people at the game this afternoon. If that's true, then at least 12,000 of them are disguised as empty seats."[28]

With the Great Depression on his presidential resume, Herbert Hoover left a meager legacy, but he did contribute his own thoughts on the longevity if not magic of baseball in America: "Next to religion, baseball has furnished a greater impact on American life than any other institution."[29] Not that major league baseball has not always been run as a business first, like in 1939 when NBC presented announcer Red Barber with a specially inscribed baseball to honor the very first television broadcast of a game — a dubious memento since it was accompanied by a bill from NBC in the amount of $35 as widely reported, including by Barber himself.[30]

Liberty Broadcasting was formed by entrepreneur Gordon McLendon in 1948. Competing with the Mutual Broadcasting System in the post-war years, Liberty had as many as 500 radio stations at its peak. Although Liberty played music and other forms of routine entertainment, it found great success in broadcasting baseball games by recreating them "live" from telegraph accounts of the games. Famed broadcaster Lindsey Nelson began his career this way.

McLendon had paid major league baseball only the nominal sum of $1,000 annually for the rights to these recreation broadcasts, which proved very popular. By 1951, the owners had caught on, so the rights fee was elevated to $250,000 with a catch: Liberty could not broadcast in any city with a minor league baseball franchise, or in the northeastern or midwestern portion of the country.[31] These restrictions and competition proved too difficult as baseball moved toward more live baseball broadcasts not only on radio but on television, too, so the network folded in 1952, just four years after it had begun.

Liberty, however, had already made its mark on baseball history, if not American history, for it found itself broadcasting the historic 1951 pennant playoff game between the Giants and the Dodgers for a national audience on October 3. Baseball fans will recognize the crazed enthusiasm of Russ Hodges, who had been calling the game for the Giants audience: "The Giants win the pennant! The Giants win the pennant! The Giants win the pennant!" Although Hodges' game call has found its way into permanent American lore with countless replays, only hometown Giants listeners actually heard that call. The national broadcast was carried by Liberty Broadcasting System and featured Liberty's own founder, Gordon McLendon, who gave a similar audio account. Although the Hodges version is more famous, the entire game featuring McLendon is the only remaining complete account of the third Giants-Dodgers playoff game in 1951, won, as the baseball world knows, by the Giants, two games to one including the stunning walk-off home run victory at the Polo Grounds courtesy of Bobby Thomson.

One reason for the sheer excitement over the Giants' eventual win was the miraculous Giants comeback that year just to get there. On August 11, 1951, the Dodgers had what seemed to be an insurmountable lead of 13½ games over the Giants, who then went on a tear. Although Brooklyn did not entirely fold, going 26–22 to close out the season, the Giants were blistering hot with a 37–7 pace to finish the year. The Giants had to win their last seven in a row just to tie, which they barely did by besting the Phillies on the last day, eking out a 14-inning win that put the Giants at 96–58, the same record as Brooklyn.

Brooklyn won the coin toss determining home-field advantage for the three-game mini-series but then remarkably gave it away when manager Charlie Dressen opted to play game one at home instead of getting the home field for the last two games. Foiling his plan, the Giants won that first game, although they lost the second, setting up the historic finale. Sal Maglie, a 23-game winner, took the mound for the Giants in that last game to face his Dodgers counterpart ace, Don Newcombe. Maglie lasted to the eighth inning, allowing just one run, but then the Dodgers scored three and took a 4–1 lead, which they held until the bottom of the ninth inning.

Newcombe was exhausted. He had already pitched a complete game followed by a long relief appearance leading up to this final showdown, which he pitched on just two days rest. With his pitching tank on empty, Newcombe tried to take himself out of the game but teammate Jackie Robinson talked him out of it. Then fate took over. Famed Dodger infielder Gil Hodges was playing close to first instead of playing off the bag to protect a three-run lead, which allowed Don Mueller to single through the gap instead of slapping into a double play. Mueller, though, would break his ankle sliding into third as Alvin Dark scored on a double by Whitey Lockman. The Giants had two runners on and needed two to tie, three to win, when Bobby Thomson stepped to the plate. Dodgers manager Dressen finally replaced Newcombe with a reliever, Ralph Branca, who, unfortunately, had a history of pitching home run balls to Thomson. Some baseball historians feel Dressen made two errors during that crucial ninth inning, one by not having Hodges play off the bag, the other in pitching Branca. Others, however, point out that the Dodgers staff was overworked and stretched thin by the pennant race, so there were few real alternatives to Branca anyway.

Branca threw a fastball and Thomson laid off. It was a strike. Branca's second pitch of the game was his last. Thomson jerked it to left, a line drive that never yielded, clearing the wall at the alleged 315-foot mark — "alleged" because some accounts place the Polo Grounds foul line in left at just 279 feet. Left fielder Andy Pafko followed the ball to the fence, but he could only watch as it sailed into destiny, a three-run game winning walk-off blast soon dubbed "the shot heard 'round the world."[32] Branca was devastated by the loss ("Why me?"), but years later both he and Thomson have virtually conceded that the Giants had been stealing signs, including Branca's final fateful pitch.

No fewer than four broadcasters called that game. One was Russ Hodges, who did the game for the local Giants fans; another was Gordon McLendon, whose rendition remains intact today. The other two were famed broadcaster Ernie Harwell, who did the game on television station WPIX, and none other than Red Barber, the voice of the Dodgers, who called the game—and the Thomson shot—for WMGM-AM: "Branca pumps, delivers—a curve swung on and belted, deep shot to left field—it is—a home run!"

Journalist Red Smith was stunned along with countless Dodgers fans. Smith wrote the following, which ran on October 4, 1951: "Now it is done. Now the story ends. And there is no way to tell it. The art of fiction is dead. Reality has strangled invention. Only the utterly impossible, the inexpressibly fantastic, can ever be plausible again." If this did not hearken, and support, Hoover's comment on baseball as a virtual religious experience, then what could?

At most it took just one day for the game to be remembered for "the shot heard 'round the baseball world," for the next morning the *New York Daily News* carried that headline, courtesy of the original famous poem by Ralph Waldo Emerson — although legend and most memories have long since dropped "baseball" as a qualifying adjective in the phrase. What happened to the Giants next? They went down to the vaunted Yankees in six games of the World Series, perhaps the only Series truly lost in history to the pennant run that preceded it.

The short-lived Liberty Broadcasting not only gave baseball and broadcasting history the only remaining full account of that playoff game, but it gave the sports world Lindsey Nelson as well. His melodious voice can still be heard in the memories of many, for Nelson did the Cotton Bowl play-by-play for 25 years, not to mention 13 years as the voice of the Notre Dame Fighting Irish and many NFL regional and network games. He also did NBC baseball broadcasts beginning in 1957. As a footnote to broadcasting history, Nelson called the first NFL football game to feature instant replay. When he died in 1995, Nelson left behind a colorful broadcasting legacy, not the least of which was his hundreds of wacky colored and checkered sport jackets for which he had become known over the decades.

While Dizzy Dean was still pitching in the 1930s, the Federal Communications Commission was formed to regulate radio, license stations, and to mandate broadcasting's service to the local communities. As it happens, it was not only the baseball owners who feared radio in the early days, the newspapers were wary, too. They refused to allow radio to read from their print editions before those papers were distributed to the public, but that in turn forced radio networks to develop their own news departments. Compounding matters for the print media and serving as a potential threat to radio, television began to take hold in the 1948 to 1952 time span. The radio networks defended themselves by entering the television market, thus NBC and CBS became early players in the television business, which soon spread to sports. By the time Dizzy was singed to do televised network baseball in 1950, baseball's golden age was nearly over.

Television, in turn, terrified the movie business. Just as baseball owners feared radio would keep fans at home, film studios believed that television could keep customers from the theater. They were right. Hollywood struggled in the 1950s as it searched for ways to compete with television. Widescreen formats, more color, and even 3-D were used to generate interest. But unlike baseball which actually benefited from fan interest enhanced by baseball on radio, there was little about television that would send viewers to the theaters. As Milton Berle, Jackie Gleason, and Sid Caesar gained traction, audiences stayed home to watch. Just as the old vaudeville stars migrated to radio in the early days, the early radio stars like George Burns and Jack Benny were attracted to television.

Baseball remained a part of radio through all these transitions, but in varying degrees. Yet it did survive, as the obituaries for broadcast legends like Harry Kalas and Harry Caray continue to confirm, partly because baseball is the game most "heard to be seen" on radio, and partly because of the nostalgic momentum that refuses to wane. Baseball still is the game of our fathers and mothers and grandparents, largely due to the legacy of radio, the pace of baseball, and the familial voices of the game's longstanding broadcasters who were as much members of the family as perhaps the family dog.

But as good as radio was for baseball, the game of baseball still had to do its part. As author John Leonard wrote, "Baseball happens to be a game of cumulative tension but football, basketball, and hockey are played with hand grenades and machine guns. This is why it plays well on radio."[34] A basketball or hockey game on the radio is a blur of words—exciting, perhaps, but the announcers project the game to the listening family, they don't *become* the family.

Baseball has also managed to not take itself too seriously—at least most of the time. It has lapses, of course, like when commissioners tinker with the game or the game's history, but the game itself is played on irregular fields with irregular fences with an irregular amount of allotted time—and it is often played with irregular characters. With 154 to 162 deliberately paced games, there is time—and therefore room—for humor in baseball. The double-talk meanderings of Casey Stengel, the oxymoronic philosophies of Yogi Berra, the tempers of Lou Pinella or Billy Martin—all are part of the game's charm, and all contribute to the success of the game on radio, where the announcers expand upon and sometimes exceed the colorful characters who actually play the game. The Stengel philosophy could be cerebral ("Most ball games are lost, not won."); sarcastic ("Can't anybody here play this game?"); funny ("He's throwing grounders."); or bitter ("I"ll never make the mistake of being 70 again.").[35]

Baseball is about personalities, about people. Perhaps this is why, at least in part, the late Commissioner Bart Giamatti's photo can be found on a boyhood dresser in a subtle scene from his actor son Paul Giamatti's feature film *Sideways*. "Baseball," observed the late Tigers announcer Ernie Harwell, "is a lot like life. It's a day-to-day existence, full of ups and downs. You make the most of your opportunities in baseball as you do in life." When Harwell received the Frick Award in 1981, he spoke of the game he loved: "Baseball is a tongue-tied kid from Georgia growing up to be an announcer and praising the Lord for showing him the way to Cooperstown."

It is no coincidence that the golden age of radio was also the golden age of baseball *on* the radio—the two matured together. While the likes of Jimmy Foxx, Ted Williams, and Jackie Robinson took the field, another lineup of stars captured America's heart: Red Barber, Mel Allen, Vin Scully, Russ Hodges, Ernie Harwell, and legions more. Mel Allen did play-by-play for the most visible team in the game, the New York Yankees, and was identified as the voice of those Yankees during much of the 1940s, 1950s, and 1960s. Ernie Harwell called games for the Tigers for 42 years, plus 13 more for other teams. Vin Scully was named Broadcaster of the Century by the American Sportswriters Association in the year 2000; in 2010 he was still sounding great as he celebrated 60 years of Dodgers broadcasting.

Baseball and broadcasting were drawn together as the years passed. Inevitably, base-

Ossie (Oswald Louis) Bluege of the Washington Senators about to tag Babe Ruth sliding into third base, circa 1925, during the period of baseball's "rabbit ball" controversy. The simultaneous emergence of Ruth and radio during the prosperous 1920s would propel baseball as sports entertainment and redefine baseball's place in American culture.

ball and broadcasting began to merge in the literal sense, as well. In 1956 the Detroit Tigers were sold to a syndicate of radio and television executives for $5.5 million; eventually CBS bought the Yankees but managed to run the team into the ground before the George Steinbrenner years.[37]

"It was all I ever lived for, to play baseball," once said the boy-wonder Mickey Mantle who perhaps never quite fully grew up.[38] In the end, the game belongs to its players, and in the beginning there was one who propelled baseball to unforeseen plateaus with such power that the momentum continues today, Babe Ruth. "Every big leaguer, and his wife," said Yankee Hall of Famer Waite Hoyte, "should teach their children to pray: 'God bless Mommy, God bless Daddy and God bless Babe Ruth.'"[39] But they, and millions more, should also pay homage to the medium that brought them into almost every home in America for nine decades and counting — radio — plus those who brought baseball on radio to life, the announcers who made the game as much an American institution as any other.

The Baseball Hall of Fame may be missing such superstars as Pete Rose, Shoeless Joe Jackson, and even Roger Maris, but it's not missing Abbott & Costello. The whole "Who's on First" episode is so distinctly American and so wholly identified with the American game of baseball that in 1956 the filmed sketch was given to the Baseball Hall of Fame in

Cooperstown, where it plays on video. In 1999, *Time* magazine named the "Who's on First?" routine as the best comedy sketch of the twentieth century. Although the routine made its debut in film, namely *One Night in the Tropics* released in 1940, its charming and hilarious wordplay proved perfect for radio and therefore has played frequently on radio over the decades. In fact, it is an early radio recording of "Who's on First?" that appears in the Library of Congress National Recording Archives.[40]

Only in America, where baseball is the game of our fathers and their fathers, all of us linked by radio broadcast tales of baseball heroes that are perennially told by those invisible family member broadcasters who call still call the game as they see it — and feel it.

9

The Quantum Leap: Television

*Baseball has done more to move America in the right direction than
all the professional patriots with their billions of cheap words.*
— MONTE IRVIN[1]

The flickering images of television came of age during the 1950s. While the first television boxes were a drably constructed amalgam that was part parlor radio and part Victrola record player combined with a fishbowl lens, the world of television would soon reform American culture. Although baseball had already matured during the 1920s and 1930s, and television gained traction in the early 1950s, there was still something missing as America crossed into the second half of the twentieth century.

That something was color — both literally and figuratively. It is widely acknowledged that Branch Rickey and Jackie Robinson changed baseball when Jackie was brought to the majors in 1947, but by reaching out, accepting, and then showcasing the black ballplayers it was baseball that was about to change America as well. Television would help pave the way.

Willie Mays, who some still say was the greatest of all ballplayers, made his major league debut in 1951. Interestingly, it was that same year, on August 11, 1951, that New York's WCBS-TV televised the first baseball game *in color*.[2] The proximity of those events may have been little more than a poignant coincidence, but the subsequent evolution of baseball and television occurred precisely when the racial fabric of American culture was moving toward integration, and their combined impact was much more than fortuitous.

Abraham Lincoln issued the Emancipation Proclamation on January 1, 1863, but racial change certainly did not occur overnight. Baseball integration seemed sudden since it came quickly on the heels of Commissioner Landis' death at the end of 1944, but baseball's desire to integrate had been evolving for some time courtesy of visionaries Bill Veeck and Branch Rickey, both of whom understood the value and the significance of African American ballplayers.

Monford "Monte" Irvin was one of the first black ballplayers to follow Jackie Robinson to the big leagues, where he batted .293 over a span of eight seasons. Irvin, who began his career with the Negro National League Newark Eagles, one day found himself hitting

.458 for the New York Giants in the 1951 World Series.[3] On August 6, 1973, Irvin was inducted into the Hall of Fame in a class that included one of history's greatest pitchers, Warren Spahn, as well as one of the all-time great position players in Roberto Clemente. Irvin was not as spectacular on the field as those two icons, and although his presence did much to spread the integration of baseball, his observation about baseball moving America (quoted at the beginning of this chapter) demonstrates an astute grasp of what baseball did for overall racial equality.

But it might not have happened that way — at least not then — without the power of television bringing the visual images of African American athletes into America's living rooms. There were no black newsmen and no widely featured black actors except for Alvin Childress, Spencer Williams, and the other performers on *Amos 'n' Andy*, which made the transition from radio to television in 1951, but they weren't even the original stars since the wildly popular radio version had featured white actors as both Amos *and* Andy.[4]

Not surprisingly, the 1950–51 network television season had many similarities to the glory days of radio. Televised programming included *The Lone Ranger, Hopalong Cassidy*, and *The Aldrich Family*. But according the Nielsen ratings, the sixth ranked television show in 1951 was NBC's *Gillette Cavalcade of Sports*. The *Cavalcade* made its network debut in 1946, but it was not about baseball, it featured boxing and is largely remembered today as the "Friday Night Fights." With its one-on-one drama, a finite ring that is easy to televise even with one camera, and great overall popularity in the 1930s, '40s, and '50s, boxing proved to be a natural entertainment vehicle for TV. Boxing shows proliferated and featured many future star announcers like Don Dunphy, Russ Hodges, Chris Schenkel, and baseball's Bob Elson who called ABC's Tuesday night fights show that was broadcast from Chicago. There were many of these boxing programs, as many as five or six network shows every week, and Gillette's *Cavalcade* was so popular that it actually appeared on two different nights each week.

By 1951–52, television *looked* even more like radio used to *sound*, adding radio stars *Red Skelton, Jack Benny*, and *Amos 'n' Andy* to the lineup of hit shows. In 1951 television also added the CBS sports offering *Pabst Blue Ribbon Bouts*, again featuring boxing, as well as still more radio stars in George Burns and Gracie Allen.[5] But 1951 was a threshold year for baseball, too, not just on the field with Willie Mays or on the radio with the Bobby Thomson blast, but on network television.

From May to September of 1951, ABC offered a prime-time weekly baseball game on Saturdays — but, very strangely, these first shows featured women players, not men. The ABC show was called simply *Girls' Baseball* and was tied to the national Women's Professional Baseball League.[6] Telecast from Chicago in 1951, the program followed one team, the Chicago-based Queens of America. In 1952 New York's Arthur Murray Girls were featured with play-by-play from boxing's great announcer Don Dunphy.

With NBC and CBS already on strong footing in the 1950s, the DuMont and ABC networks were the weakest of all four majors. ABC turned to baseball in search of unique programming and ratings, but penetrating major league baseball proved very challenging. ABC's Edgar Scherick was the original force behind the network's pursuit of baseball, but he was only able to sign the Philadelphia Athletics, Cleveland Indians, and Chicago White Sox. Then major league baseball got in the way, banning the broadcast of any games within 50 miles of any major league ballpark. Even after two decades of stunning success on the radio, baseball, an arrogant monopoly, could not get out of its own way and missed the entire national sports entertainment forest for the "trees" of local programming and gate attendance. The game was so worried about extracting a dollar from a paying customer that it resisted the whole idea of the national baseball bonanza that network television could one day offer.

ABC also had to fight a senator from Colorado, Big Ed Johnson, who just happened to be president of the Western League and therefore a staunch advocate of minor league baseball. Johnson resisted competition from televised major league games by accusing the majors of monopolistic greed and great avarice—an ironic approach since it was the very idea of competition he was attempting to avoid. The Senate did conduct hearings, and all the fodder scared off the New York Giants who had been offered a lucrative $100,000 deal for ABC to telecast just six games but turned it down amidst all the political wrangling.[7] Battle-scarred but determined, ABC pressed forward and Johnson's noise eventually subsided.

Finally ABC broke the ice, and the 1953 season opener featuring the Yankees at the Washington Senators was to be televised on April 13, 1953, with Vice President Nixon throwing the ceremonial first pitch. But the game was rained out and ABC had no back-up game to rely on, so ABC had clearly struck out, as they say, on its first viable attempt to nationally broadcast a major league game.[8] Undaunted, ABC persisted, eventually breaking through when the Indians played at the White Sox on Memorial Day of 1953. ABC managed to televise the first game of the Cleveland-Chicago doubleheader that day, but because of the league-imposed blackout in most major cities, the televised game stirred little print media interest. The *New York Times*, for example, did not even mention the threshold event at all.[9]

The *ABC Game of the Week* steadfastly held on, though, even with its broadcasts limited to outlying areas—mostly southern and rural states where viewers indeed found the games entertaining, providing the network a viable baseball foothold. Throughout the 1953 baseball season, the games that ABC was able to telecast managed to earn a respectable overall viewer rating of 11.4 even with all the blacked-out urban areas factored in.[10] But fully 75 percent of America's rural televisions were tuned in to see the real-live big league games—a stunning ratio. One reason was Dizzy Dean, the retired pitcher who had a remarkable acuity for baseball broadcasting that was delivered with a down-home delivery that spoke volumes to rural America. Moreover, Dean was still riding his on-field successes, for 1953 also happened to be the year he was inducted into Cooperstown. Dizzy Dean clearly had star power. The public knew it, the network knew it, and to be sure Dean himself knew it.

Those 1953 ratings drew attention to baseball broadcasting, and that visibility allowed ABC to garner almost 100 stations to carry games for the following 1954 season, the first full season of network telecasting. ABC also managed to add four new teams to its lineup: the Dodgers, Giants, Phillies, and Senators. According to *Center Field Shot: A History of Baseball on Television*, the momentum for baseball on national television—and for ABC—was clearly building: "When only the non–Major League markets that carried the game are considered, the *Game of the Week* was the nation's fourteenth-highest rated program—a very strong showing for a non–prime time weekend series on a weak network."

Big ratings not only draw attention, they produce sponsors, and that leads to profits.

The manufacturers and distributors of a number of male-oriented products began to notice the *Game of the Week* too, including Gillette itself, automobile companies, and the eventual perennial sports sponsors, beer producers. It was during this very period that Anheuser-Busch mogul Gussie Busch jumped in with both feet, actually buying the St. Louis Cardinals in 1953 for $3.75 million.[11] The brewing company had been struggling and losing market share to Schlitz, so Busch shrewdly stepped into the baseball fray.

As it happens, the crosstown St. Louis Browns baseball team was also floundering. In 1953, the Browns lost 100 games at a time when the seasons were only 154 games, drawing only 297,238 fans at the gate for the whole year, an average of just over 4100 per game.[12] Owner Bill Veeck could take the bleeding no longer, so after the 1953 season he sold the team, which was moved to Baltimore to become the Orioles. There was also fear of St. Louis losing the struggling Cardinals team, too, so an opportunistic August Busch stepped in, outwardly feigning civic duty by "saving" the Cardinals, but quietly engineering a cunning resurgence of his own beer company with the image of baseball. In so doing, Busch also bought the old Sportsman's Park that had housed the Browns, then renamed it Busch Stadium. These moves were a stroke of genius in several respects. First, Busch got into baseball on the eve of the television and baseball marketing explosion, and he positioned his brand Budweiser as a sports fan's beer. Cleverly, Busch also out-maneuvered major league baseball with a deft move of his own, one that would change the world of sports sponsorships forever.

Sportsman's Park was promptly renamed Busch Stadium in 1953. Busch himself had lobbied to change the name to Budweiser Stadium, but baseball in those days frowned upon naming stadiums after alcoholic drinks. He was talked out of fighting to use Budweiser in the name, so he chose Busch Stadium instead. But what about the popular Busch Bavarian Beer — didn't that count? Gussie Busch was several moves ahead. He did an end run against the league because Anheuser-Busch did not introduce Busch Beer until 1955. By then the owners were already comfortable with the Busch Stadium moniker and, more importantly, they were growing used to raking in beer-sponsor profits from television, so baseball made no waves. In 1957, just four years after the Cardinals acquisition, Anheuser-Busch topped Schlitz in sales — and has remained the leading beer producer ever since.[13]

The Korean War distracted America during the early 1950s. It also disrupted baseball by draining the game of many stars, just as World War II had done only a few years before. But by 1953 many of these players were returning to the game, beginning with slugger Ted Williams who rejoined the Red Sox in August.[14] By the spring of 1954, all the stars were home, including Willie Mays, Whitey Ford, Don Newcombe, Curt Simmons and others, sparking interest and providing more star-power for television.

By 1954 ABC was televising various games throughout a full baseball season. But success breeds competition, so in 1955 the more powerful CBS pushed its way in by featuring a baseball package of its own that included 26 games aired over 100 stations, roughly the same number of stations that ABC had garnered.[15] The CBS version of the *Game of the Week* was also blacked out in major league cities and even in minor league cities while minor league games were in progress. Ironically, baseball complained about CBS negotiating package broadcast deals, arguing that such would violate antitrust laws — all while baseball was more than happy to enjoy immunity via its own antitrust exemption courtesy of the old 1922 *Federal Base Ball* case.

CBS continued to develop its *Game of the Week* brand, and by 1956 its baseball consortium included more than 175 stations around the country.[16] By this time, all three New York baseball teams were included in the broadcasts in addition to such big market teams as the Red Sox and White Sox. All in all, CBS was able to include 13 of the 16 major league teams during the course of its broadcast season, counting the visiting teams of the various home games that were telecast. During this period CBS also began to innovate, becoming the first network to leverage its baseball product by offering a 15-minute pregame show that featured the chatty Dizzy Dean, then became the first network to offer and actually show a back-up game when the advertised contest was washed out.

The NBC television network had largely remained out of the baseball fray until 1957, when it could resist no longer and began to broadcast Saturday games. The network found four teams that still had games to sell, namely the Pirates, Senators, Braves, and the big market Chicago Cubs, and featured the established Lindsey Nelson to call the games. NBC was still playing catch-up, though, reaching 37 states with 116 affiliate stations while CBS had penetrated 42 states with a larger consortium of stations.[17] Edgar Scherick of ABC could only marvel at the growth of televised baseball. "In 1953, no one wanted us," he lamented as the stronger CBS and NBC pressed forward.

In the early years, NBC benefited from the innovations of its parent company, RCA. David Sarnoff was president of RCA during the lean Depression years, but unlike many other companies, Sarnoff's RCA kept plowing fresh research and development money into the evolving television product. Once the company's research division had acquired cutting-edge technology and legions of patents, it pressed hard to commercialize the television product. The RCA innovations were so extensive and prevalent by 1938 that the Radio Manufacturers Association began to adopt the RCA technology for a system of television standardization, which included 441 lines of dots that flickered 30 images per second.[18]

RCA also innovated a dot-sequence color system that would be compatible with the dot matrix of standard black-and-white television receivers, and as early as 1949 proposed the standardization of its system to the FCC.[19] Politics got in the way, for the FCC chose to endorse an incompatible color system developed by rival CBS. RCA sued and pled its case all the way to the United States Supreme Court, then in 1953 the FCC took another look and opted to endorse an improved version of the RCA color dot system. With that, RCA and NBC got a leg up on color broadcasting, an image that it would promote vigorously and lead to the colorful NBC "living color" peacock logo still in use today.

The television industry was booming in the 1950s. Interestingly, at that time the technology that would lead to television was already over a half century old. The cathode ray tube was developed by Ferdinand Braun in 1897, and 10 years later the tube was first used to produce crude images. Over the following years, the image dissector and iconoscope were engineered by separate approaches from Vladimir Zworykins and Philo Farnsworth. According to an article in the *Chicago Daily Tribune* on April 8, 1925, a "prismatic ring" had been invented that would soon allow the transmission of moving images called "radio movies."[20]

On September 12, 1928, the *New York Times* reported on the first televised transmission of a live dramatic performance, an experiment conducted in Schenectady, New York, whereby miniature images of the actors were successfully transmitted. "While the actors went through their parts in a locked studio room, the audience saw and heard them over a synchronized radio-television receiving set in another room in the same building," the *Times* reported. "Their appearance and voices, translated into electric impulses, were carried by land wire to transmitting station WGY, four miles away, were broadcast from there, and were picked up again at the place of their origin."[21] By 1929, the collective technology for television had advanced far enough for AT&T to actually project a live experimental image of Herbert Hoover, and throughout the 1930s RCA was very active in its R&D efforts.

RCA proceeded to obtain approval for the standardization of its television systems, although by the end of World War II there were still fewer than 7,000 television receivers throughout the United States.[22] By then, however, America had become a global leader in the development of television partly due to the innovations of RCA and others, but also partly because of World War II itself, which caused a hiatus in the innovation by European nations, especially England and Germany, both of which were fighting World War II and had little time or resources for experimental television.

The four major networks that managed to survive in the early years were CBS, NBC, ABC, and DuMont. With strong radio networks already in place, capital, and other resources, CBS and NBC were well positioned while ABC and DuMont searched for the means to compete. In 1951, while ABC was reaching out to major league baseball, the network also completed a merger with United Paramount Theaters which expanded its capital base and economic power. Strapped for cash and unable to enter the baseball bidding wars, the DuMont Network folded by 1956. But DuMont's failure was ABC's gain, for ABC picked up a number of DuMont affiliates, strengthening its base.

In 1952, UHF (ultra high frequency) channels were commercialized in addition to the VHF (very high frequency) channels as the number of stations expended across the country. The surviving big three networks thrived, for the cost barriers to entry in the television business were high and these networks already had strong footholds in technology, station affiliates, marketing, and programming. Network broadcast television continued to expand for nearly four full decades, reaching its zenith in the mid–1980s before the advent of cable began to cut into the growth of the on-air networks. During the 1978-79 season, 91 percent of the prime time audience was controlled collectively by CBS, NBC, and ABC; less than a decade later their combined portion had shrunk to 75 percent, dropping still further to just 61 percent by the 1993-94 season.[23]

Baseball would play a major role in the eventual proliferation of all televised sports. The first baseball game ever telecast was a college game played on May 17, 1939, when Princeton defeated Columbia, 2–1, at Columbia's Baker Field. New York experimental station W2XBS, which one day would become WNBC-TV, carried the game live. Just over three months later, the first major league baseball game was televised when the Brooklyn Dodgers met the Cincinnati Reds at Ebbets Field. The game utilized only two television cameras—one at ground level and one planted in the upper deck—and was called by the voice of the Dodgers' Red Barber, who also did the commercials between innings blurting out "That's a breakfast of champions" as he prepared a bowl of Wheaties cereal on camera.[24]

Eight years later, the World Series was on television when the 1947 Series between the New York Yankees and the Brooklyn Dodgers was carried live. The seven-game Series, won by the Yankees over Jackie Robinson's Dodgers, was only broadcast to the immediate surrounding New York area with Games One and Five televised on an NBC affiliate,

Games Three and Four on a CBS station, and with the remaining games offered by a DuMont station.

Television, with its moving images and visually recognizable stars, was an explosive force in entertainment, marketing, news, and politics. It is television that burns the images of history into the collective mind and imagination of America. It is unnecessary to list all or even most of those milestone events to make the point; we all know the compelling visual effects of the Nixon-Kennedy debate of 1960, Neal Armstrong's historic steps onto the moon's surface, and the chilling demise of the World Trade Center on 9/11, among scores of other threshold moments in between.

Nowhere, though, was the power of television more evident than when CBS and Edward R. Murrow took on the lynch-mob mentality of Communist-baiter Joseph McCarthy, the demagogue senator from Wisconsin responsible for the "Red" scare of the 1950s and the media black list of entertainers, newscasters, writers, and producers. Seemingly behind the fray, but still very much involved, was CBS chairman William Paley, a powerful but pragmatic media mogul who gambled on the side of free speech and news—and won when he allowed Edward R. Murrow to unleash the power of television against McCarthy, drowning the senator in his own words with a widely viewed counter-attack using video that exposed the McCarthy senate hearings for what they were, a theater of the absurd.

On March 9, 1954, Murrow, Paley, and CBS devoted the entire 30 minutes of the news program *See It Now* to the McCarthy witch hunt, summarized at the end of the show with these poignant words from Murrow who, at the time, may have been the most trusted man in America:

> The actions of the junior Senator from Wisconsin have caused alarm and dismay amongst our allies abroad, and given considerable comfort to our enemies. And whose fault is that? Not really his. He didn't create this situation of fear; he merely exploited it—and rather successfully. Cassius was right. "The fault, dear Brutus, is not in our stars, but in ourselves."[25]

The year 1954 was a watershed time for television, baseball, and baseball on television. Just four days after Murrow's assault on McCarthy, Bobby Thomson, recently traded to the Milwaukee Braves, broke his ankle sliding into second base during a preseason game against the Yankees. A youngster named Hank Aaron was assigned to replace Thomson. Aaron collected his first two hits on April 15, 1954, in a 7–6 win over the Cardinals, then slugged the first of his eventual career-record homers with a solo shot in St. Louis on April 23.

Although television and sports have enjoyed one of the most successful collaborations in history, this came about not with a sudden bang but more of a subtle evolution like the "little cat feet" that described the advent of baseball on the radio three decades earlier. Television's impact on news and politics was much more immediate if not dramatic, its images fueling both controversy and change. For example, as 1954 wore on, the Senate condemned Joseph McCarthy as a direct result of the Murrow piece from early March that same year. Elsewhere during 1954 Hollywood featured Marlon Brando in the classic film *On the Waterfront*; the first experimental hydrogen bomb was detonated; major league ballplayers unionized with the formation of the Players Association on July 12; and key sportswriter Grantland Rice, one of the pioneer voices of baseball on the radio, passed away the very next day on July 13. On the diamond itself, emerging black star Willie Mays hit .345 for the season and was named the National League MVP.

Black players were making strides just as television was making its mark on America and in the world of sports. Television was not just presenting baseball to America's living rooms, it was helping baseball to change America itself. During the seven years leading to the 1954 *Brown v. Board of Education* landmark ruling, black ballplayers continued to make headlines. Don Newcombe was named Rookie of the Year, Roy Campanella was National League MVP not once but twice, Willie Mays exploded into baseball as the 1951 Rookie of the Year, Minnie Minoso led the American League in stolen bases, Larry Doby topped the American League in home runs—and, of course, Jackie Robinson, who had started it all, continued to star for the Dodgers.

In 1948, just one year after the Robinson breakthrough, President Harry Truman issued an order formally desegregating the U.S. armed forces—hardly a blind coincidence. Certainly African Americans had fought in World War II, but Truman took the necessary step of clearing up the official records on segregation at a very opportune time. Truman was a baseball fan, so he would certainly would have observed and been influenced by Jackie's successes on and off the field.

Whether by fate, spells, or just progressive thinking, the confluence of Robinson's milestone year, Truman's order for military desegregation, the visible success of Willie Mays, especially in 1954, the 1954 *Brown v. Board* breakthrough, and the concurrent proliferation of television constituted a quantum leap for the acceptance of African American citizens. Black players were front-page news for each of those seven years from Robinson debut to *Brown,* a time when America was bombarded with home runs and showered with the class and character of Robinson, Campanella, and Mays, pulling the country closer just as racial strife off the field yanked in the opposite direction of hate, fear, and disgrace.

When the final opinion for *Brown* was written, the Supreme Court had no choice but to notice Robinson and those who had followed. Although the written opinion was extensive, the essence of the *Brown* ruling was profoundly simple, evidenced by one succinct but powerful sentence: "The separate but equal doctrine of *Plessy v. Ferguson* has no place in the field of public education." But the driving force behind that ruling is more subtle, yet just as important, as hinted by Chief Justice Earl Warren within the text of the findings. "Today ... many Negroes have achieved outstanding success in the arts and sciences as well as in the business and professional world," observed Warren, who then built the crux of the decision upon that premise.

The decision did not specifically mention baseball, probably because it was making a case for education and not sports, but the Court had to have *meant* baseball, at least in part. By 1954, *nowhere* was the success of the black man more visibly demonstrated than on the ball diamond of America's premier game, certainly more so than in business or even in entertainment during those days. The Court was saying to the world look around, observe, see what segregation did and what integration is doing now. Indeed, the Court could not have missed the success of blacks on the ball diamond, concluding that we must afford them the same opportunity as white children elsewhere, especially in the public schools. The decision continued. "...we cannot turn the clock back to ... 1896 when *Plessy v. Ferguson* was written. We must consider public education in the light of its full development and its present place in American life throughout the Nation."

The *Brown* ruling came down on May 17, 1954, just three weeks after Hank Aaron's first big league home run. Aaron's feat may have seemed inconsequential at the time and even in historic context may be little more than a poignant coincidence, but the striking on-going success of Willie Mays, who combined speed, power, and grace in becoming perhaps that best all-round baseball player in history, was neither coincidence nor merely an interesting footnote. It would be one decade later in 1964 that we would have the tools to articulate how this could be. It was then a phenomenon was defined that finds the media message is impacted, distorted, or even defined by the nature of the transmitting media itself, all as articulated by Marshall McLuhan in his 1964 book *Understanding Media: The Extensions of Man.*[26]

Television provided the means for the visible, tangible evidence that African American ballplayers, and therefore by subtle extension African American citizens, could be equal to their white counterparts. That message could also have been delivered on the radio, and in fact it was to a much lesser degree, but the visible images of equality were a profound message from the televised media that radio simply could not match. For the same reason, the visible demeanor of Richard Nixon sweating profusely while his eyes wandered sent chills through America, television betrayed Joseph McCarthy who looked as much like a dangerous kook as sounding like one, and black ballplayers on TV were given an instant national sense of credibility and acceptance.

One reason for all of this, according to McLuhan, has to do with the effort of involvement required of the viewer. Reading a book requires more effort and conscious involvement than watching a film. Although radio is more "visual" than television in the philosophical sense, the visual images in one's mind require a modicum of effort and, moreover, are a necessary function of one's own mind, life experience, and prejudices. Television, though, spoon-feeds the images and ideas in a manner that the viewer perceives as effortless. In short, televised messages are easy and very effective.

Getting closer to the specific point about racism, baseball, and television, McLuhan suggests that the specific message concerning a particularly heinous or brutal crime on the television news may convey less than what viewing the story says about a society that eagerly watches such a messy brutality at home. Television, therefore, put more black Americans into the living rooms of white America than anything else did or even could, and baseball was responsible because in those days there were almost no prominent African American stars or comedians or news people not counting sports figures (which, at the time, essentially meant boxing and baseball).

Even with the persistent message of televised baseball, however, change did not occur easily. In 1955, just one year after the McCarthy demise and the *Brown* integration decision, Rosa Parks refused to yield her seat to the white patrons of a Montgomery, Alabama, bus. Television and newsreels became the most effective medium for racial change — television was there for the marches, the speeches, and for Martin Luther King.

Before Jackie Robinson, baseball had set the national standard for "separate but equal" by overtly relegating black ballplayers to the Negro Leagues. Then Jackie and his followers, especially the great Willie Mays, became some of the biggest running baseball headlines of the early 1950s. Given the Supreme Court's long symbiotic relationship to baseball from the 1922 antitrust exemption to the 1953 *Toolson* case that revisited baseball antitrust, history can safely conclude that in 1954 when the Supreme Court noted the success of blacks in a multitude of endeavors, it must have partly meant the noble national example that was unfolding on both the baseball diamond and the front pages.

It took over 12 years after Robinson debuted for the Dodgers, but by July 21, 1959, when Boston played Pumpsie Green, every major league team had finally had at least one black ballplayer. In 1974, exactly a quarter-century later, fully 27 percent of all baseball players were African American. Baseball would be forever changed on and off the field, and its record books are still being rewritten by black players, notably the two premier marks of the game: the single-season and career home run standards. One of America's remarkable ironies, however, is that by Opening Day 2007, the number of African American players had dropped precipitously, all the way down to just 8.2 percent, an enigma partly explained by the popularity and expansion of the NFL and NBA, plus the notable proliferation of Hispanic and Asian baseball players (although in 2008 the proportion edged up to 10.2 percent).[27]

The major leagues will long be remembered for their blatant past segregation that began sometime in the nineteenth century during the time of Cap Anson's unofficial but openly stated "no blacks" rule, an exclusionary practice that extended to the new era of Robinson and even beyond. Baseball's refusal to embrace or even acknowledge the black ballplayer was an unforgivable disgrace, but to some degree that obliquity is a red herring that distracts history from an even more painful truth: baseball wasn't *setting* the segregation example, it was actually following a much larger precedent of exclusion that was long established by America itself.

The 1947 campaign proved a tough year for Jackie Robinson, for everywhere the team played, Robinson broke new ground, shook old stereotypes, and displayed great poise during a season of relentless verbal abuse. "The loneliest man I have ever seen in sports," observed New York columnist Jimmy Cannon.[28] When that first year was all over, Jackie had managed a .297 season at the plate, led the league in stolen bases, and was named National League Rookie of the Year. His dignity and many successes assured Jackie's rightful place in the national spotlight where he caught the attention of many, no doubt including the justices of the Supreme Court.

Over the ensuing years, Bill Veeck brought Larry Doby to Cleveland, followed by an aging Satchel Page and many other black ballplayers. Soon the floodgates opened, and black players flourished — but even that success did not mean racism was dead. It still is not fully quashed, but perhaps Robinson and Doby and the rest were together a brave beginning of the final end, whenever that may ultimately be. The election of actor Ronald Reagan, who knew television, and more recently the African American Barack Obama, who speaks well on television, suggest that society has been accelerating the process of acceptance with the aid of television.

Landis eventually passed away in a Chicago hospital on November 25, 1944. Five months later Jackie Robinson auditioned for the Red Sox who made no offers, while at the same time Branch Rickey was scouting two Negro League players, Terris McDuffie and Dave "Showboat" Thomas. Neither was signed, but Rickey kept looking. On August 13, 1945, Rickey, Walter O'Malley, and John L. Smith bought controlling interest in the Dodgers. Meanwhile, Dodger scout Clyde Sukeforth observed Robinson playing for the Kansas City Monarchs of the Negro Leagues, and on August 28, just two weeks after buying into the Dodgers, Rickey found himself offering Robinson the chance of a lifetime and then inked Jackie to a minor league deal on October 23, 1945.

The indisputable relationship among Robinson, *Brown v. Board*, Rosa Parks, and the progression of equality on and off the field may seem obvious in hindsight, but no one connected the dots of history better than California Congressman Adam B. Schiff in his address to Congress commemorating the 50th anniversary of the *Brown* decision:

> On April 15, 1947, Jackie Robinson would take the filed to play for the Brooklyn Dodgers—a pioneer as the first African American to play major league baseball. Robinson not only opened the door to pro sports for other African American athletes, but his remarkable accomplishment would help chip away at prejudices in the minds of Americans and jumpstart the process of dismantling existing barriers throughout our society.
>
> Adam B. Schiff, Congressman
> February 24, 2004

When Robinson himself was asked who his own hero was, he could have said Jesse Owens, Joe Louis, or maybe Satchel Paige, but instead he named Caucasian Hank Greenberg, the mild-mannered Jewish slugger for Detroit who had endured seasons of anti–Semitic hate during the 1930s and 1940s just before Jackie's own debut. Among Robinson's numerous attributes of ability, courage, and character, apparently he was colorblind, too. Maybe that places him a different class altogether, one that includes names like King and Parks and Selma, not to mention big league icon Branch Rickey and that colorful baseball champion of the downtrodden, William Veeck, Jr., who once called baseball "an island of surety in a changing world." Perhaps it is.

Fate and history often conspire in remarkable ways. Commissioner Landis died in time for Jackie Robinson to come along just as television was about to find its place in America's living rooms. The message and the medium arrived at the same time, a perfect confluence to achieve radical change. Radio, the perfect medium for the deliberate pace of baseball, had done much to propel baseball to national prominence by featuring down-home announcers who told colorful stories and became not only a part of each team they covered, but of each family that listened. Three decades later baseball would help the emergence of television, and baseball on television would take the lead in changing America.

10

The Game of the Week

On March 17, 1965, Jackie Robinson appeared on NBC television and at that moment became the first African American network broadcaster.[1] Although Robinson possessed the charisma, charm, and requisite baseball résumé, he also had a high sounding voice that did not play well from the television broadcast booth. This was nonetheless another important first for Robinson and for baseball, but Jackie would not last as an announcer because, in the end, he simply was not as skilled with the electronic media as he was with baseball.

Baseball and television would not only continue to press forward, the game would actually change television in the process. In the early days television had struggled to find its proper identity, and some of its best innovations were discovered quite by accident. In 1938, for example, the experimental NBC station in New York City "invented" televised spot news reporting on the fly when a unit operating at a local park in Queens happened to view a large fire that broke out across the river on nearby Ward's Island. The few viewers who were watching the original show from the park were no doubt surprised when the cameras quickly swung around to show the fire in progress.[2] Television executives quickly learned that news was good because it was dramatic, live, relatively easy to produce, and often very visual. Finding the news and developing a network infrastructure to process and report it, though, would be harder and require substantial investment. But news, once located, almost produced itself.

Early television found it could also develop news to telecast, which proved decidedly easier than writing and producing weekly or daily dramas. The networks began searching for news stories, and as a result President Franklin Roosevelt became the first sitting president to appear on television when NBC covered his opening address to begin the World's Fair in New York on April 30, 1939.[3]

From 1939 to 1941 the largest concentration of television receivers was in New York City where there were a few thousand sets already in use. As television searched to find itself, to develop its own "voice," there was a good deal of local programming produced, although most of it was experimental and not very good. There were no established shows as that term is used today, and certainly there was no *series* of programming in those very early days. Everything was ad hoc; viewers simply turned on the TV and saw whatever

126

potluck programming happened to be on the air at the time. The programming that *was* listed was decidedly uninspired — on Wednesday nights a weekly program was featured with this illustrious title, *The Wednesday Night Program*.[4] Over the years there would be the *Friday Night Fights*, *Saturday Night at the Movies*, *Monday Night Football*, and *Sunday Night Baseball*—but at least in these cases the viewers had a clue as to what was being offered.

In the early 1940s, the country's few operating television stations, which largely were owned by the major radio networks, especially CBS and NBC, understood the value of networking the emerging television stations around the country. In 1941, General Electric's NBC unit had three stations linked together, hooking up New York City, Schenectady, and Philadelphia — perhaps the very first television "network."[5] As it happens, NBC and CBS were both officially the first licensed commercial television stations, each receiving its government license on the same day, July 1, 1941. These two stations would become the well known anchor stations WNBC-TV and WCBS-TV in New York, but NBC would initially be more aggressive in developing a network of stations and original programming.

World War II interrupted the development of commercial television altogether. There was very little private-sector innovation during the war years, but the development of television accelerated rapidly after the war in 1946 when NBC began feeding regular programming to its embryonic three-station network, which soon was dubbed the "East Coast Network." One such program was called the *Hour Glass*, a weekly variety show, but many new programs were developed rapidly, including a crude version of a news magazine, a game show, a quiz show, a cooking show, and a the very first network soap opera called *Faraway Hill*. In May 1947, the *Kraft Television Theater* debuted, becoming the first regular network dramatic programming effort and a landmark for theatrical television.[6]

As the end of the decade approached, both NBC and DuMont (which had been licensed in 1944) gradually added new stations, even stations in the Midwest and on the West Coast, although these were not initially linked in network fashion. ABC was late getting an anchor station in New York from which it could build a viable network; CBS took a different route that focused on the development of color television in hopes in establishing a serious leg up on the competition, and as a result was slow to develop a competing network system or quality original programming. The CBS color technique, which required a spinning disc inside each television receiver, eventually lost out anyway, for it was the NBC technology developed by GE affiliate RCA that ultimately paved the way for viable color television.

CBS was discouraged by its loss in the color transmission race, but when it saw what NBC did with baseball, CBS was inspired to enter the network fray as soon as possible. Baseball, in fact, is what propelled television to the next level. The very first World Series to be shown on network television was offered by NBC in 1947 and was transmitted to the first mass audience in the history of televised programming. The Series was seen live by 3.9 million people, but only 400,000 of them were at home — the rest were in clusters of audiences huddled together at urban bars.[7] With millions of people exposed to television courtesy of the local bar and the visual drama of the World Series, interest in the new medium grew rapidly and the sales of television receivers exploded exponentially. CBS saw this growth and was afraid of being left out, so it accelerated its own business plan to catch up by developing new programming and implementing a network of stations to deliver it.

By 1948 some of what would become television's most enduring classic programs featuring top emerging stars were already under way. Ted Mack, Milton Berle, Arthur Godfrey, and the *Toast of the Town* hosted by Ed Sullivan (which evolved into the long running *Ed Sullivan Show*), all premiered in 1948. New York City was the hub of it all, for New York not only benefited from the technology of NBC and RCA and the advent of the anchor stations that provided the network feeds, but it also could exploit the vast pool of local talent provided by radio, Broadway, and off–Broadway theater that supplied a stream of actors, announcers, and even technicians, stage hands, directors, and producers. Because of these strong advantages, other cities could not develop a viable television industry to compete with New York — at least not in the early days. Chicago made an effort with its own media entrepreneurs, but was never a serious threat to the rapidly developing New York media empire. But Los Angeles would soon be different.

By the fall of 1951, Los Angeles was linked to the network programming that was originating in New York. But Los Angeles also had pools of Hollywood theatrical talent, plus one thing that New York did not have, good weather. Within one decade, the production hub for television would shift from New York to Los Angeles, a move that became largely complete with the eventual migration of Johnny Carson's *Tonight Show* to Burbank in May 1972. New York would not become irrelevant, though, for network news and a number of individual shows like David Letterman and the long-running *Law & Order* would originate there, but it would lose its dominance.

CBS may have been late to the network party, but it had solid resources and a strong radio network to draw upon. ABC was late, too, but it had enough staying power to last. The DuMont network was doomed. It *did* have early technology and was in fact the first to develop and offer a "large screen" television with a 14-inch viewing area, plus DuMont enjoyed good financing as a result of the backing it received from Paramount Pictures in 1938. But DuMont was perpetually disadvantaged since it had no existing radio network to provide credibility or the necessary captive talent pool, and therefore it also had no leverage for signing new TV stations to its network. CBS would invest heavily in programming, so although NBC had an early edge with Milton Berle, Kraft, *Dragnet*, Sid Caesar, and others, CBS was soon able to roll out hits with *I Love Lucy* and *Ed Sullivan*, and to leverage its radio advantage with shows featuring radio stars like Arthur Godfrey and Jack Benny.

Perhaps DuMont could have caught up, or at least might have remained viable as a fourth network, but then it suffered a fatal blow with an adverse government ruling. Regulations allowed each network to own five VHF broadcast television stations outright, the rest being independently owned and operated affiliates completing the vast network chain. Those five corporately owned stations provided an automatic presence in five major markets, which was a crucial foothold in the early days of intense competition. Each of NBC, CBS, and ABC was allowed to own the maximum of five such stations, but DuMont was not because, as it happened, DuMont's financial backer Paramount also owned stations, so the government would not let DuMont add more, leaving it at a permanent disadvantage in the major market cities. Then the problem snowballed because Paramount, sensing the implications of this deficiency, refused to provide further financing to DuMont.

DuMont pressed on, though, determined to survive by producing cheap programming. It had moderate, albeit spotty, success with such diverse shows as the *Cavalcade of Stars*, which featured Jackie Gleason and an early version of the "Honeymooners" skits; *They Stand Accused*, a courtroom drama set in Chicago; and the well-known children's show *Captain Video*. But these cheaply produced programs gave the network a low quality image, exacerbated by an often-cited anecdote from the DuMont drama *Rocky King, Detective* where during one live episode a dead body rose up, dusted itself off, and walked from the set while still on camera. The network's news efforts did not fair much better. *The Walter Compton News* originated from Washington, D.C., but was broadcast on only two stations in 1947.[8]

Partly because of its financial straits and resultant seat-of-the-pants productions, the DuMont network was quick to learn the value of sports programming, again because sports are relatively cheap and easy to produce — especially the ones that require only one camera like boxing or wrestling. DuMont offered some boxing, especially in New York with the emerging Chris Schenkel behind the microphone, but it could not consistently compete with the plethora of boxing shows offered by the other major networks.[9] Instead it relied upon professional wrestling, an amalgam of sports, entertainment, and something of a Greek tragedy as the good guys faced the bad guys in the ring. Chicago's Jack Brickhouse, who would become one of the classic long-running baseball announcers for the Chicago Cubs, was one of the early DuMont wrestling announcers when he called play-by-play from Chicago's Marigold Garden every Saturday night for six years. Wrestling in those days consisted of some colorful monster characters bashing each other in small arenas where the fans sat very close to the ring. It brought in a few dollars, but it did little to advance the image of the DuMont network. Faced with insurmountable obstacles, DuMont exited the network television business in 1956.

The ABC network struggled, too, but managed to survive due to its five anchor VHF stations, a viable radio network to rely upon, a successful merger with United Paramount Theaters that provided capital, and some very astute programming moves. One of the best ABC programming decisions was to acquire the television rights to Walt Disney in 1954, allowing it to ride the success of the Disney animated films and positioning itself just one year before the opening of a soon-to-be American institution, Disneyland. ABC also completed a deal with Warner Bros. Studios, assuring it a stream of original quality programming, especially popular westerns like *Maverick*. Conglomerate ITT, and later industrialist and movie mogul Howard Hughes, made runs at acquiring ABC, but the network continued to go it alone.

For almost 30 years ABC was mired in third place in a three-way contest, but it still managed to remain a viable network competitor. It never had a number one rated show until *Marcus Welby, MD* during the 1970-71 season, but it did garner a definable audience by offering the *Movie of the Week* and the occasional dramatic programs that were somewhat edgy like *Mod Squad*, *The Rookies*, *The FBI*, *Rat Patrol* and a very quirky production of *Batman* with Adam West. Sports, however, would definitely lead ABC out of the doldrums. It was during the 1971-72 season that a revolutionary new concept cracked the top 25 shows for the first time, *Monday Night Football*. But ABC did not simply televise a football game, it recognized the pageantry of the NFL and the entertainment power of the sports announcing team, so it turned *Monday Night Football* into a weekly entertainment extravaganza that took up an entire evening of programming, was easy to produce, and was immensely profitable. In 1974, CBS had owned eight of the top 10 rated shows on television, and ABC had precisely none. By 1975, ABC offered five shows in the top 10, including the number two and three slots.[10]

Although now identified with baseball, the original *Game of the Week* did not offer baseball at all, but football. As early as 1950, the ABC network offered a weekly 30-minute program of highlights for a specially targeted college football game.[11] ABC continued to experiment with major sports programming by offering a more extensive highlight film of Notre Dame football games. ABC did not televise a professional football contest until 1959 when it produced a late night Saturday video replay narrated, in part, by a young Howard Cosell.

Monday Night Football was the inspiration of a dynamic ABC executive named Roone Arledge, who would change sports and television so dramatically that *Life* magazine would list Arledge as one of the 100 most important Americans of the twentieth century. Arledge almost single-handedly lifted ABC as a forceful competitor to both CBS and NBC, and he did it originally with sports and then again with news when ABC had him run the news division in 1977.[12]

Not only did the whole concept of *Monday Night Football* come from Arledge, but the idea of sports as genuine entertainment did, too. He packed the announcing booth with three personalities, not just the usual one or two announcers. One voice that Arledge took a particular chance on was the acerbic, verbose, and colorful Howard Cosell. But the team also struck gold with former Dallas Cowboys quarterback Don Meredith, whose infectious southern drawl, down-home personality, and good humor gave life to the football banter in the booth. Although he was not Dizzy Dean, many of those Meredith qualities were very similar to Dean's and they played just as well on television partly because of it.

Educated at Columbia University, Arledge got his first job, somewhat appropriately, at the struggling DuMont network. He was not there long enough to make an impact because of an intervening stint in the military, but perhaps he got a competitive taste for broadcasting's underdogs. Arledge was eventually introduced to Ed Scherick at ABC, a network with a loose enough management structure to allow the flow and implementation of creative ideas. Still in his late 20s, Arledge encouraged ABC to not only televise more sports, especially college football, he campaigned to make the broadcasts more interesting and, where possible, to also appeal to female viewers. Soon ABC found itself immersed in programming that featured college football, AAU events, and even the Olympics. Remarkably, televised sports had made their debut at the seminal 1936 Berlin Olympics, but by the time Arledge and ABC covered the games, television coverage had come a long, long way. In 1936, an collection of RCA and Farnsworth equipment was used to generate blurred images at 25 frames per second. Although 72 hours of those Olympics were shown, there were not seen by many, for viewers had to be present at a special viewing booth installed in either Berlin or Potsdam.[13] Arledge utilized multiple cameras, announcers, color, and overall cachet to Olympics coverage for ABC, taking the art and science of televised sports to new levels of entertainment. Then ABC accepted another Arledge brainchild that would propel the network's sports image: *Wide World of Sports*, complete with its "thrill of victory, agony of defeat" tagline. ABC was rapidly developing a brand for itself as the most innovative, if not the best, sports network.

Monday Night Football was a leading innovation for sports programming because it was in prime time, not on the weekends, and offered an entertaining trio of broadcasters. The focus on entertainment offended some sports purists at first, but it soon became the model for successful sports programming, beginning four decades ago and counting, most recently with the ABC-Disney-ESPN corporate triumvirate. When Arledge was asked to run the ABC news division in 1977, he again offended tradition by making news entertaining, then discovered, quite by accident, the notion of *Nightline* which evolved from the nightly recap of America's hostage citizens being held by a hostile Iran for over a year, an emotional story that captured the hearts and attention of American viewers back home. When the hostages were released upon the election of a new, tough talking President Ronald Reagan, America was already so addicted to news programming in the late night slot that the nightly hostage recap continued on as the *Nightline* news magazine wrap-up for decades to come. And *Monday Night Football* would spawn more sports, like the occasional *Thursday Night Football* and eventually ESPN's *Sunday Night Baseball*.

Would America accept baseball on a national Sunday night telecast? Baseball, of course, had really started all this with the successful telecast of the 1947 World Series. Chance would play its part, too, like stumbling upon Howard Cosell or lucking into *Nightline* by accident — both of which were really a function of Branch Rickey's "luck is the residue of design" axiom and no one made luck happen better than Arledge.

Baseball would also be propelled not only by the extended drama and excitement of the 1947 World Series, but also by the 1951 Bobby Thomson home run blast that is still shown today as part of nearly every serious baseball retrospective that finds its way to television. The Thomson home run itself was an act of fate (aided by the stealing a few signs, according to recent sources), as was the timely emergence of Willie Mays who brought speed, flashy play, and renewed interest in the game just as television itself was emerging. But another innovation would change the face of baseball on television, and it was no accident. It was also in 1951 that Chicago's independent station WGN decided to place a camera in the distant outfield stands, far from home plate. Interestingly, WGN first tried this new angle on a Little League game before offering it during Cubs telecasts. This "center field shot" provided an unobstructed comprehensive view of the pitcher, batter, catcher, and umpire. The viewing fans were brought virtually into the game by simply showing them that angle, now a standard feature of any well produced baseball broadcast. The impact of that singular baseball broadcasting technique was so significant that it served as the title to a leading retrospective book about baseball on television, *Center Field Shot*.[14]

Baseball on television would continue to be boosted by the Chicago approach originally implemented by William Wrigley when radio had been emerging three decades earlier: embrace the broadcasting to billboard the games and generate fans, attendance, and gate receipts. When the rest of baseball had feared radio as a competitor, Wrigley, a born marketer, used the media to his advantage. His son P.K. Wrigley specifically followed that model when television emerged, even as baseball was again nervous about the effect of television on attendance.

Wrigley turned to William Eddy, an expert on the emerging television medium, to develop the best ways to translate baseball to television. This was 1945, very early in the process. It was also the last year the Chicago Cubs would find themselves in the World Series, which may have been more than a footnote to history since World Series excitement likely spurred early enthusiasm from Wrigley and others just as television was on its way.[15] Due to the efforts of both Wrigley and Eddy, Wrigley found himself with a thoughtful roadmap of producing and directing baseball games for television — even before games themselves were being televised. One of these innovations was the concept of remote television production. It was not practical to build a television transmission facility every time a baseball game was to be played, so Wrigley pioneered the remote production vehicle with an elaborately equipped truck dubbed in its early days as the "Blue Goose." Not only would the remote television truck be instrumental in televising baseball and other sports, it would become a great addition to the business of televised news.

Immediately following the successful telecast of the 1947 Series, Wrigley and WGN featured the Cubs on television for a number of games in 1948, followed by the broadcast of every Cubs home game for the 1949 season. In the tradition of his father, Phillip Wrigley was eager to sell the Cubs' broadcast rights to stir interest in the team and he typically charged less than the other big market teams in New York and, eventually, Los Angeles. By 1960 the Cubs were also seen playing several games on the road, with most road games being televised by the end of the decade.

Just as Wrigley had planned, television not only failed to keep fans at home, it helped drive attendance at Chicago's fabled Wrigley Field. When the first Cubs games on the radio were broadcast in 1925, the Cubs set an all-time attendance record in 1926 at Wrigley Field. In 1927 the team home attendance topped the one million mark for the first time ever at 1,159,168, which was almost double the major league average that year of 663,740. In 1920 and 1921, Cubs attendance had actually been below the league-wide average, and in 1925 it was only a little higher: 622,610 vs. 544,213.[16]

In 1945, the year the Cubs last appeared in the Series, home attendance was relatively strong at 1,036,386. Attendance remained very good even as games were televised, exceeding the one million mark for four of the next five years beginning in 1948.[17] Ten percent of all U.S. television sets could be found in the Chicago metropolitan area in 1948 (18,500 sets in Chicago city proper), and the first regular "television guide" publication debuted in Chicago on May 9, 1948.[18] Television must have had a positive impact on Cubs' attendance since the team itself was woeful by then, going just 64–90 in 1948 and 62–92 in 1951. Both attendance and the team would be weak for the remainder of the 1950s and most of the 1960s until the storied 1969 Cubs won 92 games only to fall to the miracle Mets that year; attendance, though, would jump by 60 percent to 1,674,993. These also happened to the glory days of famed baseball broadcaster Jack Brickhouse, whose enthusiasm and cheerful "hey-hey" home run call carried the team through many good and mostly bad years from 1947 to 1981 when he announced over 5,000 baseball games on television, more than anyone else.[19]

WGN television was especially busy during these early days, for it not only televised the Cubs home games beginning in 1948, it also broadcast all the White Sox home games, as the Cubs and Sox alternated their home-away schedules. Sox attendance traditionally lagged the Cubs, but then the White Sox attendance also surged when television came along, surpassing the one million mark for the first time in 1951. In fact, Sox home attendance would exceed both the one million mark and the league-wide average for seven straight years from 1951 through 1957.

By 1949, national interest in televised baseball was growing, again bolstered by the World Series, a five game contest won by the Yankees of Joe DiMaggio over the Dodgers and Jackie Robinson who was the National League's MVP and its leading hitter at .342.

In what could have been a lasting boon to the weak DuMont network, DuMont was awarded the right to televise all the Yankee home games during the 1949 Series. CBS, meanwhile, covered the Dodgers' home games. Both networks debuted a new split screen technique which proved especially useful to baseball, allowing the viewer to see the usual pitcher-batter angle and also the runner, if any, on first base. And both networks also borrowed WGN's center field shot technique, although CBS used it more frequently than rival DuMont did, the latter feeling the new perspective was confusing to viewers.[20]

With national interest growing in the new phenomenon of television, and television discovering how to best exploit sports entertainment, the national game of baseball was a natural beneficiary of the concurrent technological and marketing innovations of television. National reviews for the 1949 Series were good, but not yet stellar, as noted by this excerpt from *Center Field Shot*:

> The Series' growing TV reach meant comments on the new techniques might come from cities throughout the East and Midwest. *Variety* summarized the mixed reactions of viewers from New York ("solid job"), Chicago ("didn't measure up to our local coverage"), Detroit ("good job, but plenty of gripes heard"), Boston ("fans stunned by overall pickup quality"), Cleveland ("Series not so good, 'ours was better'"), Cincinnati ("Cameras performed 'swell job'"), and St. Louis ("compared favorably").[21]

The cool Chicago review may have been biased, but it likely was also jaded by the high quality baseball coverage that had already been emanating from WGN for the better part of three years at that point. But the overall acceptance of these baseball telecasts inspired continued national coverage of the World Series. New York's WOR and WFTZ from Philadelphia televised the 1950 Series between the Yankees and Phillies with the usual big three networks all taking the feeds to a national audience.

Baseball did its part in 1950, too. On February 7, Ted Williams became the highest paid baseball player in history when he inked a $125,000 deal with the Red Sox; the Yankees signed an irascible rookie named Billy Martin who debuted on April 18 with two hits in one inning; Ralph Kiner went on a home run tear that included two grand slams in three days in May; pitcher Bob Feller notched his 200th win; Dodger Gil Hodges tied a major league record with 17 total bases in a game against the Braves; Roy Campanella slugged three straight homers in a game, each one with Hodges already on base; Joe DiMaggio become the first player to slam three home runs in one game at Washington's cavernous Griffith Stadium — all of them over 400 feet; and rookie Yankee hurler Whitey Ford nailed nine wins in a row as of September 25 during the New York pennant run.[22]

The 1950 Phillies were surprising enough to be dubbed the Whiz Kids, their 91–63 record good enough to take the National League pennant from the star-studded Dodgers. Big Del Ennis sported a .311 average with 31 home runs and 126 RBIs, Richie Ashburn slugged .303, and pitcher Robin Roberts had a 20-win season. Even Eddie Waitkus contributed, playing in every game that year and winning the Comeback Player of the Year Award — he had been shot by a fan the year before, an act of fate that later would inspire the story for one of baseball's most compelling motion pictures, *The Natural*, the fictional story of a returning baseball phenom at the close of his career.

Managed by Eddie Sawyer, the Phillies were good but not good enough to best the Yankees under Casey Stengel. New York won 98 games in 1950 behind the likes of Phil Rizzuto, Yogi Berra, Hank Bauer, and Joe DiMaggio — all of whom hit over .300 — plus rookie pitching sensation Whitey Ford. The Whiz Kid Phillies were swept by the Yankees in the Series, and indeed 1950 would be their only pennant. When asked why the talented Phillies could never win more than just the one pennant, Riche Ashburn's response was terse but poignant on many levels: "We were all white."

So were the Yankees, among others. New York would not feature its first African American player until eight years after Jackie Robinson when catcher Elston Howard appeared in 1955. A confluence of threshold events had led to the integration of the major leagues, such as the fortuitous death of Commissioner Landis and the star qualities offered by the first black player Jackie Robinson, and television itself played a major role as the rest of America watched the likes of Robinson, Doby, Campanella, and Mays circling the bases while Don Newcombe was pitching the Dodgers into the World Series. It was undeniably difficult to hide an all-white team on the national stage offered by television.

Elston Howard had turned down college scholarship offers to play in the Negro Leagues, where he roomed with Ernie Banks and played under Kansas City manager Buck O'Neil. The Yankees would sign Howard and African American Vic Power, but they traded Power away before he ever got to the batters box. "They were waiting for me to turn white, and I couldn't do it," Power reportedly charged.[23] Howard, though, would star for the Yankees from 1955 to 1967, appearing in 10 different World Series and nine All-Star Games. Elston Howard homered in his first World Series at-bat, which poignantly came off Don Newcombe. Howard's number 32 was retired in 1984.

As baseball continued to morph on the field of play, the televising of big league baseball evolved rapidly as new techniques were tried and then improved upon. The 1950 World Series introduced the use of a high almost overheard camera angle that showed the whole infield. A third base camera was utilized to show the pitcher and the baserunner in the same shot, rendering the split screen unnecessary. Moreover, a new lens was introduced that could show tight close-ups, which brought an intimacy to the players and the game.[24] Since the players are not hidden by helmets as in football, the tight shots made them not only more accessible, but more familiar to the viewing audience. This innovation was thought to be among the most influential in the early days of baseball broadcasting.

By 1951, the World Series would help inspire another innovation: coast-to-coast live television coverage. The games had been offered nationally before, but not live, not everywhere, and not all at once. To do so would require a good deal of investment and technological know-how included a sophisticated network of relay facilities to send the broadcast images 3,000 miles from one coast to another. Both the technology and requisite investment would come from a source not commonly associated with television: AT&T. According to its own website, among other sources, AT&T designed, built, and operated the national cable and microwave relay system that made true network television possible with genuine national live telecasts. The system was tested on September 4, 1951, when an address from President Harry Truman was carried coast-to-coast via the AT&T transmission system.[25]

Normally associated with phone lines and cell service, AT&T nonetheless has a history of television innovation. It was the company's Bell Laboratories that first demonstrated the working idea of television on April 7, 1927. And in July 10, 1962, it would be AT&T's threshold Telstar Satellite that would transmit the first satellite television broadcasts, setting the stage for world sporting events like the boxing matches of Muhammad Ali in the 1960s and 1970s, and live Olympics coverage in years to come, not to mention the ability to transmit world news instantly, like the 1969 moon landing and legions of threshold events from the Iran hostages to September 11, 2001, and the rest of what would become televised world history.[26] It all would have started with the 1951 World Series between the Giants and the Yankees — except for one thing.

Yes, the 1951 Series inspired coast-to-coast live baseball coverage, and so the techniques, the investment, and the AT&T networking were all in place on the eve of the World Series. Fate, though, would intervene to find the Giants in a dead-heat National League tie with the Dodgers, each team with a 96–58 record at the close of the regular baseball season on September 30. The Dodgers had come from behind twice in their last game on September 30 to tie the Giants, setting the stage for the dramatic 1951 playoff series between the Dodgers of Jackie Robinson and Bobby Thomson's New York Giants. CBS could not resist the ready-made drama, transmitting game one after wrangling the rights to do so from ABC. NBC managed to nail down the rights to the other two games, and so NBC and CBS shared the drama of not only the playoff games but the live national telecast courtesy of AT&T's just-installed national microwave relay system. NBC got the best of it, showing Bobby Thomson's historic walk-off home run at the Polo Grounds that changed the course of baseball history on October 3, 1951.

Neither baseball nor sports programming would ever be quite the same. With technology and marketing dollars driving further investment, baseball on television would thrive during the 1950s. It had traveled a long road of innovation already, of course. The coast to coast microwave networking was only the most recent advance to a long chain of events that perhaps began with the single iconoscope camera that broadcast the very first major league baseball game on television on May 17, 1939, to the orthicon and image-orthicon cameras of the 1947 World Series, which worked better in low light and were capable of capturing wider angles and using telephoto lenses for close-ups.[27]

By the 1970s, most games were using four or five cameras, but the networks were devoting many more cameras to key games of national interest. NBC deployed 13 cameras to cover the 1983 All-Star Game, and by 2006 Fox was using 28 cameras to do the All-Star contest. In 1984 ABC introduced the "super slo mo" camera for the baseball playoffs, then NBC responded with an even better technology for the 1984 World Series that was able to slow the action down three times as much as ABC could.

In addition to Bobby Thomson's playoff "shot heard round the world," and the national relay network, 1951 also brought color television to baseball, although very little of the country was even equipped to see it. The very first games shown in color were Dodgers baseball games during the last two months of the 1951 regular season by a CBS network that was aggressively touting its spinning-wheel color technique — although that approach would lose out in 1952 to the NBC color technology developed by RCA and adopted industry-wide.[28] NBC would then debut its color system nationally for the 1955 World Series featuring the Yankees and Brooklyn Dodgers.

Television graphics, a necessary addition to both news and sports, would evolve, too. The original white lettering super-imposed at the bottom the screen was washed out, seemed flimsy to the viewer, and sometimes even flickered or was out of balance on the screen. But it was there and it brought a certain "coolness" factor for the viewer as baseball batting averages appeared on the screen. By the mid–1960s these images were matted over the game in a different process that made them bolder and more authoritative. The process began to become electronically generated by the early 1970s by means of an electronic character-generator device that had a modicum of stored memory. By the time of the 1975 World Series featuring the "Big Red Machine" Cincinnati Reds—the Series where Boston catcher Carlton Fisk is still seen waving his own home run into fair territory—the screen graphics had become yellow, less washed out, and could be easily changed and updated as the game went on.

The use of graphics got a huge boost when computers appeared in the early 1980s. These computers enhanced the use of statistics in a way that became so useful to sports analysis that it developed its own identity, sabermetrics.[29] Baseball, with its myriad numbers and stats throughout the history of the game, benefited the most among major team sports. Television benefited, too, since it could show, twist, invert, re-work and study all these emerging statistics on the fly.

From the pale, sometimes cock-eyed labeling of the early 1960s to the plasma explosion of color graphics, screen-crawls on the top and bottom, and eye-popping bursts of color like on the set of ESPN, the use of imagery in sports has evolved beyond even the wildest imaginations of those who once were glued to the black-and-white picture tubes of the 1950s. But there was still more to come: better sound. The advent of wireless microphones allowed television to capture game sounds on the field, enhancing the crack of the bat and the braying calls of the umpire. The field mikes also helped produce a stereo sound effect that one day would burst into family rooms with a sophisticated, computer chip surround sound system that pulls the viewer almost into the live crowd at the game—not to mention enhancing the sounds of the game itself. Sub-woofers and surround sound bring a new dimension to the crack of the bat and, in the NBA, the reverberating thump of thundering dunks has become unmistakable.

Both sports and news continued to exploit the television medium. By the time of the 1952 presidential conventions, there were an approximately 17,900,000 television sets in use in America that reached an estimated 60 million viewers.[30] Paul Levitan, the director of special events for CBS-TV guessed that it would take 22 years of speeches for a politician to reach all those voters through conventional campaign stumping—a notion that has been the cornerstone of national politics ever since.

As it happens, the Republican National Convention was in Chicago that year where WGN television, riding its string of innovative baseball successes, installed three large (24-inch) television screens in the courtyard at Tribune Tower, where the passing public could keep an eye on the live convention. The following day, though, the national convention was pre-empted by our national game, for those same sets were used to show the baseball All-Star Game as it was played in Philadelphia.[31]

NBC paid close attention to the combined powers of television and baseball. By the summer of 1956, NBC found itself paying an eye-popping sum of $16,250,000 for the exclusive television and radio rights to the World Series and All-Star Games for five straight years beginning in 1957. The $3,250,000 annual rate was close to three times the previous record for similar rights. The NBC deal knocked Mutual Broadcasting from its own World Series radio deal, and for the first time since 1939 Mutual would be shut out of the Series. On the baseball side, as much as 60 percent of that broadcast revenue would find its way to the players pension fund.[32]

That was a good week for NBC—not only did the network win the bidding for the package of baseball classics, but that same week NBC drubbed the CBS juggernaut *Ed Sullivan Show* in the ratings when Steve Allen hosted the "king," Elvis Presley, to take

55.3 percent of the viewing audience compared to 39.7 percent for Sullivan. It was NBC's best showing against Sullivan in two years.[33]

NBC had already landed a weekly Saturday game from major league baseball when NBC was awarded the Series and All-Star deals, symbolically exacerbated by the Elvis coup that was more like a sharp stick in the eye. The two powerhouse networks NBC and CBS were squarely pitted against each other in a ratings war over content, especially baseball. Desperate to catch up, CBS countered with a move of its own, Sunday baseball, announcing in December 1957 its own plans to televise a regular Sunday afternoon "Game of the Week" beginning in 1958. The CBS games featured a five-team lineup from major market cities: the Indians, White Sox, Yankees, Phillies, and Reds.[34]

Baseball would continue to be concerned about gate attendance, however. In 1957 televised major league games were blacked out within a 50-mile radius of the home cities, which seems absurd in the modern world of broadcasting where ratings are driven by the big market television sets tuned to the home-team games. CBS announced that its Sunday games would not be shown in areas where even minor league games were playing, a move meant to placate the minors that were severely threatened by the proliferation of televised major league games.

In 1946 there were only 15 network programs shown during a whole week of prime-time broadcasting from the combined four networks, and two of those were NBC's *Gillette Cavalcade of Sports* that usually featured boxing. By 1949 there were ten *times* as many shows offered in prime-time evenings, over 150 per week. In addition to Arthur Godfrey, Ed Sullivan, band leader Fred Waring, and a number of emerging classic shows like *Candid Camera* and *The Original Amateur Hour*, there were 11 sports offerings, none of which featured baseball: eight showed boxing or wrestling, while two featured roller derby.

There was baseball in the daytime, though, and overall major league attendance did drop during the early years of televised baseball. Total league attendance reached a then all-time high of 20 million fans in 1948 but it had dropped to just 14 million only five years later in 1953. National League president Warren Giles was publicly concerned. "We'll be playing with only 500 people in the stands and everybody else watching on TV," Giles warned.[35] Given the facts known at the time, it was a rational fear, but was it also reasonable? These were the same initial fears about radio, but baseball on radio was thriving in the 1940s including the peak attendance year of 1948. By 1953, perhaps fans were willing to stay home to watch baseball on television, but in 1953 many were just watching television — period. By then the medium had become the entire message, at least for a while. Television was not just a new toy for baseball, it was a revolutionary innovation that finally was in wide national distribution. Just as radio captured the nation's attention when it first appeared, and color television did it all over again in the late 1950s to early 1960s, the advent of television in the first place was an unprecedented milestone that thoroughly engaged the American public. Of course people stayed home — they could not keep their eyes off any TV screen, whether it showed baseball or not.

Walter O'Malley's Brooklyn Dodgers were a powerhouse team that won the pennant four times in the five years from 1952 through 1956. In those days the typical price for a Dodgers ticket was $2.00. The team averaged about 1.2 million paid fans per season, generating gate receipts of around $2.4 million.[36] But the foreseeable future was not bright, for they played in an aging stadium, Ebbets Field, which had a small capacity at 32,000. Moreover, the fan base of middle class ticket buyers was also eroding as more of them were moving out of Brooklyn during the American exodus to the suburbs during the 1950s.

O'Malley was both a pragmatist and a visionary. He saw the coming problems of both Ebbets Field and Brooklyn itself, but in the meantime he also perceived the potential of television. By the mid–1950s the Dodgers were televising over 100 games per year, with TV rights generating $800,000 annually — an amount equal to one-third of the total gate receipts, the equivalent of 400,000 extra fans per year. O'Malley was especially intrigued by televising road games, for they would generate revenue and stimulate interest in the team that would carry over to the homestands without cannibalizing home gate receipts. But there was one problem: it was expensive to lease long-distance phone lines, which were a pricey luxury at the time. Producer Tom Villante solved the problem by creating a virtual co-op to share the cost among teams, prorating the costs according to the portion of games shown by the respective teams involved. O'Malley bucked the trend and became an early advocate of baseball on television. Eventually CBS and NBC caught on, pressing each other to land more and more rights deals to televise baseball nationally as the 1950s wore on.

Baseball, with its deliberate charm and alluring intervals begging for homespun tales of the game, was truly a team sport that was built for radio. But the magical powers of television were overwhelming America; viewers could not get enough of this new phenomenon, and it began to overwhelm radio, as well. It took radio's stars like Jack Benny, the *Amos 'n' Andy* characters, and the popular sit-com invention of Mrs. Goldberg, and it even stole the wistful magic of seeing baseball in the mind's eye.

Soon television took the radio sports announcers, too, like Red Barber, Vin Scully, Jack Brickhouse, and perhaps the one who set the standard for television banter from the broadcast booth, Dizzy Dean, who left the radio booth twice — once to take the field and pitch four shutout innings for the hapless Browns in 1947, and then to do the *Game of the Week* for television starting in 1950. When Dizzy was asked why he gave up his successful radio broadcasting for television, his down-home explanation also portended the advent of televised baseball at radio's expense: "I'm through talking about things folks ain't seeing."[37]

$$\boxed{11}$$

The Great Home Run Chase

Have faith in the Yankees, my son.
— ERNEST HEMINGWAY, *THE OLD MAN AND THE SEA*

Television could not save the Brooklyn Dodgers. But it did impact baseball history in profuse ways, even contributing to the westward migration of the Dodgers and other big league teams.

As the 1950s progressed, television impacted the game both directly and indirectly. When the newly transplanted Milwaukee Braves found themselves with a brand-new 43,000 seat stadium and enough space for a 10,000-car parking lot, they captured the attention, if not the imagination, of the Dodgers.[1] The automobile helped propel those Braves to more spacious confines. American's traffic would soon be the bane of Brooklyn since it was the eventual suburban flight and the western migration, enabled by a massive new interstate highway system, that was about to change America, baseball, and most certainly the Dodgers.

"They brought me up to the Brooklyn Dodgers, which at that time was in Brooklyn," said Casey Stengel, summarizing his own promotion to the big leagues while rubbing an open wound that still hurts in the Flatbush neighborhoods.[2] In true Stengel fashion, his simplistic observation was at once ridiculously profound. Although the Braves' move to Milwaukee, and in particular their ensuing success, had caught the eye of Walter O'Malley, other acts of fate would be needed before his Dodgers' relocation to California could become a reality. For one, commercial air travel had to become much more accessible, which it was beginning to do by the end of the 1950s; moreover, a workable highway system had to be in place or developing rapidly, which also was underway. Then, when coast-to-coast television technology finally became feasible, the fate of the Dodgers was duly sealed.

During the summer of 1954 the air waves were filled with two things on radio: baseball and an emerging craze called rock and roll propelled by the likes of Bill Haley, whose "Rock Around the Clock" may have been the first genuine rock song, and Elvis Presley, a new heart-throb who would impact music, television, and America with his unprecedented popularity on the heels of his first release, "That's All Right," on Sun Records.

Thus the urban neighborhoods in New York, Baltimore, Philadelphia, and Boston were alive with the summer sounds of rock and roll and baseball, all while there were great changes lurking in the baseball winds.

Postwar America was transforming rapidly as the country spread its wings and migrated westward. In a few short years both the Dodgers and Giants would relocate to California, due in large part to a mostly forgotten summer day that would transform America: June 29, 1956, the day that President Dwight Eisenhower signed the Federal-Aid Highway Act. With that stroke of Eisenhower's pen the federal interstate highway system was born.[3] Thereafter the Brooklyn Dodgers would enter the home stretch of a historic exodus to sunshine, fame, and baseball fortune.

Secretary of Commerce Sinclair Weeks publicly called the highway bill "the greatest public-works program in the history of the world." The Act launched a revolutionary $33,480,000 road building program — expressed in 1956 dollars — that would propel American automakers, reshape the North American landscape, and eventually lead to America's unique dependence on oil, first from Texas and Oklahoma, then the likes of Venezuela and Saudi Arabia less than two decades later. The new highway system was planned to provide a 41,000-mile network of limited access roads — no stoplights or inter-sections — to link nearly every American city and town that had a population of more than 50,000.[4] Roads, television, and parking (or lack thereof) would soon impact baseball geography.

In 1952 the Braves had been ensconced in Boston, but the Boston Braves drew little more than flies with a paltry gate attendance of 281,000 for the entire year, just over 3,600 lost souls per game. This was even fewer than the 1888 Dodgers, then called the Brooklyn Bridegrooms, had drawn. The very next year, the 1953 Milwaukee Braves saw 1.8 million fans pour into their new stadium, then the team eclipsed the two million mark for each of the next four years. Walter O'Malley's Dodgers were still holding their own, drawing 1,088,000 in 1952, about 37 percent higher than the league average at the time.[5] But by 1954 the league had caught up, and in 1957 the league average exceeded the Dodgers' attendance level for the first time in 20 years.

Mediocre performance was not O'Malley's baseball style, so he was hardly content with just beating the averages. At the same time, it was clear the Dodgers would not likely draw many more than one million fans to their aging Ebbets Field. But could Ebbets be refurbished? Rebuilt? At what cost? And where would the cars park? This, after all, was the densely packed borough of Brooklyn set within the guts of the New York urban sprawl. Yes, public transportation was very accessible, but what about all those cars and highways, not to mention the romantic promise of a distant land called California? The Braves had found both fame and fortune by moving west, albeit only to Milwaukee; O'Malley would do the same for his Dodgers — and then some.

The Dodgers won the pennant in 1955, then bested the vaunted crosstown Yankees in seven hard-fought games for their first World Series title in history. The Dodgers won 98 games that year, buried the transplanted Braves by 13½ games, and featured such stars as National League MVP Roy Campanella, slugger Duke Snider, Gil Hodges, and 20-game winner Don Newcombe. But attendance did not budge at all from 1954 to 1955 and was actually less than it had been in 1951, a foreboding signal of things to come if the Dodgers' on-field performance were to drop off again — as it surely would one day. But what could go wrong? Duke Snider had just led the league with 136 RBIs, Roy Campanella was MVP, and Don Newcombe led the league in winning percentage with a stunning 80 percent win ratio. Fate would take Roy Campanella off the field in 1958 when a car crash paralyzed the three-time MVP, but there was more. Something larger, more lasting, and potentially damaging to the Dodgers was beginning to take shape in their own backyard.

On Opening Day, April 17, 1956, a surging star from the Bronx slammed two monster home runs in Washington against the Senators. Both blasts by Mickey Mantle were said to exceed 500 feet, and one may have been the longest home run ball ever hit into the right field bleachers at Griffith Stadium.[6] Mantle would slug many storied home runs in Yankee Stadium and elsewhere, but Griffith Stadium provided the backdrop for some of the biggest, including what still may be the longest home run in the history of the entire major leagues. Exactly three years before, on April 17, 1953, Mantle had launched a reputed 565-foot moon shot that exited Griffith Stadium altogether, first by clearing the 50-foot-high left center field wall, then nicking a beer sign 460 feet from home plate before clearing the 55-foot left field bleachers on its way to 434 Oakdale Street.[7] The Mantle missile was retrieved by a surprised 10-year-old, Donald Dunaway, who then traded it back to Mantle for a signed replacement ball—completing a round trip of about 1100 feet in one day, perhaps a baseball record in its own right.[8]

The primary point, though, is not about interesting baseball trivia, it concerns image, cachet, and an inescapable change of the baseball old guard, all portending a great baseball metamorphosis precisely at the dawn of television's early glory days. A timely accident of fate, it was during this baseball juncture that transcontinental television was just beginning to develop. First demonstrated successfully in September 1951, the advent of coast-to-coast television would not only enable movie capital Los Angeles to supplant New York as the nation's television hub, it would also allow the migration of eastern baseball teams just when they would be able to enjoy a surge in home attendance with eager new fans while expanding both their local and national visibility via the power and compelling images of television. With American working people in search of jobs and alluring California weather just as the new interstate highways, automobiles, and television itself were all reaching westward, baseball was sure to follow. And it did.

On February 20, 1953, Anheuser-Busch bought the Cardinals just as the rival St. Louis Browns were going broke and heading the other direction to Baltimore, but the soon-to-be-Orioles were the exception. On March 18, 1953, the Boston Braves obtained permission to move west to Milwaukee. In a symbolic baseball brawl that erupted on September 6, 1953, the local Dodgers and Giants had a hardball donnybrook that featured Giants manager Leo Durocher taunting the Dodgers as crybabies. It was a colorful neighborhood spat, but all too poignantly both teams would soon be gone from New York. In 1953 the Dodgers lost the World Series to the Yankees, the fifth world title in a row for this newest popular rendition of the Bronx bombers. Then, on November 9 that same year, the Supreme Court affirmed baseball's bizarre antitrust exemption, validating the unbridled power of the baseball lords which would allow them to hoard players and to manipulate national television deals with impunity just as television was taking its own quantum leap forward.

In what could have become a watershed moment for Brooklyn, the Dodgers signed future Hall of Famer Roberto Clemente to a minor league deal in February 1954, but Clemente would never wear Dodger blue because Brooklyn would lose him to the Pirates in a 1955 baseball draft. Meanwhile, another youngster was serving notice with his very first home run on April 23, 1954. It was Hank Aaron, who was wearing a Milwaukee Braves uniform and would bring still more success to the transplanted Braves for years to come. The new kids like Aaron and Clemente were changing baseball, and two of the best were on other New York teams. The 1954 National League batting champion Willie Mays was named league MVP as a member of the Giants, and in 1955 Mickey Mantle slugged home runs by the bunches for the rival Yankees, hitting one from each side of the plate during a game in May, then launching another 500-footer in June, all en route to an American League home run title. The tides were turning, but the Dodgers still had one last hurrah left in them for 1955, the year they won 98 games and finally captured their first World Series—and the only world title they would bring home to Brooklyn.

The Dodgers did not exactly fade in 1956, for they still took 93 games and the pennant away from the Braves by just one game, but Mantle and the Yankees nonetheless took center stage. Mantle slammed homers from both sides again on May 18 (and yet again on July 1), and 12 days later he almost became the only man to hit a fair ball over the roof of Yankee Stadium, clunking a tape measure shot off the distant upper deck facade.[9] Stopped just 370 feet from home plate, the ball was still 117 feet off the ground, a mere 18 inches from leaving the stadium altogether—it was the stuff of legends while the Dodgers were growing short on lore as the Yankees thrived.[10] The Yankees finished strong in 1956, winning the pennant and ultimately burying the Dodgers 9–0 to take the pivotal Game Seven of the World Series. Don Newcombe's dual MVP and Cy Young Awards followed his 27 regular season wins, but even he was overshadowed by Yankee Don Larson's historic World Series perfect game on October 8, 1956. American League MVP Mantle did his part, too, contributing a rare Triple Crown season that topped all players in *both* leagues in all three categories: batting (.353), RBIs (130), and home runs (52).

On October 11, 1956, just after losing the Series, Walter O'Malley publicly denied a pending move away from the looming shadow of the Yankees to Los Angeles. But then, on October 30, the Dodgers sold Ebbets Field. Yes, the team leased it back through the remainder of the decade, but the proverbial "handwriting on the wall" was coming into a most foreboding focus. On December 13 the Dodgers traded fabled Jackie Robinson to the crosstown Giants, but Jackie retired before ever taking the field for his new team. Meanwhile, Phil Rizzuto was released by his Yankees, too, but the team did not dump him altogether. Rizzuto soon found himself in the broadcast booth with legendary baseball announcers Red Barber and Mel Allen.

The following year was like rubbing salt on a festering Dodgers wound, for the prospering Milwaukee Braves bested Brooklyn to take the 1957 National League pennant behind the league-leading 44 home runs of Hank Aaron. Overshadowed by banner years from Ted Williams (league hitting and slugging leader), Mantle (MVP), and Rookie of the Year Yankee newcomer Tony Kubek—who would later become an even better announcer than player, winning the coveted Frick Award—there was another greenhorn player with sullen eyes and a reluctant smile, Roger Maris, who clubbed his first major league home run on April 18, 1957. Soon Maris would switch uniforms, donning Yankee pinstripes just in time to change the baseball world, and television would be there not just to show it, but to make an impact. The storybook 1961 home run chase between teammates Mickey Mantle and Roger Maris provided unprecedented theater for baseball broadcasting, and none of baseball, television, or Roger Maris would ever be quite the same.

The dual baseball machinations on the field with the game's new stars and transformed teams, and concurrently off the field with the accelerating evolution of live media coverage, would be held together by the games' colorful announcers who were the enduring glue of baseball broadcasting. The 1961 annals of baseball history would not be relegated to mere dusty pages lost somewhere in distant vaults of time and posterity, it would be given eternal life through the voices of the game's enduring announcers. Two of the best would find themselves witnessing the transformation of baseball through the 1950s and into the watershed moments of the 1960s, all before an age of American innocence would be forever tarnished by assassinations, racial revolution, Vietnam, Watergate, and at least two discredited presidents.

For six consecutive decades fans experienced their Dodgers through the eyes and voice of their team, Vin Scully. Virtually synonymous with the Dodgers name, Scully first called games for Brooklyn beginning in 1950.[11] It was an exciting yet disappointing debut season, though, with the heroics of Roy Campanella, Gil Hodges, Duke Snider, Jackie Robinson, and Don Newcombe falling just two games short as they watched the Phillies take the pennant. Scully then witnessed the fateful 1951 season when the Dodgers came up short against the Giants in 1951, the year of Bobby Thomson's homer in the stunning National League finale. The very next year, though, Scully called an eventful 1952 Dodgers season that lasted all the way to the final out of World Series Game Seven against the Yankees when Brooklyn finally lost the seventh game, 4–2.

Scully's smooth voice sparkled with baseball excitement, and while he was clearly identified with Dodgers blue, Scully was never fully a "homer." Scully announced the game with the enthusiasm of a fan and the professionalism of a journalist, all while making a specific effort to avoid the word "we" in referring to the Dodgers, even though the team was as much his as anyone's. That style served him well, for Scully became an acclaimed national announcer notwithstanding his Dodgers roots, calling games for CBS and NBC including ten different World Series, 18 no-hit games, and even three perfect games, one each by Don Larsen, Sandy Koufax, and Dennis Martinez. Not only was Scully the American Sportscasters Association Broadcaster of the Century, he was anointed by historian Curt Smith as the #1 baseball announcer of all time. "The consummate professional," explains BaseballLibrary.com, "he [Scully] is as knowledgeable as he is lyrical, weaving accurate play-by-play with understated color in a calm resonant voice that is a joy to hear."[12] Moreover, Scully did it primarily as a solo announcer, a rarity in the modern broadcast booth where two and sometimes three voices are used to describe the game.

Born near the Bronx in 1927 just two years prior to the great stock market crash, Scully lived through the Depression and World War II before taking the Dodgers microphone for the first time in 1950 while still only 22 years of age, sharing the task with established announcer Red Barber before going solo in 1954. Scully had just played center field for Fordham University in New York, where he also helped launch the school's own FM radio station, then suddenly he found himself calling games for the storied Dodgers franchise. Scully suffered through five disappointing baseball seasons, some of them pennant-winning years that came up short in the post-season, before the Dodgers finally won it all in 1955. The young Scully was all "Brooklyn," through and through, but when push came to shove, he was more about the Dodgers than geography, and he left for Los Angeles with the team before the 1958 season. In the New Millennium of league expansion and franchise free agency in all the major team sports, it is difficult to fathom the sweeping import of the Dodgers' westward journey. Before 1958, the western-most major league baseball team in the United States was in Kansas City, where the Philadelphia Athletics transplanted themselves after the 1954 season, making the exodus to California both radical and heartbreaking for those back in Brooklyn.

Until the substantial commercialization of air travel, a West Coast big league team was not practical. Each Dodgers road trip would have taken much too long via the train, while eastern teams would have invested days just to get to Los Angeles and, once there, would have found no other nearby teams to play. National television did its part, too, with coast-to-coast hook-ups keeping teams from being totally lost in the western abyss. Scheduling was difficult even with air travel, since in 1958 every other National League team was at or east of the Mississippi River — most of them substantially east of it — except for the other West Coast transplant, the San Francisco Giants, who also had just moved. Starved for baseball, southern California readily embraced the Dodgers and Scully, whose voice was heard by millions in and around the Los Angeles area.

National television broadcasts would have emerged sooner or later anyway, but without them appearing when they did, Vin Scully may never have been the well known national announcer he ultimately became — and maybe he would not have been named baseball's greatest ever. When the Dodgers arrived in southern California, there were few television sets but plenty of radios. There were also many, many cars and not much public transportation. The Los Angeles Memorial Coliseum, where the Dodgers played for four full seasons beginning with the first home game of 1958 on April 18, was situated only three miles southwest of downtown L.A., immediately adjacent to USC. A mammoth stadium that opened in 1923, the Coliseum was a classic design of ancient Roman influence. Its capacity of 74,000 in 1923 was enlarged to 105,000 in 1952, and there was room for plenty of parking.[13]

Built for football and track, the stadium had to be retrofitted to accommodate major league baseball. Even so, the dimensions were reminiscent of the elongated Polo Grounds with a left field line of just 250 feet in 1958 while left center and center were a distant 425 feet and right center farther still, a full 440 feet from home plate.[14] The very short left field also sported a 40-foot fence to partially compensate for the distance, giving it a shortened version of the Green Monster effect of Boston's Fenway Park. The 1958 Dodgers opened their season in San Francisco against the transplanted Giants, losing to the Giants, 8–0. However, it would not take long for the Dodgers to make a substantial mark in Los Angeles, for in 1959, their second season in California, they won the pennant with a mark of 88–68, two full games over their thorn-in-the-side Braves, then took the World Series from the 1959 "go-go" Chicago White Sox (after winning two games of a best-of-three season-ending playoff). The team's success coupled with the capacity of the gigantic Coliseum helped the Dodgers set all-time attendance records; the three games in L.A. averaged over 92,000 fans each, while the Game Five standard of 92,706 still stands as a major league record.[15]

The Dodgers hitters would remain prodigious enough behind Duke Snider and Gil Hodges, while their brash young pitchers would prove more than worthy. The youthful power pitcher Don Drysdale would make his mark, leading the entire major league in strikeouts at 242, far ahead of his American League counterpart Jim Bunning's 201 for the Tigers, and teammate Sandy Koufax would tie Bob Feller's single-game strikeout record by fanning 18 Giants batters on August 31, including 15 of the final 17 hitters he faced.

The sale of Chavez Ravine from the city of Los Angeles to the Dodgers paved the way for a new Dodgers Stadium, but not before a challenge to that sale went all the way to the United States Supreme Court where the city, and the Dodgers, ultimately prevailed. Back in New York, the Dodgers exodus was still a nasty pill that was not going down easily. In 1958 Congressman Emmanuel Cellar backed a bill to subject major league baseball to U.S. antitrust laws, but it gained no traction. The baseball antitrust exemption would be the subject of many battles for years to come, but the sports tides would continue to drift the way of protectionism with Congress soon passing the Sports Broadcasting Act of 1961 to effectively exempt the NFL and other leagues from antitrust laws in the packaging and selling of national broadcasting rights *en masse*, a practice that otherwise would have been deemed a conspiracy in restraint of trade had the teams attempted to combine their efforts to sell such rights collectively.

Baseball itself did not need the Sports Broadcasting Act, although one day the law could regain relevance if baseball ever loses its overall exemption. But the Dodgers would survive the political assaults from New York and the various threats against its antitrust immunity, and so a new and long lasting chapter of Dodgers history was allowed to begin.

The Dodgers immediately benefited from three attributes that eastern teams could only dream about: California weather, beaches, and Vin Scully in the booth. All three would impact the evolution of baseball. Years later, one survey conducted to find the most important Dodger of all time actually named someone who had never swung the bat even once for the Dodgers: Vin Scully himself. Columnist Rick Reilly echoed the thoughts of many when he concluded that "Vinnie *is* the Dodgers."[16]

Importantly, the success of Vin Scully was partly born of an unintentional throwback to the very roots of baseball broadcasting and the evolution of baseball itself: the radio. One reason was Scully's talent, his incredible baseball savvy boosted by his "next door" tone and affable voice. But the southern California weather and beaches would play a role, too. The Coliseum, where the Dodgers first landed after moving, was so vast and elongated that many fans were seated far, far from home plate. They developed the habit of bringing their popular transistor radios to the game where Scully's voice remained firmly ensconced in their ears.[17] And then there were the beaches—Californians spent vast amounts of time outdoors hiking, running, camping, and soaking up the California sun at the area beaches where the radio would inevitably be turned to Vin Scully and the Dodgers. Ironically, this produced the same effect that the Dodgers experienced in the early days of Flatbush decades earlier when Dodgers games could be heard everywhere in the urban neighborhood. Even as radio proliferated, Dodgers attendance soared. In 1959 they passed the two million mark for the first time, double their 1957 attendance in Brooklyn.[18] As the 1960s emerged, the California beaches were alive with baseball through the resonant voice of Vin Scully. The Dodgers, baseball, and "Vinnie" himself, all surged together largely due to the magic of baseball broadcasting.

By the time the Dodgers left the Coliseum for their own new digs at Chavez Ravine, the Los Angeles fans were so addicted to Scully's voice that they carried on the tradition of clinging to their radios at the ballpark. Importantly, in addition to sunshine, Scully, and radios, Dodger Stadium also had a special rare commodity that trumped what most eastern teams could offer, land. The stadium was built on a 300-acre parcel, bigger than Disneyland in nearby Anaheim. It could seat 56,000 fans but, importantly for Los Angeles, the stadium grounds could accommodate 16,000 cars. When Dodger Stadium opened in

1962, attendance surged again, surpassing 2.7 million, well over double the league average of 1.14 million.[19] Remarkably, it was the first privately financed baseball stadium since the 1923 opening of Yankee Stadium — a poignant coincidence given the emergence of the Dodgers and Yankees as formidable teams when the 1950s morphed into the 1960s, both those storied teams contributing to the history of baseball broadcasting with Vin Scully in California and Mel Allen who would oversee Yankees and baseball history from his vantage point in New York.

When Mel Allen died on June 16, 1996, he left behind a 60-season career that not only witnessed some of the most storied of all baseball history but also helped influence it. Born in 1913 as Melvin Avrom Israel — the name change would come in 1943 at age 30 — Allen grew up in Birmingham, Alabama, then attended the University of Alabama where he cut his teeth broadcasting for the Crimson Tide.[20] By age 24 he had become a staff announcer at CBS, and 41 years later Allen would be the first winner of the coveted Frick Award for broadcasting, an honor he shared with icon Red Barber, who had occupied the booth with Allen when Barber left the Dodgers for the Yankees. Mel Allen called Yankees games for over 20 years during a span from 1939 to 1964, minus time off for the armed forces during World War II.[21] He was there long enough to announce 15 world championships for the fabled Yankees, including perhaps the most storied season since the Murderers' Row era of Ruth and Gehrig.

There are two years in baseball lore that simply stand on their own with no introduction — a phenomenon only found in the history of major league baseball and no other American team sport. Those years were 1927 and 1961, two separate seasons that require neither introduction nor explanation in the context of baseball. Mel Allen was a 14-year-old Alabama boy when Ruth made his imprint on 1927, but he was a virtual part of the 1961 version that saw a three-way home run chase among the fair-haired boy-wonder Mickey Mantle, the quiet and seemingly sullen Roger Maris, and the ghost of a long-deceased George Herman Ruth. Many fans pulled for their personable hero Mickey Mantle to oust the Holy Grail of baseball's record books, Ruth's mystical 60 homers, while legions of baseball purists actually rooted for Ruth, preferring to preserve the most revered of all baseball standards for posterity. However, very few, if any, actually supported Roger Maris in his own quest for baseball immortality.

These two seasons of all seasons—1927 and 1961— had something else in common, too, for it was during both years that the reach of baseball broadcasting touched the game itself. Just as radio emerged in the 1920s during the dawn of Murderers' Row to spread baseball past the stadium walls and even beyond the cities themselves, television was finding its legs just as Mantle and Maris put on a baseball show for the ages.

Perhaps "1961" really began earlier, as soon as December 11, 1959, when an unheralded trade involving the Yankees and Athletics sent emerging slugger Roger Maris, who hit 16 homers that year, to New York.[22] It was a move that would soon impact baseball history, and it would take place under the nose of another broadcasting icon making his own mark 3,000 miles away from Vin Scully's Dodgers, Mel Allen. In 1960, the first season of the Maris-Mantle duo, Mel Allen and the Bronx were treated to a preview of the milestone season to come, although no one could have predicted the breadth and impact of that pinnacle year of baseball records and lore. In 1960 the Yankees took the American League pennant again, the tenth time in 12 years that New York earned a trip to the World Series. Mickey Mantle would not disappoint, besting Maris' 39 homers with 40 of his own to lead the American League. But Maris would flex his own baseball muscle, driving in 112 runs, topping not only all other Yankees but everyone in the league.[23] Neither player individually would best his National League counterpart, though, for the Cubs' young phenom Ernie Banks would crush 41 long balls to top both leagues while the perennial slugger Hank Aaron would knock 126 runs across the plate.

Roger Maris did enough damage to win the America League MVP, however, while he and Mantle, Moose Skowron, and Yogi Berra led the Casey Stengel Yankees to the World Series with a stellar 97–57 regular season mark, the best in either league. The 95-win Pirates were not far behind, though, and by the time autumn arrived their own featured slugger would prove too much to handle. Although Roger Maris would slam a two-run blast in Game One of the Series, that would be matched by a two-run jack by the future Hall of Famer Bill Mazeroski as the Pirates took the first game. Mantle entered the fray in Game Two, crushing two home runs for five RBIs in a 19-hit Yankee victory. Mantle, Bobby Richard-

New York Governor Alfred E. Smith at the opening of Yankee Stadium (April 18, 1923), the original "House That Ruth Built." When Babe Ruth doubled Yankees attendance at the Polo Grounds in 1920, Ruth's first year as a Yankee, the seeds were sown for a new ballpark. Yankee Stadium was the first triple-deck baseball facility and the first ballpark to be called a "stadium." It opened to a staggering official crowd of 74,200 in 1923. During a game in late September 1966, while under ownership of the CBS Network, the Yankees drew only 413 fans, its smallest gate ever, contributing to the firing of legendary broadcaster Red Barber who had noted the paltry attendance on the air.

son, and hurler Whitey Ford shone in Game Three, a 10–0 pasting of Pittsburgh. The Pirates, who also featured batting champ Dick Groat (.325) and future Hall of Famer Roberto Clemente, would not fold, forcing a Game Seven that produced one of the most dramatic finishes in Series history. The slugfest was tied 9–9 in the ninth inning when Mazeroski stepped into the batter's box and unloaded a game-winning solo shot to take the World Series title in storybook fashion. Captured on national television, the Mazeroski blast is still played over and over, and remains regarded as one of the defining moments of baseball post-season history.

That shot by "Maz" made him an instant baseball legend. It was this singular home run that stood out among 138 big league homers hit by Mazeroski, all for the Pirates, plus a stellar fielding career, that ultimately led Mazeroski to the Baseball Hall of Fame in 2001. But there may have been something else at work, namely, the magic of television. Bill Mazeroski is in the Hall of Fame, but Roger Maris is not. There are several factors often cited for this oddity, such as Mazeroski's defense and Roger Maris' allegedly uninspired overall body of work, notwithstanding his near mystical 1961 season. But the facts betray the baseball logic — although they may have been jaded by the impact of television, since Maris proved anything but popular or photogenic.

By all apparent standards, Bill Mazeroski was an outstanding player and a great ambassador for the game. There are few, if any, who suggest he should not be in Cooperstown, but the mystery lingers why Maris himself is not. Bill Mazeroski played in 2,163 games over 17 years, a very long career.[24] Roger Maris played for fewer years (12 seasons), but he slugged 275 home runs, almost exactly double the Mazeroski total.[25] The two were closely matched in RBIs (851 for Maris and 853 for Maz), as well as sporting identical career batting averages at .260 each. Maris' career on-base percentage was .345 compared with .299 for Maz, and Maris compiled a .476 career slugging mark against Mazeroski's .367.

As for an overall body of work, there are few players in major league history who compare with Roger Maris, for Roger appeared in seven World Series, winning three of them, while Mazeroski was in two, winning both. And Maris did not just go for the ride with those great Yankee teams, he was a big reason for their greatness, plus he did it once again for the Cardinals where he also won a Series in 1967. Maris was also the league MVP not once, but twice, beating out baseball legend Mantle for the American League honors in back-to-back years, 1960 and 1961.

And then there was "1961" itself, the year that not only needs no further description, it defies it. Bill Mazeroski clubbed one spectacular home run in 1960 (after hitting an unremarkable 11 homers during the regular season), but Maris slugged an entire miracle season in 1961 when he slammed 61 long balls to best Mickey Mantle in the great home run chase that went down to the wire, ultimately beating the ghost of Babe Ruth and changing the baseball record books forever. In 1961, Maris singularly clubbed almost *half* of Mazeroski's career total of 138 homers, all in the pressure-cooker Bronx before what was often a national television audience. And lost among those 1961 homers were a stunning 142 RBIs for Maris during a year when Maz had had just 59 even though he played nearly a full season (152 games).

Most telling of all is that the Hall of Fame displays the *bat* Maris used to hit the infamous home run #61, the ball itself, and Roger's 1961 home jersey — but not Maris. He held the home run record longer than Ruth did, 37 years vs. 34, and Maris remains the last holder of that revered mark before the steroid era.

So what? Was Maris' 1961 season merely a career aberration to be discounted by baseball history? It was unique, to be sure, but there was nothing "mere" about it. Over his entire career, Maris slammed one home run every 18.5 at-bats, while Mazeroski's career produced one home run in 56.2 at-bats, making Maris' ratio about three times as prodigious as that of Maz. So what happened? Why no Maris in the Hall? One reason is fate. Maris was the first to beat Ruth's total in the 162-game era, and that nuance was held against Maris but has never been a material factor in analyzing or accepting subsequent single-season home run records (all of which now carry some form of steroid taint), or any other season-long record, for that matter. In being the first to down Ruth, the less-than-popular Maris was not perceived as breaking the baseball Holy Grail mark, but rather as desecrating it. And among those who may not have cared about ancient baseball history, most had been rooting for Mantle to break the mark, not Roger Maris.

But there is another factor, a lurking reason behind all the other causes: television. The lens was friendly to the affable Mickey Mantle and Bill Mazeroski, but Maris' personality ranged from boring to stubborn to hostile. As the summer of 1961 heated up as baseball headed into July, the Maris-Mantle home run chase was beginning to look like a viable two-way assault on the Ruth record. When a New York reporter, Joe Trimble, directly asked Maris whether he could break the fabled 60-homer mark, Maris was less than hospitable. "How the fuck should I know?"[26] Mantle was glib, good looking, and carried a boyish charm that the media loved — and that played well on television. In the end, Maris was almost the baseball version of Richard Nixon during the televised 1960 presidential debates with John Kennedy. Television's role in the 1960 election is now legendary and often repeated. Nixon had a dark complexion and a non-engaging personality, and he appeared nervous on television. With a five o'clock shadow, sweaty brow, and shifty demeanor, Nixon was a profound contrast to the youthful, sunny, glib, and good looking John F. Kennedy. To make matters worse, Nixon had been sick and looked gaunt yet he refused to wear television make-up, then he found himself sweating under the lights as though he was on a political hot seat.[27] As it happens, he was. Long-time CBS anchor/reporter Charles Kuralt observed that Kennedy's smooth and engaging performance had transformed television into America's new political front porch.[28] And Nixon did not play well on this televised stoop.

The similarity between those 1960 debates and the great home run chase of 1961 is striking, both happening during the same era of black-and-white television with its harsh lighting and images. Maris had dark, almost sunken eyes. He was gifted with neither a quick wit nor engaging charm. When contrasted to the brightly poised Mantle, Roger Maris seemed even less personable, and the television camera flashed those differences across America. Kennedy and Nixon actually debated four times, but after the first, polls showed that television viewers believed Kennedy had won — yet those who only heard the exchange on radio, where the "focus" seemed more on issues that on persona, had still believed Nixon was the winner.[29] Did the same phenomenon influence the perception of Maris in the context of baseball history? It almost certainly did. Maris won on the facts — 61 homers — but Mantle won the battle of posterity, a beloved icon enshrined in Cooperstown along with Ruth, leaving Maris as the odd man out.

Maris was chasing the record of a baseball god which jaded viewer impressions in the first place, and then, to make matters worse, Commissioner Ford Frick fueled the flames of negativity when he announced that any new mark would be tarnished by the 162-game season of 1961. The Ruth standard was set during the 154-game era, so Maris was not only perceived as the villain, but thanks to Frick he was seen as cheating history, all of which only made Maris more withdrawn and even less personable. In truth, Maris may not have been very engaging but he was not a villain, either. He was a very good young baseball player with a very big job to do. Maris understood that he was not well liked, which made him sometimes even more acerbic, which seems reminiscent of heavyweight champion George Foreman's later dilemma when he faced Muhammad Ali in Zaire, Africa, in 1974. Ali was charming, funny, engaging, and outspoken, while Foreman was perceived as withdrawn and sullen — the villain — even though in truth Foreman was then, and continued to be for decades, a particularly likeably guy.

When Frick announced on July 18 that unless the new record was broken in the old season quota of 154 games, the new mark "will not be the official record," his reactionary edict applied to both Mantle and Maris.[30] Whether it would have impacted Mantle and the game the same as it affected the eventual record-holder Maris will never be known, but certainly neither Maris nor history would be the same thereafter. Frick never affixed an official asterisk to the Maris record, but his statement was the reason the fabled asterisk grew from legend to virtual fact.

One week after Frick's proclamation, Maris launched not just one or two, but *four* home runs during a doubleheader thrashing of the White Sox. That effort put Maris a full 27 games ahead of Ruth in his quest for baseball immortality. By July 26, both Mantle, with 39 homers, and Maris, at 40, were far enough ahead of Ruth that the Frick warning could possibly be mooted long before season's end.[31] Mel Allen, who was calling the Yankees games at the time, had never relied on his famous home run trademark call "going ... going ... *gone*" so often, as the powerful Yankees of Mantle, Maris, Moose Skowron, Yogi Berra, and Elston Howard clubbed an American League team record 240 long balls during that threshold season of 1961 — a record that stands, interestingly, without the taint of a real or imagined asterisk. "How about that?" Mel Allen must have thought, for when something really spectacular happened on the field of play, whether by the defense or otherwise, he would often punctuate it with that resonant trademark expression of his own baseball wonder.

As the summer of '61 wore on, Maris and Mantle were forced to endure not only the chilling effect of Ford Frick's public statements, but also another indignity as the conspiracy theorists began to emerge, rousing public speculation that the official 1961 ball was livelier than the 1927 version, which had the effect of keeping Ruth himself in the great home run chase, too. Tests on the ball did suggest it might be zippier, but they were too inconclusive to support the lively ball theory.[32] That did not stop Dizzy Dean, by then a widely followed baseball broadcaster, who was much less scientific but decidedly more emphatic when he said that the ball was so lively he could feel "its heart beating in his hands."[33]

By September 11, 1961, with Maris at 56 long ball blasts and Mantle at 53, the nation and the world were captivated by the three-way Maris-Mantle-Ruth struggle as national television and international radio following the drama. But then, on that very same day, Mantle developed an infection that stemmed from a medical mishap when the needle from a flu shot accidentally hit bone.[34] Mantle's assault on Ruth thereafter faded while Maris continued to press forward even while his own pace was slowing as the season wound down.

The 154th game of the '61 Yankees season was played on September 20. Maris connected on a Milt Pappas pitch for home run number 59, but a very long, slightly foul drive was as close as he would come to number 60 that day, putting Ford Frick's edict into play. The very next day, though, Frick was already backpedaling when he announced that the eventual new home run mark, if it were to happen, would stand as a "162-game record" — whereupon he expressly denied that an official asterisk would be utilized.

When the 1961 season finale arrived on the first day of October, Maris was tied with

Ruth at 60 homers with just one more game left to take the all-time lead. At home against Boston, a fourth-inning Maris shot sailed into baseball destiny and clanked into the record books when it finally came to rest in the right field seats at Section 33, Box 163D.[35] It was a historic Yankees moment, but the voice of the Yankees, Mel Allen, did not call it for the radio. Although he was present in the booth, Allen was not announcing that particular inning.

The Maris record and ensuing baseball debates largely overshadowed the overall Yankees season of 1961, a monster year when they compiled a lofty 109–53 record behind the combined 115 home runs and 270 RBIs from Mantle and Maris alone with another 71 total long balls from Elton Howard, Yogi Berra, and Moose Skowron — not to mention a dominant 25–4 mark from starting pitcher Whitey Ford. Then those powerful Yankees went on to best Frank Robinson's Reds in the World Series, four games to one, sealing their lasting legacy.

Perhaps clubbing those 61 homers was the easy part. Maris was also forced to endure the lively ball accusations and resultant testing ordered by American League president Joe Cronin and National League president Warren Giles, the 154-game qualifying comments from Ford Frick, and baseball purists who could not abandon the ghost of Ruth. But his own teammate Mickey Mantle, the sentimental favorite of many, stood up for Roger Maris, publicly calling him baseball's best all-round player and then endorsing the new record accordingly: "I really believe that the 61 homers was the greatest feat in baseball history," said the gracious Mantle.

The 1961 season was an MVP year for Maris, his second in a row, but the relentless criticism weighed heavily on him. Baseball's spring training of 1962 found Maris even more withdrawn as he dismissed youngsters in search of an autograph, often signed his name with just an "X," declined interviews with the press, and once openly cursed columnist Oscar Fraley of United Press International. Although Mantle may have been gracious, the voice of the Yankees was not amused. "Maris has a lot to learn about warmth, appreciation, graciousness, and that sort of thing," said Mel Allen. The voice of the Yankees was piling on, essentially calling Maris cold and ungracious, further damaging the Maris legacy.[36]

Television did Roger Maris no favors as it made him into a Nixon-like target for the whole country to see. With the help of the television lens, Maris was transformed from a shy ballplayer to one that was sullen and gaunt, even withdrawn, irascible, and insulting, while the camera caught it all in dingy black-and-white splendor. Just as with the Kennedy-Nixon debates and other key watershed moments, the medium had largely "become the message" for Maris and baseball, too.

Soon, though, it was Mel Allen's turn to be rocked by the Yankees. In 1964 the team suddenly fired Allen as its broadcaster, stunning both Allen and the baseball world. Although still popular with the public, Allen became despondent and was unable to step into any team's broadcast booth for all of 1965, 1966, and 1967. He tried doing play-by-play work for the Indians in 1968, but it was not the same. Those distant magical Yankee moments were gone forever. In 1977, Allen turned to a half-hour baseball recap show called *This Week in Baseball*, which found broadcasting legs with Allen continuing to host it through the 1995 season. At one point it was the highest rated regular sports show around, giving Mel Allen one more turn at baseball immortality.

Baseball historian Curt Smith recounted the aftermath of Allen's dismissal from the

Yankees, which had not only come without warning but also without benefit of any corresponding public announcement or explanation. "They left people to believe whatever they wanted — and people believed the worst," Allen lamented. Ironically, the public itself then became jaded, just as audiences had done with Maris. Quoting *Sports Illustrated*, Smith continued, "Allen became a victim of rumors. He was supposed to be a drunkard, a drug user. Neither rumor was true, but he couldn't fight them. It was as if he had leprosy."[37]

That is how Maris looked and often felt: like a leper. But Maris and Mel Allen were by no means the only baseball icons to struggle with the media. When the Yankees had gotten off to a slow start in the 1958 World Series, manager Casey Stengel was confronted by a television reporter who asked whether the Yankees were choking. "Do you choke on that fucking microphone?" Stengel tersely replied, just before he turned away from the camera and condescendingly scratched his own derriere in plain view. Recognizing the incumbent power of the media and its televised images, Stengel promptly elaborated, "When I cursed I knocked out their audio and when I scratched my ass I ruined their picture."[38] Yet another defining moment in baseball broadcasting.

The individual players and managers were not the only ones with broadcasting issues, of course. Sometimes it was the baseball media itself. In 1952 the Liberty Broadcasting System filed a $12 million federal antitrust lawsuit in Chicago against major league baseball, naming 13 teams and the presidents of both leagues as defendants. Liberty explained that it was being forced out of its baseball *Game of the Day* radio broadcasts. Liberty president Gordon McLendon held a news conference where he publicly charged that major league baseball had denied Liberty's access to 13 big league clubs despite being the highest broadcast bidder. The lawsuit claimed that baseball had awarded "game of the day" broadcast rights to competing Mutual Broadcasting System, alleging that the "operators of organized baseball were engaged in a continuous conspiracy to monopolize and restrain competition in broadcasting and recreating play-by-play accounts of professional baseball games." The Liberty lawsuit sought actual damages, including lost profits, of over $4 million, which under federal antitrust laws could be trebled to over $12 million.[39]

The Liberty action had been doomed from the start. Not only was baseball still exempt from antitrust laws stemming from the 1922 *Federal Base Ball* decision, but Liberty was stretched thin financially. McLendon was a free-wheeling young broadcasting entrepreneur who had founded a Dallas radio station when he was just 26 years old. His mission was to broadcast big league baseball games every day. Beginning in 1947, he arranged to pay major league baseball the nominal sum of $1,000 per year to recreate play-by-play from ticker-tape reports of East Coast games, which he topped off with dubbed sound effects like the crack of wood on the ball and "spontaneous" roars of a recorded crowd. The idea was a big hit, but perhaps McLendon had grown his radio empire too quickly, reaching a network of 458 stations which was second in size to the established giant Mutual Broadcasting. Strapped for cash, he sold half of Liberty to a Texas oil investor for $1 million in 1951. But the minor leagues began to complain that big league baseball on local radio was impeding their own attendance, so the major leagues hiked the annual fee threshold from $1,000 to $225,000, then restricted the areas where Liberty could broadcast games, thus protecting the minor league system. McLendon answered with a desperate antitrust suit, but a year later Liberty was bankrupt anyway.[40]

In 1946 the Yankees had become the first big league baseball team to enter into a local television contract, selling the rights to televise their games for the tidy sum of $75,000.[41] In 1958 the Yankees would sell 140 games for over $1 million, but a half-century later the Yankee broadcast rights would balloon to $52 million per year.[42] Lucrative television deals would begin to drive the availability, image, and profitability of all major team sports, especially baseball and football on the heels of the Sports Broadcasting Act of 1961 that allowed the NFL to package its broadcast rights in bundles without violating antitrust laws. The Act allowed the same for other sports, including baseball, although major league baseball did not really need the added legislation because of its own long-standing antitrust exemption.

Baseball on radio would never disappear for the same reasons it had taken hold during the early days of the 1920s and 1930s in the first place. Baseball was still the perfect game for radio, and baseball, with its many games during a long season, was often available for listeners in the car, on the beaches, and at work — especially in garages and among trades people with the flexibility to keep the radio nearby.

Television would change the game immeasurably, often in unforeseen ways. Ratings would drive the frequency of night games, change the game times for World Series contests, bring superstar status to the recognizable players seen almost daily from spring to fall, cause light standards to be installed at Chicago's Wrigley Field in 1988, and become the Waterloo downfall of many like Dodgers' executive Al Campanis, who inexplicably ambushed himself on national television with racist remarks explaining "why blacks do not have the tools to be baseball managers" during an eventful episode of ABC's *Nightline* on April 6, 1987. The very next year television would assist colorful NFL broadcast analyst Jimmy "the Greek" Snyder to do his own similar crash and burn, when he found himself commenting on the alleged evolutionary physical traits of African American football players. Television would continue to spread ill-conceived comments for years to come to the chagrin, for example, of ABC simulcast personality Don Imus, who once blurted on camera that the Rutgers University women's basketball team looked like "nappy-headed hos."

But the stoic images of Roger Maris not only harken much about broadcasting the game, those televised impressions of Maris helped alter the history of the game. If the personable and popular Mickey Mantle had broken the Ruth mark instead of the decidedly sullen Maris, would there have been any lingering issues about legitimacy, asterisks, or Cooperstown?

A similar battle of personalities, almost entirely driven by television, would play itself out again on the baseball diamond during the 1998 rendition of the Mantle-Maris battle when Sammy Sosa and Mark McGwire duked it out for the home run crown and a new baseball home run record. The summer of 1998 is now tarnished by the steroid era, but at the time Sosa was extremely engaging, even playful, while McGwire, though not a villain, was more down to business and less outgoing. McGwire outdueled Sosa that year, but many would remember the smiles and antics of Sammy more fondly — at least until he feigned a lack of English at the subsequent Congressional steroid hearings, itself a dubious threshold moment for baseball on television.

12

Holy Cow

In 1947 the "point-contact" transistor amplifier was invented as the direct result of research conducted by three Bell Laboratories scientists who would eventually receive the Nobel Prize in Physics (1956) for their efforts. They were members of a "solid state physics group" at Bell Labs, charged with replacing the cumbersome vacuum tubes that were used inside radio and television receivers.[1] Their solution was a compact, efficient solid-state replacement — and thus the "transistor" was born.

When the solid-state transistor was commercialized for radio, the portable transistor radio swept across America, including the L.A. Coliseum and beaches of southern California where it helped spread the popularity of Beach Boys music, Vin Scully, and baseball. Bell Labs patented the new device and then unveiled a prototype during a news conference on June 30, 1948. The first practical application of the transistor to radio was accomplished by Texas Instruments in 1954 with a Regency TR-1 model driven by four Texas Instruments' transistors and manufactured by the Regency division of a company in Indianapolis called "IDEA."[2] (Note: The 1978 Intel 8086 microprocessor had 29,000 transistors; the 2003 Intel Pentium-4 had 55 million.) Remarkably, the major radio manufacturers were not interested. Only when the Texas Instruments model sold 150,000 units at $49.95 (well over $300 each in current dollars) did others, like Raytheon and Zenith, begin to follow. When Japanese manufacturers lowered the price to under $10 in the 1960s, the transistor radio exploded in popularity.

Why was the transistor so revolutionary? Without transistors, the broadcast signal sent to the radio receiver had to be amplified by means of the vacuum tube system in the chassis. The tubes were relatively large, unwieldy, needed lots of electricity, and sometimes burned out like a light bulb. As a result, the original portable radios were big (the size of a toaster oven), heavy, and needed two kinds of batteries, one to heat the tube filaments and one to power the signal circuits. The transistor radio was not much larger than a couple of cigarette packs and weighed eight ounces or less. Some could fit inside a shirt pocket and all operated on standard flashlight batteries — although the square-shaped nine-volt battery would soon be invented specifically for transistor radios.

While the transistor radio may have accelerated Scully's popularity by spreading his voice across southern California, Scully himself supplied the necessary talent. In many ways Vin Scully was a broadcasting enigma. His career spanned well over half a century, but even after 50 years the award-winning broadcaster Dick Enberg could still observe that Scully goes "against the flow," calling him "deep and authentic, oblivious to fad."[3] Vin Scully won every sports broadcasting award worth winning. The press box at Dodger Stadium was named for him and, remarkably, the Dodgers print ads often featured Vin Scully's name ahead of the team name.

Sixty seasons after Scully announced his first Dodgers game, the *Wall Street Journal* ran a piece on September 3, 2009, finding Vin Scully to be the most verbose of all the *recent* baseball announcers. The survey was based on words spoken during one full non-scoring inning, and though limited in scope and less than scientific, it reveals an interesting comparison among major contemporary broadcasters. Scully led everyone with 143.51 words clocked per minute, while the second-place Dan McLaughlin of the Cardinals came in much lower at just 109.93. The Royals' Ryan Lefebvre was under 100 at 96.71 and the Braves' Chip Caray was measured at just 78.80, but they were both virtual chatter boxes when compared to Ken Harrelson of the White Sox who spoke 70.90 words per minute, Gary Thorne at 66.97 for the Orioles, or the Padres Mark Neely at 61.64. Last place was Duane Kuiper for the Giants, who offered a paltry 55.44 words per minute for his listeners. Both New York announcers were in the bottom half, with the Yankees' Michael Kay and the Mets' Gary Cohen both logged at just over 73 words.[4]

Scully, though, remained the only major baseball broadcaster to still work alone, partly explaining his proclivity as a fundamental need for words to fill air time, but conversely Scully's gift for gab may be the likely reason he needed no partner in the first place. Going solo for an entire ballgame is very difficult for obvious reasons, there being no one to share ideas with or to engage in conversational chatter while someone else helps carry the load. But there is one overriding benefit if one is able to do it: the *perceived* conversation thus comes between the broadcaster, Scully, and each listener, inevitably personalizing the broadcast like none other. When others are in the booth, the listener or viewer eavesdrops on their conversation, but does not participate in that banter the same as when the announcer speaks directly with the audience. This likely contributes to Scully's overwhelming, and enduring, popularity among his audience members—in short, he engages them directly.

The "voice of the Dodgers," however, was not merely verbose all those years, he was also glib. "He pitches as though he's double parked," Scully observed while watching Cardinals' fireballer Bob Gibson shut out the Dodgers in 1972. "It's a mere moment in a man's life between an All-Star Game and an Old-Timer's Game," Scully once said, showing his philosophical side.[5] Broadcasting baseball for the better part of six decades, Vin Scully could not help but learn to fall in love with the game of baseball. "Football is to baseball as blackjack is to bridge," he said fondly. "One is the quick jolt; the other the deliberate, slow-paced game of skill. But never was a sport more ideally suited to television than baseball. It's all there in front of you. It's theatre, really."[6] Although reflecting on televised baseball, Scully was also really describing baseball on the radio. It is a game that is easy to visualize from descriptive words. The NFL and NBA games are exciting, to be sure, but they can also be a blur on the radio. As noted, baseball's pace is "quintessential radio."

Football and basketball do better on television because of their respective fast action. Because the eye can pick up and discern the frenzy faster than it can be described, both sports feature speed and action in an almost video-game style. Scully was impressed by how the one-shot image of baseball can be captured on the screen, and he is right from the perspective of a baseball purist — but baseball is not especially entertaining on television for the same reason that it works so well on radio. The old black-and-white images of baseball on television were necessary to see the game, but not particularly appealing to the eye. Some of this changed, though, with the advent of color television. But baseball experienced a quantum leap in visual appeal when wide-screen high-definition television began to display the stunning beauty of both the ballparks and the game itself, even though football and basketball are played "horizontally" in the footprint of the wide screen image.

Scully understood the romance, wistful images, and historic perspective of the game. He loved baseball and baseball players. Although Scully grew to dislike the loneliness of road games — and he took many hundreds of road trips during his career — he still professed his love for the game: "I really love baseball. The guys and the game."[7] It is no wonder that Scully's antithesis was a boxing-turned-football man, Howard Cosell, who not only spoke slowly, deliberately, and often *down* to his audience, he did not particularly like baseball players: "I have found most baseball players to be afflicted with tobacco-chewing minds."[8]

Cosell, though, added commentary, controversy, and color first to his boxing broadcasts, then to NFL games thanks to ABC's *Monday Night Football* inspiration, and eventually to baseball as well. Just as Scully perpetuated the one-man booth, others were bringing in whole teams to replicate the successful banter that had evolved among Howard Cosell, Don Meredith, and Keith Jackson, the latter supplying the original play-by-play for the Monday night NFL games. The typical baseball broadcast grew to feature two announcers, one to call the play-by-play and the other to add "color." The color man is usually a former player who provides special insight to the game and shares a number of stories from his playing career and baseball history.

What makes a good announcer for baseball? Mitch Rosen, program director for WSCR sports radio in Chicago, which carries White Sox games in addition to a full lineup of sports talk, says "teach me something." Rosen feels the good announcers are conversational, fan friendly, and can bring insight to the game, with the best ones having a personality that extends beyond the mere play-by-play delivery to become "a summer friend" for the listener.[9]

Announcers like Jack Buck, Harry Caray, Mel Allen, Jack Brickhouse, Vin Scully, and others became that summer friend during the long baseball season. The color man grew from Phil Rizzuto to Don Drysdale, Tony Kubek, Joe Garagiola, Joe Morgan, and many others, including one, Bob Uecker, who actually enhanced his prolific broadcast career by making fun of his less-than-modest baseball prowess on the field.

Phil Rizzuto played 15 years for the Yankees, winning the league MVP in 1950, but he experienced a resurgence after his retirement like few others in pro sports when he went on to broadcast Yankees games on radio and television for 40 years beginning in 1957. Rizzuto brought energy and warmth to the booth, adopting the "holy cow" exclamation even before Harry Caray made it famous in St. Louis and Chicago. He would chomp on cannoli between innings and even make fun of himself leaving the game early by referring to his anxious wife Cora or the crowded George Washington Bridge, which was on his way home.

On the field Rizzuto had played with many of the Yankee greats. His rookie year

1941 was the fabled season of Joe DiMaggio's 56-game hitting streak, described by Ted Williams as perhaps "the greatest batting achievement of all." Over the ensuing years Rizzuto played alongside 1942 MVP Joe Gordon, Nick Etten who led the league in RBIs in 1945, Allie Reynolds, Johnny Mize, Whitey Ford, Hank Bauer, Yogi Berra, Ralph Houk, future American League president Bobby Brown, and the darling of the Yankees, Mickey Mantle. But in the broadcast booth, Rizzuto's lineups were just as impressive, with broadcast partners like icons Mel Allen (1957–64) and Red Barber (1957–66) in addition to Joe Garagiola, Bill White, Bobby Murcer, Jim Kaat, Billy Martin, Tom Seaver, and others.

Rizzuto saw and called much of baseball history during his Yankees tenure behind the microphone, like the infamous pine-tar game when George Brett went ballistic on national television. But perhaps no moment was bigger than the Roger Maris home run on October 1, 1961, when Rizzuto was working the game for WCBS Radio: "Here's the windup, fastball, hit deep to right, this could be it. Way back there. Holy cow, he did it! Sixty-one HOME RUNS! They're fighting for the ball out there! Holy cow!"[10]

In 1964 the Yankees lost the World Series to the St. Louis Cardinals, and then endured a 12-year Series drought. When they finally made it back in 1976, Rizzuto was there, too, broadcasting for NBC network television alongside Joe Garagiola and Tony Kubek where he again participated in baseball history. The 1976 NBC broadcast was the last to feature the local broadcaster of each pennant winner, after which the network stuck to its regular national announcers.

Rizutto was charming, silly, fun, and excitable. He was a great player, a great broadcaster, a great fan, and a great teammate. That latter trait, ironically, seems to have contributed to the end of his broadcast career. When Mickey Mantle died in 1995, the corporate suits at WPIX — or maybe it was the Yankees brass, who had the right of approval over their broadcasters— refused to let Rizzuto, the quintessential Yankee, fan, broadcaster, and teammate, attend the funeral. They demanded that he broadcast a road game in Boston instead, which devastated Rizutto, who initially obliged but could take it no more and left the booth during the game. He announced his retirement soon after that, although fan reaction and the voice of reason eventually won his job back again for the 1996 season. But it would not be the same. Perhaps Rizutto should have known better. After all, he had already seen the cold heart of corporate broadcasting at work when Mel Allen was unceremoniously fired on December 17, 1964. The media, of course, is a business, complete with the incumbent glory and failings of any bureaucratic enterprise.

Radio may have gained traction gradually like Frick's "little cat feet," but television burst onto the scene in "living" black-and-white splendor. In 1925 most baseball executives, except for William Wrigley and later Larry MacPhail, had feared that radio would one day empty the stands. They were wrong, for radio broadened baseball's appeal and caused an upward jolt to the attendance figures. Television would eventually prove different, yet the owners would find themselves not caring. The difference was money.

At first television hurt the minor leagues, where local fans could suddenly watch actual big league games instead of going the local ballpark. But it also had a depressing effect on major league baseball itself. In 1947, the year of Jackie Robinson's debut, all of major league attendance was at 19,874,539. In 1949, when there were fewer than four million TV sets in the United States, the big league gate was at 20 million. Just twelve years later, the magical season of 1961, total attendance was actually lower at just 18,894,518.[11] Television gained popularity in the interim, causing big league attendance to plummet to only 14 million in both 1952 and 1953, evoking the angst of National League president Warren Giles who feared, "We'll be playing with only 500 people in the stands and everybody else watching on TV."[12] Gate receipts rebounded only after the Maris-Mantle duel when attendance ballooned to 21,375,215 in 1962, then it crept gradually higher through the 1960s, reaching 27,229,666 at decade's end. The year of the next major home run milestone (Hank Aaron's career mark) in 1974, after the big leagues began to expand with more teams, attendance was up to 30,025,608.

Although both television and attendance were mostly on the upswing from the 1970s until the 1994 labor action and unprecedented cancellation of the World Series, the growth of gate receipts was dwarfed by the exponential increase in television money that was pouring into major league baseball. During the 20-year span ending in 1990, the national television revenue to the big leagues grew 1,742 percent. While attendance figures almost doubled during the same span, national TV money exploded by a factor of ten times. Not coincidentally, so did player salaries, keeping exact pace expanding by an almost identical 1,741 percent.[13] This was not merely a coincidence, although the similarity in those numbers is striking, for it was broadcasting that began to drive those salaries in the first place.

Expanding the ratings was one reason, but little of that would occur without the necessary technical advances to make television broadcasts more interesting. At first, even the worst flickering images were fascinating to watch, but soon the one-dimensional nature of the baseball broadcasts grew monotonous. Fortunately for television in general and baseball in particular, portable radios were not the only things growing smaller. Ironically, the television sets themselves started with small screens but then got bigger, but on the other end of the spectrum were the television cameras. They began to shrink as early as 1957, as noted by an NBC *Game of the Week* representative who stated that the camera operators "would be equipped with an ultra-portable (cigar box size) camera that 'can even be carried into the dugout to get a picture of Casey Stengel twitching.'"[14] The "twitching" comment is especially charming in the context of baseball history, hinting at why baseball, a game of great humor with very colorful personalities, became the national sport in the first place.

Even the idea of placing a camera on the field, let alone in the dugout with Stengel himself, was a breakthrough innovation. A 1957 pre-season game in Houston between the Indians and Giants featured a bulky caged-in camera about a dozen feet behind the home plate umpire. Hugh Beach, producer-director for the CBS counterpart to NBC's *Game of the Week*, was especially exited about the on-field experiment and the future of baseball broadcasting: "Never before in the history of big-league baseball have so many fans been given so close a view." Others, though, feared that television might be criticized for placing too much emphasis on camera gimmicks instead of reporting the game itself. "We are certainly not going to neglect the coverage of baseball games just to get cute with cameras," reported the *New York Times*, quoting one concerned official. But NBC's Harry Coyle noted the importance of technological progress, saying, "We had only three cameras covering baseball back in 1947, two of which could be expected to go on the blink during any game."[15] A former director for the CBS games recounted how cameramen sometimes didn't even know where first base was in the early days of television, and well into the 1950s there was still much debate about much the broadcasters should — or should not — talk during broadcasts.

The talking debate seems incredulous given modern sports broadcasting techniques that engage two or three commentators at once, thus relegating dead air on radio and television entirely to the distant past. The *Times* quoted broadcast icon Mel Allen, who was skeptical about too much talk: "When the TV picture tells the whole story, no talk is needed. But, let's say there is a ground ball to the shortstop that on TV looks like a routine play; but, at the last moment the ball takes a bad hop. The viewer on TV can't see this. So the announcer should then tell what happened."[16]

But focusing only on New York, Chicago, and the national networks fails to tell the whole broadcasting story. In the late 1950s there were eight National League teams, and five of them still televised no home games at all. The search for modernized stadiums and expansive parking lots was driving much of the baseball business more than the emerging implications of television. In the 1950s Los Angeles, San Francisco, Milwaukee, Baltimore, and Kansas City all lured teams in search of new audiences and exciting new stadiums to boost revenues, yet few teams were considering the long term implications of television on the revenue stream. One reason is that for most ballclubs there was no meaningful television revenue in the first place. According to journalist John Helyar's 1994 study of the business of baseball, *Lords of the Realm*, broadcast rights accounted for just 17 percent of baseball revenue in 1956; moreover, there was still little material improvement nine years later, as "even in 1965, only four teams topped $1 million in local annual broadcast revenues: the Yankees, Mets, Dodgers, and Astros."[17] Houston, a new expansion team at the time, reported the most television revenue at $1.8 million while the Senators enjoyed the least at just $300,000. The Cubs, even with their large market, WGN television, and the Wrigley family's vision, were still just average in 1965 at $500,000 per year.

As the 1960s emerged, skeptical owners largely looked down on the idea of local big league broadcasts, for they still were unable to reconcile the issue of broadcasting versus gate attendance. The owners were less concerned about networks, though, even though the networks would pay teams based on the frequency of their national appearances. In 1964, when the New York Yankees were the biggest draw, there were many such appearances by the nationally followed Yankees who were still riding the coattails of their legend, lore, and high profile players. The total network payments to the Yankees in 1964 were still just $550,000, but that sum was five times the amount paid to the next highest teams, the Cardinals and the Phillies, a ratio that was at the very least intriguing.[18] The Cardinals, interestingly, then beat the Yankees in the 1964 World Series, the effective end to Yankee dynasties until great New York teams would return many years later; but even at that time the Yankee television revenues would remain relatively golden.

After 1964, televised baseball took a quantum leap in revenues and importance, but it started with an unlikely source, the NFL's brash young commissioner, Pete Rozelle. When Bert Bell died in 1959, the National Football League was left without a commissioner. In January 1960, the owners surprised the sports world by turning to Pete Rozelle, who was just 33 years old at the time but had already compiled a worthy sports resume. Rozelle had begun his sports career as a student publicist for his own school's football team at the University of San Francisco, after which he marketed Melbourne's 1956 Olympics for a Los Angeles public relations company, then became a dynamic general manager for the struggling Los Angeles Rams football team which he soon turned into a sparkling business success. Even so, Rozelle's youth got in the way, for according to published reports (from ESPN and elsewhere) it still took 23 ballots for the owners to turn to Rozelle who, after that many votes, may have been a compromise candidate.[19]

Whether a political compromise or not, Rozelle was nonetheless a savvy public relations executive, and he not only knew football, he was very interested in the emergence of sports broadcasting. At the time, baseball was making early inroads with local and national telecasts, but the rival American Football League, a competing start-up that was an aggressive marketer, had managed to cut some promising television deals that Rozelle astutely saw as the future for NFL football's own revenue streams. The AFL model was to package its team rights and sell them together to network television, an approach Rozelle felt could be even more successful with the more established and visible NFL. But there were significant roadblocks in the way, for in those days the NFL had only 12 teams playing a 12-game season, with few of them having television deals or even knowing much about television. Attendance wasn't very good at NFL games so the owners had to be convinced that television would not make it worse. And one more thing: Rozelle's concept of expanding the AFL approach by bundling, selling, and sharing television rights and revenues was a likely violation of federal antitrust laws.

The Sherman Act of 1890 was established to punish and prevent the monopolistic trusts of early mega-entrepreneurs like Rockefeller's Standard Oil and Andrew Carnegie's steel companies. There were provisions in the law that not only gave the federal government enforcement authority, but the Act also provided civil causes of action and treble damage penalties for cases brought and won by wounded competitors and the general public. There were two elements of the Act to contend with, one punishing monopolists and one addressing antitrust violations. Illegal "monopolies" occur when one enterprise attains dominant control of a market through illegal or illicit means, but an "antitrust" violation occurs when two or more enterprises conspire to injure competition. An antitrust violation is officially defined as "a contract, combination, or conspiracy to restrain trade," and it does not require proof that an entire market is dominated, just that the conspirators got together and injured competition in some way.

At least until 2009, when the NFL began to argue before the Supreme Court that its multiple teams all act together as one giant entity (*American Needle v. NFL*) (an argument the NFL eventually lost), professional sports leagues comprising multiple independently owned teams were always deemed to be multiple entities acting in concert. In such case, the Rozelle television scheme to prepackage and market all the television rights deals together would indeed be a "contract, combination, or conspiracy" in restraint of trade. Rozelle and the NFL found this out the hard way after inking a network television contract with CBS, only to have it voided by a federal court. Undaunted, Rozelle began to lobby Congress to modify the antitrust laws specifically for national broadcast rights, arguing that the law as written would prevent the NFL from showing more games on a national basis. Congress agreed, passing the Sports Broadcasting Act of 1961 (15 USC 1291), exempting professional sports leagues from federal antitrust provisions that otherwise would block the leagues from bundling and selling their team broadcast rights in one package, even though that would prevent individual teams from negotiating their own deals with network competitors.

Rozelle displayed great political acumen in obtaining the new law, which required a good deal of savvy and deal making, a skill that Rozelle put to good use five years later when two of the most powerful members of Congress were from the same state, Louisiana: Senator Russell Long and Congressman Hale Boggs. First elected to the House in 1941 where he helped pass the interstate highway system bill in 1956, Boggs participated on the Warren Commission in 1963 to 1964, and served as majority whip from 1961 to 1970, just as the Sports Broadcasting Act was being passed.[20] By 1966 the NFL sought to merge with the competing AFL which had put a dent in NFL ratings with such high-flying teams as the New York Jets and Oakland Raiders, but it needed another Congressional exemption from the antitrust laws. The House Judiciary Committee chairperson, Emanuel Celler, whose committee oversaw such antitrust matters, never would have approved such a move since he held a grudge against teams and sports leagues in general for the departure of his beloved Brooklyn Dodgers.[21] So Rozelle sought the help of Boggs who amended the Sports Broadcasting Act with a one-sentence modification to allow the NFL-AFL merger with antitrust impunity. It is no coincidence whatsoever that the next NFL expansion team was the New Orleans Saints, awarded by the NFL on November 1, 1966 — the day after Halloween, which just happens to be All Saints Day.

"Congress sanctioning the single-network deal is the most significant thing Pete [Rozelle] ever did," said Art Modell, a former NFL owner of the Cleveland Browns.[22] The stunning success of NFL national broadcasting after 1961 was a stellar model for all leagues, including baseball which, conveniently, already had its own antitrust exemption. Perhaps to hedge baseball's own bet, major league baseball was nonetheless included in the Sports Broadcasting Act exemptions, although in all likelihood baseball would not have needed the additional legal protection at the time. But baseball did notice how the NFL was exploiting television, and that did make an impact on how the game approached broadcasting. Rozelle's original pact with CBS was for $9.3 million over two years, revenue that would be shared equally among the NFL clubs.[23] This was far short of the multi-billion dollar deals 30 and 40 years later, but it laid the groundwork for one of the great value-added approaches to sports leagues: television and revenue sharing. It must have been a hard sell for Rozelle at first, for he had to talk the big market teams into letting go of their own lucrative television deals. They did, and the rest became a very lucrative chapter in the history of sports broadcasting. Under Rozelle, the NFL then leveraged its new national exposure and revenue streams to expand from 12 teams to 28 clubs during his tenure, thus multiplying league profits even more.

None of this was lost on major league baseball. While the Yankees were reaping a nice $550,000 for their own broadcast rights in 1964, this was nothing compared to the multi-million-dollar deals the NFL was raking in with a different philosophy: the rising tide lifts all boats. When Tigers owner John Fetzer rocked the baseball boat by encouraging the game to follow the NFL model, the league soon inked a $5.7 million deal to feature an ABC version of the *Game of the Week*. Baseball was still lagging football, but it was learning, for the biggest factor behind such a quantum leap was that the owners, for the first time, would allow these national broadcasts to be viewed in big market cities. No longer was baseball willing to protect the existing big or small market franchises at the expense of losing a major national revenue stream. Major league baseball had experienced an epiphany. Under this new deal, each baseball team received $300,000, which was three times what the average had been when the teams were left to their own individual broadcast negotiating. Only the Yankees would get less, but over time the Yankees would certainly make up for it through a strong national draw and some very astute television moves by future owner George Steinbrenner.[24]

ABC, however, did not prove very successful in developing ratings and sponsors for baseball. After the 1965 season, NBC won the bidding and took the national broadcasting away from ABC, showing its own broadcasting and negotiating skills by landing the entire baseball package including the All-Star Game, the World Series, and the *Game of the Week*. At $11.8 million per year this new NBC deal was much more lucrative than the ABC contract had been, and baseball was on its way. That number expanded to $49.5 million for the 1969–71 rights package, then exploded yet again to $92.8 million by the end of the 1970s.[25]

Baseball had come a long way. As recently as 1955, the *New York Times'* Jack Gould had been lambasting how baseball appeared on color television. "During the course of the afternoon, the sun and clouds kept moving and the shadows lengthened," he wrote, describing the color telecast of the Yankees-Dodgers game on September 28, 1955, the first-ever World Series game to be shown in color. "This led to constantly changing lighting conditions with which the color cameras could not fully cope." Most shots, Gould complained, were marred by harsh tints that wore on one's eyes, then Gould confessed he was personally glad to return to the more comfortable black-and-white images of baseball. Gould actually was so worked up over the broadcast that he took a shot at seasoned broadcaster Mel Allen, too. "Before he [Allen] tired out a bit, he had one of his characteristic afternoons, a matinee of the cliché," complained Gould, who went on to ridicule Allen's redundancies like "a ballplayer's ballplayer" or overstatements like "America's greatest classic." The second half of the game was called by Vin Scully, clearly a favorite of Gould, who affectionately reported that Scully "let the Yankees and Dodgers play the game, which was refreshing."[26] Perhaps Scully had not yet perfecting his league-leading verbose style.

Over and above the passage of the Sports Broadcasting Act, the year 1961 proved a landmark for sports and other broadcasting. It was on April 29 that ABC's long-running and acclaimed *Wide World of Sports* debuted, followed less than two weeks later by FCC chairman Newton Minow's historic observation about television as a "vast wasteland." By July 11, 1962, the Telstar I satellite began its first transatlantic transmission, and by 1963 television was finding its legs in every venue from music to news, drama, and sports, with each of the following milestones taking place in 1963 alone:

June 7:   the Rolling Stones debuted on television
Sept. 2: the network evening news was expanded to 30 minutes from 15
Sept. 7: the Beatles made their first United States television appearance
Sept. 7: *American Bandstand* moved to California and was shown weekly
Nov. 22: the aftermath of the John F. Kennedy assassination, funeral, and Jack
     Ruby murder of Lee Harvey Oswald, which itself was captured on television[27]

It was also in 1963 when the NFL expanded its national broadcasts, chef Julia Child debuted on television, Virginia Graham began to host the groundbreaking daytime talk show *Girl Talk*, and *Let's Make a Deal* began a 16-year daytime run.[28] Television was not only finding itself, it was taking quantum leaps precisely when Roger Maris broke the vaunted Ruth record (1961), Jackie Robinson was inducted into the Baseball Hall of Fame (1962), Willie Mays dominated the All-Star Game (1963), the Mets played their last game in the Polo Grounds (1963), and the Yankee World Series dynasty was ended by the Cardinals (1964).

By 1965, televised baseball was good enough to spur controversy over how the game was being called by the umpires—a debate that would gain momentum every year until major league baseball finally considered limited instant replay review in 2008. Again following the lead of professional football broadcasts, baseball utilized the isolated camera during an ABC nationally televised game between the Mets and Giants at Shea Stadium on April 17, 1965. This telecast also featured slow motion and videotape—both of which concerned baseball purists who felt that television could second-guess and one day overrule or replace the umpires. Although many of these concerns proved accurate as technology improved, none of those fears were realized during that first game. Indeed, the video replays confirmed the accuracy of the umpires, as reported by the *New York Times*: "The anticipated spectre of the camera disputing umpire's calls did not occur. Runners who were called out were really out; the camera was either too far away from the plate or did not have the proper angle."[29]

By then the isolated camera and video replays were common in football and accepted by the viewers and media, who felt that the diversified nature of the action, which was hard to follow in the blur of activity on the field, was good for football but not appropriate for televised baseball. "There is nothing that complicated in watching a baseball game," wrote the *Times*, "the spectator only needs to follow the ball." The *Times* conceded that once the isolated camera caught an interesting big lead off first base by Giants runner Jim Hart, who was then picked off by the Mets catcher who had seen the same thing, all of which was caught by the isolated camera.[30] But the *Times* found this less than compelling and dismissed it, missing the point about this being an exception that should have proven the rule of sports and baseball coverage. Soon such video angles and replays would be at the heart of all baseball telecasts, not just an infrequent diversion.

Viewers, sponsors, and team owners were not the only ones noticing the impact of broadcasting on the game and its revenues. In 1965 the players took note, too. The Players Association was still weak in 1965, at that time devoting much of its attention to funding a modest player pension plan. There was virtually no baseball free agency in those days, major league baseball was exempt from the antitrust laws, and the players union had not yet aggressively wielded the labor laws in any meaningful or adversarial way. For 11 years the player pension plan had been funded by a 60 percent share of broadcast revenues from the World Series and All-Star Game. This had amounted to a nominal source of income until 1965, when suddenly the pension share jumped to $1.6 million. But this sum itself was not the problem, it was the rate of expansion that both caught the players' attention and elevated the concern of the owners. Pitcher Robin Roberts, a player rep from the National League, confided to other players that he could see the number escalating to almost ten times that amount at $15 million annually or more. But he was also becoming discouraged, since the players received no benefit from the ABC television deal that did not include the All-Star or World Series games. Roberts resigned as a player rep, but he continued to influence his successor and even asked if he could attend the player rep meetings at Houston in late 1965, where Roberts floated the idea of hiring a full-time director for the union.

A union search committee was formed comprised of Roberts, his successor rep Bob Friend, Harvey Kuehn, and Jim Bunning.[31] Kuehn had been the AL Rookie of the Year in 1953, led the league in number of hits four times, and later was Manager of the Year in 1982. Bunning was a dominant pitcher who hurled a no-hitter in 1958 for Detroit and then pitched a perfect game in 1964 for the Phillies, before winning a Kentucky seat in

Congress in 1986 and then being elected to the Senate in 1998 where he remained until deciding to retire at the end of his last term in 2010.[32]

At first the committee and its new leader, former legal counsel Judge Cannon who was close to the Pittsburgh ownership, mostly maintained the status quo, afraid to rock the boat because there was always a perception that the owners might yank the pension plan altogether. The owners, after all, were known for being both tough and reactionary, a rather dangerous combination where the players were concerned. After the 1957 season, for example, Mickey Mantle was offered a pay cut for not winning the rare Triple Crown, even though 1957 was in many ways a better Mantle year, and after the 1966 season the Yankees fired sportscasting great Red Barber for asking the television camera to scan the vast number of vacant seats at Yankee Stadium — an impressive array of 66,587 *empty* seats, to be sure, during one fateful day in September.[33] The Yankees said it was for Barber's broadcasting "style," but no credible baseball source believes that whitewashed version. A multi-decade broadcasting career that in many ways helped invent sports casting itself was flushed because of one alleged miscue — and the retribution of a reactionary management team still worried about the effects of television on attendance. Armed with the antitrust exemption and an iron-clad reserve clause, the owners had little to fear from the players, and their willingness to wield the proverbial ax showed it.

If sports managers and coaches are destined to be fired often, sports broadcasters might be a close second. Many have longevity, of course, but many more are summarily dismissed at the whims of management when the perceived right time comes — as it inevitably does for most. The modern sports announcer is not employed directly by the local team, but is hired by the sports broadcasting station that carries the games. However, the typical rights contract between the station and the team gives the team management the right to approve or disapprove of the announcers who call its games. This has a chilling effect on what the local announcers say about the team, creating a dilemma for those who want to criticize the club for the betterment of the team or to appease the listeners who are thinking the same thing. There is no similar formal control over national broadcasts, giving the national announcers more independence and objectivity, but there nonetheless are powers of persuasion that can be effective.

One baseball broadcaster who experienced it all was the fabled Harry Caray, whose resonant "holy cow!" still reverberates among the hallowed memories of older baseball audiences throughout the Midwest. Harry began broadcasting St. Louis Cardinals games in 1945, and within a few years he was featured on the flagship station KMOX, which led the largest network of baseball broadcasts in the country, flinging Harry's voice and Cardinals lore throughout the middle part of the country. Harry Caray was an outgoing, hard drinking, lover of baseball, a unique broadcaster by any measure — but most of all he was a showman. Harry often pushed the envelope on air, daring to criticize where others feared to tread. Known for his seventh-inning renditions of "Take Me Out to the Ball Game," Harry Caray was an entertainer who clearly loved the game of baseball.[34]

Harry Caray spent much of his early career calling the games of Cardinals' Hall of Famer Stan Musial, then later he broadcast St. Louis games during one of the team's most productive eras that featured such Cardinal stars as Bob Gibson, catcher Tim McCarver (later a nationally known broadcaster himself), Ken Boyer, Curt Flood, Lou Brock, Orlando Cepeda — and even Roger Maris, who helped power the Cardinals to the World Series in 1967 and 1968. But the real stars for both seasons were slugger Cepeda who in

1967 was the first unanimous MVP in National League history, speedster Lou Brock who stole 52 bases in 1967 and 62 more in 1968, Curt Flood (.335 batting in 1967), and power pitcher Bob Gibson whose feats from the mound are more than legendary. Bob Gibson won just 13 regular season games for the 101–60 Cardinals in 1967 (having missed almost two months to a broken leg), but he won three World Series games that year against Boston, giving up a total of just three runs on 14 hits for all three games combined, leading the Cardinals to the world title. The nearly unhittable Gibson was even better in 1968, winning 22 games (13 by shutout), leading the league in strikeouts (268) and ERA (a sizzling 1.12) en route to both the Cy Young Award and league MVP honors. Then he was matched against Tigers' sensation Denny McLain (31–6) in the Series, getting the best of McLain twice before losing the final contest as the Tigers eked out a Series victory in seven games.

Harry Caray was there through it all, riding the Cardinals success from the booth, cheerleading the team and belting out his trademark "holy cow" at key moments when he chose to punctuate his home run call that began with "it might be, it could be, it IS." But Caray also invited controversy with his candid style whereby he thoroughly identified with his teams, broadcasting in the first person "we" while referring to the other team as "they." He was a homer, but only from a fan's perspective, not management's, for Harry could not restrain himself when stupid mistakes were made on the field or otherwise. Suddenly, while on top of the baseball world, Harry Caray was fired in 1969 — the news reportedly came by telephone, reaching Harry in a saloon.

Why was Harry Caray fired by the Cardinals? This has proven to be one of the mysteries of baseball broadcasting. No one seems to be sure, but most stories point to a number of personal indiscretions. Stan Musial once called Harry a "party animal," so maybe his overall lifestyle was part of the cause. Those who believe sexual indiscretions were the reason point to stories about an affair with the wife of August Busch III, essentially the top boss' daughter-in-law. Others believe that Harry finally proved to be a risky loose cannon who was too much for the Cardinals management. Harry himself publicly preferred the affair version, finding it more flattering.

Another possibility — sheer speculation — might have had something to do with Curt Flood. Harry was fired in October 1969, the same month that the Cardinals shocked baseball by dumping outfielder Curt Flood, who was traded to the Phillies for Dick Allen. Flood was devastated and soon sued major league baseball to reverse the game's bizarre antitrust exemption that allowed owners to treat players like chattel or, as Dick Allen himself put it, like slaves. Harry was a fan, an emotional person who could criticize the players but who also loved those players. Could this trade have inspired Caray to say something to management?

Most likely there was no single cause, although the affair, if there was one, may have been the last straw among a string of annoyances. Harry was already a rock in management's shoe, but the affair would have provided the leverage to push him out the door. Chicagoan Charlie Finley then hired Harry to do Oakland games in 1970, but it took Harry less than one year to irk Finley, so Harry lasted only one season with the Athletics. "That shit he pulled in St. Louis didn't go over here," explained Finley, a rough and tumble businessman who had little patience for the likes of Harry Caray's antics.[35]

Harry landed in Chicago to broadcast White Sox games beginning with the 1971 season. He was paired with outspoken former Red Sox star Jimmy Piersall, together making an acerbic but very entertaining broadcast team. The pair proved a little too entertaining when team play was criticized, and Harry was again fired, this time by John Allyn of the Sox. Then baseball man Bill Veeck, himself a showman in the P.T. Barnum mold, bought the White Sox and rehired Caray. Veeck is the man who once featured midget Eddie Gaedel at the plate for the St. Louis Browns, got the idea for ivy on the outfield wall at Chicago's Wrigley Field, once put the White Sox players in shorts, and installed the exploding scoreboard — so the act of hiring Harry back was hardly out of character.

By 1982 Harry was gone again, but this time he left on his own for the crosstown Chicago Cubs, where Harry's career began all over again on superstation WGN-TV where fans across the country could follow the Cubs and Harry Caray. By this time Caray was a caricature of himself, his massive black-rimmed glasses are still a trademark, still spoofed in 2010 and counting on NBC's *Saturday Night Live*. At Wrigley he continued a tradition that had begun with the Sox, leading the entire crowd in a rendition of "Take Me Out to the Ball Game" after the top of the seventh inning. Harry had often sung the song to himself, but one day Veeck got the idea to pipe it live into the stadium and the rest is baseball history. The Cubs still follow the tradition, even though Harry himself died in 1998 at just 78 years of age, by featuring celebrity singers to carry on, including these, among hundreds:

Jack Black	Russell Crowe
Mel Gibson	Cuba Gooding, Jr.
Julia Louis-Dreyfus	Jay Leno
Bernie Mac	Ann-Margret
Bill Murray	Jeremy Piven
Harold Ramis	Tim Robbins
Muhammad Ali	George Foreman
Chuck Berry	Peter Frampton
Mark Cuban	Donald Trump[36]

Some stars with Chicago roots have appeared multiple times: Jim Belushi (3), John Cusack (5), John Mahoney (3), Joe Mantegna (4), Gary Sinise (4), Vince Vaughn (4), and others. And some have included the biggest names in baseball broadcasting: Jack Buck, Bob Uecker, Ernie Harwell, Chip Caray, and Vin Scully. Those performances were not always a good time, though. Mike Ditka butchered the song as bad as anyone, and Richard Dreyfuss, who had not even seen a baseball game since 1988, was wholly clueless.[37]

But Harry pressed on. As he aged, he began to mispronounce player names and other words, slaughtering the English language, which the fans actually found charming, not offensive. In addition, Harry could not resist saying various words backward, just for kicks. He opened a highly successful restaurant, which still exists north of Chicago's Loop, and his statue now stands outside Wrigley Field. Harry Caray was one of a kind, leaving a long and storied broadcasting legacy in two major cities, not to mention the contributions of his son Skip, the voice of the Braves, and grandson Chip, who also did Cubs games for years and then became a national baseball voice as well.[38]

Harry Christopher Carabina — Harry Caray — died on February 18, 1998. A Ford Frick Award winner, Harry offended some, annoyed many, and was the hero of many more. Lost in the hoopla during his life and at his death, though, was Jack Brickhouse, who had broadcast thousands of Cubs games on television beginning long before Harry arrived, and who was a very classy announcer admired by everyone who knew him — so much so that Brickhouse still is regarded by many Chicago purists as the real voice of the Chicago Cubs.

> *Booze, broads and bullshit. If you got all that, what else do you need?*
> — Harry Caray[39]

13

Seashells, Balloons, and Walk-Off Home Runs

I don't believe what I just saw!

— JACK BUCK, 1988[1]

Everyone's favorite uncle around Chicago was a steady broadcaster named Jack Brickhouse. He was a wonderfully nice guy with a low-key delivery who may have seemed a little dull to some, but he was genuine, accessible, and nonjudgmental. His "hey, hey" home run call still echoes faintly through the confines of Wrigley Field, where Jack first called a Cubs game in 1942. He would not announce his last Cubs game until 40 years later, suffering dozens of futile seasons in between, even counting the Cubs' ill-fated 1945 trip to the World Series, where a goat was blamed not only for that loss, but for all lost Cub seasons thereafter.

Brickhouse was mostly a television man broadcasting legions of baseball games, including early assignments for both the White Sox and the Cubs—over 5,000 televised games in all.[2] In 1948, nearly ten percent of all television sets in the United States were in the Chicago area, and WGN television was a leader in early programming. Jack was not originally from Chicago, however; he was yet another baseball man with ties to downstate Peoria where he grew up. In 1924, at just eight years of age, Jack was listening to Illinois play Michigan on the radio when he heard Red Grange, "The Galloping Ghost," score four touchdowns in fewer than 12 minutes of playing time. At that moment the legend of Grange was born, and Jack Brickhouse learned he wanted to be a sports announcer.[3] Over the years he would do just about everything that the stations would ask, including wresting and later a 24-year plum job calling Chicago Bears games with Irv Kupcinet — a Chicago gossip columnist known in national entertainment circles as "Kup"—during the smash-mouth Bears years of Dick Butkus, Gale Sayers, Mike Ditka, and a promising rookie named Walter Payton.

But baseball and Jack Brickhouse were made for each other, and Jack soon became identified with the Chicago Cubs. He lived and died with the team, which in those years mostly involved the latter during a remarkable string of poor Cubs seasons. During his

168

tenure he saw the debut of the fabulous rookie shortstop Ernie Banks who was the first African American Cub, then Jack witnessed Ernie's entire career pass by without winning a pennant. The very first baseball game telecast by satellite was the Telstar broadcast of the Cubs-Phillies game on July 23, 1962, with Jack there at the microphone perched in front of the television cameras.[4] When the great collapse of 1969 saw the Mets come from behind in September to take the pennant and World Series, Jack suffered with all the Cubs—it was as hard on Jack as anyone.

That same year, 1969, would be Harry Caray's last season in St. Louis where he had been a Cardinals fixture for 25 campaigns. Harry would then begin his journey to Chicago's South Side following a one-year stint in Oakland. When he arrived on Chicago's North Side to do Cubs games in 1982, Harry brought his wild and colorful persona, the big black glasses, perpetual tan, luminous white hair — and an ebullient personality brimming with eccentricities. Harry was all personality in contract to the subdued delivery of Jack Brickhouse. Nonetheless, the stellar career of Brickhouse can never be taken from him, for Jack was a long-standing, loyal pro, but Harry was the singing cheerleader who got the statue at Wrigley. Harry deserved his acclaim, but Jack's legacy deserves better than most remember. But all is not fair, as they say, and that applies to love, war, and certainly baseball.

Another great pro who is largely unsung, at least outside Houston, is Milo Hamilton, a Ford Frick Award winner with more than 60 years in broadcasting. Born and educated in Iowa, Hamilton called games for six different big league teams before settling in with Houston in 1985, where he found a quarter-century home as the voice of the Astros. Before that he had stops with the Browns, Cardinals, and Cubs in the 1950s, then the White Sox, Braves, and Pirates during the 1960s and 1970s. From 1980 to 1984 he was back with the Cubs again, a span that included Ryne Sandburg's rookie season and a good Cubs team that almost made the World Series in 1984.[5] During those same years in Chicago, Hamilton also called NBA games for the Bulls, a time when his voice became associated with a new basketball phenomenon named Michael Jordan. A member of the Texas Baseball Hall of Fame, Milo Hamilton was born to broadcast — as a young man he was awarded a degree in radio speech from the University of Iowa and never looked back.

By 2009, Hamilton's broadcast career had spanned numerous baseball milestones including 11 no-hitters, five grand slams by Ernie Banks in one season, Hank Aaron's 715th home run, Barry Bonds' 70th in 2001, and Roger Maris' historic 61st homer in 1961—with Hamilton recreating the latter from a Western Union ticker. Just as importantly, Hamilton won the Texas Toy Cannon Award (named for Astros great Jimmy Wynn) for his community service and a lifetime of raising funds for the March of Dimes, American Cancer Society, Leukemia Society of America, and others.[6]

What was Hamilton's secret? "Preparation," according to an interview in 2010. Add a resonant broadcast voice, a love for the game, and unique insight, and one gets a 60+ year career in baseball broadcasting — almost all of it in the big leagues. "Dead air is not always bad," Milo adds, emphasizing the importance of the game over needless chatter, even in the booth.[7] Milo was around long enough to have re-created road games in the early days, adding sound effects like striking a metronome with a pencil, playing the national anthem in an echo chamber, and announcing lineups with his head in a waste basket to simulate a distant stadium announcer. While broadcasting for WCFL in Chicago with Bob Elson, Milo added curtain-call cheering for the radio as reports came in of

Roger Maris' landmark 61st homer in 1961—then rode the elevator from the studio at Chicago's Merchandise Mart where other riders were perplexed at how he "got back from New York" so fast.[8] As of 2010, Milo Hamilton owned the second longest tenure in baseball broadcasting (including a 26+ year run for the Houston Astros), just behind the soon-to-retire Vin Scully.

If luck is truly the residue of design, as baseball sage Branch Rickey believed, then many baseball broadcasters are living proof. At one time or another most had been in the right place at the right time, yet making their own way, like when the engineer Harold Arlin first stumbled into the KDKA studios in Pittsburgh just because he was curious. Some also had history thrust upon them for the same reason, which is what happened to baseball legend Jack Buck during the first game of the 1988 World Series. Already a sea-soned announcer who had one of the more recognizable baritone voices of the baby boomer generation, especially among sports fans of course, Buck gained sudden national fame for his exuberant home run call on October 15, 1988: "I don't believe what I just saw!" Buck exclaimed, not once but three times. "I don't believe what I just saw!" Neither did Dennis Eckersley, the veteran starter-turned-closer for the Oakland Athletics, who found himself facing pinch-hitter Kirk Gibson in the bottom of the ninth inning, his team leading Tommy Lasorda's Dodgers, 4–3, with two outs and a runner on base.[9]

Oakland had scored all its runs during the second inning when Jose Canseco had clubbed a grand slam off rookie starter Tim Belcher, who was on the mound because the Dodgers' ace Orel Hershiser was fully depleted after pitching in no fewer than four games during a tough playoff series against the Mets. Led by sluggers Mark McGwire and Jose Canseco, the 1988 A's also featured pitching sensation Dave Stewart, who had notched consecutive 20-win seasons, rendering Oakland a formidable opponent. The Dodgers' best weapons included Hershiser, who wasn't even pitching that night, and a banged-up slugger Kirk Gibson, the National League MVP who was on the bench with two bad legs due to an injured right leg and a pulled left hamstring.

Gibson simply could not run at all and did not expect to play. According to Vin Scully, Gibson was not even able to leave the bench for pre-game introductions. To make the game even more improbable, Eckersley had already nailed 45 saves during the 1988 season and was ready to face pinch-hitter Dave Anderson, who sported a journeyman .249 average, when suddenly manager Lasorda pulled Anderson for the noticeably lame Kirk Gibson.[10] Since Gibson could not run the bases, not even to first, Lasorda was clearly going for the win with one swing, challenging his slugger with a long-ball-or-nothing assignment.

Eckersley had downed the first two batters in the ninth, but then he walked Mike Davis. With a man on, Lasorda had a sudden inspiration—put the game in the hands of his MVP dynamo Gibson, who then limped to the plate and proceeded to work the count all the way to 3-and-2 as millions of nervous viewers watched. At that point first base was open because Davis had stolen second on the 2-and-2 count after Gibson managed to foul off several pitches, grimacing in pain each time. Eckersley chose to challenge Gib-son, who connected on the next Eckersley delivery, launching the ball toward the right field stands and into baseball destiny. Aptly described as a genuine "limp off home run," Gibson indeed hobbled around the bases as Jack Buck nearly climbed out of his skin call-ing the improbable watershed moment to a national audience for CBS Radio.[11] That home run not only stole a victory in Game One of the Series, it may have won the whole World

Series altogether, for the powerful Athletics never really recovered from that defining moment, losing the championship in just five games. Jack Buck was not only on hand, his stunning reaction has endured as one of the most memorable home run calls in the history of baseball broadcasting. It can still be seen and heard on numerous websites featuring the CBS radio feed.

Also present for the Gibson miracle was Vin Scully, calling the game for national television. "Trying to catch lightning right now," said Scully when Gibson hobbled to the plate. Moments later baseball history had been changed. "She is gone," Scully announced, emphasizing "gone," but then he fell silent, allowing posterity to sink in, uninterrupted, for the television audience. The exuberance and dejection of both teams needed no further words. Eventually Vin Scully broke the silence with his final take: "In a year so improbable the *impossible* has happened."[12] Indeed.

Jack Buck's journey to that magical Gibson moment and beyond had begun, in part, by accident. Buck had fought in World War II and was injured, receiving a Purple Heart for his trouble. It was only after the war that he became a student at Ohio State and did a sports show for campus station WOSU, after which Buck was hired by nearby WCOL radio to call Ohio State football and basketball games.[13] When WCOL landed the broadcasting rights to a local Cardinals minor league team, two things happened at once: Buck shifted to baseball and he began a long affiliation with the Cardinals organization. That relationship continued when Buck began calling games in Rochester for another Cardinals affiliate, and his connection to the organization was further strengthened by a number of commercial assignments for Anheuser-Busch. By 1954 he found himself behind the big league microphone in St. Louis alongside veteran announcer Harry Caray.[14]

At first, Buck and Caray were not a good fit for each other, but they made it work and remained paired for 15 years with Harry providing the glitz and glamour, Buck the stability and professionalism. When the Cardinals removed Buck for a brief experiment in 1960 to team Joe Garagiola with Caray, the mistake was obvious. The two were reunited for the 1961 season, where they continued together through the 1969 campaign, after which Harry was finally dumped. With Harry gone, Jack Buck became the top Cardinals broadcaster. After an unsuccessful pairing with Jim Woods, Buck was teamed with a former Cardinals player, Mike Shannon, who proceeded to stay at Buck's side until Buck could go no longer.[15] Jack suffered from Parkinson's, shaking noticeably but still able to call games with a solid voice before passing away in 2002. He died at the Barnes-Jewish Hospital at the age of 77.

Partner Mike Shannon had become a great companion and friend to Jack Buck. Shannon was born in St. Louis, where he later became the starting right fielder for the Cardinals, contributing a two-run jack against Yankee great Whitey Ford when the Cards took the World Series in 1964. In 1967 Roger Maris took over in right, so Shannon moved to third base where he again brought success, contributing home runs in the 1967 Series also won by the Cardinals, and again in 1968 off Mickey Lolich although St. Louis lost that Series to the Denny McLain Tigers. Kidney problems forced Shannon off the field and into the booth, where he continued as a fan favorite with his down-home delivery that produced hundreds of quotes reminiscent of Yogi Berra and Dizzy Dean, such as "A hit up the middle right now would be like a nice ham sandwich and a cold frosty one," or "It's raining like a Chinese fire drill," or "He's madder than a pig caught under a barnyard gate," or "I just want to tell everyone Happy Easter and Happy Hanukkah."[16]

When Jack Buck died, he left behind Mike Shannon, a wardrobe of plaid sport coats, an infectious smile, millions of fans, and an enduring broadcast legacy that was also beginning to include son Joe Buck. Jack had become a companion to legions of listeners, especially shut-ins, truck drivers, and motorists who listened faithfully to the radio. His voice reached far beyond St. Louis, and not only when he did national baseball broadcasts or was paired with Hank Stram to do NFL football on the radio. "Whenever I hear him, it reminds me of home," said one-time Cub third baseman Bill Mueller. "He was on all the time. He was just soothing to hear. You find yourself driving through the city of [St. Louis] and you hear his voice, and it brings you back to when you were a little kid growing up and it's a good feeling."[17] In the Midwest, one station you could almost always pick up on your AM radio was KMOX out of St. Louis. And KMOX meant Jack Buck and St. Louis Cardinals baseball.

In some ways Jack's voice carries on with son Joe Buck, who achieved his own high degree of success in the world of baseball broadcasting. On the eve of the 2009 World Series between the Yankees and Phillies, Joe and partner Tim McCarver, a former Cardinals catcher, were about to broadcast their twelfth World Series nationally for the Fox network. Although he continues the Buck legacy, Joe became a deserved broadcasting star in his own right, with many younger viewers knowing Joe without recalling his father Jack at all. Even before the 2009 Series, Joe and Tim had already called 59 World Series games together, more than the three Series called by either the McCarver–Jim Palmer–Al Michaels trio in the 1980s (plus part of the 1995 Series) or the team of Vin Scully and Joe Garagiola, also during the 1980s.[18]

Joe Buck was born into a large family of eight children. Joe enjoyed following his father through the world of baseball; he admired Jack, and sought to become a broadcaster in his dad's footsteps. His influential father helped Joe get started, of course, but like most successful father-son legacies, the son had to earn it after that. Joe did. In 1996 he became the youngest national announcer for World Series telecasts since Vin Scully in 1953. The Fox ratings exploded with Joe Buck and Tim McCarver, and that influenced the Fox corporate decision to embrace baseball and invest in the World Series broadcast rights. Jack's advice to son Joe, among other things: "Keep your volume low, repeat the score, don't treat it like *War and Peace*."[19]

Ironically, it was Jack Buck who had originally been teamed with Tim McCarver for the Fox telecasts starting in 1990. But Jack and Tim had bad chemistry together, and that led to Fox removing Jack after fewer than two years. Jack had not been at his best on television anyway, and preferred radio where he excelled like few others. "In television, all they want you to do is shut up," Jack Buck reasoned. "I'm not very good at shutting up."[20]

Mike Shannon and Tim McCarver not only had ties to the Cardinals and the Buck family, both are outstanding examples of the emerging role of the color commentator — retired players who bring an array of personal experience, insight, and stories to the broadcast booth. Dizzy Dean had been one of the first superstar players to achieve a high level of success in the broadcast booth. Although he was retained because of his baseball skills and fame, Dean was not really a "color commentator" as that term would later be used; he had a gift for gab that enhanced his own playing career, stories, and credibility. During the 1940s, 1950s, and even much of the 1960s, most pro athletes were not very good in the booth. They were stilted if not stoic and typically had no training in public speaking or broadcasting.

One of the first genuine color commentators was former Dallas quarterback Don Meredith on *Monday Night Football*, while one of the first in baseball was Don Drysdale, a former Dodgers pitcher with an impressive on-field resume and a smooth voice in the booth. Drysdale, a big man at 6'5", not only threw hard, he was known for his aggressive brush-back pitches. The 154 batters he hit is still a modern-era National League record. Teamed with Hall of Famer Sandy Koufax, the two became one of the most dominant pitching duos in the history of the major leagues. In 1962 Drysdale won 25 games and the Cy Young Award, he was also the Dodgers' best hitter for average in 1965 with a .300 mark, and in 1968 his 58 consecutive scoreless innings established a new record. Drysdale was an outstanding athlete, and history sometimes overlooks his remarkable hitting ability. In 1965, when Drysdale was the only player on the Dodgers to bat .300, his slugging average that year was .591, on the strength of his seven homers, an impressive total for a pitcher. He was often used as a pinch-hitter throughout his career.[21] Remarkably, Drysdale never missed a start as a pitcher. He led the National League in games started every year from 1962 through 1965, plus led the league in innings pitched three of those years.[22]

Drysdale also had an eye for the camera during his pitching days in Los Angeles, often appearing in various television shows like *The Brady Bunch* and *You Bet Your Life*. When he retired in 1969, he promptly entered the broadcast booth, announcing games at various times for the Dodgers, Angels, and White Sox — and sometimes nationally for the ABC network. Drysdale had started his pitching career in Brooklyn, where he won 17 games the year before the club moved to Los Angeles. He had a great deal of history and baseball color to draw upon beginning with those early days with Duke Snider. In the booth, Drysdale proved to be good natured, fan friendly, and very knowledgeable. While his delivery was well polished and made for easy listening, at first Drysdale had to make a few adjustments. He later confessed, for example, to feeling foolish about interviewing players and asking them questions to which he, as a former player, already knew the answers.

Former Oakland Raiders football coach John Madden took the color role to new levels of entertainment with his enthusiasm, funny stories, and "telestrator" drawings that were hastily scribbled all over the screen. Madden not only knew football, he knew how to entertain, and that made John Madden a very popular broadcaster. At the same time that Madden was providing energy to NFL football, former Marquette University coach Al McGuire displayed the same entertaining approach for NCAA basketball games, as the two former coaches reinvented the color commentator role for television.

Al McGuire was a talented coach and proved to be a gifted commentator. He was charming, fun, and spoke with a thick New York accent that personified his Big Apple toughness; yet his delivery was sometimes self-deprecating and almost always conveyed with a wink behind his voice. McGuire salted his delivery with legions of creative metaphors that brought originality and verve to each McGuire telecast. When the game ended, McGuire would announce "the carnival gates are closed" or simply sigh, "tap city." Easy opponents were "cupcakes," close games were called "white knucklers," big men were "aircraft carriers," and a satisfying win was savored with "seashells and balloons."[23]

Winner of an NCAA basketball title for Marquette in his final year of coaching, McGuire approached broadcasting with a seasoned perspective and gracious humility that revealed a love not just for the game of basketball, but of people — often accented with a dash of street smarts, such as, "All love affairs end. Eventually the girl is gonna put curlers in her hair." He even had an air of Yogi Berra wisdom about him, with such gems as "Fifty percent of the doctors in this country graduated in the bottom half of their class." But he did not hold it against them, sometimes adding, "I think the world is run by C students." McGuire was entertaining and likeable, perhaps because of his Stengel-like introspective. "A team should be an extension of a coach's personality," McGuire would say. "My teams were arrogant and obnoxious."[24]

Like many sports stars, Al McGuire grew up poor. He was the son of Irish immigrant who ran a saloon, which is where McGuire got much of his early education before starring in basketball at St. John's University where he was captain of a 26–5 team that won third place in the 1951 NIT Tournament — in those days the NIT was the premier post-season basketball tourney.[25] He spent a couple years in the NBA with the New York Knicks and Baltimore Bullets, where he soon displayed the quintessential McGuire humor. One story says he talked his way onto the court to stop Hall of Fame guard Bob Cousy, who McGuire promptly fouled the next six times Cousy touched the ball.

Paired with Billy Packer for some of the best NCAA telecasts for NBC, McGuire was there when Magic Johnson and Michigan State downed Larry Bird's Indiana State team for the 1979 NCAA title in one of the greatest matchups in the history of college hoops. That game "put college basketball on its afterburner" McGuire insisted over the years.

Al McGuire was just 72 years old when he succumbed to leukemia in 2001. While he never called baseball games and never played baseball at any meaningful level, he was cut from the same colorful cloth and Stengel and Berra with a sincere intelligence and a unique style that would influence sports broadcasting in the years and decades to follow, especially the use of color commentators. It is also significant, as well as poignant, that many of the attributes of successful team sport participants and broadcasters beg the colorful down-home colloquialisms of baseball more than any other sport, often emulating the game's wonderful wordsmiths including Berra and Stengel as well as its colorful announcers like Harry Caray, Mike Shannon, Ralph Kiner — and one of the best of baseball's eccentric broadcasters, the inimitable Bob Uecker, a color man who emulated both the intelligence and self-deprecation of Al McGuire.

Outstanding color commentators have emerged for all the major team sports, such as Phil Simms and Joe Theismann in football, Hubie Brown, Doug Collins, Reggie Miller, and Charles Barkley for NBA basketball, and a litany of successful baseball announcers from Tim McCarver to Joe Morgan, Jim Palmer, Lou Piniella, and many more. But none of them was more unique, if not uniquely suited, than baseball's Bob Uecker.

If there are no second acts in most American lives, as F. Scott Fitzgerald once cynically noted, Bob Uecker must surely be an exception to that rule. A very good defensive catcher with a gun for an arm, Uecker hit over .300 three different times — all in the minor leagues.[26] Uecker signed with the Milwaukee Braves organization in 1956. He did club a three-run ninth-inning shot late in 1964 to help power the Cardinals to the National League pennant, and in 1967, his last year in the league, he had a five–RBI game against the Giants while wearing a Braves uniform.[27]

In 1971, less than four years after his retirement from major league baseball, he displayed a remarkable sense of humor with the comedic timing of a pro while he was a broadcaster for Milwaukee Brewers games.[28] He was soon doing color — and very colorfully — commentary for ABC's *Monday Night Baseball* during the 1970s followed by a similar stint for NBC during the 1990s. Uecker's deadpan delivery, self-deprecating humor, and hilarious baseball stories left fans laughing everywhere, including the *Tonight Show* with Johnny Carson, where he was a frequent guest, a very big hit, and a favorite of Carson who began introducing Uecker as "Mr. Baseball." Uecker then leveraged his fame and popularity into many other television appearances, including a recurring role in 115 episodes of the sitcom *Mr. Belvedere* from 1985 to 1990, plus two published books titled, somewhat appropriately, *Catch 222* and *Catcher in the Wry*. He also was featured in the 1989 hit film parody *Major League* starring Charlie Sheen, Tom Berenger, Corbin Bernsen, and Rene Russo, followed by two sequels in 1994 and 1998.

Reflecting on his own baseball career highlights, Uecker noted two: "I got an intentional walk from Sandy Koufax and I got out of a rundown against the Mets." He joked about one alleged award he received in Philadelphia, "Bob Uecker Day Off," exuding a trademark theme of futility that found its way into many of his stories. "One time I got pulled over at 4:00 A.M.," Uecker said. "I was fined $75 for being intoxicated and $400 for being with the Phillies." Uecker insists that his 1965 baseball card had no picture on it; he admits he led the league in "Go get 'em next time"; and notes that in 1962 he was named Minor League Player of the Year — he was playing for the Mets at the time.[29]

Uecker poked relentless fun at himself and rose to the top doing it, but others were much more kind and effusive in their genuine admiration. Notes the Radio Hall of Fame: "In 1971, Uecker was hired by the Brewers to provide color commentary alongside announcers Merle Haron and Tom Collins. One day Uecker was left to do play-by-play coverage and his talent could not be denied."[30] Uecker was a career .200 hitter, but he proceeded to become the voice of the Brewers franchise for well over three decades — especially remarkable since he never played for the Brewers. Yes, Bob came up to Milwaukee from the minors, but the team was the Braves where he played for many seasons, including his last after the Braves had long since moved to Atlanta, with tours of duty at St. Louis and Philadelphia in between. But he identifies with Milwaukee and vice versa, so Bob Uecker inevitably became the face and voice of the franchise where he developed a platform so unique that he soon drew national attention.

Although he is a virtual comedian on the talk show circuit, when Uecker calls baseball games he can be clever and glib, even funny occasionally, but for the most part he is all business — a seasoned pro behind the microphone. Howard Cosell, who did nationally televised baseball with Uecker and Keith Jackson, admired Uecker as a broadcaster and as a person. Uke, as some called him, transcended baseball and broadcasting, and has been largely admired as a genuine person and a consummate professional behind the microphone.

Baseball broadcasting became fertile ground for other ballplayers, again as real broadcasters and not just color commentators. Two of the best on the networks were Tony Kubek and Joe Garagiola, both of whom would become Ford Frick Award winners.

Kubek, who was Rookie of the Year in 1957 with a .297 average for the Yankees, played in the same era as Bob Uecker — and Kubek happened to be from Milwaukee. By 1958 Kubek had earned the starting shortstop position, contributing to a wonderful double play combination with Bobby Richardson at second base for eight seasons. Kubek set a Yankees record for hitting doubles as a shortstop, and he played on six World Series teams. In 1960, the year of Bill Mazeroski's famous home run and Pittsburgh's world title, Bill Virdon slapped what looked like a double play ball that took a nasty hop that hit Kubek in the throat, keeping the eighth inning of Game Seven alive for Mazeroski. Ironically,

1960 had been Kubek's best all-round year at the plate when he played in 147 games, batted .273 with a career high in both home runs (14) and RBIs (62). His best average came in 1962 at .314, but then he was drafted into the reserves and then called up by the Army. He was never quite the same when he returned.[31]

Kubek soon suffered from back problems and was forced to retire at just 29 years of age. His bad back and neck sent Kubek to the Mayo Clinic in 1965, where he learned of a defect in his vertebrae that likely was caused by an injury playing touch football while in the Army. The Mayo doctors told Kubek that a collision could paralyze him, so he hung up the baseball spikes, retiring before the 1966 season as a two-time All-Star with a .266 career batting average and .980 fielding percentage. A clutch hitter who could spray the ball everywhere, Kubek had been a highly touted Yankee prospect. He could play virtually any position, and often did just that, replacing an injured Mickey Mantle in center or playing short, second, third, or even right field.[32]

While Tony Kubek was a wonderful and successful baseball player, he became an even better broadcaster. With sandy hair and a square jaw, Tony projected a smooth fan-friendly voice and called the game with candor and, where appropriate, due criticism. For 30 years Kubek was an analyst for the Yankees, Blue Jays, and nationally for the *NBC Game of the Week*. Said Hall of Fame president Jeff Idelson, after Kubek's 2009 Ford Frick Award: "In the days before all-sports TV networks, Tony brought baseball into your living room every Saturday afternoon for almost three decades. His straightforward style, quick and detailed analysis and no-nonsense commentary on the game's nuances gave viewers an insider's look at what the players were experiencing on the field."[33]

In the television booth, Kubek was first an analyst for back-up games beginning with the 1966 season. His talent was undeniable, so by 1969 he was promoted to do the primary games where he was teamed over the ensuing years with such luminaries as Jim Simpson, Curt Gowdy, Bob Costas, and Joe Garagiola. Kubek broadcast 11 World Series, 14 American League Championship Series, and 10 All-Star Games nationally for NBC television. And he worked the very last *NBC Game of the Week*, which was telecast on September 30, 1989.

Through it all, Kubek's personal favorite partner was the veteran Curt Gowdy, a virtual cowboy and outdoorsman from Wyoming, who made his mark when he was chosen from hundreds of applicants to become Mel Allen's 1949 partner in the Yankees booth. By 1951 Gowdy had become the play-by-play voice of the Boston Red Sox, where he remained behind the mike for 15 years.[34]

Like many of his radio counterparts, Gowdy had a resonant voice. In his case it was also rather nasal, yet very distinctive, sounding a bit like actor Dick Van Dyke. Virtually any sports fan over the age of 45 would be able to recognize Curt's seductive low-key delivery. The first game Gowdy ever called was a high school football game in Wyoming. It was 1943, the teams had six players each, it was below zero on the field, and there were only 15 people in the stands. By 1946 he was broadcasting for a station in Oklahoma City before brashly applying for the Yankees job in 1949.

Gowdy left the Red Sox in 1966 to do NBC's *Game of the Week* nationally, where he called games with Tony Kubek, among others. But he later would call the Boston years as the happiest in his life. When Gowdy died in 1986 at the age of 86, the *Boston Globe* quoted NBC chairman Dick Ebersol who called Gowdy "one of the greatest sports broadcasters in history."[35] Like Kubek, Gowdy had a bad back, and he struggled with it so much that he missed the entire 1957 Red Sox season. Like Kubek, Gowdy won the coveted Ford Frick Award, but Gowdy's sportscasting went far beyond baseball. He won 13 Emmy Awards and became the first sports broadcaster to earn the Peabody Award. He not only called 16 World Series, he was on hand for nine Super Bowls and 12 Rose Bowls, he called the NCAA Final Four on 24 occasions, and did the Olympics eight different times. Many sports fans, however, remember his long stint hosting *American Sportsman*, ABC's national show that focused on hunting and fishing, hearkening Gowdy's outdoor roots from his youth in Wyoming.[36]

Football fans will not only remember Gowdy's Super Bowl work, including the watershed Super Bowl III when the Jets and "Broadway Joe" Namath stunned the football world by upsetting the favored NFL Colts, but the most devoted viewers also recall that it was Gowdy in the broadcast booth when the NFL's infamous "Heidi game" went dark on November 17, 1968. It was a classic match-up between the scrappy high-flying Oakland Raiders against the legendary New York Jets led by marquee quarterback Joe Namath. With 65 seconds left, kicker Jim Turner booted a field goal to put the Jets ahead, 32–29. NBC then cut to a commercial, but the game never returned. With neither explanation nor warning, the next programming the football viewers saw was the image of Heidi, the story of an orphaned Swiss girl. While Heidi herded her goats on national television, the Raiders took a 36–32 lead on the arm of quarterback Daryle Lamonica, then recovered a fumble on the ensuing kickoff and scored again — two touchdowns in nine seconds.[37] The game also featured 19 penalty flags that chewed up 238 yards and, unfortunately, lots of time, causing the game to exceed its allotted time period. NBC chose to resolve the programming conflict by cutting to its regularly scheduled *Heidi* film. When NBC was excoriated for that move, it was the last time an NFL game in progress would be yanked without further updates or explanation.

Curt Gowdy was one of the greatest and most diverse sports broadcasters, but baseball was in his blood. While with the Red Sox he announced Carl Yastrzemski's first plate appearance in a Boston uniform and called icon Ted Williams' last at-bat, a poignant, storybook career walk-off home run that Gowdy himself remembered as "one of the big thrills of my life."[38]

While doing the *Game of the Week*, both Kubek and Gowdy would cross paths with another great announcer, Joe Garagiola, a consummate baseball man with an engaging, fan-friendly demeanor that played very well on television. He was also a comedian, not as self-deprecating as Bob Uecker, but he told funny stories, always about baseball and often about himself. If he was not a model for Uecker's own approach to humor, Garagiola certainly influenced the evolution of the color commentator. But Garagiola's fame had an auspicious and decidedly controversial beginning.

Joe Garagiola had been a boyhood friend of Yogi Berra.[39] At just 16 years old, Joe was lifted from sandlot ball by a Cardinals visionary named Branch Rickey, who lured the youngster with a $500 bonus. It would take Garagiola four years, two in the minors and two more in the military, to make the major leagues in 1946. The very next year in 1947, the historic season of Jackie Robinson's debut, the Dodgers played a May series in St. Louis against the Cardinals. The ensuing encounters between Robinson and Garagiola would change Joe's life.

The 1947 baseball crowd was largely skeptical about black major leaguers, with players and fans alike openly hostile to Robinson. In St. Louis, the home field crowd at

Sportsman's Park had been officially segregated until 1944 — which may seem surprising since St. Louis is a northern industrial town, but the city is nonetheless parallel to portions of Kentucky and Virginia and is as close to Memphis as it is to Chicago. In Robinson's first trip to the plate in St. Louis, he and the opposing catcher Garagiola got into a verbal confrontation. Joe was still only 21 years of age, while Robinson, though a rookie, was noticeably older at 28. Jackie was no wallflower, either, and Branch Rickey had not signed Robinson because he was a pacifist; rather, Rickey had been attracted by Robinson's great strength of character. By the time Jackie encountered the young Garagiola on the field, Jackie had already spent two years in the Army during World War II as a second lieutenant, where he did not see combat but did make waves by refusing to sit in the back of a seg- regated bus, got court-martialed for his trouble, then was acquitted but subsequently discharged anyway.[40]

The 21-year-old Garagiola got more than he bargained for with Robinson. When Joe trash-talked Jackie, shouting to the infield and baiting Robinson about his alleged weak hitting, Jackie asked the brash catcher about his own average. Joe was hitting about 100 points lower than Robinson at the time, but said the difference was only because Jackie could run faster. "No matter how fast you run, Joe," countered Jackie, "you couldn't hit as much as you weigh." Robinson failed to get a hit that day, but he did walk and make it to third, then burst home to score, racing past Garagiola at the plate. Some say that it was this Cardinals series, where Jackie stood up to the white Italian Garagiola in a hostile environment, that provided a needed watershed moment helping Jackie to gain the respect of his own teammates, many of whom had still harbored their own doubts.

Later in the season, Garagiola grounded to short and spiked Robinson's foot at first base. Robinson was not injured but he felt Joe had done it on purpose. The next time Jackie took the batter's box he made a comment to the catcher Garagiola. Joe responded with a racist remark, at least according to Robinson's recollection, and the verbal alter- cation began to escalate. When the umpire stepped in, Jackie laughed, which incensed Joe. Robinson popped out, but his next plate appearance produced a prodigious home run to tie the game, which evoked far-away cheers in, of all places, the Polo Grounds, where a small crowd was gathered for a Negro League game.[41] Many in the all–Negro audience had portable radios, so they soon heard of Jackie's homer thanks to the miracle of baseball broadcasting.

Over the years Garagiola would defend his conduct toward Robinson, describing Jackie as a hard-nose competitor, the type of player who would have received Garagiola's trash talk regardless of color, which is precisely what Joe said happened. Although the series of incidents would both perplex and haunt Joe, he nonetheless became a likeable, funny, and skilled national baseball announcer for NBC. Ironically, during a Cardinals game in Brooklyn during the early summer of 1950, Garagiola found himself legging out a bunt with Robinson racing to cover the bag. As Joe lunged toward first base, he saw Robinson's foot out of position and swerved to avoid yet another collision, lost his balance and tumbled to the ground, separating Joe's shoulder. Joe would only play 30 games that year and got traded to Pittsburgh — largely because of his effort to *avoid* injuring Robin- son's errant foot at first base.

Although Garagiola would do well for the Pirates in 1952, the years were catching up and retirement was fast approaching. By 1955 Joe was out of baseball and beginning his broadcasting career, where at first he called games for the Cardinals, then was tapped for the *Game of the Week* in 1961, the year of the Maris and Mantle showdown. Four years later Joe became the voice of the Yankees, replacing icon Mel Allen, while still doing national games for NBC from 1961 to 1988. Joe was so popular that he became one of the few sports announcers to transcend sports broadcasting when he did a stint hosting NBC's powerhouse *Today Show* from 1969 to 1973. When the imminently likeable Joe Garagiola became an author, his first effort, *Baseball Is a Funny Game* became an immediate hit and still ranks as one of baseball's best-selling books.

While the original baseball announcers in the1920s were sometimes prone to dead air, the art of storytelling would soon become one the mainstay attributes of the great baseball announcers. Although many successful baseball broadcasters could tell wonderful stories, few could do so with the style and humor of Garagiola and Uecker. Both were catchers, as it happened, which means they knew and played the game with intimate knowledge and respect; both were average or sub-average big leaguers; and both played off their own limitations to entertain their audiences. Some broadcasters proved to be consummate reporters, like Vin Scully or the Cubs' Pat Hughes, a solid professional who handled the laboring oar alongside former third baseman Ron Santo, a blatant "homer" known to live, breath, groan, and die with each play in the Cubs booth. Santo's plaintive cry "OOOOhhhhhhh, Noooooooh" was evident when left fielder Brant Brown dropped a easy fly ball that would have preserved a 7–5 Cubs lead over the Brewers late in a three-way wild-card race with the Giants and Mets on September 23, 1998. Milwaukee scored three runs on that miscue, winning the game.[42]

There are many unabashed homers, of course, who regularly refer to the team as "we." Some of those became caricatures of themselves, which is what happened to Harry Caray, one of the great ones who slipped off the deep end during his later years in the booth. Harry Caray was mostly liked by the fans, virtually admired on Chicago's North Side, but the players did not care for him since he was not only critical but contemptuous. Relief pitcher Jim Brosnan wrote a baseball exposé that called Harry a "Tomato-Face," an overt put-down of Harry's red, cherub face that was also a subtle slam at Caray's reputation as a heavy drinker.[43] When teamed with baseball's bad-boy Jimmy Piersall to call White Sox games in 1977, the year of the free swinging "South Side hit men" of owner Bill Veeck, Harry was so critical of the team that even the affable Veeck cringed. On the North Side, the Cubs had been criticized and ridiculed for decades (although not by the straight-arrow announcer Jack Brickhouse), so Harry's act was much better received by the frustrated fans at Wrigley Field.

Both on the field and in the booth, baseball has a remarkable acuity for father-son combinations. Jack and Joe Buck are perhaps the most successful father-son duo. In Harry Caray's case, he spawned, quite literally, son Skip (actually Harry Jr.) who would call over three decades of Atlanta Braves games beginning in 1972, and grandson Chip, who broadcast televised Cubs games for five years before joining his father in Atlanta, after which he was signed by TBS to be the lead announcer for national telecasts. Chip, unfortunately, was not always well received by the media. During the baseball playoffs of 2009, the *New York Daily News* ran a scathing piece. "He's erratic. That's being kind."[44] The article speculated that the reason TBS kept Chip on amid a sea of mediocrity or worse, was his ties to two ghosts, Chip's late father Skip and grandfather Harry.

Harry's reach was still being felt, even in death. Chip called him "the ultimate fan," son Skip explained. "He never sugar-coated the pill." But even Skip lamented the clown-like caricature that Harry had become in his last years behind the microphone, especially after he came back from a stroke suffered in 1987. Harry had become "a caricature with big glasses, the Bud Man, saying 'holy cow' and shouting 'Cubs win!'" Skip conceded just after Harry's death in 1998.

As baseball's color commentators developed further, television technology continued to evolve throughout the 1960s and beyond, bringing the game closer to the viewers at home. The changes were pervasive and rapid, striking fear among some, including the media philosopher Marshall McLuhan who in 1969 pronounced, "Baseball is doomed."[45] Like with the alleged death of Mark Twain, McLuhan's report on the demise of televised baseball, if not baseball itself, was largely "premature." Although the game struggled with low scoring due to the dominant pitchers of the era, and met stiff competition from the NFL and later the NBA of Michael Jordan, television continued to adapt, learning how to better understand, capture, and broadcast the unique game of baseball.

As the 1970s progressed, televised baseball began to use up to seven cameras, one placed at each of first base, third base, home plate, center field facing back toward the plate, left field, and also one more focused on each dugout for reaction shots of players and the manager. Soon all the cameras were able to process slow motion video replays. At the same time larger lenses were showing more of the batter, color quality improved, and two-color video graphics emerged.

Televised baseball experienced a quantum leap on October 21, 1975, during a singular moment that would reveal the dramatic power of baseball when viewed with a sense of perspective commensurate with the explosive nature of the game itself. That night, the powerful Cincinnati Reds of Tony Perez, Johnny Bench, George Foster, Ken Griffey, and Joe Morgan held a three games to two edge as the World Series moved back to Boston, where the Red Sox had to wait out three days of chilling rain before trying to even the Series. The Reds' Gary Nolan was assigned to face a tough Boston lineup of Fred Lynn, Jim Rice, Boston legend Carl Yastrzemski — and tenacious catcher Carlton Fisk.

The Sox took an early 3–0 lead for pitcher Luis Tiant as Lynn blasted a three-run shot to right. But the prodigious Reds clawed back, taking a 6–3 lead through their half of the eighth inning. Then the game *really* began. With two outs and two men on, pinch-hitter Bernie Carbo ripped a 425-foot bomb to center, tying the game at 6–6.[46] No one could score for two more innings, but even then the players knew this game was becoming something special. When he came to the plate in the tenth inning, the Reds' Pete Rose reportedly turned to the catcher Fisk and said, "This is some kind of game, isn't it?" The Reds almost mounted a threat in the eleventh with Ken Griffey on first when Joe Morgan crushed a liner to right. Instead of clearing the wall, however, Morgan's ball was run down by the sprinting Dwight Evans, who not only made a one-hand catch but also managed to spin and gun down Griffey for a rally-killing double play. Said Joe Garagiola: "Well hit, right field deep ... Evans is going back, back near the wall and... Oh what a catch he made! What a catch by Dwight Evans and it's a double play...."

Then came the bottom of the fateful twelfth inning. Carlton Fisk, a very big man for a catcher, lumbered to the plate. Not wanting to fall behind in the count, pitcher Pat Darcy challenged Fisk with a high fastball. Fisk connected, launching the ball high, deep and down the line. Would that ball stay fair for a dramatic come-from-behind win, or would it simply drift foul for a harmless long strike? If a home run ball could be redirected on the fly, Fisk did it. With the Boston crowd in a collective frenzy, Fisk himself drifted down the first base line as if to get a head start on destiny. He jumped excitedly with anticipation while waving his arms toward fair territory, willing the ball to do the same. This was not simply an extraordinary moment for baseball, it was a watershed image for television that wreaked of drama and excitement. Coming in crucial Game Six of the World Series before a national audience, it would influence future broadcasts of post-season baseball.

Fate not only intervened with Fisk's fly ball, it had already influenced the televised images. With more cameras in place, there were more shots to choose from, but the right shot still had to be captured and the director still had to choose that image for the viewing audience. Consistent with the trend to utilize more televised angles for the Series for the Fenway games, NBC had the foresight to placed a camera inside the left field Green Monster scoreboard wall. However, operator Lou Gerard ignored instructions to follow the ball while leaving the lens focused on the animated Carlton Fisk. While Gerard later explained how at the last second he had simply been distracted by a rat and therefore had failed to follow instructions to track the ball, the totality of the circumstances and the weight of history and credulity suggest otherwise.[47] Which is more likely: a rat suddenly appears in the twelfth inning at precisely the right defining moment and then actually *distracts* the cameraman in the face of the explosive crowd and the drama of Fisk's animated attempt at baseball sorcery — or could it be that Gerard himself was simply distracted, perhaps frozen, by one of the greatest scenes in the history of baseball as it unfolded before his very eyes? There is an axiom in law, science, and history that the simplest explanations are almost always the right ones. Even if a rat had appeared on cue, would it really have distracted a seasoned cameraman focused on one of the greatest all-time baseball moments? Had such a rodent fallen directly onto Gerard's lap it would not likely have influenced events as much as the on-field drama itself did.

As the fateful Fisk shot to the stands began to descend, it clanked off the foul pole — really the "fair pole" — and indeed landed in baseball posterity. The impossible had happened again, a walk-off foul ball had been willed fair — and it all unfolded through the televised lens of history. But even with that, the moment was not over. Fisk circled the bases, still flinging his arms and jumping with excitement. Thereafter, baseball would deploy more cameras and would be more sensitive to the human side of the game, especially for home runs — the players, and not just the play, would thereafter become the story.

Broadcast on both television and radio by NBC, the 1975 World Series not only produced compelling television, it was announced by a who's who of sports broadcasters. Curt Gowdy and Joe Garagiola shared play-by-play duties, as Tony Kubek provided the color commentary. This would be the last Series called by Gowdy, however, with Garagiola taking over for NBC as its lead announcer beginning in 1976. It would also be a last hurrah for NBC radio, with CBS picking up the World Series rights for ensuing years. Also in the booth for the 1975 classic were local team announcers Ned Martin and Dick Stockton for Boston and Marty Brennaman for Cincinnati.

A week after the Series ended, NBC was stunned by its own ratings success. The seventh game had apparently garnered a prime-time viewing audience of 71 million, which made it the second most watched sporting event in history at the time, trailing only Super Bowl IX. The impressive audience was lured by a number of factors like the possibility of Boston finally winning the Series, not to mention the overall cachet of a Game Seven showdown. But the biggest catalyst had to be the drama of Game Six itself with Fisk's homer, shown over and over during the ensuring hours leading up to Game Seven. With estimates of about 367 million viewers for the whole Series, NBC began to rethink its approach to baseball programming in the wake of the Fisk heroics and how his now infamous walk-off home run had been televised. It had been about Fisk the player, not the ball itself.

Another factor behind the broadcasting success of the 1975 Series was prime time. Because of two rain postponements early in the Series, for the first time ever there were five World Series games shown to a prime-time viewing audience. Moreover, CBS had beaten NBC in the network ratings wars for 1974, but the 1975 World Series would help propel both ratings and dollars for NBC. It was also a good sign for the third network, ABC, which sought to capitalize on its early *Monday Night Football* successes with a bold leap into prime-time baseball, which had already announced the planned telecast of 16 Monday night baseball games during the ensuing 1976 season.

History now regards 1975's Game Six as one of the greatest World Series games ever played, some calling it *the* greatest of all time. But it is also seen as one of the best broadcasts of all World Series games, and probably was in fact the best that had been telecast up to that time. Fisk, fate, and NBC's Harry Coyle comprised much of the reason behind such success. Coyle had been directing baseball games for television since 1947 — seeing televised games even before he could afford a TV at home. When the 1975 Series came about, Coyle and Executive Producer Scotty Connal implored NBC to devote its best technicians and to place a camera in the Green Monster wall. It all paid off "Branch Rickey" style, with the luck of the Series' dramatic images being the residue of NBC's design, largely at the hands of Harry Coyle.

Coyle publicly backed up cameraman Lou Gerard's nightlong battle with rats behind the Green Monster. Maybe the vermin story is true or perhaps it is at least partly true. Whatever the real reason, Gerard, the consummate professional, could not keep his eyes off Fisk, which meant the rest of the world was watching the catcher's antics, too. Fortunately, the "rest of the world" included Harry Coyle, whose eye caught the Fisk body English drama, causing him to keep that camera angle for the viewing audience. "That type of shot is a director's dream," he said, understating history.[48]

More than a decade later, when Kirk Gibson made his own improbable assault on history, the cameras followed not just the ball, but Gibson as he triumphantly did a limp-trot around the bases, pumping his arms in victory. Those cameras were glued to Gibson in no small part because of what the networks learned about featuring the human side of baseball, a sport that by its nature lends itself to such singular moments. Interestingly, Jack Buck found himself calling that Gibson blast and "not believing what he just saw" because CBS had picked up the Series rights just after the 1975 Series, rendering that year's fall classic a milestone for myriad reasons.

Ironically, according to Milo Hamilton, a number of radio announcers, including Jack Buck and Milo himself, began to avoid television broadcasting in the 1990s. "In television," says Milo, "the truck does the game." Ironically, after Fisk, Gibson, and others, the television director began to take charge and the announcers were forced to follow the lead, while in radio it is still the announcer who compiles the visual images of the game as it unfolds for the audience, leaving more creativity and a personal touch for the radio broadcaster.

Just one night after the Fisk spectacle in 1975, the Red Sox lost that World Series in Game Seven behind a timely Joe Morgan single in the ninth inning. Once again history had slipped from the team's grasp as it had done so many times before and after — until Boston finally prevailed in 2004.

> *That foul tip bounced up and caught him right in the groins ... and that'll really clear your eyes out.*
>
> — Mike Shannon[49]

14

All's Fair in Love and Baseball

Baseball, my son, is the cornerstone of civilization.
— DAGWOOD BUMSTEAD[1]

Baseball is Peck's bad boy. It is an irreverent game, a team sport made of one-on-one confrontations that grew up while America was emerging as an industrial power. Its deliberate pace was largely responsible for the game's success on radio, and the radio announcers who evolved contributed to baseball's stature as our national pastime. America listened, especially young boys who hung on every pitch, first during the myriad day games during the early twentieth century, but then by clutching their transistor radios under the pillow as night games became more prevalent. And so it was, even listening to baseball on the radio became an act of subversion, corrupting young fans across the country with the lure of baseball after bedtime.

The impious game of baseball did not disappoint. From stolen signs to spitballs, grease balls, corked bats, the manipulation of outfield shapes and walls, and even tampering with the rules, no organized team sport has been more vexatious than baseball. Perhaps its lack of uniformity is partly to blame — no other major sport besides golf is played on an irregular field — which may invite mischief more than other sports. Opened in 1923, the original Yankee Stadium was constructed with a sub–300-foot right field almost certainly to exploit the power of its left-handed slugger George Herman Ruth, who had shown a remarkable proclivity for pulling balls into the right field stands while playing at the elongated Polo Grounds. Whether in the form of Boston's Green Monster wall or Wrigley's ivy or any number of other oddities, baseball's topography has influenced the game from its earliest days when prairie grass and horses were part of the terrain. Sometimes these nuances serve the game well, but other times they are exploited at the expense of history. The television camera lodged in Boston's left field wall, the one that so poignantly captured the dramatic body language of Carlton Fisk's World Series home run, certainly exploited the uniqueness of Fenway in a harmless way, while in New York a sign-stealing system that relied on a hidden center field spyglass during the 1951 season was anything but benign, for it likely influenced the game itself by aiding Bobby Thomson's pennant-winning walk-off home run.

Such baseball monkey business is not entirely frowned upon by baseball history, although in recent years major league baseball has taken itself more seriously, if not too seriously, perhaps at the expense of baseball's spontaneity and its swashbuckling American image. Over the ensuing decades of baseball broadcasting, the game's announcers have not been immune to baseball's mischievous legacy, sometimes taking on a measure of baseball's personality themselves. Who could be more irreverent, for example, than Bob Uecker? Who could be more mischievous than Harry Caray? Or funnier than Joe Garagiola, more acerbic than bad-boy Jimmy Piersall calling White Sox games, or more spontaneous than a young Ronald Reagan improvising a near-record number of fabricated foul balls to buy time when the news feed of the Cubs game he was announcing had been interrupted?

Baseball has traditionally embraced chicanery — deception being the whole point of the curve ball, the hidden-ball trick, or an intentional drop of the occasional infield fly ball, an act of subversion that ultimately necessitated the infield fly rule. Even when such shell games are contrary to the rules, however, baseball has been less judgmental than other sports. Spitballs, stolen signs, corked bats, brushback pitches, and excessive pine tar have all been forgiven as part of the game itself, even in the face of various fines, ejections, and suspensions.

As the reach of the television lens improved, it began to both reveal and influence the art of baseball skullduggery. Pitchers scuffing or otherwise doctoring the balls are forced to be more careful, and players discussing strategy during a trip to the mound have all taken to covering their faces with their gloves when speaking, presumably to foil lip readers who may be lurking in the opposing dugout if not in the broadcast booth. Sometimes the captured images can be priceless, like Lou Piniella ripping a base from its roots and tossing it with contempt, or Graig Nettles who once sprayed superballs across the infield when his supercharged bat exploded, or Sammy Sosa splintering his bat to reveal an illegally corked implant in front of the umpires and the ubiquitous television lens.

One unforgettable miracle of television and pine tar led to the explosive reaction by Kansas City third baseman George Brett after he slammed a dramatic two-out home run in the ninth inning at Yankee Stadium on July 24, 1983, driving in two runs to take a 5–4 lead over Billy Martin's Yankees. Brett demonstrated understandable excitement over his timely home run, but that was nothing compared to what the camera would soon capture. Brett had not yet rounded the bases when Martin approached the umpires to complain about Brett's bat; Brett was already in the dugout when the umpires ruled that the bat was illegal, since the pine tar on the handle allegedly extended too far up the barrel. Then, when the umpires took the home run away altogether, Brett erupted, exploding from the bench in full gallop toward the umpires, eyes bulging with a frenzied anger in full view of the television lens.[2] That pine tar incident remains as one of the more entertaining episodes in the history of baseball broadcasting. Although the league would later reinstate the home run by ruling the bat had not broken the "spirit" of the rule, the vision of George Brett's eyes nearly popping from his head remains an indelible image of sports frustration, perhaps the ultimate reaction shot for television.

Even the owners themselves are not above manipulation. Freezing African American players out of the big leagues was certainly a manipulative act, as was lowering the pitcher's mound in 1969 for the purpose of leveling — somewhat literally — the playing field by reducing the dominance of big league pitching, which was beginning to over-whelm baseball offense, excitement, and the game's entertainment value for most of the viewing audience. From the perspective of baseball scoring and entertainment, no year was worse than 1968 when the official mound height was 15 inches and pitchers ruled the game. Denny McLain won 31 games for the Detroit Tigers and Bob Gibson pitched 13 shutouts for the St. Louis Cardinals that same year. Moreover, Gibson struck out 268 batters that season and topped the National League with an ERA of 1.12. Cleveland's Sam McDowell fanned even more at 283 while teammate Luis Tiant logged a league leading 1.60 ERA. Remarkably, the American League batting champion, Boston's Carl Yastrzemski, barely broke .300 that year, his season mark of .301 being the lowest league-leading average in history. Perhaps most telling of all is that pitchers McLain and Gibson, not everyday hitters like Billy Williams, Hank Aaron, or Rod Carew, were named the MVPs of their respective leagues.[3]

As a result, baseball Rule 1.04 was amended to lower the height of the mound to 10 inches, a five-inch drop.[4] The following season in 1969, no pitcher registered an earned run average under 2.00, and although McLain would again lead the American League in victories, his 24 wins were well off his blistering 1968 pace. The Twins' Rod Carew led the AL in hitting with a much loftier .332 average, and the league MVPs were sluggers again, Harmon Killebrew who launched 49 home runs for the Twins and Willie McCovey who clubbed 45 long balls in a Giants uniform.[5] The trend continued. One year later in 1970 the best ERAs were 2.56 (Diego Segui for Oakland) and 2.81 (the Mets' Tom Seaver), while the Braves' Rico Carty hit for a major league high average at .366, a full 65 points over AL leader Yastrzemski's mark from the year before the mound was lowered.[6]

Although there have been occasional rule changes for myriad reasons in all sports, like the NBA three-point line or the two-point conversion rule for the NFL, baseball has enjoyed a longer history of such changes. There was a time when a one-bouncer into the stands was a home run, for example, and on December 10, 1972, the oft-maligned des-ignated hitter rule was added to create still more instant offense, at least for the American League. Before 1920, the spitball had been a legal pitch, then in 1920 Ruth was sent packing to New York and the spitball was suddenly banned as the leagues discovered a new way to sell tickets: baseball offense, especially the home run ball. There are dozens of other examples including the infield fly rule, the number of allowed strikes and balls, and so on.

Sometimes the law of unintended consequences would also come into play. The des-ignated hitter rule not only added offense, it completely changed the way games are man-aged in the American League and tampered with the American League record books, putting AL pitchers at a disadvantage while bloating the batting records of AL hitters. Perhaps the lower pitching mound contributed to another phenomenon — the prolifer-ation of towering pitchers. Standing at least 6'5", Don Drysdale was a giant in his day, but as time wore on the modern-day pitchers have grown taller, with a plethora of hurlers standing 6'6" or more, including the 6'10" Randy Johnson. As of 2008, nine super-tall pitchers at 6'9" or more had appeared in the majors, but most of them had done so in recent years. Randy Johnson himself entered the league in 1988, but seven others began in the 1990s or later. Just one super-tall pitcher had appeared before Randy Johnson — Johnny Gee, who played from 1939 to 1946.[7] This phenomenon is partly because all athletes have gotten bigger, stronger, and taller over the years, but some of it is a function of physics. The tall pitchers simply have an advantage of physics, that is, an advantage to those who used to deliver from a higher mound. Two things happen when pitching at a downward angle from a higher release point: one, the ball travels toward the batter at a sharper angle, making it harder to evaluate and to hit squarely, and two, there is a slightly longer arc to the release of the ball which generates more torque and enhances pitch speed. Also, when a pitcher is taller this arc is larger by its nature, generating torque in its own right.[8] Tall pitchers are not always better or even good — some observers have noted that it seems to take them longer to fully develop — but they appear to have an inherent physical advantage, rather like left-handers do when pitching to left-handed batters, except that theirs is vertical.

Over the years, though, most great pitchers were shorter, of course. Sandy Koufax was shorter than his teammate Drysdale, but at 6'2" he still had good height for his era. Flame throwing Bob Gibson was just over 6'1", Bob Feller 6'0", Pedro Martinez 5'11" and Cy Young Award winner Steve Stone measured in at perhaps 5'10". Stone, interestingly, manipulated his own career, deliberately squeezing several of his best remaining years into one. Steve Stone pitched in the majors from 1971 through 1981, winning the Cy Young Award in 1980 with a sparkling 25–7 record for the Orioles, including one stretch of 14 straight victories. Stone was a cerebral player who remains very analytical. The year before, in 1979, he was a mortal 11–7 although he was seventh best in the league in hits allowed per 9 innings. It was that year when Stone purposefully opted to go for the gold by pitching a vast number of curve balls. He knew it would take a toll on his arm, but Stone threw more than 50 percent curve balls that season, not only wining 25 games but also leading the league in winning percentage. But he was right about his arm — Stone had only one mediocre year left, winning just four games in 1981 with a 4.60 ERA. "I knew it would ruin my arm," Stone said. "But one year of 25–7 is worth five of 15–15."[9]

Stone's insight has served him well, first as a pitcher, then as a superb baseball broadcaster. As a player, Stone's baseball idol was Sandy Koufax himself. He says he read the Koufax autobiography numerous times and even changed his jersey to Koufax's number 32. Stone also was attracted to the metaphysical approach to baseball if not life, meeting with a psychic and adopting meditation and other self-inspirational techniques. Between stints with the Giants and Orioles, Stone spent three years in Chicago, one for the Sox and two with the Cubs (1974–76). After retiring, Stone soon found himself in the television booth on Chicago's North Side with none other than Harry Caray, where Stone began as a color commentator for the Cubs' flagship station, WGN-TV.

Steve Stone's partnership with the flamboyant, unpredictable Harry Caray was a marriage made in baseball heaven, Wrigley Field. Smooth, steady, and still insightful, Stone was the rudder to Harry's flailing paddles. When Harry meandered, Stone skillfully kept the viewers focused on the game while still allowing for Harry's antics. Stone saw the humor in Caray's nonsense, but instead of ridiculing it, he seemed to appreciate its uniqueness. The pair stayed together for 15 years, complementing each other and becoming one of the most successful broadcast teams in the country. Stone's cerebral approach to baseball was even better applied to broadcasting where he amazed viewers with astounding insight into the future, suggesting not only what hitters, pitchers and managers should do, but predicting what they actually *would* do at multiple key moments during the course of a game.

Eventually the brilliance of Steve Stone would catch up to him, becoming his Achilles heel when team management began to feel his candor and insight were making Cubs manager Dusty Baker look bad. At first Stone noticed more and more managing mistakes, then he began to predict opposing manager moves in real time during games; ultimately he could take it no more, openly criticizing Baker and the team. When the Cubs slipped out of contention with a 12-inning loss to the Reds late in the 2004 season, Stone all but blamed their leadership — or lack thereof — on the field of play. Cubs management was not up to the criticism, especially since Stone was almost entirely right, so barely a month later Stone found himself resigning. Baseball had come a long way from when a frustrated Dizzy Dean could leave the booth to go pitch a few innings, to more recent years when a thin-skinned corporate management could not handle intelligent criticism of its own field general's widely televised miscues.

Steve and Harry were not together for every season. In 2000 Steve Stone had left his telecasting post during a hiatus for health reasons, but he was back by 2003. During his broadcast tenure, Stone would be an eyewitness to one of the most exciting years in baseball history, the great home run chase of 1998, a national baseball extravaganza unlike any other since the Maris-Mantle battle of 1961. This time, though, the home run season of the ages would not involve teammates, but rather would be played on a national stage between two prodigious sluggers on fiercely rival teams, the Cubs and the Cardinals. While Jack Buck called that fateful season for Mark McGwire's Cardinals, Harry Caray and Steve Stone relished the home run barrage of Sammy Sosa.

From a team perspective, the 1998 season would actually be the year of the Yankees, who won a staggering 114 games during the regular season, and it would be an individual breakthrough year for Mark McGwire with his 70-homer milestone. But in many ways the outgoing slugger Sammy Sosa stole the show, for after all, it was Sosa, not McGwire, who captured league MVP honors that season. When Sosa slammed 20 home runs in the month of June, it was a major league record, a remarkable feat never achieved by the likes of Ruth, Gehrig, Mays, Mantle, or Aaron.[10] As the season unfolded, it was apparent that 1998 could become a very special year, a point that grew more and more obvious as the year wore on, especially since home runs make great television, a point discovered with Carlton Fisk's body language during the Boston-Reds clash in the 1975 World Series.

McGwire had already clubbed four homers when his deep 424-foot blast on April 14 portended a barrage of tape measure shots in 1998. Indeed, during that same game, he smashed two *more* mammoth home runs, a second off pitcher Jeff Suppan before crushing a 462-foot blast courtesy of reliever Barry Manuel. On May 12 McGwire outdid himself with a stunning 527-footer, followed four days later by a 545-foot moon shot off Livian Hernandez. Then, on May 19, McGwire served up another three-homer game, but this time they were all 440 feet or longer. On June 8 McGwire hit a more-human 356-footer off Jason Bere, but then started a ridiculous streak of 16 straight homers from June 10 to July 28 that all sailed over 400 feet.[11]

By September 5, when McGwire clubbed number 60, it was clear there would soon be a new home run king. "Wake up, Babe Ruth, you're about to have company," Jack Buck announced over KMOX. "And his name is Mark McGwire."[12] Two days later, when number 61 caromed off a Mike Morgan pitch to pass Ruth and tie Roger Maris, Buck could hardly contain himself. "Lookit there. Lookit there. Lookit there. McGwire's number 61. Flight 61, headed for Planet Maris. History. Bedlam. What a moment. Pardon me while I stand to applaud."[13] McGwire kept going, of course, entering uncharted territory with home run #62 just one day later on September 8, when he a slapped an 88-mile-per-hour fastball off the Cubs' Steve Trachsel. But Cub Sammy Sosa continued to dog both history and McGwire, and on September 25 Sosa actually became the first major leaguer to reach 66 homers in a season, a feat that would land his black bat into the Hall of Fame. But McGwire refused to fade, clubbing his own #66 just hours later on yet another day that he would he hit three, followed by two more the next day to close the season with five historic home runs in just two days.

The 1998 race had begun with a barrage from McGwire who had slammed 24 homers by May 24. But Sosa had then countered with a blistering pace of 20 homers in 24 games. As the two sluggers faced off during the season, fan and media interest soared. McGwire was named by *Time* as its "Hero of the Year"; Fox television's national baseball ratings were up 11 percent for the season; and according to the *New York Times*, baseball benefited by an estimated $1.5 billion in new proceeds from all the Sosa-McGwire excitement.[14] Broadcaster Tim McCarver released a book called *The Perfect Season*, and baseball attendance shot upward.

The live gate attendance at all major league baseball games had inched upward after World War II, but it was not always a steady climb. It eclipsed 20 million for the first time in 1948 but slumped in the 1950s precisely when television began to proliferate. By 1952 and 1953, attendance had dropped by one-third from its peak and actually ended the decade lower than where it had begun. The year following the historic Maris-Mantle home run duel saw a sharp jump, then, as the big leagues added more expansion teams, gate receipts began to accelerate, rising by almost 50 percent from a decade low in 1961 to a record 27,229,666 by 1969.[15] By then the extreme newness of television had worn off, so TV was again billboarding games just as radio had done four decades before, fueling fan interest and boosting attendance rather than competing with it.

When the 1970s began, baseball made a radical move almost entirely driven by television. Major league baseball recognized that the big money ratings were in prime time. Day games for the Fall Classic generated viewers of course, but not as many as the league would like; moreover, many of those viewers were young children, shut-ins, and the unemployed, not the kind of viewers that advertisers preferred. On October 13, 1971, the World Series debuted in prime time. The Pirates won Game Four at home by a narrow 4–3 margin over Baltimore and eventually came from behind to win the Series in seven games after having lost the first two contests.[16]

Ratings for that 1971 World Series leaped ahead, recovering from a weak 19.4 rating with a 53 share in 1970 to notch a 24.2 rating and 59 share for the 1971 Series—an especially impressive turnaround given that both pennant winners were smaller market teams. The rating figure is a way to measure households owning a television expressed as percentages, thus the 24.2 "rating" meant that 24.2 percent of all households with a television were tuned to that program, in this case it was the average of programs comprising the 1971 World Series games. The "share" measurement pertained more to the televisions that were actually turned on and being viewed, also expressed in percentages, so that baseball's 59 share meant that 59 percent of all televisions in use were actually tuned to the 1971 Series.[17]

The top-rated television show for all of the 1971-72 network season was the innovative CBS program *All in the Family*, which turned in a spectacular 34 rating for the season, meaning that 34 percent of all households with a television actually had the TV on and tuned to that program. The *Flip Wilson Show* was a distant second that network season at 28.2. Had the 1971 World Series been a full-season program, its 24.2 rating would have earned eighth place for the year, an extremely good showing. By contrast, baseball's lower 19.4 World Series rating one year before would not have placed the 1970 Series in the top-25 shows, and that was a year when even the pedestrian country music comedy of *Hee Haw* nailed a 21.4.[18]

The trend continued for NBC, which carried the Series during the first seven years of the decade, with the World Series rating expanding to a robust 27.5 in 1972 as Charlie Finley's Oakland A's defeated the Reds in seven games. The next year was even better when the Series registered a Nielsen rating of 30.7 as America watched the Mets lose in seven games to the A's, an entertaining chip-on-the-shoulder team that featured Reggie Jackson, Jim "Catfish" Hunter, Joe Rudi, Bert Campeneris, Rollie Fingers, and Ken Holtzman. That 30.7 would have landed the Series in a close second place for the entire 1973-74 television season, barely behind *All in the Family* at 31.2.[19] With the pitcher's mound lowered, scoring and home runs up, and the World Series in prime time, major league baseball was basking in an economic bonanza.

But was this resurgence enough to carry baseball through an entire season, let alone a full decade? League-wide attendance at the ballparks would indeed drift higher throughout the 1970s, starting the decade at 28.75 million total fans and ending with a figure of 43.55 million, an increase of more than 51 percent.[20] To some degree, an overall resurgence in baseball may also have been fueling the World Series ratings, but even so, it would take televised night games to capture the full benefit. It is likely that both factors were feeding each other, but the conclusion was clear and unavoidable: baseball was back.

Baseball broadcasting in the early 1980s would benefit from renewed fan interest, more televised night games, and better broadcasting technology as color television improved, instant replay became more sophisticated, and the national announcers grew more and more polished in the booth. By 1987 attendance would spike to a record 52 million, more than doubling over the prior 20 years, but, somewhat curiously, national interest in televised baseball would begin to slide again. The ABC and NBC networks began to alternate the Series telecasts beginning in 1979, then baseball granted the Series rights to CBS starting in 1990 for four straight years.

Although the 1980 World Series ratings were a powerful 32.8 (and a lofty 56 share), which would have topped the 1979-80 prime-time network season and was good enough for a solid second place for the 1980-81 season, by 1982 the Nielsen numbers were dipping to 28.0, plunging to just 22.9 for the 1984 Series, the lowest rating since 1970.[21] Why?

Competition. In the early 1980s cable television began to take hold, not only with the upstart CNN cable news channel owned and spearheaded by a baseball man, Ted Turner, but also the embryonic ESPN. Viewership was simply being diluted because audiences were finding more choices on television. Moreover, a fourth on-air network, Fox, was gaining traction, spreading the TV audience further.

Even the audience that was left had been in decline. In 1979 a survey conducted by *TV Guide* indicated that 49 percent of American viewers were watching less television.[22] That same year, ESPN was launched, and almost immediately it became the largest cable channel, carried by nearly every cable system and accessible to over 57 million viewers.[23] Ted Turner's Cable News Network (CNN) was a quantum leap of television and technology that was launched just one year later in 1980 with the support of two major sponsors willing to gamble on Turner, cable, and news: General Foods and Proctor & Gamble.[24] Ironically, that same year was when television news icon Walter Cronkite retired from CBS network television, a point even more profound in hindsight than it appeared at the time. With Cronkite out and Turner's CNN on the rise, it was apparent that both television and America were changing radically.

American viewing habits were becoming more edgy. Cable provided more freedom from broadcast regulators, and certainly more choices. Network television was forced to keep up. In November 1980, CBS nailed a broadcast home run of its own. An earthy prime-time soap opera had debuted on April 2, 1978, flaunting sex, money, and power like never before on network television. America was quickly hooked, as *Dallas* became a stunning hit for CBS. When the slippery, seedy oil tycoon character J.R. Ewing, played by Larry Hagman, was shot by an unknown fictional assailant, tension and viewers mounted as the dramatic crime came to a head. When the perpetrator was finally revealed during a show in November 1980, CBS rewrote the broadcasting record books with a *Dallas* episode that snared a 53.3 rating with an astronomical 76 share.[25]

Sports became edgier and more controversial, too, featuring not only the loud mouth quantum leap of boxing and entertainment, Muhammad Ali, but also Howard Cosell, the announcer who "told it like it is" with enough acerbic wit, lofty ego, and cerebral candor to land a key anchor role on *Monday Night Football*. Sports were clearly going prime time, too, but would they be able to keep up with all the other programming?

When the 1985 fall television season began, NBC was in its 60th year — and it had never, ever, finished first in the network prime time ratings for a whole broadcast year. This was especially remarkable since at the time there had been only three networks in existence since the distant demise of the old DuMont network. But 1985 would be different with NBC capturing the prime-time crown for the first time, although network television overall continued to struggle with the proliferation of cable. NBC raised its advertising rates that year, but both ABC and CBS were forced to cut theirs by 1986-87.[26]

Sports programming, including the popular NFL, was not immune. Although the 1985 Chicago Bears football team crushed the league with a bone-jarring defense, it featured a plethora of colorful personalities like quarterback Jim McMahon, the beloved Walter Payton, "Danimal" Dan Hampton, the wild-eyed Mike Singletary, William "Refrigerator" Perry, and even their coach, the unpredictable and imminently entertaining Mike Ditka. That Bears team was even edgier than the hit show *Dallas*, and they drew ratings like flies to honey — and football. But even they could not save the NFL from the cable dilution. In 1986, for the first time, all three networks experienced difficulty selling sports programming. Even advertising rates for the vaunted NFL dropped for the first time, a full 15 percent lower in 1986 alone.[27]

The networks became more aggressive. Two things never before shown on TV over the course of four decades suddenly appeared in one year, both during 1987: exposed brassieres for a Playtex commercial and condoms. If that were not enough, Rupert Murdoch, the controversial financier who already owned 20th Century–Fox, dove head-first into the television business with a ground-breaking fourth network, Fox Broadcasting. That same year, with over 50 percent of American households were equipped with cable, Murdoch was diluting what was left of the free on-air television market.

Then came the VCR recording device. Even those who still watched network television could record shows and skip the commercials. In 1982 only 4 percent of homes had a VCR device, but just six years later in 1988 nearly 60 percent had one. Cable was still expanding rapidly, and by 1989, it was exploiting the pay-per-view revenue streams that only cable could provide. In July of that year, the networks turned in a record low performance against cable, capturing only 55 percent of the viewing audience. But one network player, Rupert Murdoch, knew how to compete, and the Fox Network was rapidly becoming the edgiest of the four networks behind its sarcastic hit show with a cult following that would last two decades and more, *The Simpsons*.[28]

America became fearful of schlock television, and the government fought back with the Children's Television Act that mandated certain minimum levels of educational programming for children. But then something else happened that would change the viewing world dramatically: reality television.

Fate and misfortune would conspire to reshape cable television news just as CNN was celebrating its first full decade of operation. In January 1991, the Gulf War exploded in the Middle East and on cable television, especially on CNN, the only news organization capable of executing a full-time, full-scale account of the Iraq invasion with its embedded reporters, some of whom were actually in Baghdad where images of tracer bombs lit up the nighttime desert sky. Fearing accusations of exploiting the war, many advertisers stepped back, hurting television revenues on both network and cable channels. But cable still benefited, because legions of remaining viewers who had not yet bought into the CNN model were suddenly, irreconcilably, hooked.

War, as it happens, offers the ultimate in dramatic reality programming, so CNN took a massive leap forward with its compelling around-the-clock images. Hooked on cable, news, and reality, viewers craved more, which they soon received later in 1991 with the invention of Court-TV and its 24-hour live drama of real trials courtesy of a joint venture called Courtroom Television Network.

The following year, network television, and NBC in particular, would suffer another blow: the retirement of late-night television icon Johnny Carson. Cronkite and Carson were gone, while Homer Simpson, MTV, Fox, and "reality programming" were in. It was inevitable, perhaps, that sooner or later the "reality" part of reality programming would itself be manipulated. In 1993, the news magazine program *Dateline NBC* showed a dramatic on-camera explosion of a GM truck during a story about safety issues—but the explosion, as it happens, was not a real event. It had been staged. Noticeably unimpressed with NBC's notion of manipulated news, General Motors pulled its NBC news advertising, dealing the network a blow against its credibility and budget.

But some television innovators, first Ted Turner, then Fox, and even NBC by 1992, did recognize a programming phenomenon that would help boost, if not redefine, sports programming on television. Simply put, sports provide reliable reality television at affordable costs of production. All sports, baseball included, are essentially reality TV, staged programs driven by real events that supply the excitement and drama.

As 1993 unfolded, not only were 98 percent of American households equipped with at least one television, but 64 percent of households—almost two-thirds—sported at least two, one reason that the anticipated final episode of the hit television comedy *Cheers* could draw 93.1 million viewers in 1993 after an 11-year run.[29] As television was becoming a bigger and bigger force of American commerce and culture, and as channels and networks proliferated, television craved more and more content.

Ted Turner was the first to recognize this trend and to specifically address it with sports programming. In his early years Turner worked for his father's billboard business where he learned much about business in general and advertising in particular. Later he acquired that business, called Turner Advertising Company, after his volatile father shot himself in 1963.[30] By then Ted was a superb but aggressive businessman with a flair for advertising and promotion. Seven years later, when Turner Advertising was the largest advertising company in the South, Ted bought a local UHF Atlanta television station, WJRJ, partly to fend off the insurgence of television as a competitor to the billboard business. It was a small independent station and not a network affiliate, so it needed programming but had a modest budget. Turner's first idea was to acquire and show legions of old television programs, which were very cheap but had an established audience. Soon, though, Turner began to search for alternate programming. The eventual answer was down the street, the Atlanta Braves baseball team.[31]

After buying another local UHF station, Charlotte-based WRET, Turner changed his company's name and focus. The new Turner Communications Group was losing money in 1971, so Turner augmented his programming with the purchase of old black-and-white motion pictures. With color television proliferating, Turner was able to acquire these black-and-white films on the cheap; he bought them rather than renting or licensing them, showing these movies over and over without paying royalties. Finally Turner's group broke even by 1972. Then the FCC made a few regulatory changes, allowing cable operators to acquire far-away signals from other stations. Turner, who had instant classic programming to offer, was a willing and opportunistic seller, and so Turner Communications earned a profit of $1 million in 1973.[32]

Selling programming to cable operators around the country was already becoming very lucrative when Turner seized upon another opportunity. When RCA launched a major communications satellite in 1975, Turner jumped in with both feet, renting a channel for his own company TCG. He built a large satellite dish in rural Georgia to distribute his television signal and programming to cable operators across the country.[33] Still hungry for programming, Turner suddenly spied the Atlanta Braves baseball team. The Braves were losing money and rumors swirled about their possible departure from Atlanta, which already was their third home city after leaving Boston and then Milwaukee. By this time Turner had become adept at acquiring cheap, losing properties with an eye toward turning them around with his savvy and innovation.

Turner paid just $10 million for the Braves in 1976 — a team that would be worth in the neighborhood of the league average $482 million by 2009.[34] When Turner bought the Braves, he was still just 37 years of age but was already a nationally known media mogul. He publicly affirmed his trademark desire to win on the field, but Turner had more in mind than just baseball. He was, after all, in the media and entertainment business, so he saw the Braves as ready-made reality programming. Once the team was in place, it virtually produced itself, playing 162 regular-season games every year, nearly three hours of prospective television each time, into eternity, all for the price of $10 million.

With the Braves floundering, major league baseball approved its brash new team owner, but many league insiders would soon regret the move. Turner did to baseball what he had already done for sleepy local television, rocking the big league boat with new ideas and an irreverent distaste for stodgy rules. On the field Turner jumped at a new opportunity with the advent of free agency and the demise of the reserve clause courtesy of Andy Messersmith and Dave McNally. Suddenly he could go after other players to stock his struggling team, so Turner landed the first of the first, signing pitcher Andy Messersmith himself. The other owners were already annoyed by, if not fearful of, this new free agent beast, when Turner rubbed salt in the wound by giving Messersmith jersey number 17 with a new name on the back: "Channel," meaning that when the centerfield camera showed Messersmith pitching on the mound, the audience saw "Channel 17" on his back.[35] Turner also baited the league commissioner, Bowie Kuhn, by openly violating league rules against player tampering when he lured another free agent, slugger Gary Matthews, to Atlanta. Turner openly railed against Kuhn and his archaic rules, fuming at baseball's winter meetings with a variety of public outcries. Turner had to be physically removed — by his own people — but the damage was done. Kuhn suspended Turner from baseball for the entire 1977 season, a year that Turner spent sailing, wining the America's Cup in yacht racing for good measure.

But Turner's revitalized television empire, the newly named WTBS, continued to thrive and became the first cable station to be delivered to audiences via satellite. With classic television shows and movies, plus the Atlanta Braves baseball games, Turner fed programming to cable stations around the country, virtually inventing the "superstation" concept. By 1976, when he bought the Braves, Turner's superstation was worth an estimated $40 million. Energized by the sports programming concept, Turner also bought the struggling NBA Atlanta Hawks basketball team, expanding his sports programming even further.

By 1979, WTBS was broadcasting 24 hours every day, flinging its multifarious programming across the country. The Atlanta Braves became a household name, almost America's team, with games available to a majority of U.S. households. But then the world scoffed more than ever. The very next year Turner found another source of cheap reality programming, one that also produced itself after an initial investment: television news. The traditional networks were barely making money with news and they already had a stranglehold with their nightly television newscasts. But Turner was undaunted, launching Cable News Network, CNN, in 1980, aided by cash raised from selling his Charlotte station WRET for $20 million.[36]

Others took note of Turner's sports programming success. In 1993 Visa anted up $3 million to sponsor the 1996 Summer Olympic Games, to be hosted by Atlanta, the hometown of Turner's TBS, CNN, Braves, and Hawks. That same year, the still fledgling Fox Network shocked sports broadcasting by landing the NFL rights to broadcast National Conference football games, wresting the rights from long-time NFL network broadcaster CBS. Meanwhile, the 1994 Winter Olympics became the most watched television event in history with 204 million American viewers, partly aided by the drama of skating rivals Tonya Harding and Nancy Kerrigan.[37]

Also in 1994, reality television received an explosive but dubious boost when football star O.J. Simpson was chased down and then tried for the murders of his wife Nicole and her friend Ron Goldman. The famous white Bronco car chase of June 1994 was watched live by 95 million viewers.[38] The subsequent trial, which began in January 1995, offered 133 days of live courtroom testimony that blended sports, courtroom drama, and reality television like never before.

Meanwhile, there was no major league baseball on television — or anywhere — from August 1994 to April 1995.[39] The most brutal labor stoppage in major league history was decimating the game and, even worse, angering fans across America. There was no big league ball to be found anywhere — except, of all places, PBS, the Public Broadcasting System. Filmmaker and historian Ken Burns had produced one of the most complete, most dignified, and most romantic of all visual baseball anthologies, his 10-part *Baseball* documentary that aired on public television throughout the month of September 1994. More than 43 million people tuned in to at least parts of the landmark PBS showing, proving that baseball was not entirely dead even though it had disappeared from view in 1994.[40] The mini-series was a smash television hit, but the real series, the World Series, was nowhere to be found in 1994. For the first time ever, the fall classic had been cancelled. ABC and NBC were big losers, too, for they had launched a joint venture with major league baseball called the Baseball Network, which promptly lost $95 million in advertising revenue.[41]

The World Series had been manipulated before, of course, when the Black Sox threw the 1919 Series to the Reds as part of a gambling cabal. Baseball was an irreverent affair around the turn of the twentieth century, as gambling was prevalent — often in the stands during the games themselves. According to Roger Abrams, law school dean, baseball historian, and baseball arbitrator, even the very first World Series in 1903 may have been influenced by gamblers. Over the eons baseball tampered with the length of the series, which in some years had been a nine-game extravaganza. But until 1994 no one had ever cancelled the Series due to a baseball labor dispute; the fans were not quick to forgive those who did, largely blaming both players and owners.

The 1981 players strike had lasted seven weeks, but baseball and the World Series had survived the ordeal. Not even 9/11 could keep baseball on the mat, as the Mets and Liza Minnelli showed a televised world stage on September 21, 2001, just 10 days after the World Trade Center attacks. Her stirring rendition of Frank Sinatra's trademark song "New York, New York" during the seventh-inning stretch of the Mets' first post-attack home game (against the Braves) was an in-your-face statement for baseball and for America. That watershed event was already one of baseball's defining moments, one of the most profound in baseball's history, when the very next inning catcher Mike Piazza slammed a two-run game-winning exclamation point over the Shea Stadium wall. With the great home run chase of 1998, Barry Bonds' new single-season homer mark during 2001 itself in the books, and September 11 reclaimed by the Mets and Liza Minnelli on worldwide television, baseball was truly back.

But this time baseball's resurgence would be marred like never before. The game was about to be excoriated on national television, in Congress, and across the front pages in a public flogging that was more relentlessly severe than anything since the Watergate hearings in Congress during the summer of 1973.

Rumors of steroid use in baseball had begun to swirl during and after the Sosa-McGwire-Bonds years of the great home run chase. Baseball players were beginning to look like linebackers and home runs were being crushed at record paces not only by the superstar sluggers but also by ordinary position players, even slap-hitter infielders, all during an era when major league baseball lacked a serious testing program for performance-enhancing drugs. More and more tangible evidence that those rumors could be true began to surface, like when the state police in Boston discovered steroids and needles in a vehicle owned by a Boston Red Sox infielder, or when a Florida Marlins clubhouse employee found six vials of steroids in one pitcher's locker.

In 2002, following Barry Bonds' 2001 assault on the record books, one-time MVP

Ken Caminiti publicly estimated that "about half" of all major leaguers were using some form of anabolic steroids. Two years later, on October 10, 2004, Caminiti was dead due to a litany of issues that included an enlarged heart and a drug overdose, perhaps cocaine, for which he had tested positive just days earlier. He was only 41 years old.[42] Then came Jose Canseco, the former slugger, one-time teammate of Mark McGwire when the two played for Oakland, and a home run hitter himself. Already an outspoken "bad boy" of baseball, Canseco took those steroid rumors and placed them on the *New York Times* best-seller list with the release of his steroid exposé *Juiced* in February 2005.

With *Juiced* about to hit the shelves, Canseco was spread over the airwaves even as baseball and others denigrated Canseco's story as shameless self-promotion. Long-time CBS correspondent Mike Wallace aired a story on Canseco's accusations during a watershed *60 Minutes* piece for CBS television. Canseco had named names, big ones, and pulled no punches. Soon many of the biggest of those named players found themselves being grilled by Congress on television. All initially denied such steroid use, and some, notably Mark McGwire, just stonewalled it. Rafael Palmeiro was especially indignant on camera: "I have never used steroids. Period. I don't know how to say it any more clearly than that. Never."[43]

About six months later, during the summer of 2005, Palmeiro failed a league drug test conducted under a new steroid policy, forcing him to revise his adamant statement. Canseco, meanwhile, told countless stories of steroid abuse at the major league level, including his own, admitting that he took banned anabolic steroids and human growth hormone during his entire 16-year career than ended in 2001. In August 2005, Canseco was on *60 Minutes* again, reporting that he, himself, had actually injected Mark McGwire, Palmeiro and other players with steroids.

Following the initial *60 Minutes* story, the House Government Reform Committee lambasted baseball during its all-day, nationally televised hearing that lasted a grueling 11 hours. The Committee attacked baseball's weak steroid policies and the evasive testimony from such stars as McGwire, Palmeiro, Sammy Sosa, and pitcher Curt Shilling. "I have not been reassured one bit by the testimony I have heard today," announced Congressman Stephen Lynch, who went on to denounce the myriad loopholes in baseball's testing policy at that time.[44]

Not even baseball's powerbrokers were immune from Congressional contempt. Commissioner Bud Selig and union leader Donald Fehr were taken to the woodshed for baseball's joke of a testing policy, which never even contained penalties for first-time offenders until just before the 2005 season — but even then the penalty was just a 10-game suspension. This was barely a wrist slap when compared to the far more serious two *years* imposed by the International Olympics Committee.

If all that were not enough, in March 2006 Penguin Group's Gotham Books published *Game of Shadows*, an exhaustive third-party exposé of BALCO and Barry Bonds, written by award-winning investigative reporters at the *San Francisco Chronicle*. Baseball was not only embarrassed, but indeed humiliated by the relentless barrage of incriminating evidence. The sport was taking a hit in the pocketbook where it counts: attendance, sponsors, and television ratings.[45]

Partly to rebuild its credibility, and partly to gain political support to finally impose tougher standards and penalties, baseball decided to bite the bullet on March 30, 2006 (the very same month that *Game of Shadows* debuted), when Commissioner Selig retained the highly respected former Senate Majority Leader George J. Mitchell, then a lawyer in private practice at the mega law firm DLA Piper US LLP, to investigate the use of steroids in the major leagues. Mitchell and his staff proceeded to interview over 700 people and sift through 115,000 pages of documents in compiling a book-length 400+ page official report on the use of performance-enhancing drugs by major league baseball.[46]

The highly anticipated Mitchell Report was formally issued on December 13, 2007. Even its title seemed thorough and daunting: *Report to the Commissioner of Baseball of an Independent Investigation into the Illegal Use of Steroids and Other Performance Enhancing Substances by Players in Major League Baseball*. The report essentially indicted baseball, the players union, the underworld that supplied illegal performance-enhancing drugs such as the now infamous Bay Area Laboratory Co-Operative (BALCO), and legions of individual players. The steroid scandals that broke on and around the turn of the New Millennium have been exhaustively reported, but why did it happen in the first place?

The players union resisted testing efforts, a remarkable position given the health and welfare of its members was at issue. The Mitchell Report specifically concluded, "The Players Association was largely uncooperative." And it scolded the Association for interfering with the Mitchell investigation. "The Players Association sent out a memorandum that effectively discouraged players from cooperating. Not one player contacted me [Mitchell] in response to my memorandum."[47]

In the face of mounting evidence of juiced players, the players union fought drug testing and the league did not aggressively take that issue to the mat. Baseball attendance plummeted in 1994, the year of the strike, and did recover in 1995. It did not reach pre-strike levels until the Sosa-McGwire year of 1998 when the entire nation was energized by home runs. Television ratings for baseball are skewed by the game's localized television deals and can be somewhat hard to evaluate, unlike in football where fewer games per season and more definable network deals make NFL comparisons easier to define and analyze. But taking the World Series as a proxy for national fan interest, it is clear that viewer attention has been in a strong downtrend since the late 1970s.

In 1978 an exciting Dodgers-Yankees Series drew 44.3 million viewers, a total that would never again be reached. By 1989 that number would plummet to just 24.5 million, especially since the Bay Area Series between the Giants and the Athletics was geographically challenged and was of less interest to national viewers. Viewership would drop into the 20 millions again in 1993, and would never again hit 30 million. While the Series was canceled altogether in 1994, there was a one-year resurgence in 1995 to 28.97 million viewers with average rating scores of 19.5. Still, the overall trend was in steep decline even though the Yankees were featured in four out of five years up to and including 2000. As the steroid controversy emerged with Canseco, Bonds, *Game of Shadows*, and all the rest, the public lost faith and interest in big league ball. Viewership for the 2002 World Series dipped under 20 million, only about 40 percent of what it was in 1978. The numbers were down to 17 million in 2005 and a paltry 13.6 million viewers in 2008, with an 8.4 rating and 14 share compared to a 32.8 rating and 56 share in 1980.[48]

What happened? More cable, more channels, and more choices, including a surging NFL and an NBA energized by the Michael Jordan era, contributed handily. The 1994 labor action and World Series debacle was more like the final dagger than the overall cause, but the ensuing fan disgust heightened concerns among the baseball owners. Did baseball invent the steroid crisis to boost fan interest? Not likely, but when the players themselves discovered steroids and the league then discovered the home runs they produced, the ensuing headlines, and the energized 1998 regular season that was unlike any other in almost 40 years, it was too easy and too tempting to look the other way. But baseball took such indifference a step further by seemingly digging its head into the sand in the face of mounting evidence that directly pointed to the contamination of major league ball.

The great steroid era desecrated the game, diluted records, tarnished the feats of Hank Aaron, Roger Maris and even Babe Ruth, and ruined countless careers and lives. There is no better evidence of baseball's misplaced values than what happened to Barry Bonds himself in 1998, which is to say, nothing. One of the most talented players in big league history, a virtual throwback to his own Godfather Willie Mays, Barry Bonds turned in a spectacular 1998 season when he hit .303, slugged 37 home runs, and made the All-Star team for the eighth time — yet no one even noticed. Two players who later would be in the middle of the steroid quagmire, Sosa and McGwire, stole all the headlines and records. Sammy Sosa hit five more homers than the all-time Roger Maris record, yet he did not even lead the league in 1998, settling for second place behind McGwire's unprecedented 70.

According to the *Game of Shadows*, excerpted in a *Sports Illustrated* article that preceded the book's publication, Bonds played in a three-game series at St. Louis in May 1998 and received a surprising education about the power and influence of baseball's home run ball. During those three days Bonds took a back seat to a Cardinals fan frenzy as Mark McGwire slammed his 21st homer of the season, a 425-footer on May 22, followed by two more shots the next day, one of them a spectacular 477 feet, followed by still another on May 24. Discouraged, Bonds himself would soon fall victim to the steroid pandemic.[49] Bonds should be accountable to baseball and history, of course, but was he not really a victim, yet another casualty of baseball manipulation? Baseball's "take no prisoners" approach to hardball has long been a part of the game's legacy. The leagues turned to offense and home runs many times over the decades, subsidizing both with rule changes, equipment changes, the lowered pitching mound, designated hitter rule, smaller parks and, ultimately, juiced players.

The 1998 home run barrage produced some of the best baseball television ever, but there is no free lunch in life or baseball. Once fans realized they had been duped, they lost interest at alarming rates. Yes, the 2009 World Series produced bigger ratings as the Yankees finally won again, but will this be an exception that proves the underlying rule? The follow-up baseball spin produced such headlines as "2009 World Series Posts Biggest Year-to-Year Growth in History." And to be fair, this was an impressive 39 percent increase over the 2008 numbers that had produced an 11.9 rating with an average audience of 19.4 million. But 2008 had been especially dismal, so a rebound was not unexpected, and, after all, 2009 featured the Yankees and Phillies, an entertaining match-up of big market teams. Moreover, the ratings and viewership were still low by historic standards, with the 11.9 rating tied for fifth lowest since 1968.[50]

Perhaps most disturbing for the baseball television numbers was its head-to-head confrontation with the NFL, where the 2009 World Series fell astonishingly short. Crucial Game Four of the Series happened to fall on a Sunday during the beginning of the NFL season. The regular-season match-up between the Packers and Vikings drew a television audience of 29.8 million, compared to the 22.3 million who were watching the World Series. Yes, the NFL game was especially interesting for it featured quarterback Brett

Favre on his new team against Favre's former team, the Packers. Still, it was nonetheless a regular-season contest, but as the football game entered prime time after 7:00 P.M. Eastern Time, its viewership actually expanded to 36.3 million.[51]

Ironically, by the New Millennium, our esteemed national game had begun to visibly suffer from a lack of national interest. But among all the team sports, baseball still plays best on radio. And by 2009 the game had largely repaired its gate attendance woes suffered during the mid–1990s. Although no team topped the four million mark in 2009, fully nine teams surpassed the three million season attendance threshold, including Milwaukee among the perennial big winners like the Yankees, Mets, Dodgers, Cardinals, and Cubs. Although 2009 attendance was down 6.58 percent from 2008, the season bore the brunt of the severe 2008 national recession and, even so, the league did manage to surpass the vaunted 70 million mark in total attendance for six straight years.[52]

Perhaps all is fair in love and baseball, at least more than with other team sports, but manipulation comes with a price, especially when a manipulated public recognizes itself as the victim. But one venue where manipulation has done nothing but improve the game's enjoyment is television itself, where adding color in the 1950s, then replay, and more recently the boxed strike zone overlay have improved baseball telecasts and increased the viewing enjoyment of those who still follow the game. Adding to the game's broadcast appeal is the advent of high-definition television. Although HD certainly enhances the imagery of NFL games, it brings the stunning beauty of the major league ballparks into the home, enhancing the visual quality of baseball on television in its own unique ways. Baseball may have been built for radio, but HD-TV seems to have been invented for baseball — and that is good for the game, the fans, and the sponsors who discovered, among other things, the viability of virtual advertising. Television technology may have contributed the superimposed yellow first-down line for NFL games, but baseball's slower pace and extended focus on the batter was a natural for superimposed signage directly in the viewer's line of sight. Baseball's pace was not only built for radio, but later it proved a natural for virtual advertising.

15

A Word from Our Sponsor

The very first radio commercial occurred in 1922.[1] Commercial sponsorships would impact sports like no other driving force during the second half of the twentieth century and into the New Millennium, but getting there was a near-mystical story of confusion, innovation, and, ultimately, marketing and technological genius.

Early broadcast sponsorships were a mystery to most of baseball. Owners were obsessed with stadium attendance, sometimes to the point of keeping games off the air altogether. But even when baseball relented, it had no idea what kind of value that sports broadcasting could offer. Larry MacPhail inked a deal with WOR, a major 50,000-watt station in New York, to carry Dodgers games, then signed an impressive array of sponsors like General Mills, Mobil Oil, and Proctor & Gamble. But most owners who followed, even including MacPhail at first, did not grasp the full picture. Initially they sought only to recapture enough lost revenue from perceived lower ticket sales due to the radio and television cannibalization of the games as an entertainment product.[2]

As television became viable in the late 1940s, two large market teams, the Brooklyn Dodgers and the Chicago Cubs, understood and embraced the idea of sports television. The Dodgers would broadcast more than 100 games per year as the 1950s emerged, and Phil Wrigley's Cubs believed that television would hook the community on his baseball product. Wrigley, already an astute marketer and advertiser with his chewing gum empire, felt that television could create new fans, especially women and children who watched afternoon Cubs games.[3] The kids would grow up to become paying customers and the moms would get hooked on baseball. Both eventually happened, for the children indeed grew up as fans and, over the decades, baseball began to count large numbers of women among its staunch fan base.

One phenomenon that facilitated television marketing, especially advertising to women as well as fostering the idea of celebrity endorsements — all of which would drive sports marketing in the closing decades of the twentieth century — was a television breakthrough called *The Goldbergs*. In 1928 a Bronx housewife named Gertrude Berg stumbled into radio, where she began to write and perform a daily 15-minute radio sitcom that debuted in 1929. The show was about an immigrant Jewish family that was so likeable, and so distinctly American, that it was embraced by all of New York for 18 years on radio—then the show jumped to television. "For millions of Americans," *Life* magazine wrote, "listening to *The Goldbergs* ... has been a happy ritual akin to slipping on a pair of comfortable old shoes that never seem to wear out."[4]

The fictional matriarch Molly Goldberg became a national icon, a bit of Oprah Winfrey and Martha Stewart rolled into an All-American homemaker image in the form of a Jewish mother. When the show debuted on CBS network television in 1949, the actress Gertrude Berg already had a following of millions. As it happens, the show always began with the Molly Goldberg character chatting through her apartment window to the neighbors in the next apartments and, sometimes, directly to her audience. It was a natural set-up for product endorsements, so Molly began to do live commercials, in character, to begin the show, raving about Sanka coffee as a decaffeinated wonder, giving "decaf" a serious boost in credibility and acceptance. The show ended its long run only when one of the key actors was blacklisted during the 1950s McCarthy baiting.[5] CBS dumped the show and its popularity in 1951, then it went to NBC for a year and ended on the DuMont network in 1954. But its influence had already been made. And noticed.

Just 10 years later, New York's WOR-TV, the same station that MacPhail had signed for the Dodgers, became the first to broadcast a program that was *only* a commercial—and the "infomercial" concept was born.[6] Television, in the meantime, continued to evolve both technically and as an advertising juggernaut. In 1964, the year that 73 million viewers watched the Beatles debut on the *Ed Sullivan Show*, NBC was third in a three-network race for prime-time audiences. CBS was charging $50,000 per minute for advertising in prime time, ABC took in $45,000, and NBC was able to charge the least at $41,000 per minute. Then NBC made a concerted commitment to color, and by 1965 touted itself as the "full color network" with no less than 96 percent of its programming broadcast in color, including sports events. In 1966, an article in *New York Times Magazine* conceded what was becoming the obvious: "TV is not an art form or a cultural channel; it is an advertising medium."[7] Sounds a bit like the Internet in general, and Google in particular, in the twenty-first century.

To expand the television audience, attract advertisers, and generate ad revenues, television had to grow, adapt, and continue to improve technically. Color broadcasting of sports events began early but was not widespread; it did not start with NBC, but rather began when a CBS affiliate did color telecasts of Dodgers baseball games during the latter two months of the 1951 season. The first use of color during a nationally televised baseball game, though, was in fact by NBC when it broadcast the 1955 Yankees-Dodgers World Series.

Graphics were soon added, but in the early days they depicted just names or statistics, like a batting average, superimposed on the screen in what was a very washed-out image. Those images cleared up some in 1965 when the graphics were matted over the game picture. When baseball went to more night games to enhance ballpark attendance, television was forced to respond. Night games were harder to telecast, especially by means of the early cameras that needed a great deal of lighting. By 1967, Boston's WDHD utilized new RCA TK-43 "big tube" cameras that could operate in lower light, which made the telecast of night games more attractive, and feasible.[8] Meanwhile, during the 1970s the graphics morphed from white to yellow, which seemed less washed-out, before being enhanced by an electronic character generator that had stored memory and could therefore be rapidly updated and used more frequently, if not also more creatively.

Stereo television was introduced in the 1980s, giving TV a boost in sound quality and capabilities. Wireless microphones were placed at key positions to capture the compelling sounds of sports, especially the umpire, the distinct crack of a home run ball off the bat, and even a runner's foot thumping the bag at first base. When computers also emerged in the 1980s, baseball, a game replete with statistics and numbers of all sorts from the early 1900s, embraced "sabermetrics" more than ever. By the late 1990s, graphics were used 200 or more times per game, almost all of them devised on the fly during the game as the need dictated.[9]

When Fox debuted as a fourth television network in the fall of 1986, this new network searched for ways to distinguish itself much like NBC had embodied color telecasts years before. One way was to produce creative but decidedly edgier programming.[10] Fox Television was part of Rupert Murdoch's News Corporation, where Murdoch was known for marketing, controversy, and taking chances. In fewer than 20 years, Fox went from a television novice to become the highest rated broadcast network for the age 18–49 audience. Fox then achieved the number one overall ranking by the 2007-08 broadcast season, partly by offering racier programs to young adults, and partly by offering a growing sports programming lineup.

Fox had begun with a stake in the movie business through 20th Century–Fox, before it purchased many television stations including several in major markets like New York City (WNEW), Los Angeles (KTTV), Chicago (WFLD), and Houston (KRIV). Fox was aggressive and creative, but not always successful. It lured the acerbic but funny Joan Rivers from her position as guest host — and heir apparent — position with NBC's *Tonight Show*, but she could not sustain an audience against her former mentor Johnny Carson. Rivers ultimately failed at Fox, but Fox stumbled upon a successful replacement guest host in Arsenio Hall. Fox continued to roll out cutting-edge programming in prime time like *Married ... with Children*, followed by hits with younger audiences like *Beverly Hills 90210* and *Melrose Place*. In 1989 Fox tried a mid-season 1989 replacement series with the animated, sarcastic, politically irreverent *The Simpsons*, which broke into the top–30 ratings. Television would never quite be the same.[11]

As the 1990s unfolded, while Fox was a large owner of stations and entrenched with gutsy programming, it was still a distant fourth, and barely noticed, in what had become a four-network race. Then Fox did the unthinkable, winning the rights to NFL broadcasting, wresting football away from CBS for the first time since 1955. Many thought Fox would fail and that the NFL had lost its senses, but along with these NFL rights came seasoned broadcasters in John Madden, Pat Summerall, and Terry Bradshaw.

But Fox did not rest on its NFL laurels. During the 1990s Fox and its spinoff Sportvision invested heavily in television graphics, inventing some creative applications for sports. Although some were simple gimmicks, others proved to be innovative and wildly popular with viewing audiences. Fox was a pioneer, for example, in its use of pictorial graphics to visually track key elements of games in progress.

Then Fox engineers came up with an ingenious way to overlay visual graphics into the game itself — not shown over the game, but actually appearing to be "in" the game. Sportvision, a company that was spawned by and then spun off from Fox, developed and exploited the requisite technology that would revolutionize football telecasts: the yellow first-down line. That yellow line stretching across the field of play was used to show the first-down threshold, but the technical challenges to making it seem *under* the players and not on top of the screen were complex. The line debuted not on Fox, but on ESPN during its broadcast of a Ravens-Bengals game on September 27, 1988.[12] When that yellow first-down line soon became an indelible part of NFL and NCAA football broadcasting, the technology spread to other creative uses for other sports.

As of 2009, that seemingly simple first-down stripe required eight computers and a full tractor-trailer of technical equipment, plus a staff of four people to run it all. Not only does the line have to appear to run under the feet of the players, it has to self adjust to the camera positions and angles—otherwise the stripe would simply be out of place or running the wrong way almost all the time. To do the job, a special device is mounted on each of the television cameras, the sole purpose of which is to record every movement the camera lens makes and to send that coded data to the computers 30 times per second.

All in all, there are eight complex hurdles that the yellow first-down system has to solve on the fly. Four of these, for example, are (a) knowing where the first-down threshold is at all times; (b) understanding that football fields are not flat but are slightly curved, then adjusting accordingly 30 times per second; (c) maintaining the illusion of the line under the officials, the players, the ball itself, and even a passing bird; and (d) compensating for other myriad graphics that are flashed over the screen on a regular basis.[13] To make all this work, a virtual field has to be fed to the computer network — actual pregame measurements are made and fed to the system for analysis later, so that when all the data is processed, the line itself can be "painted" across the field. To maintain the illusion of a line running on the field and under everything else, the computer system essentially has to eliminate a precise amount of yellow color on a perfectly calculated sliver of anything that actually runs across where the fictitious line supposedly is on the field — and must do so in flashes of real time as those things move about. If that is not hard enough, the system also has to adjust for clumps of moving dirt, snow, mud, and rain. The whole task seems insurmountable, but determined Sportvision technicians made it work.

So what does a yellow first-down stripe have to do with baseball broadcasting? A great deal, as it happens. Elements of the same technology are used for the Fox HitZone that shows a hitter's relative strength though a superimposed strike zone, and especially for the FoxTrax process that follows an actual pitch through or around the strike zone on its way to the catcher. The superimposed strike box is used to mark a two-dimensional strike zone and then analyze a moving ball through or near it. To do so, the box comprising the zone has to be adjusted for the strike zone itself and the angle of the camera. To do that, Sportvision developed its own "PITCHf/x" system (pronounced "pitch-effects"), which measures the position of a baseball to within a half-inch of where the ball actually travels, beginning where the pitch starts to break, about 40 feet from home plate. The system has to calculate the ball position, speed, deceleration, trajectory — and indeed a changing trajectory like that of a curve ball or slider.[14] A comet-like trail visually follows, and marks, the path of the ball on its way to the plate, past the batter, and into the catcher's mitt — often shown from an angle behind the pitcher in full view of the batter.

By the end of the 2007 baseball season, Sportvision had special PITCHf/x cameras installed in all but two major league parks. As the 2008 season began, Sportvision was prepared to track every major league pitch thrown in every ballpark for the entire year. But not only does the PITCHf/x system track the ball visually, it also calculates the types and location of all the pitches, then can plot them on a graph for visual interpretation. To do so, each pitch must be identified. Was it a curveball, a knuckleball, or a fastball — and if the latter, was it a traditional four-seam fastball or a sinkerball two-seamer? By 2009, Sportvision was tracking eight different pitches: fastballs, sinkers, curveballs, sliders, changeups, split-finger fastballs, cut fastballs, and knuckleballs.[15]

Three top executives from Fox Sports and News Corporation had formed Sportvision. While at Fox Sports one such founder, Stan Honey, was the driving force behind the development of a comet-like glowing trail to a moving hockey puck. The intent was to make hockey more palatable for television, where the small puck rocketed around the ice and was hard to see, especially during lightning fast scores. The comet puck was highlighted like a shooting star in real time, tracking blue at speeds under 70 mph, but turning hot red when the puck was rocketed at faster speeds. Fox had won the rights to broadcast NHL games in 1996, and its hockey tracker was ready for 1998. It took $2 million and a team assembled by Stan Honey from both Stanford Research and an in-car navigation company to bring the comet-like puck online. Although it was a novel approach to sports broadcasting and a technical marvel, it was perceived as gimmicky and distracting and was not especially well received by viewers, even though the puck was in fact easier to see. But Fox knew it had developed something of value, and instinctively believed it could be further developed to revolutionize sports broadcasting. Sportvision was spun off with its first round of venture financing in 1998, the same year the yellow first-down marker debuted.[16] Additional rounds of financing followed as new technologies developed, such as the virtual strike "K-Zone" and a RACEf/x system for NASCAR broadcasting.

In 2002, the widely followed trade magazine *Street & Smith Sports Business Journal* credited Sportvision with having created no fewer than eight of the most important technological innovations in televised sports since 1939. As part of its own 25-year anniversary retrospective, ESPN itself ranked the yellow first-down line as the seventh biggest sports media innovation during its 25-year existence, even ahead of instant replay and sports talk radio.[17] Unlike that superficial hockey comet trail, the yellow linemarker seemed to be part of the field. In short, it clearly looked as though it belonged there, largely due to the technological genius that made the illusion of it as part of the field seem viable.

All of these technical innovations would forever change how all sports are viewed on television. But there was one more use that had not yet been exploited, which would have particular application to major league baseball. Advertising.

To be more precise, virtual advertising would change how baseball is viewed, marketed, and sold for television. "It's the most astonishing kind of advertising technology I've ever seen," confessed David Verkin to the *New York Times* in 1999.[18] Verkin was speaking as the CEO of a New York firm in the business of buying commercial time and ad space for others. The virtual ads are a now-you-see-it, sometimes-you-don't foray into the world of advertising, where stadium signage appears on television but not in the stadium itself. More accurately, these ads "appear to appear" on television, since in reality they exist nowhere except in a computer and on the TV screen itself.

In the fall of 1999, three major league teams participated in a virtual ad program, the Padres, Phillies, and Giants.[19] Viewers have since grown used to seeing virtual ads in sports everywhere, often not even realizing they are in fact fictional parts of the visual terrain. But they did not begin with sports at all. Regular entertainment programming in foreign countries had been inserting products and ads in post-production for years.

But sports are live events, so inserting virtual ads on an otherwise blank wall behind home plate would take a great deal of technology, akin to the rubric of physics and media that goes into the K-Zone tracker or the NFL yellow first-down line.

The key to making these ads palatable to viewers was to make them a "virtual part" of the stadium. Ballpark ads have appeared since the beginning of baseball, even in the minor leagues where ads have historically rimmed the park, even appearing on buildings across from the outfield, like the somewhat famous Budweiser rooftop sign that WGN-TV viewers saw over the Wrigley Field left field wall for years. Enter the yellow-line technology where ads seemingly are placed on a wall behind the batter in full view of the center field camera shot. But since this ad is behind the batter, it has to look like it is in the actual real background for viewers to accept it.

The advantages of virtual advertising go far beyond simply the obvious. Clearly they are easier to install — no one has to go to the stadium and paste or paint an actual sign. And they are easier to change for the same reason. This is where marketing and technology truly join forces; if the ads can be removed easily, why not switch them often? Different ads can appear in different innings, or even with each pitch if it were not so distracting to keep making changes. Taking the process a step further, these ads can be specially targeted to the viewers. For a national broadcast, viewers on the East Coast might see billboarding for Wise potato chips while at the same time fans on the West Coast could be looking at Laura Scudder's brand.

The first-ever virtual advertising in the United States came as a product placement, but not for a sporting event. The first such efforts were an experimental broadcast on the UPN network during a prime-time television series called *Seven Days*. Such advertisers as Coke, Blockbuster video, and Evian bottled water participated in the experiment whereby the viewing audience saw virtual bottles of Evian next to a water carafe, a Blockbuster video appearing to lie on a desktop, and so on.[20]

These types of ads are especially useful in the age of video recording and playback, where traditional commercials are often skipped over. The virtual ads and product placements are, again like the NFL yellow line, a part of the landscape. The public is growing even more tolerant of these images because actual billboard ads are becoming more prevalent, appearing on the floor in airports, bathroom walls, blimps, and projected onto ceilings and buildings.

At the beginning of 2010 there was still considerable debate over whether virtual ads and virtual product placements would have a meaningful place in regular entertainment programming. But since actual product placements have a role in Hollywood feature films, it is likely some form of virtual placements will continue to develop on television — especially since so many viewers can electronically skip regular commercials via recorded programming. In the age of fast-forwarding, the best way to display the "ad" or the product is in the program itself. If a Ford model is used as the car of choice in a crime drama series, for example, why not have an occasional Ford billboard turn up in the program?

In a 2009 story on the emergence of virtual ads, the *New York Times* quoted Paul Schulman, an executive at a unit of Omnicom, who took the position that virtual ads work best in televised sports events.[21] When an ad for a product can appear on the wall behind the batter, it is on screen for several seconds or even several minutes during a game. Then a new ad can magically appear. Ads can even be separated and specially targeted based on location of the viewer. Without the Sportvision type of technology, this would all be hypothetical, for the ad has to look real and seem as though it is really behind the batter and not an overlay on the front of the televised image, which in essence it really is.

In effect, audio "virtual ads" have appeared in baseball for decades. Mel Allen cooperated by announcing the "Ballentine Blast" for home runs, a paid nod to the Ballentine Beer sponsorship slipped into the context of the game. Allen did the same for cigars, too, with his "White Owl Wallop," but he was not the only announcer to play along. Red Barber promoted a classic brand of cigarettes with his "Old Goldie" home run call, and several announcers, including Harry Caray, have contributed variations of Budweiser's scripted "This Bud's for You."[22]

Money talks, so advertising will always find a way. Remarkably, though, even radio did not discover the obvious connection at first. Radio was commercially viable and ready to appear around the country by 1920, but at first the concept of commercials as that term is used today was prohibited. The first commercial, per se, was in 1922, and it was more of a commercial disguised as a program along the lines of what would now be referred to as an infomercial. But once the advertising genie was out of the bottle, there was no putting it back. Wheaties hit it big with a catchy musical commercial in 1926; Sunoco Oil was an early radio sponsor in 1932; Colgate sponsored the first daytime serial program in 1933; Jell-O sponsored the *Jack Benny Program* in 1934; and in 1935 Lever bath soap began to appear in five-minute ad formats.[23]

Meanwhile, none other than Tyrus Raymond Cobb pioneered another form of "product placement" advertising: the celebrity endorsement. Perhaps the best pure hitter in baseball history, in 1950 Ty Cobb was named by *The Sporting News* as the most important player in the first 50 years of major league baseball, ahead of Ruth, Gehrig, and Cy Young.[24] Cobb led the league in batting for nine straight seasons, hit .350 or more 11 years in a row, hit over .400 three times including .420 in 1911, and retired with a .367 lifetime average, a record that many believe will never be broken.[25] In 1907, Cobb garnered his first commercial endorsement, the first of its kind for an athlete, when he signed on with Coca-Cola, the emerging soft drink company with roots in his home state of Georgia. Cobb knew the early Coke owners, so he did not stop with the endorsements, he also became a large investor, making far more with his Coke stock holdings than playing baseball. He also invested in the early automobile industry. Cobb's investments were the largest contributor to a sizable $12 million estate accumulated by the time of his death in 1961.[26]

One of the most successful early product endorsements is one that did *not* happen. The Baby Ruth candy bar, which is still a successful product now owned by Nestle, was introduced by Chicago's Curtiss Candy Company in 1920. Babe Ruth himself had nothing to do with the candy — officially — but unofficially the bar almost certainly exploited Ruth's name for free. Curtiss Candy had been founded in 1916 with an uninspired "Kandy Kake" bar. By 1920, Babe Ruth was setting records, reinventing baseball as a home run game, and inspiring the construction of the original Yankee Stadium, which would open in 1923 as the true "House That Ruth Built." Curtiss Candy suddenly thought up the Baby Ruth bar, but insisted that its brand was inspired by President Grover Cleveland's daughter Ruth, who died at age 12 in 1904, long before the company was founded and a full 16 years before the bar was introduced. Confirmed by a plethora of historic commentary, if not the sheer logic of greed, the obvious intent was to exploit the biggest name in the country at the time, Babe Ruth. The Babe never officially endorsed the bar and was never paid a royalty. Curtiss Candy almost certainly stole it, misappropriating Ruth's image and misleading the public, who largely identified the bar with the slugger Ruth. Adding insult to injury, Ruth did launch his own bar with a 1926 endorsement deal, but was sued by Curtiss for infringing on Curtiss' own "Ruth" mark. Curtiss won, leaving Ruth not only without any compensation for the hot selling Baby Ruth bar, but without the right to use his own name to sell his own candy.[27]

The court decision against Ruth was technically correct, but only because it was founded upon a false premise in the first place. By analogy, a man named McDonald would not now be able to start a hamburger chain named McDonald's, even if he were a famous athlete, because that name is already owned, registered, taken, and used in commerce for the same purpose. The difference is that the company McDonald's bought the original name while Curtiss stole theirs. But the courts in those days were not only unsympathetic to rights of publicity, they ware largely unaware of such a thing. The success of movie, television, and sports stars has subsequently changed the paradigm dramatically. Imagine a new "Mikey Jordan" bar hitting the market at the top of Michael Jordan's career without a challenge from Jordan, or a "LeBron Bar" that paid no royalties to NBA superstar LeBron James. In today's sponsorship environment, such results would be unthinkable.

Not so during the 1920s. The Baby Ruth bar was so successful that new factories had to be built just to keep up with demand. They used up to six train carloads of peanuts every day, which was about 150,000 pounds. By 1927 — the front-page year of Ruth and Murderer's Row — Curtiss owned the largest candy facility in the world. Its Baby Ruth plant operated 24 hours a day and needed a fleet of 54 trucks to bring in the raw materials and to distribute the finished bars. It was the largest selling five-cent candy bar in the United States.[28] When Curtiss began to sponsor a CBS radio show called *The Baby Ruth Hour* in 1929, the scheme had come full circle. But Ruth never made a cent from the exploitation. Ironically, Nestlé's Baby Ruth bar became the official candy bar of major league baseball in 2006, which means that Nestlé actually paid baseball for the right to use Ruth's name in conjunction with big league ball.

It was 1925, precisely during the Ruth candy bar revolution, when President Calvin Coolidge observed, "the chief business of the American people is business." Major league baseball had already transformed itself from a game to a business, beginning when the Cincinnati Red Stockings made themselves into a professional organization in 1869.[29] Although prize fighting had been something of an entertainment business for years, the National and American League peace treaty in the early 1900s transformed baseball into what would become known as a genuine sports industry. Business, of course, is driven by profits, and profits are the product of revenue and growth. Ticket sales, endorsements, media rights deals, concessions, and sponsorships are the driving forces behind the business of sport.

Baseball cards featuring players emerged in the United States during the 1880s as premium items sold in conjunction with tobacco products.[30] This was a business model reminiscent of the original Wrigley chewing gum, which had been a novel premium item for soap product sales. Just as the gum soon supplanted the soap, baseball cards took on a life — and value — of their own. Eventually the cards would be a source of licensing income to baseball and the players, but the big money would clearly be driven by the media.

By 1950, major league baseball had cut a $6 million multi-year deal with Gillette to sponsor the All-Star Game.[31] Three years later in 1953, Gussie Busch dropped all pretenses and moved his beer company directly into the business of baseball by inextricably tying Budweiser and then Busch to the St. Louis Cardinals. Buying the Cardinals, naming the ballpark Busch Stadium, and launching Busch Beer proved to be a product tie-in of big league proportions, turning a good beer business into an empire and a sports advertising juggernaut.

In 1956 baseball announced a $16.25 million pact with NBC for the rights to televise both the All-Star Game and the World Series for a period of five years.[32] Riding a wave of sports advertising success, in 1960 Gillette completed an $8.5 million package with ABC to televise a series of sports programming including football and the lucrative *Friday Night Fights* boxing shows, while maintaining an affiliation with major league baseball with a 25-week installment of the baseball *Game of the Week* on Saturday afternoons.[33] ABC paid $5.7 million for the *Game of the Week* telecasts beginning in 1965, but the players were getting nothing directly from it — a point not lost on Robin Roberts and the Players Association.[34] Yes, the players were receiving a cut of the World Series and All-Star Game broadcasting, but not these regular weekly telecasts. Still, the geometric increase in baseball salaries would be driven by multi-million-dollar broadcast rights, deals that one day would reach into the billions of dollars.

James Farrell, among others, have duly noted that television advertising soon became a primary force behind big league baseball; some have narrowed that observation to beer advertising in particular.[35] Eberhard Anheuser bought the Bavarian brewery in 1860, renaming it the E. Anheuser & Co. His son-in-law, Adolphus Busch, joined up four years later, and the firm was renamed the now familiar Anheuser-Busch. The famous eagle and capital "A" logo began to appear in 1872, and in 1876 the Budweiser brand was introduced. Michelob was launched in 1896, and by 1901 the company was producing one million barrels of beer annually. In 1920, when Prohibition began, the company was forced to diversify into root beer, yeast, ice cream, grape beverages— and even a non-alcoholic version of Budweiser. Prohibition lasted 13 years, and when it ended the company returned to its brewing roots and also introduced another icon, the Budweiser Clydesdale horses. When the Busch family bought the Cardinals, they had difficulty renaming their park after an established beer, namely Budweiser, so they simply gave it the family moniker Busch Stadium — and then they introduced Busch Beer in 1955.[36] By 1997, worldwide sales of Anheuser-Busch beer products would reach 100 million barrels annually, and in 2003 Bud Light became the top selling beer in the United States. As of 2009, the two best selling beers in the world were Budweiser and Bud Light, due, in no small part, to sports marketing and television.

In 1945 Narragansett Beer sponsored the first telecasts of Boston Red Sox games, a year when there were only 7000 working TV sets in America.[37] In 1947, half of all television sets sold in Chicago were to local bars sensing the use of TV and sports to attract customers. Hamm's, Blatz, Old Style, and many other beers got into the sports advertising act. In 1970, tobacco giant Philip Morris bought Miller Brewing and considered launching a Marlboro brand beer. The company averted that potential disaster, while at the same time identifying sweeping trends to low-calorie beer. To counter the potential "sissy" image of so-called light beers, Miller commercials featured two of the toughest, manliest, former athletes it could find, Dick Butkus and Bubba Smith, who argued the two strongest attributes of Miller: "tastes great" or "less filling." From 1973 to 1983, there were 81 different commercials using that theme, some featuring former baseball players like the irascible Billy Martin and the inimitable Bob Uecker.[38] In 1984, one Miller ad showed Uecker in a bar wearing an ugly checkered sport coat and pretending to be Whitey Ford.

But something else happened in 1984 that would reshape sports-related marketing for a quarter century and beyond. During the third quarter of the Super Bowl, Apple Computer unveiled a 60-second commercial with noticeable Orwellian overtones called simply, "1984," which introduced the revolutionary 128K Macintosh computer with graphical user interface, listed at a then stunning price of $2,495 each. Due in large part to its Super Bowl exposure, sales far surpassed expectations when they reached 75,000 units in the first month after the ad ran.[39] This innovation — the use of novel commercials introduced at the Super Bowl — would transform the Super Bowl into an annual showcase for new and unique commercials that, for some, would surpass the entertainment value of the game itself. Ten years later, personal computers outsold television sets in the United States.[40]

With the Super Bowl's mega-status in sports, entertainment, and advertising, the loop of sports and marketing had come full circle. Sports had begun to "sponsor" the ads. The distinction is further blurred with virtual advertising in the background and naming rights to stadiums, now known, variously as of the start of 2010, as the Cell (U.S. Cellular Field where the White Sox play), Miller Park (Brewers), Tropicana Field (Rays), Comerica Park (Tigers), Coors Field (Rockies), and Petco Park (Padres). Some baseball teams still feature the old-fashioned names like Yankee Stadium, Fenway Park, and Dodger Stadium. There are two hybrids of a sort, Busch Stadium and Wrigley Field, the latter name dating to 1926 although it, like Busch, was named after the owner and was not really a naming rights deal. At the beginning of 2010, 57 percent of all major league ballparks had name sponsors, fewer than in the NBA (79 percent) or NHL (90 percent), but more than the NFL (50 percent). The average rights deal among all major American sports amounted to $2.9 million per year, with the highest at $300 million over 30 years for the football's Houston Texans.

Naming rights deals turn entire stadiums into giant billboards for the two or three million fans who pass through the gates at most major league stadiums each year, but these corporate sponsorships are also propelled by television where the name of the park is stated and shown numerous times throughout local and national telecasts. Ad rates, and to a degree naming rights, are driven by viewers, and television viewers are measured by the rating services, notably the famous Nielsen ratings generated by the Nielsen Company in Northbrook, Illinois. Nielsen television ratings are "captured, housed, and stored" in systems retrieved from about 25,000 metered households, but the company does much more. Besides processing data from 1.6 million handwritten paper diaries during crucial sweeps periods, the firm can analyze its data in very sophisticated ways to learn whether children watch cartoons with the parents, what zip codes are tuned into what football games, whether pet owners prefer situation comedies, and so on.[41]

According to Nielsen's own website, the company measures over 40 percent of the world's TV viewing audience, a daunting task since many homes now have multiple television sets, each with access to 100 or more channels. Arthur Nielsen introduced the first monitoring device in 1936 when there were only 200 television sets in the world. When it developed the forerunner to its current ratings system in 1950, the average American household had just one TV, if any, and only three network channels to select from. The company is now a giant research firm that measures product sales, market share, distribution, price and merchandising conditions in retail outlets as well as tracking television viewers.[42]

A sample of the highest rated shows in a season includes *I Love Lucy* (1952–55), *Gunsmoke* (1957–61), *The Beverly Hillbillies* (1962–63), *All in the Family* (1971–76), *Dallas* (1980–82), *Cheers* (1990–91), *Seinfeld* (1994–95), *ER* (1995–97), and *American Idol* (2004–09), some reappearing on top again in subsequent years. Comedy and drama shared the top honors for decades until a new phenomenon of "reality programming" emerged in its current form with *Who Wants to Be a Millionaire?* in 1999 and *American Idol* in 2004.[43] No sports program has ever made number one, but these shows are prime time and customary sports programming does not lend itself to that formula. *Monday Night Football* does appear in prime time, but it never made the top 10. But sports are reality programming and they do play a huge role in television viewing habits and media revenues. When 9/11 bumped the NFL season a week, it sent the Super Bowl into the February sweeps period where it remains, virtually assuring a sweeps victory for whatever network televises the Super Bowl that year. A similar effect has evolved for the World Series during the November sweeps period, although World Series ratings have not dominated in recent years as much as the Super Bowl does.

By 1993, 98 percent of all households in America had at least one television, and 64 percent had two or more. The following year, 204 million U.S. viewers watched at least some of the Winter Olympics, making those games the most-watched event in the history of television to that point.[44] In recent years ESPN has been a big player for cable sports broadcasting while the Fox television network has made its mark in traditional football and baseball broadcasting. Fox not only seized its NFL broadcast rights in 1993 with a four-year $1.58 billion deal for NFC conference games, it began to feature major league baseball games in 1996 and presently has baseball rights extending through 2013, guaranteeing that the All-Star Game and World Series will be on Fox throughout. Including additional playoff games awarded to TBS, major league baseball has reportedly signed aggregate television deals for $3 billion during that period.

Bringing its own edgy brand to baseball, Fox began its telecast efforts with a catchy slogan: "Same game, new attitude." Unabashedly mining for ratings, Fox monitored the baseball schedule of major markets in New York, Los Angeles, and Chicago. If a game combined teams from two of those markets, Fox wanted it.

Fox would telecast many key games, of course, but none was stranger than the now infamous Steve Bartman game that seemed to mystically deny the Cubs their best shot at the World Series in decades. On October 3, 2003, the Cubs were leading the Marlins 3–0 in the eighth inning of Game Six of the National League Championship Series, when a high fly to left came straight down toward the left field wall. Cubs left fielder Moises Alou seemed to have a bead on the ball, jumped, and was thwarted by a fan who reached and bobbled the ball. The fan was Steve Bartman, a 26 year old from suburban Northbrook, Illinois, who actually played varsity baseball for nearby Notre Dame High School. The Cubs were up on the Marlins three games to two, and a win that night would have sent them to the World Series. Mark Prior was mowing down the Marlins with a three-hit shutout at the time, but then the wheels came off. Instead of registering an out — although there is no guarantee that Alou could have caught the ball — the Marlins went on to score eight more runs to win the game. They also won the NLCS, for the Cubs not only failed to win Game Seven that year, they did not win another playoff game for years, at least through the 2010 season, even though they made the playoffs two more times during that stretch. They were swept both times. The Bartman game made for great television, though, the image of Bartman's blooper replayed thousands of times.

The Cubs were riding a wave of renewed popularity behind the pitching of Kerry Wood and Mark Prior, which had not only made the Bartman game more crucial, it created a great deal of friction between the Cubs and their neighbors. The big bone of contention was those rooftop bars across the street from Wrigley where hundreds of fans watched games—not for free, because they would pay up to $150 per ticket to watch from these unusual vantage points—but the bars got the money, not the Cubs. This however, would certainly not be the first case over broadcast rights. Indeed, the control and ownership of broadcasting has been the subject of numerous lawsuits, notably including a scuffle among the Chicago Bulls, NBA, and WGN-TV when the NBA wanted to take away local broadcast rights to sell them to the networks during the Michael Jordan heydays. But the Cubs case would be one of the more unusual, because fans had been watching games at Wrigley Field from their neighboring apartments for decades. No one complained. But when the apartment dwellers built viewing stands on their roofs and began charging big money, it caught the attention of the Cubs who already suffered from a small stadium and little room to expand on Chicago's North Side.

In 2002, the Cubs sued the rooftop owners in Federal District Court, alleging various equitable claims, including trademark infringement and copyright infringement, because these rooftop bar owners were also showing the games on television as part of the ticket price package. The case was alive during the Bartman playoffs, but was settled in January 2004 with an agreement to pay the Cubs a royalty license fee in ticket sales.

Steve Stone, longtime broadcast partner to Harry Caray, was there for much of the Cubs' resurgence and tribulations during these years, including the Bartman debacle. But Stone stood up for Bartman, dispelling those who were tempted to invoke the alleged Cubs' Curse of the Billy Goat from 1945. "Steve Bartman did not give up the four hits ... later. He did not make the error at shortstop. Steve Bartman did not cause the Chicago Cubs not to go to the World Series. The Florida Marlins did."[45] But Stone remained critical of team manager Dusty Baker and the team itself, not just for the 2003 collapse but a number of miscues that seemed to continually hurt the team. After the 2004 season, Stone announced he would not be back. It appears he was not technically fired, but it does seem that he was forced out.

Money still talks. In 1958, all ad expenditures in radio and television totaled $2 billion combined, a very healthy number for the times. Less than a half-century later, Fox and TBS would shell out $3 billion just for the rights to major league baseball alone. The explosive growth in broadcast payments became one of the driving forces behind the exponential increase in ballplayer salaries, yet in 1982, there was a suit filed in Chicago by major leaguers to prevent the broadcast of their games without their further permission—and payments. The Seventh Circuit Court of Appeals ruled against the players in 1986, reminding them that they were employees subject to "work for hire" rules, thus ending one of the brasher double dipping attempts in sports memory.[46] The court was saying that, for the time being, the baseball dog would still be in charge of the tail. By 2009, however, the broadcasting tail may have won out in a different way when an interesting inversion was observed and reported that major league baseball on the radio offered more commercials than actual baseball. The *Hartford Courant* ran a story about two games on July 18, 2009, the Red Sox against the Blue Jays on WTIC radio and the Yankees against the Tigers on WPOP. In an hour of listening, the commercials had actually won out over baseball.[47]

As any business matures and becomes more and more lucrative, competition grows fierce from new entrants into the marketplace. At one time the baseball team owners were individual business people like William Wrigley, Charles Comiskey, Charles Finley, and Connie Mack. But as the stakes grew higher, driven largely by broadcasting, corporate ownership began to surface. In 1964, the CBS network bought the New York Yankees, setting into motion a quantum leap series of events where the media would take a larger stake in sports than just revenue from commercial advertising. Sports are part of the entertainment business, so it is no wonder that the entertainment business would take serious note.

16

Wagging the Dog

While baseball broadcasting matured as both an entertainment medium and a lucrative business, money and sponsors proceeded to exert more and more influence over the broadcasting process. Eventually broadcasting began to sway the game of baseball itself with night games, promotions, on-field ads, and even instant replay plus ultra-sophisticated computer graphics.

Minor league games, especially the road games, continued to utilize re-creations for their radio listeners well into the 1950s, just as the majors did in the very early days of baseball broadcasting. The fans at home perceived little to no difference, but these studio renditions comprised a virtual symphony of sounds that had to be produced and performed with a great deal of precision and, in many cases, an indelible love for the game. Not only did the announcer have to simulate the baseball excitement of the moment, but all the usual background sounds had to be carefully orchestrated to include the ballpark breeze, the crack of the bat, the slap of a fastball into the catcher's mitt, and different cheers, jeers, ooh's and ah's of the crowd which, of course, had to be modulated between the home and away fans, the home crowd always needing to "cheer" much louder.

In addition to calling the game, entertaining fans, and doing promos and commercials, the announcer had to be proficient in reading Teletype shorthand on the fly as it came over the wires, which looked something like this when it arrived:

Burton up.
B1OS.
B2LO.
S1C.
S2 Foul.
Out. Flied out to right.[1]

This rather stark descriptive information would be processed by the announcer and translated into an intelligible narrative with the requisite sense of excitement and urgency: "The hitter Burton steps into the batter's box. He takes a pitch outside for a ball. Here's the pitch — LOW — for a 2–0 count. He takes the next pitch for a called strike. Foul ball, the count is 2–2. A swing and a fly to right — *caught* for the out." The broadcaster, of course, had to pause during intervals between windups, and the more creative announcers

213

could add the sound effects, excitement, and more colorful details along the way. For example, he might add the right fielder charging the ball, the pitcher shaking off the catcher, and other embellishments—much like Ronald Reagan's efforts in creating game content to retain his audience while the Teletype went dead.

Sometimes personal conflicts would arise between the Teletype operators and the announcer, and if something was amiss the announcer might take subtle, or sometimes more direct, jabs at the technical people feeding the information. If that offended the Teletype people, which it occasionally did, the tension could escalate, sometimes inspiring the Teletype operators to omit important information like a runner being picked off base, thus requiring the announcer to improvise on the fly if something relevant followed like a home run or a sudden third out.

Creating realistic sound effects became something of an art form, with small sticks or miniature wooden bats striking the Teletype paper rolls for a dull thud, striking another bat for a wood-to-wood sounding clash, or clanking something metallic. It all happened in a small broadcast room with one announcer, a bevy of sound effects, and no home viewers—collectively amounting to "virtual baseball."

Decades later, the process of producing a baseball telecast would evolve into a technically complex amalgam of baseball, entertainment, and commercial sponsorships all orchestrated on the fly with the concurrent efforts of dozens of people behind the scenes. In the summer of 1998, *Popular Mechanics* approached announcer Jim Kaat, a former big league pitcher announcing Yankees games at the time, to do an article about all the mechanics of broadcasting a live game. Kaat allowed a magazine creative director and some photographers to follow him around one day before, during, and after a Yankees broadcast. Doing about 100 games a year, Kaat felt the whole process would be routine but, as he later reported the assignment "would turn into a marathon of epic proportions and one of the longest broadcasting days of my career."[2]

The day they chose was July 20, a Yankees doubleheader in which the first game went 17 innings. New York was looking to break a three-game losing skid, even though the Yankees enjoyed a 14-game lead in first place. As Kaat and Ken Singleton called the game, viewers at home were entertained by two experienced commentators watching and announcing a big league game. What they did not see was the telecasting extravaganza that had to be managed to perfection among scores of trained technicians. According to Kaat in his *Popular Mechanics* piece, the whole process to produce and air the game took over a hundred people and 14 cameras, not to mention several days of preparation such as research on the Tigers, the Yankees' opponent, which in that case had been conducted by the producer Leon Schweir. Then, when the Tigers arrived at the stadium, Kaat himself would dig for breaking news or other inside info, especially concerning the opponent. He spoke to managers and trainers from both teams to verify injury reports and know the available pitchers. Being a former player with long-time connections, Kaat also worked the current players and coaches for information, stories, and back stories; discussed the pending start with the designated pitcher; and investigated the umpiring crew, especially the tendencies of that day's home plate umpire. With less than three hours before game time, all the announcers, producers, the director, tape and graphics operators met to review the day's planned broadcast, especially the scripted commercials, plugs, and promos that had to be slipped into the telecast.[3]

Before each televised game starts, the broadcast choreographer and the producer plan the introductory graphics. If the game is an expected pitching dual between ace starters, then the two pitchers are shown, perhaps together on split screen, as the audience is teased about the upcoming contest. The choreographer will cue the audio people if or when he needs music, and he will monitor the 14 camera shots, constantly selecting which feed should be sent live from moment to moment. Each show is a virtual circus of on-camera and back-stage performances, yet there can be still more. None of this addresses the use of replay, rain delays, or for that matter the post-game show, a production in its own right.

The modern production of a televised baseball game is of course a distant cry from the emergence of baseball on the radio in the 1920s when stations did not pay for broadcast rights at all. At first, the team owners were afraid of radio, but even when they embraced it they did so reluctantly and were simply happy to billboard the games, hoping to boost traffic through the turnstiles. Henry Ford entered into the first major sponsorship when he agreed to pay $400,000 to sponsor four years of World Series games beginning with the 1934 Fall Classic.[4] Even in 1951, when Liberty broadcast on radio the infamous Bobby Thomson walk-off homer to win the pennant, Liberty had paid not one cent for the rights. Liberty just showed up and broadcast the game, as no one seemed to mind. By 1993, however, CBS was committing over $50 million per year to major league baseball for the radio rights to six years of select games.

In 2001, the 50th anniversary of the Bobby Thomson pennant blast inspired a parade of retrospectives and commentary. *Sports Illustrated* ranked it the second greatest sports moment of the recently concluded twentieth century, just behind the "miracle on ice" 1980 Olympic hockey victory by the United States over the dominant Russian team.[5] It made for compelling video and even better audio, with "the Giants win the pennant" still reverberating through baseball posterity.

History later revealed that the Thomson epiphany was likely the partial product of baseball larceny. The Giants had developed a practice of stealing the opposing catcher's signs by means of a hidden telescope beyond the outfield wall, probably manned by one Henry Leonard Schenz, a utility infielder who had spent four years with the Chicago Cubs where he first honed his scope-aided, sign-stealing skills. The Wrigley Field scoreboard that loomed over the center field wall provided a good hiding place and surveillance post.[6] Of course, stealing signs required more than just watching through a telescope; someone had to understand the signs, decipher their code, and convey it somehow to the batter—a process that was not without flaws. Then, of course, the batter still had to execute. It's one thing to know an inside fastball is coming, another to actually do something about it. According to history and subsequent admissions by Thomson, it appears that Thomson knew what Ralph Branca was going to throw in the pinnacle 1951 playoff game. Back-up catcher Sal Yvars told the *New York Times* in 2001, a half-century after the blast, that he was the one assigned to relay the coming pitch to the batter, in this case Thomson.[7] Branca's second pitch to Thomson was a high fastball inside, and Bobby yanked it hard to left, over the wall, and into baseball destiny. Whether by hook, crook, stolen signs or not, that home run changed baseball history and created great broadcasting drama for the audiences at home.

"What's he mad at me for?" Yvars protested. "I was just the messenger." The scheme ran this way: Schenz (and later Herman Franks) picked up and read the sign from the outfield, then relayed it by buzzer to the dugout. Yvars would do nothing if it was a fastball, but if a curve was coming he would casually toss a ball into the air. Interestingly, stealing signs was permissible in 1951.[8] Major league baseball did not proscribe such thefts until 1961, but the stigma of Thomson's larceny continues to hover over one of baseball's defining moments.

The Thomson drama was not just one event, although it may be remembered that way now. In fact it was the culmination of an incredible run by the Giants to overtake a 13½ game Dodgers' lead in the standings as late as August 11. Then the Giants won 37 of their next 44 games to finally tie Brooklyn on the last day, to force the infamous tiebreaker, with both teams finishing the regular season at 96–58 thanks to a final-day Dodgers victory over the Phillies in 14 grueling innings.[9]

Thomson's home run only had to clear the Polo Grounds' left field wall just 279 feet from the plate, but it became an instant classic and is still known as "the shot heard round the world," a description that pays apt homage to one of the most American of all events, the first shot fired at the Concord Bridge triggering the Revolutionary War that was later memorialized by Ralph Waldo Emerson's descriptive poem where the line was first coined.

Perhaps as significant as the Thomson "shot" itself was to baseball, the historic drama was captured for eternal posterity by no fewer than four broadcasters. NBC televised the game nationally, featuring Ernie Harwell's resonant "It's gone!" just as Thomson's bat cracked against the Branca fastball. Red Barber, calling the game for the Dodgers over WMGM-AM radio, reported with decidedly less emotion, "It's in there for the pennant." On the other side of that pinnacle moment was Russ Hodges, who announced the contest for Giants fans on WMCA-AM. Normally very officious and not prone to excitement let alone exuberance, Hodges even-handedly reported Thomson's trip to the plate but soon found himself caught up the energized moment, his voice helping to memorialize the blast for all of baseball eternity:

> There's a long drive. It's gonna be it, I believe ... THE GIANTS WIN THE PENNANT! THE GIANTS WIN THE PENNANT! THE GIANTS WIN THE PENNANT! Bobby Thomson hits into the lower deck of the left-field stands! The Giants win the pennant and they're going crazy, they're going crazy! Ohhhh-oh.!!![10]

Hodges was not the only sportscaster to shout "the Giants win the pennant," but it is this rendition that remains the call of the century, even though it was originally heard only by the local audience of Giants fans tuned into the game. The Liberty Radio Network carried the game for a national audience where many more heard Gordon McClendon with a similar "Giants win the pennant" shriek. Although Hodges' exclamation would become history's favorite, McClendon's call remains the only complete broadcast account of the entire game. With a few more moments to reflect, sportscaster Red Barber finally described the Thomson shocker as "utterly impossible" and "inexpressibly fantastic." Surrendering to history, Barber conceded, "The art of fiction is dead." Little did Barber realize just how right he may have been.[11]

Some believe that Thomson's feat was the greatest single baseball event of the twentieth century, including *Sports Illustrated*, in its ranking just behind the 1980 Olympic hockey final. But many other moments may have been equal to the occasion, although before 1950 they were relegated to print accounts only and thus somewhat lost to posterity. The Giants' pennant-winner was a major event, of course, but it's impact has long endured partially because of the Hodges excited call, memorialized forever, together with the familiar televised image of Thomson crushing Branca's pitch to left field, captured for all of posterity by NBC television.

Was television the most significant change to major league baseball during the twentieth century? A 1999 piece in *Baseball Weekly* concluded that Jackie Robinson topped the most *important* list of changes in baseball during the century, while pegging the advent of television as second.[12] But as important as Robinson was, his individual landmark appearance triggered a revolution, but television itself *was* a revolution.

The issue of "importance" may actually pose the question unfairly, since modern baseball is the profound product of both those epiphanies, one distinctly breaking ground on the field of play, the other off. Without Robinson and those who followed, baseball "the game" would have suffered immeasurably, not to mention the continued negative impact of such overt racism on all of America. But television was highly significant, especially if the measure is baseball as an entertainment medium. Without television, player salaries and team values could not have experienced quantum-leap advances; ticket sales would likely have suffered without the billboard effect of television promoting every baseball team 154 times (now 162) per year; and without it, even the abject pre–Robinson "whiteness" of the game would not have been so starkly exposed.

Robinson's own travails as the leader of a major sports movement deserve every accolade that posterity can offer, but his personal place in history is somewhat fortuitous, since after the death of Commissioner Kenesaw Landis, the race barrier was destined to be broken by Branch Rickey or Bill Veeck. Cleveland owner Bill Veeck had already been trying, so eventually it may have been Larry Doby, Satchel Paige, Roy Campanella, or Minnie Minoso to have made history as the first African American major leaguer — although certainly no one would have done it better than the talented, classy, and even-tempered Robinson. In hindsight, television was inevitable, too, assuming the inevitability of science in general. Even without television, baseball may have fared the best of all the major team sports since it plays so well on radio; but baseball without television would be a much different spectacle and, who knows, may not have maintained itself as a premier sport in the face of competition from football and basketball.

Before television, baseball had become the top team sport in America, and in many ways baseball became a metaphor for America itself. *After* television, baseball was able to maintain a significant hold on America, and at least maintain an argument for its claim as America's game. In the early years, it was baseball and boxing that gained the most exposure from television, with baseball enjoying many of the sports broadcasting "firsts" as the twentieth century progressed. But by the 1960s the NFL was entrenched in television, then Magic Johnson, Larry Bird, and Michael Jordan did the same for the NBA as the 1980s emerged.

Television may have become the ultimate tail wagging the sports dog, because broadcasting has continually been the most important influence over baseball itself, changing it from a day game to largely an evening entertainment vehicle, affecting the pace of the game, the salaries, and now even the rules as instant replay creeps its way into the baseball culture. Although night baseball is largely associated with the threshold World Series night games in the early 1970s, the very first televised night game had actually occurred years before in June 1941 at Ebbets Field.[13] The lighting was difficult but proved better than expected, surprising the handful of viewers who saw the game, yet it would be years before there would be enough television sets to matter, let alone influence the game itself.

The introduction of color into television was another quantum leap for broadcasting and baseball and it, too, occurred sooner than many would expect. In August and September of 1951, CBS experimented with color telecasts of Brooklyn Dodgers games while trying to promote its own color technology over that developed by RCA.[14] Ultimately, archrival NBC, thanks to its affiliation with RCA, was the first to show a nationally televised game in color when it telecast the 1955 World Series between the Yankees and Dodgers. Again, there were so few sets in those days that baseball itself was largely unaffected. However, eventually baseball uniforms and even stadium seats would become more colorful specifically to make a better impression on color television — and of course stadium advertising would proliferate and become more colorful as well, for much the same reason.

Technology would push televised sports forward at an accelerated pace during the 1960s. In 1967 RCA introduced the "big tube" TK-43 camera which could perform in limited lighting conditions, at once improving the quality of both nighttime and color baseball telecasts, a major leap forward that would indeed influence baseball itself with a vast proliferation of televised night games in the 1970s.

On May 24, 1935, the struggling Cincinnati Reds, a perennial last-place team, made a desperate move to regain attendance with the first of several night games played under the lights at Crosley Field. The team's GM Larry MacPhail took a page from the minor leagues by offering night games to boost interest if not attendance. Night baseball proved more than just a gimmick, for the 20,442 Reds fans who came that first night comprised the biggest Cincinnati crowd in years. The experiment was so successful that the Reds played a number of night games that year and eventually eked out a modest profit for the season.[15] Interestingly, the minor leagues had been experimenting successfully with night games for years, but soon major league night baseball and television would deal a severe blow to the minors.

The very next day, fate and posterity were at work. On May 25, 1935, a fading Babe Ruth was in a Boston Braves uniform when he slammed three home runs in a game against the Pirates, the final shot being the last home run of his entire career. In true Ruthian fashion, that last blast went out with a proverbial bang, for it was the first homer ever to clear the right field stands at Forbes Field in Pittsburgh. The end of the Ruth era was a blow to major league baseball, but the game, duly transformed by Ruth himself into a great showcase of stars and power, managed to survive. That same year Hank Greenberg drove in 170 runs for the first-place Tigers, who went on to defeat the Cubs in the World Series after drawing a million fans during the regular season. And of course Lou Gehrig, Joe DiMaggio, Jimmy Foxx, and others would continue to pick up the slack. Perhaps none was individually as prolific as Ruth, but there were more of them delivering great baseball moments, and the major leagues would continue to on, surviving even the Great Depression.

Night baseball had arrived in the big leagues just as Ruth was leaving, one major era ushering out the other on virtually the same day, all within 24 hours of each other. Although night baseball continued to proliferate at the major league level, initially it had little effect on the minor leagues which, for the most part, were deliberately situated in other markets. But then television discovered night baseball. When broadcast icon Red Barber called a crudely televised Dodgers-Reds game played during the daytime on August 26, 1939, only about 400 television sets were tuned in.[16] Less than two years later in June

1941, the first major league night game was televised. By 1947, the owners were hotly debating whether to televise the World Series. Some owners were worried that television could have a chilling effect on league-wide attendance, but others like the Cubs' Wrigley and Veeck in Cleveland, felt that television would continue to billboard the game and expand the fan base much the way radio did in the 1920s.

Although the 1949 World Series between the Yankees and Dodgers was still a day contest, something happened in Game Five that would portend a new era in baseball broadcasting: the Ebbets Field lights were turned on. Game Five as it happens, was the final deciding game as the Yankees took the championship; when the lights came on in the ninth inning it was the first artificial lighting ever for a World Series contest.[17] Interestingly, night broadcasts on television did not take the same path as radio broadcasting almost two decades earlier. With owners fearing radio, only the World Series was initially broadcast over the airwaves, for although many owners thought radio could keep fans away from regular-season games no one seriously felt that World Series attendance could suffer. But television was different. It debuted with local teams and the World Series followed. Although the first televised night game was in 1941, the World Series remained a daytime extravaganza until the 1971 World Series.

Bobby Thomson and the Giants did more than alter the 1951 pennant race. Together they may have been the first broadcasting domino that would propel a series of events in the advent of televised sports, especially baseball. The major leagues had already discovered the entertainment value of home runs when they banned the spitball and began to embrace the long-ball antics of Ruth in 1920, reaffirming that conviction when the pitching mound was lowered in 1969 to recapture lost audiences bored by the grueling one- and two-run baseball games as the 1960s wore on.

As early as 1959 television was conceding the marquee value of home runs themselves. At that time a brief but now classic show called *Home Run Derby* debuted. It featured major stars slugging for home runs against each other for prizes and was filmed at the West Coast Wrigley Field, a Los Angeles version of Chicago's Wrigley. The batter was allowed three "outs" per inning, an out being any ball hit except for home runs, plus any strike, whether by foul, called strike, or a swing and miss. Two batters competed against each other for a total of nine such "innings," each inning comprised of three outs for that batter.

Many of the genuine stars of the era participated, such as Hank Aaron, Duke Snider, Ernie Banks, Wally Post, Willie Mays, Harmon Killebrew, Rocky Colavito, and Mickey Mantle. The winner continued on, facing another batter during the next episode. Each episode winner received $2,000, a tidy sum for those days, while the loser was paid $1,000. But each participant received an extra bonus of $500 if he could hit three homers in a row. Nineteen different players competed, with Hank Aaron winning the most contests, pocketing $13,000 during six straight victories.[18]

Television was there for nearly every significant baseball moment, from the 1950s forward, including games featuring Dodger Jackie Robinson, the Bobby Thomson pennant-winner, Roger Maris' 61st home run, Carlton Fisk's "body language" home run shot during the classic 1975 World Series against the Reds, Hank Aaron's blast to break Ruth's lifetime homer mark, and hundreds of other milestones. The home runs especially, brought good drama to the screen, taking just enough time for an exuberant home run call by the announcer, adding to the entertainment value of the moment.

Early television, of course, was making its mark in every venue, not just baseball, boxing, and a surprising number of pro wrestling matches. Television also featured early dramatic shows, much comedy, and news. Inevitably, television played a role in making the news, too, a historic point that was punctuated by Edward R. Murrow's *See It Now* report exposing Sen. Joe McCarthy as a Communist-baiting menace to America and the Constitution. It was a watershed moment for television, and television has been a part of history ever since, including its role in the 1960 presidential election, then flashing the Vietnam War before the eyes of a war-torn America, the 1968 political marches and riots, the 1969 moon landing, and Hank Aaron's home run that finally bested Babe Ruth's lifetime mark.

History suggests that when baseball needed a boost, the game would embrace offense, especially home runs. When Ruth went to the Big Apple stage in 1920, the spitball was banned at the same time, and home run totals exploded. The 1961 season was a milestone in baseball history and televised sports entertainment with the Maris-Mantle home run chase against each other, as the ghost of Ruth added drama and excitement to the entire year. As pitchers grew better and big league pitching caught up to the hitters, batting averages and home runs suffered, leading baseball to lower the pitching mound in 1969. When labor strife and a canceled World Series brought baseball to a standstill in 1994, the game floundered until the great home run chase, part two, when Sammy Sosa and Mark McGwire chased Ruth and Maris for a national television audience.

Bobby Thomson's mystical home run may have done for televised baseball what Edward R. Murrow did for network news less than three years later on March 9, 1954. Neither television nor baseball would ever be quite the same thereafter.

The first televised baseball game, a contest between Princeton and Columbia, was presented by the forerunner to WNBC-TV in New York on May 17, 1939, although almost no on saw it. Later that same year, the first major league game was shown, a Dodgers-Reds game announced by Red Barber on August 26, 1939. The game featured only two cameras, one in the stands near home plate, the other in the upper deck at third base next to Barber.[19] By 1947, the year of Jackie Robinson's debut for those same Dodgers, television sets with five-inch and seven-inch screens were selling off the shelves in record numbers. Just as baseball attendance gained a boost when radio helped the game find new audiences, television brought baseball to still more and attendance surged again. The year was capped by the first mass TV audience to see a major league game when the 1947 World Series, sponsored by both Ford and Gillette, was televised locally in New York where 3.9 million viewers caught the parts of the Series.

In 1950 the first All-Star Game was televised, which happened to be at Chicago's Comiskey Park that year. The next year, 1951, not only brought the Bobby Thomson blast, it featured the first game televised in color (by CBS on August 11).[20] Then in 1955 the first color telecast of the World Series was offered.[21] As early as 1962, the first satellite broadcast of a game took place, a contest from Chicago featuring the Cubs and Phillies. Two years later the first game distributed on cable TV took place when the Cubs met the Dodgers in L.A. on July 17, 1964. When Commissioner Bowie Kuhn endorsed the first World Series night game on October 13, 1971, baseball took a quantum leap that was more than just a televised game, it was impacted by the medium itself.

The media was clearly capable of influencing the game of baseball, whether by impacting attendance, dictating night games, or ultimately favoring baseball offense. But on July 16, 1956, the tail was finding a new way to wag the dog when two radio executives heading an 11-member syndicate bought the Detroit Tigers for a then record price of $5.5 million, a package that also included Detroit's Briggs Stadium, named for the selling Briggs family which had been affiliated with the Tigers for decades. At the time, Fred Knorr, just 42 years old, owned the Knorr Broadcasting Company which, in turn, owned and operated four Michigan radio stations. His partner John Fetzer, age 55, headed Fetzer Broadcasting with radio interests in Michigan, Illinois, and Nebraska.[22]

An interesting footnote to the Knorr-Fetzer purchase is found among the identities of the other syndicate members, one of whom was singer and Hollywood star Bing Crosby, who already owned a piece of the Pittsburgh Pirates. Other baseball moguls in the making included retailer R.F. Woolworth and Lehman Brothers partner Joseph A. Thomas.[23]

The following year aging player Phil Rizzuto sent a demo tape of himself as a baseball broadcaster, hoping to catch on with Baltimore after his playing career. A sponsor for Yankees broadcasting caught wind of it and insisted the team hire Rizzuto, who proceeded to call Yankees games in 1957, where he remained for 40 years. With Rizzuto on board and the 1961 home run season in the books, CBS television began to look at the Yankees as more than just content. After the 1964 season, the media giant bought 80 percent of the team for $11.2 million, then fired broadcast icon Mel Allen.[24] The following season would not prove very lucky, for the Yankees finished in the second division of the American League in 1965, the first time in four decades. Then baseball instituted its amateur player draft for the first time, making it harder for the Yankees to simply spend themselves out of a hole. So they did even worse in 1966, finishing in last place for the first time since 1912, then they dumped the legendary Red Barber. Some say that Barber was fired because he noted during one broadcast that there were only 413 fans in the 67,000-seat Yankee stadium, but at the time there also had been friction brewing among Barber, Rizzuto, and the lively Joe Garagiola in the booth. The attendance barb may have simply been the last straw among a number of growing issues.

By the spring of 1965 television had discovered the value of an isolated camera to pick up additional details of the game and its players. One of those "little details" soon included reading the catcher's signs, as ABC discovered when its announcer Joe Garagiola, a former big league catcher, rather easily deciphered the Mets' signals during a game with the Giants in April 1965. One finger was for a fastball, two meant a curve, and three indicated a change-up. Garagiola soon concluded that the second sign in the series flashed by catcher Chris Cannizzaro was the live sign, causing co-announcer Chris Schenkel to issue a disclaimer to viewers who might think Joe was in on some kind of broadcasting conspiracy since the Mets were being shut out, 4–0.[25] Most likely, it was the dominant pitching of young Giants starter Juan Marichal that had shut down New York that day, not Garagiola's playful code breaking.

Technology continued to influence television, and baseball telecasting would find new ways to impact the game on the field. In November 2007, when major league baseball began to study the official use of instant replay to review certain aspects of games in progress, it was about to close a 43-year loop that began at ABC with its *Game of the Week* telecasts in 1965.

Instant replay was first widely used to entertain home audiences during the telecast of football games, but it soon made its way to big league baseball games where issues of trapped balls, foul balls, missed tags, and home runs were difficult to catch in game-speed real time. Replays made their way to the World Series when NBC used them for the Fall Classic broadcasts in 1968 and 1969. At first the replays were a curiosity, mildly interesting but not used a great deal. Since viewers were not used to them, the replays came with a printed graphics disclaimer denoting the shots as replays on the screen to avoid viewer confusion. Replay became more and more a part of the game, dissecting plays and umpire calls; by the 1990s there would be over 100 such replays shown on a typical network telecast of a baseball game.

Baseball may be a deliberately paced game with only spurts of action on the field, but it is played with a rather small ball that travels at high speeds in a very large area. Even trained and experienced umpires can have difficulty discerning fair and foul balls, fan interference, home runs, close plays on the bases, and the like, so replays naturally began to expose a number of missed calls. For myriad reasons of politics, tradition, and logistics, major league baseball resisted the formal use of the replay system in reviewing and possibly reversing on-field decisions by the umpires, even though the NFL had been using it with reasonable success since 1999.

The use of official replay to review calls began as early as 1986 for NFL games, but there were fewer cameras, the technology was less sophisticated, and there was little direction on how to deploy it during games.[26] At first only the officials themselves could initiate a review and overturn themselves, but the results were spotty and inconsistent. By 1992 the NFL concluded that the replay system did not provide enough value for the trouble, and the league abandoned it until better technology and a more refined system of coaching challenges was implemented in 1999. Even then there were problems, like officials failing to grasp and consistently apply "indisputable evidence" standards, but soon the system began to work, enhancing fairness on a dependable basis.

Interestingly, the final piece that made the NFL system viable was not a computer, digital technology, or other high-tech application, but the pedestrian red flag thrown from the sidelines by a challenging coach. The NFL originally tried vibrating pagers to the officials, but sending the message, recognizing the vibrating challenge, and overcoming technical difficulties made the process cumbersome and unreliable. It was soon scrapped for the simple red flag, which solved everything and had one more benefit for television: the dramatic flair of a red flying protest flag sailing defiantly onto the field.

In August 2008, major league baseball announced a plan whereby all televised games would be monitored by a technician and one umpire supervisor offsite at Major League Baseball Advanced Media in New York. Baseball, however, elected to play the whole review process much closer to the vest. There are no dramatic flags or even manager challenges in the same formal sense as with the NFL. And so far very few baseball game events are reviewable in the first place. The umpire crew chief decides whether to review a call, which at first included only the home run determination. So with that first tepid foray into the replay world, baseball became the last major sport to invoke a review system.

If any of the major sports could argue against the need for such replay during the regular season, it would be baseball. With its 162 games, there is a reasonable statistical likelihood that blown calls will even themselves out over the entire season. This has been the tradition of the game, but the baseball marathon season argument loses its teeth as the pennant races heat up and the playoffs begin. In the NFL, replay is crucial because a blown call could tip one game; in a football season of just 16 total games, the statistical impact is the same as robbing a baseball club of 10 wins. But during or near the baseball post-season, the importance of each call and each game is significantly greater, yet baseball showed a remarkable resistance to post-season reviews.

During the 2009 baseball playoffs, fate and television conspired to expose the fallibility of umpires and the importance of replay review. Viewing audiences and the press torched major league baseball for butchering key post season calls, including the *Los Angeles Times* in a piece on October 28, 2009:

> The postseason also has been about CB Bucknor, who blew *three* [emphasis added] calls at first base in one game between the Angels and Boston Red Sox, and Tim McClelland, who blew two calls at third base in one game between the Angels and Yankees, and Phil Cuzzi, who blew a call that quite possibly cost the Minnesota Twins a victory in their series with the Yankees.[27]

Undaunted, Commissioner Selig continued to resist the expansion of instant replay for the impending World Series, which he concluded would be a knee-jerk response to what the *Times* reported as a "rare and sudden epidemic of high-profile blown calls."[28] The baseball umpires are good at what they do, but that is not the point. Nearly everyone agrees the umpires make the right calls most of the time, even 99 percent of the time, as Angels manager Mike Scioscia observed during the 2009 playoffs. But with big money, baseball history, and baseball integrity hanging in the balance, those other 1 percent of calls will increasingly become the ones that count. After all, most plays are routine where the calls are easy. Baseball being a game of momentum where one extra baserunner and one less out could propel an inning, a game, and even a whole playoff series, the replay debate will not end until a more equitable review process is invoked and consistently applied.

When the 2009 playoffs began, major league baseball's timid review system limited the reviewable events to just three: fair or foul home runs, whether a possible home run actually cleared a fence, and whether there may have been fan interference. During the 2009 regular season, 58 such baseball plays were reviewed and 20 of those (34.45 percent) were reversed, thus changing the game in some tangible way on 20 occasions.[29]

The Fox network, which carried the World Series in 2009, announced it would cover the games with 20 cameras, all equipped with recording capabilities to capture replay if necessary. But with all that equipment and commensurate technology, baseball would be able to review and reverse a home run call, but it would *not* be able to assess whether a runner touched home plate or a myriad other possibilities that might be resolved by replay. Although some arguments about the more limited cameras and technical capabilities during locally televised regular season games have merit, the same arguments are not compelling for playoff and World Series contests. Viewers remained skeptical, and the *Los Angeles Times* drove the point home: "If the World Series at all resembles the first two rounds of the baseball playoffs, an umpire will make a bad call, a call so bad that instant replay will reveal the error for all of America to see, in living color, in high definition, and within seconds. The manager will charge onto the field to argue. The umpire will defend his call. The game will go on. The error will not be corrected."[30]

Technical broadcasting capabilities continued to progress and enhance the telecast of all sporting events, including baseball. In 1969, Neil Armstrong not only walked on the moon, but his steps and threshold statement "one small step for man" words were televised live, transmitted a quarter million miles back home to an anxious audience.

From that night forward, America has continued to ask the relentless rhetorical question, "If they can put a man on the moon, why can't they... [fill in the blank with cures for cancer, instant replay, testing for steroids, or any other topic of debate].

One of the most significant innovations in television arrived at the close of the twentieth century with the advent of digital television and high-definition (HD) broadcasting. The requisite precision of sports, each contest offering its own "game of inches" claims to fame, were a natural beneficiary. The first HD telecast of a big league baseball game took place on September 16, 1997, when an Orioles-Indians contest was transmitted to a select group of journalists and executives gathered at the National Press Club in Washington, D.C. HD television is particularly well suited for baseball, where a small ball travels great distances and bang-bang plays are made on the basepaths.[31] On HDTV the field is wider and more complete, the clarity of the action is better, and for entertainment purposes the breadth and beauty of the ballparks as part of the entire baseball experience are greatly enhanced.

Neil Armstrong's quantum leap was not the only epiphany of 1969. That same year produced Woodstock and other cultural milestones, including its own impact on the game of baseball. While this was Harry Caray's last broadcast year in St. Louis, opening the door to Jack Buck and those who followed, it was also the first season of a lowered pitching mound necessitated by the paucity of baseball offense that had kept getting worse through 1968. It was also the first year of a baseball playoff system, spreading championship hopes, the most valuable of all sports commodities, among more and more teams. Sports are entertaining, but pulling for the home team is much more than just amusing, it stems from an intense identity with one's own team, city, or favorite players. If there is no hope of winning — this year or next — then discouragement sets in. Discouraged fans do not watch baseball games as much as those still clinging to that ephemeral commodity hope. When there were just eight or ten teams in each league, and one of them opened an insurmountable lead on the second-place club, the excitement of the season was extinguished until the World Series. But with divisional play, playoffs, and a wild-card formula, there remains a mathematical chance for success that extends "hope" well into the season for many, many teams and fans.

Television executives and sports moguls both recognized that with so much league expansion, the waning product called hope had to be repackaged and resold. The NFL is particularly known for its Byzantine playoff formulae. With just three or four games left in any given season, there is usually some Rube Goldberg series of mathematical anomalies that could result in most teams still making the playoffs. Note also the implied redefinition of "success." With 30 or so clubs in each major team sport, expectations of a world championship are decidedly dim for any given team. Although lip service is given to the eternal quest for such nirvana as the Super Bowl, the Stanley Cup, the NBA title, and the most enduring of them all — the World Series championship — the real quest for most teams each year is to "make the playoffs." It is a brilliant shift in sports entertainment, for most teams have at least some shot at the playoffs, rendering many more games important if not crucial, and thus there is more drama to sell to more viewers. And once a team is in the playoffs, the entire "hope" formula starts all over as teams jockey for home field, and better playoff seeding, each one with a justifiable shot at the world title, or at least to "go deep into the playoffs."

The lucrative marriage of baseball playoffs and television was inevitable, but it received a special, albeit accidental, boost during the summer of 1967. As fate would have it, the All-Star Game that year was played in Anaheim, California. As was the tradition — an overused word that often gets in the way of progress — that game was played and televised during the daytime hours. It began at 4:15 P.M. Pacific Time, and soon fate would intervene again. That 1967 All-Star Game extended to extra innings — lots of them — which with the three-hour time difference were seen by TV viewers on the East Coast in prime time. It did not end until Reds' slugger Tony Perez launched a 15th inning home run, giving the National League a one-run advantage in a close game that was then saved by a promising young power pitcher named Tom Seaver. Television executives then received an important surprise that, in some ways, is reminiscent of Yogi Berra's observation about baseball in California: "It gets late early out there." According to a 2008 piece carried by the business website *MarketWatch*, baseball and TV have become a dysfunctional marriage with television influencing the game in many profound ways. The network executives were immediately surprised to learn the ratings for their 1967 summer classic: the longer the game went, the higher the ratings climbed. Indeed, the aggregate ratings for the game went up each half hour as the time-zone differential pushed deeper into prime-time viewing on the East Coast until, in the end, the game mustered a stunning 25.6 rating with a 50 share of the television market. All in all, 50 million viewers saw the game, a record that was particularly impressive since 1967 was during the teeth of the pitchers' era of low scoring and largely boring baseball.[32]

The NBC network had discovered a much-needed antidote to baseball apathy: prime time. The 1968 game was played in Houston, when the same phenomenon occurred: as the East Coast slid into prime time, the ratings expanded dramatically. In 1969 baseball again tried a strictly daytime All-Star Game, but the ratings suffered. Starting in 1970, the peak year for All-Star Game ratings with a 28.5 and a 54 share, every All-Star Game would be played — and telecast — at night.[33] This was an inspired epiphany, but even night games could not overcome the saturation of baseball on TV, so ratings would weaken steadily until the game could achieve only an 8.4 rating with a 15 share. With so many games televised, and with the advent of free agency and the interleague play, the mystique of the All-Star Game contest had evaporated. In short, the All-Star Game itself had become rather boring.

The owners could not help but notice the impact of night games, so some continued to look for baseball gimmicks to enhance interest, attendance, and viewership. One innovative owner, the colorful Charles O. Finley, experimented with yellow bases during the Athletics home opener in 1970.[34] He also invented the idea of ball girls retrieving foul balls and even experimented with colored baseballs. In 1971 Finley paid his own players to grow big mustaches, the eccentric handlebars providing an entertaining look reminiscent of baseball's old-time persona. In 1974 Finley signed world-class sprinter Herb Washington, who scored 29 runs, without ever coming to bat, as a pinch-runner. He also gave one of his star pitchers a nickname just because it sounded good; thus John Odom had suddenly become Johnny "Blue Moon" Odom.

Commissioner Kuhn, a stuffed shirt with no sense of humor, and the maverick Finley, whose baseball life was something of an irreverent put-on, clashed for years. Finley was originally a Chicago businessman, and he saw the world differently than most. After the A's won the World Series, Finley took a number of baseball men around Chicago, including a stop at the famed Billy Goat Tavern, a dive located on lower Michigan Avenue near the Tribune Tower. There his guests were shocked to see his actual World Series trophy on display. When they expressed their surprise and asked about whether Kuhn knew where the trophy was, Finley's answer was concise: "Fuck him."[35]

In 1976, players Messersmith and McNally toppled the baseball reserve clause. With free agency about to redefine baseball salaries, and with two World Series titles under his belt, Finley threw in the towel, opting to sell three of this star players—Joe Rudi, Rollie Fingers, and Vida Blue—to the Red Sox and Yankees for a total of $3.5 million in cash. When Commissioner Kuhn voided all three transactions as "not in the best interests of baseball," Finley was livid. He sued Kuhn for arbitrary and unreasonable conduct, but the courts were reluctant to intervene in baseball's right to govern itself, even thought the "best interests" clause was grotesquely vague on its face.[36] Charlie Finley lost, but he still got his licks in, publicly calling Kuhn the "village idiot" before apologizing to "village idiots everywhere."

Kuhn, a lawyer by trade (whose own post-baseball law firm would later go bankrupt amidst a number of billing scandals due in part to his flamboyant partner Harvey Meyerson), had no qualms about pushing around his own team owners like Finley and the equally recalcitrant Ted Turner. But even the aloof Kuhn could not control the power of the television networks. When the 1970 All-Star Game ratings exploded to the upside, the networks insisted on having World Series night games to boost ratings and revenues. Baseball, sensing an opportunity to line its pockets with television rights fees, readily conceded. Kuhn authorized World Series night games beginning in 1971, and then, to quiet baseball purists and other critics, showed up for the cameras wearing no overcoat, even though the October night temperatures were virtually freezing.[37]

Ted Turner impacted both baseball and television like few others, maybe more than anyone including Bowie Kuhn. When Turner's father committed suicide in 1963, he left the 24-year-old Ted with a family billboard business and a mound of debt. Turner was a quick study, and he noticed that most ad dollars were beginning to chase television and radio, not outdoor billboards. So in 1970, Turner plunged into television, buying local Atlanta station WJRJ, an ultra-high frequency channel that had very little to offer in entertainment. At the time, in fact, it was losing $600,000 per year, a huge sum for then 31-year-old Turner.[38]

With WJRJ on board and bleeding red ink, Turner not only needed programming content to sell, it had to be cheap programming. Initially he showed old-time television re-runs, the model used today by many local stations that run such timeless shows as *I Love Lucy, Leave It to Beaver, Dick Van Dyke, Andy Griffith*, and other offerings from the early 1960s. When cable TV got a boost from the Federal Communications Commission with a 1972 ruling that allowed cable operators to import signals acquired from distant markets, Turner saw an opportunity. But with cable television came a need for still more content. Turner embraced two forms of broadcasting that could produce themselves: news and sports. Neither required a script or costly weekly production budgets. The games, and the news, just played themselves out—they key was in capturing that content in the first place. In 1976 Turner bought the Atlanta Braves for an estimated $10 to $12 million, then began to distribute Braves games on what would become one of the original cable superstations.[39] Baseball fans around the country began to see and to follow Braves games. This was a big gamble by Turner, for 1976 was the beginning of baseball free agency that would soon lead to skyrocketing player salaries. But Turner remained a step ahead, as overall television revenues would grow as fast or faster than player salaries.

By the end of 1976, the station was renamed WTCG with its signal beamed by satellite to four other cable providers in Nebraska, Kansas, Virginia, and Alabama. The superstation concept was born. In those days most people around the country could see only one baseball game per week from whichever network was running a Saturday version of the baseball *Game of the Week* telecasts. But now much of the country could see the Braves—*and* whoever they played, meaning every other National League team — over 150 times a year.[40] Meanwhile, in late 1975, Turner noticed HBO's effort to link satellites and television to capture and provide the globally anticipated Joe Frazier–Muhammad Ali title fight dubbed the "Thrilla in Manila." But Turner's interest was not inspired so much by sports as it was by the news element of that worldwide event, not to mention satellite's ability to reach around the globe with live programming. Four years later, in June 1980, Turner embraced news like no one had ever done when his Cable News Network became a reality. CNN debuted with two monster sponsors in General Foods and Proctor & Gamble, plus 1.7 million cable subscribers.[41] It was anything but easy, however, with revenues falling short of forecasts while expenses soared, squeezing profits and spooking Turner's lenders who began calling the loans. He successfully refinanced, but only at exorbitant interest rates that ran as high as 18 percent.

CNN covered world news on the fly, and it often looked like the patchwork it was with some ridiculing its call letters as the "chicken noodle network." But gavel-to-gavel coverage of national political conventions brought credibility, and its ability to stay on the air when President Ronald Reagan was shot in 1981 gave CNN a leg up when it was the first to report that Reagan had indeed been injured, while the other networks showed their regular programming. CNN would limp along for a decade, but the first Gulf War convincingly propelled it to the forefront.

The superstation carrying Braves games and other programming was soon renamed WTBS, its current moniker. It made $18 million in 1981, throwing off enough cash to fund CNN and other Turner enterprises. By the 1981-82 network season, WTBS was as big as the rest of the cable industry combined when measured by advertising revenues. It already reached 26 million homes across the country, but the Turner empire would continue to grow for two more decades.[42]

Turner was the first to hire baseball's new crop of free agents after pitcher Andy Messersmith defeated baseball's reserve clause in arbitration. So Turner inked Messersmith, then set about courting another star, San Francisco's Gary Matthews. When the Giants accused him of tampering with the rules, Turner feuded with Commissioner Kuhn and got himself suspended for a year. By 1986 Turner acquired the MGM film library, after which he founded Turner Network Television (TNT) to show old movies, but it soon also featured pro wrestling, NBA games, and NASCAR events.

By 1991, on the heels of the Gulf War, *Time Magazine* had named Turner its Man of the Year. Neither cable television, news, nor baseball would ever quite be the same. In fact, the Turner superstation model of baseball and cable would be followed by others. The *Chicago Tribune*, which already broadcast Cubs games by means of its profitable WGN radio and television stations, bought the Cubs team outright on June 16, 1981, for $20.5 million. WGN was proceeding to build its television station into a national superstation and saw the Cubs as a lucrative brand that would attract national viewers. It added Bulls basketball games and Michael Jordan during the peak of the Jordan years, a property that was so hot that it inspired an antitrust action among the Bulls organization, WGN, and the National Basketball Association, when the NBA tried to reign in its game telecasts to resell them to national networks like ESPN and Turner's TNT. The case produced a nasty fight, but was eventually settled with WGN retaining the rights to some of the Bulls games.[43] Meanwhile, the Mets were following the same business plan with New York's WOR, as did the Yankees with WPIX. The broadcasters had shifted dramatically from carrying games to influencing the teams — and baseball — directly.

Just after Turner launched Braves games on WTBS, in 1978 Bill Rasmussen from Bristol, Connecticut, who had worked in communications for the New England Whalers hockey team, dreamed up the idea of a national cable sports network. With financing from Getty Oil, of all places, the "Entertainment Sports Programming Network" became a reality. In the early 1980s, cable sports network ESPN was operating at a loss although it had acquired a foothold in 23 million homes. In 1984, ABC bought ESPN outright. Then broadcast giant Capital Cities Group bought ABC and expanded ABC's already successful *Monday Night Football* into *Sunday Night Football* as well. Two years later, ESPN completed a $400 million rights transaction to televise major league baseball games.[44]

In August 1995, Disney bought the entire Cap Cities entertainment conglomerate including ABC and ESPN. Disney recognized the strong brand that ESPN had become and began to invest heavily in sports programming. By 2006, investment banking house UBS estimated the value of the ESPN property alone at $28 billion, close to half of Disney's entire market capitalization at the time of $70 billion. By 2008, ESPN was reaching 94 million homes with programming from 65 different sports including NFL and major league baseball games. Coming full circle in the broadcast world, ESPN also launched ESPN radio, a consortium of 700 radio stations with 350 full-time affiliates offering NBA and major league baseball games, among others.[45]

Soon many of the top media empires not only offered sports programming, but also owned the sports properties themselves. By the New Millennium, not only did Turner (by then owned by AOL Time Warner) own the Atlanta Braves and the *Chicago Tribune* (with its broadcast superstation WGN) control the Cubs, but Rupert Murdoch's News Corporation, owner of the Fox Television Network, owned the Los Angeles Dodgers, having acquired the team from Peter O'Malley for an estimated $350 million. At the same time, Rogers Communications owned the Toronto Blue Jays, and Walt Disney Co. itself had added the Los Angeles Angels to its roster of brands.

Sports programming had experienced exponential growth from the 1960s forward, but it was not always a smooth progression. One of the more enduring gaffes of baseball and television, for example, occurred on April 6, 1987, when Dodgers executive Al Campanis appeared on ABC's *Nightline* program with Ted Koppel. Campanis, who was then 70 years old and looked like a deer in headlights as he fielded questions, found himself making a unfortunate reply to Koppel's inquiry about a paucity of black managers and executives in major league baseball. "I truly believe," Campanis replied, "that they may not have some of the necessities to be, let's say, a field manager or perhaps a GM."[46] Koppel, a news man, then gave Campanis a chance to either clarify or dig deeper, and his guest blundered into the latter with a diatribe about how black people are wonderful and make great athletes, but may not have the necessities to be baseball managers, front office people, or executives in general, whether at baseball teams or banks. Two days later, Campanis was gone from the Dodgers, the very team that had embraced an African

American to break the color barrier in 1947 — a remarkable baseball irony that had played itself out on live national television.

But corporate ownership influenced the game in more ways than spectacular gaffes and historic irony. Chicago's Wrigley Field had been without lights since the structure was built in 1914, and in the 1980s it was the last big league baseball venue to offer only day games— that is, until August 8, 1988.[47] The Cubs had played at Wrigley for 72 straight years without lights, but the *Tribune* knew that night baseball could offer a radical increase in viewers, ratings, and advertising dollars, so it almost immediately began a campaign to change Cubs history. Overcoming day baseball purists, recalcitrant Cub fans, hostile neighbors who lived in the Wrigleyville area of Chicago's North Side, and local politics, the *Tribune* finally prevailed when the Cubs hosted the Mets on August 8, 1988 — a game that was rained out by the fourth inning, pushing the first official night game to the following evening with a 6–4 win over the Mets.

Corporate bottom-line management driven by television revenues was behind the Cubs' transition to night baseball. The very next year, in 1989, baseball's network television contract was up for renewal. Television revenue and player salaries had grown exponentially over the two prior decades, almost in lock step, both increasing just over 1,700 percent. Television had nearly killed the minor leagues, and it caused major league attendance to drop from 20 million in 1948 to 14.4 million just five years later. But once it began to showcase the game, attendance began to grow. The corporate tides were rising, and they were clearly lifting all boats.

Baseball revenues continued to bring profits and skyrocketing salaries, but as the 1990s approached, public cynicism over money began to tarnish the game's appeal. The labor action of 1994 brought the clash of money and baseball to a head, dealing a final blow to the disgruntled public when the 1994 World Series was canceled. Billionaire owners were squabbling with millionaire players over money at the expense of the game and the fans— money that was coming from those same fans in the first place. Baseball suffered. In 1991 over 35 million viewers watched the game's flagship spectacle, the World Series, on television, but the ratings would drop dramatically. One year later only 30 million watched, which sank to 24 million one year after that. The next year was 1994 when the number of viewers was actually zero since there was no Series at all. Viewership inched up to 28 million the next year in 1995, but a steady decline once again ensured.[48]

With baseball's image, ratings, and revenues all suffering at once during the mid–1990s, the game nonetheless experienced a sudden resurgence in 1998. Baseball was back for the same reason that had allowed Ruth to ignite the Murderers' row in the 1920s and for Mantle and Maris to propel baseball into the 1960s: home runs. By 1998, home runs were being captured in living color, often by big-screen television sets. Adding to the excitement, that season's historic home run chase between the Cubs' Sammy Sosa and the Cardinals' Mark McGwire was actually a three-way contest against the ghost of Ruth himself. The inevitable televised drama gripped an entire nation. Baseball, at last, had lucked out, or so it seemed. The headline of a *New York Times* article on September 4, 1998, said it all: "A Sport Is Reborn — the Home Run, America's Signature Feat, Invigorates Baseball; September's Aura Restored to Fans."[49] When that article ran, Sosa was at 56 homers and counting while McGwire was about to go for the vaunted number 60. Sosa would actually made it to number 66 ahead of McGwire, but the latter pushed the envelope still further, achieving home run number 70 — a feat that no human had ever come close to achieving, not Ruth or Gehrig or Foxx or Greenberg, Willie Mays, Hank Aaron, the golden boy Mickey Mantle nor the sullen Roger Maris or even the acerbic Barry Bonds at the time.

The *Times* referred to the home run as America's signature feat. Indeed it is. A great success in business, publishing, cinema, music or even war is often called a home run. Even a long NFL touchdown pass is referred to as a home run ball. For the better part of a decade, beginning perhaps a couple years before the Sosa-McGwire barrage, baseball gave Americans what they craved: spectacular home runs. Those long ball shots played well on television, taking upward of four seconds to unfold in their full splendor of crushing sports achievement. Baseball may have originally been a game built for radio, but television was built for the home run spectacle — especially widescreen HD.

But all that glitters is not always golden or even pure where baseball is concerned. Evidence of steroids in baseball during those years is pervasive and has been widely reported. The most exhaustive and probably the most reliable is the Mitchell Report, an investigation conducted by former U.S. Senator George Mitchell at the request of Commissioner Bud Selig on March 30, 2006. That report was compiled after Mitchell's team conducted over 700 interviews, 68 with players, and the review of over 115,000 hard-copy pages of documents and 20,000 more electronic pages. The report pointed fingers at many, notably the Players Association, which it described as "largely uncooperative." Many were to blame, Mitchell concluded, including the players, the major leagues, and the players union itself. Among its many findings, the Mitchell Report came to a stark but inevitable realization: "The use of steroids in Major League Baseball was widespread. The response by baseball was slow to develop and was initially ineffective. For many years, citing concerns for the privacy rights of the players, the Players Association opposed mandatory random drug testing of its members for steroids and other substances."[50]

There is no evidence of an overt conspiracy among baseball, its players, and the suppliers of illicit drugs, but once the players discovered steroids, it is clear that baseball was unresponsive, perhaps blinded by the lure of the home run ball, ratings, money, and the resurgence of the game itself in the wake of the 1994 labor wars. In view of all that has surfaced since 1998, the circumstantial evidence of an implied conspiracy as everyone looked the other way in the face of burgeoning records, ratings, and revenue is compelling. It is not only possible, but perhaps likely that, in the end, corporate profits and television drama may have contributed nearly as much to baseball's great steroid era as the drugs themselves. Such would be the ultimate irony of the tail wagging the baseball dog, of the media exerting so much influence over the game that baseball itself became distorted.

Perhaps baseball innocently ignored the threat of steroids, at least at first, feeling that steroids would not produce the expert hand-eye coordination that is necessary to hit a curveball or wicked slider. The other sports leagues, not to mention the Olympics, have long tested for performance-enhancing drugs. But baseball is more a game of inches and skill rather than bulk, so maybe the major leagues can be given a pass — but only up to a point. There comes a time when the obvious becomes patent, even to a foolish observer, and when self-interest and greed become blinding and destructive — all because the added power and stamina of the steroid monster enhances the existing skills of an established home run power hitter.

For the first 95 years of the twentieth century, a 50-home run season was achieved only 18 times in total, four of which were by Ruth, none by then reigning lifetime record-holder Hank Aaron. From 1995 to 2007, a blink of history that may have encompassed most of the steroid era, the 50-homer plateau was achieved 23 times. Even more compelling, 60 homers were reached six times in just four short years—1998 through 2001— all by just three players, Sammy Sosa (three times), Mark McGwire (twice), and Barry Bonds (once). All three players were National Leaguers, which may have no significance except, fortunately, to leave some of the American League records undistorted by the steroid era. Roger Maris still holds the record for most AL homers in a season; Hank Greenberg the most AL homers for a first baseman; Mickey Mantle the most for a switch-hitter; and both Jimmie Foxx and Hank Greenberg the most for an AL right-hander. Even four National League home run marks survived the steroid onslaught: Ernie Banks still holds the mark for homers from a shortstop (47 in 1958), Rogers Hornsby the most at second base (42 in 1922), Mike Schmidt (48 in 1980) at third, and rookie marks for Frank Robinson and Wally Berger with 38 homers each. Ironically, Mark McGwire still holds the American League rookie mark with 49 jacks for Oakland in 1987, when steroids were not likely a factor.[51]

In the wake of the steroid era, the New York Yankees successfully launched the YES (Yankees Entertainment and Sports) Network in 2002. But World Series ratings have continued to drop, slipping to just 15 million viewers in 2006 and only 13 million in 2008. Major media conglomerates have begun to exit team ownership as a business model strategy. In 2004, News Corp. sold the Dodgers, and in 2007 Time Warner (the successor to Turner) unloaded the Braves for $450 million—selling the team that Ted Turner had originally purchased for about $12 million in 1976. Disney sold the Los Angeles Angels of Anaheim in 2003, and even the *Chicago Tribune*, a bankrupt media giant at the time, at long last sold the Cubs in 2009.[52] Media ownership allowed big business to avoid the broadcast rights fees, but corporate America found itself with little patience or taste for the escalating player salaries that ensued.

By the spring of 2009, a third of all major league baseball franchises were experiencing a decline in value. League-wide, average values actually went up one percent, but that was largely because the Yankees' pegged value jumped by 15 percent to a staggering $1.5 billion due, in part, to their new stadium. The ten teams that declined in value comprised the biggest aggregate loss since 2004. Teams in regions of high unemployment in the post–2008 Great Recession were hit hard, with big drops in value suffered by the Nationals, Tigers, and Indians.[53]

Baseball in the New Millennium will not go away, but it will need to earn its keep the hard way in the aftermath of the steroid era. There will be no artificially cheap home run thrills to boost national ratings and attendance, and the economic impact of the recent Great Recession could be felt for years. As noted, television may have been the second most important factor in baseball during the twentieth century (behind Jackie Robinson's assault on the color barrier), but the steroid revelation may already be one of the most pervasive events of the twenty-first century. Fate and technology may help mitigate baseball's misfortunes, however. As also noted, major league baseball plays especially well on high-definition television where colorful fields, an appealing variety in stadiums, close-ups of players who are not concealed by helmets, and the great American spectacle of double plays, strikeouts, and home runs are exploited to the fullest in front of virtual advertising that cannot be fast-forwarded into oblivion.

Yes, ratings and profits and ego and greed all contributed in varying degrees to the steroid era. But just as radio elevated baseball as an entertainment juggernaut and television later propelled it to new heights, it appears that widescreen HD splendor will help bring the game back from the depths of the steroid debacle. The media money tail may still wag the baseball dog from time to time, but so far none of the media, steroids, or the big league brass has managed to kill that dog altogether.

17

The Prodigal Game

As October drew to a close with the 2009 World Series underway, Suzyn Waldman became the first woman ever to broadcast a game in the Fall Classic. Hired as a television analyst by owner George Steinbrenner, Waldman had been associated with the New York Yankees for over two decades, working games in various capacities, including play-by-play duties, for both WFAN and the YES network. Waldman became a national analyst for WCBS radio in 2005, so when the Yankees made it back to the Series in 2009, she was ready to make history.[1]

Lesley Visser had been the first woman to cover the World Series as a reporter when she handled the 1990 World Series for CBS. On August 3, 1993, Gayle Gardner made history as the first woman to do major league baseball play-by-play when she called a Rockies-Reds game for Denver's KWGN-TV. That same year Andrea Joyce became the first woman to co-host network coverage of the World Series. Then, in 1995, Hannah Storm became the first woman to act as a solo host for a World Series game.

It took a number of years for the progression to become complete, but Waldman's eventual Game One appearance was both historic and symbolic, visibly bringing the game forward to twenty-first century standards of broadcasting equality. But change does not come easy for the nation's most enduring team sport. Over the decades baseball found it difficult to embrace African American ballplayers, instant replay, steroid testing, interleague play, free agency — and even radio when it first appeared in the 1920s and, for some teams, well into the 1930s. Yet baseball would enigmatically tamper with other rules and traditions with abandon, giving the game a distinct Jekyll & Hyde personality, such as the lowered pitcher's mound, the designated hitter — in one league and not the other, no less — and a gimmick that desecrates the very spirit of success: awarding the World Series home-field advantage not to the winner of the most games, but to the team from the league that was to the winner of a mid-season exhibition game.

Instant replay reviews could easily reverse a plethora of blown umpire calls, like those blatant gaffes during the 2009 playoffs, although an argument can be made for shunning replay during the regular season. With 162 games, there is ample time for missed calls to even themselves out, giving baseball a more flawed yet human side while not necessarily distorting history. But that same argument cannot be applied to the post-season where missed bases and tags, as well as fair, foul, and home run balls, can make all the difference in one game, a series, and therefore posterity. There is no rational justification whatsoever for baseball's approach to the summer All-Star Game whereby the winner determines home-field advantage for the game's signature fall moment, the World Series—except for one misguided purpose.

The All-Star Game influence over the real championship series was a contrived gimmick enacted to bring relevance to a wholly irrelevant All-Star contest. But the proper solution is not to demean the World Series in exchange for artificially invoking a modicum of relevance to the All-Star break; it would have been to either leave the All-Star Game alone or improve it, or to dump it altogether. First played to spice up Chicago's Worlds Fair in 1933, baseball's All-Star Game was an inspired innovation for its day. The very first game was played at Comiskey Park on July 6, 1933, having been dreamed up by *Chicago Tribune* sports editor Arch Ward as part of Chicago's Century of Progress fair. The All-Star Game understandably became a big hit with fans for decades.

With the advent of free agency, interleague play, and the proliferation of baseball on television through multiple cable outlets, the relevance of the All-Star contest could not help but diminish. Fans could watch any team and any player almost at will on television, and in every major league city they could see multiple stars from the other league during several interleague games throughout the middle part of summer. Moreover, after the season expanded to 162 games, player salaries exploded, the stakes grew higher for players and owners alike, and player apathy set in for All-Star duty. The players began to prefer the brief mid-summer break for tired arms and sore backs rather than to travel, pitch, or hit during an exhibition game. Many began to dream up injuries and other excuses, creating friction among the players, teams, the league itself, and the fans.

Concurrently, another contrivance was generating interest among fans and players alike: the home run derby offered as part of the All-Star Game package.[2] It did not require hard slides, pulled hamstrings, or extra work for weary pitchers. Developed almost entirely for the television audience, the 2009 home run contest, played and aired in July on ESPN, drew a 10 share, meaning 10 percent of all televisions in use were tuned to the game. More importantly, it bested all broadcast programming that night among the coveted adult bracket of 18 to 49 year olds.[3] Players enjoy the competition and fans love the drama of long balls crushed by the best home run hitters of the day.

Rating shares for the All-Star Game have dropped precipitously from the high 40s and low 50s in the 1960s and 1970s to just the teens in the New Millennium. Not since 1999 has the game scored a 20 share or better, settling in around 15 for six years running. Relative to other shows, though, the 2009 All-Star Game still did relatively well in the ratings and was the most watched such contest since 2002, providing the most obvious reason for its continued existence: television money. But at what overall cost? The post-game spin described the 2009 All-Star Game as "the sixth most watched sporting event of 2009," at least through July when it was played.[4] But it was a deceptive sixth place. The Super Bowl audience was six *times* as big and the NCAA championship game was larger by about three million viewers. Yes, the game was watched by 14.6 million on Fox, but *America's Got Talent* drew 13.5 million that same week on NBC while the sit-com *Two and a Half Men* pulled 9.1 million for CBS. The game makes money for baseball and the networks, but the players object to playing, the game itself is rather boring and still irrelevant despite the World Series gimmick, and the ratings trend is distinctly downward.

In 1960 the All-Star Game drew a 50 share, peaking with a 54 in 1970. By 1990 its share was down to 33, then 23 in 1996, 18 in 2000, and 15 in 2009. Although 15 percent of sets were tuned in, that means 85 percent of televisions in use were showing something else.[5] Yet the game continues, largely because it produces itself and can still draw more viewers than most top regular programming like *Royal Pains* (6.23 million), *The Bachelorette* (8.01 million), and *Wipeout* (7.69 million).[6] But it is still largely irrelevant, disdained by the players, and distorted by its contrived World Series relevance.

Making the All-Star team is a privilege, and virtually all players regard it as an achievement, an honor. But actually playing in the game at the expense of extra rest during a 162-game marathon season is not the best option for most. The All-Star Game served its purpose, providing a glimpse of players from other leagues when television was either non-existent or a lesser factor, all when the regular season and expanded play-offs were less grueling.

But in spite of the All-Star Game, there are reasons to believe baseball itself could be on the rebound. One of those reasons can be traced to television technology. Just as baseball crept into radio "like little cat feet," there may be a new marriage of baseball and high-definition television that is subtly boosting the game. By 2005, almost all televisions being sold were of the flat-screen variety, nearly all with the theater-wide format, and many with very large screens of 42 inches or more.[7] Analog TVs were being replaced in droves before the federal government got into the act by mandating the HD digital format in 2009. In 2004, DVD video disks outsold VHS tapes for the first time, but by 2009 DVDs were being pushed aside by other electronic recording capabilities, computers, and even portable devices like Apple's iPod.[8] As fate would have it, the widescreen digital television brings expansive baseball fields into the home complete with their inherent beauty. The wide-shot format captures the whole field of play where plays can be seen from multiple angles. While all sports benefit from the HD phenomenon, baseball is among the biggest beneficiaries with its deliberate play, cathedral stadiums, and long-ball style played out over a mammoth field that is 100 feet deeper than a football field and nearly three times as wide.

In 2002, Fox broadcast the entire World Series in high definition, portending extraordinary things to come for baseball on TV. But advanced technology not only changes the shape and suitability of the televised image, it can enhance availability. Sophisticated cable and satellite systems, for example, make the MLB Network possible by providing access to multiple games. The MLB Network was conceived in 2008 as a consortium among the major leagues and multiple minority owner providers such as DirecTV (16.67 percent), Comcast (8.34 percent), Time Warner (6.35 percent), and Cox Communications (1.98 percent). The new network anticipates subscriber fees of over $152 million and ad revenues of $65 million by 2015, giving the venture a substantial enterprise valuation in the range of $1.2 billion.[9]

Ironically, the 2007 season was the last for the Braves on the TBS superstation, the Ted Turner brainchild that jump-started modern-day baseball broadcasting. TBS had provided the Braves and their opponents, at first all the National League teams and then interleague opponents, but with the MLB Network fans do not have to wait for their own teams to appear on a game-of-the-week format or show up as a Braves opponent. Radio may be back, too. In 2009 the Atlanta Braves radio network counted 152 stations strewn across the southern United States, including one station in the Virgin Islands.

With its MLB Network in place, baseball decided to broadcast the Hall of Fame induction ceremony live for the first time ever, suggesting that baseball may find more and more ways to exploit its own network capabilities. But the game is facing a growing quandary that can only become more controversial as time progresses — the Hall of Fame itself. The Hall is an independent institution not under the direct control of major league baseball, but tradition has forged a symbiotic relationship that will face a burgeoning dilemma as players from the steroid era become otherwise eligible for induction.

The great steroid era will soon lead to the great baseball dilemma, a brewing conflict made inevitable by a distortion of history that begs for resolution: baseball has embraced the performance records of the steroid era but not the players who set those records. History may not be kind to the game if that paradox is not resolved. But how can it be?

When Barry Bonds set the single-season home run record at 73, he supplanted both Mark McGwire and the pre-steroid marks of Roger Maris and Babe Ruth. One option would be for baseball to revoke that record, but there are dozens of marks set by different players for multifarious reasons during the steroid years. Negating each one fairly would be virtually impossible since it cannot be determined which players and records were truly tarnished. Another approach could be to qualify those marks with a steroid-era asterisk, but even that is not a viable solution for the same reason.

Will sports history be left to beg the ultimate steroid question — how can baseball embrace the steroid records but not the players who achieved them? And how does baseball determine which players were clean and which were not? Published reports suggest that Barry Bonds was tainted by steroids — and even Bonds admits to using steroids, he just maintains it was "accidental." Mark McGwire has finally conceded his own steroid use, in 2010, after staying mum about it during the prior Congressional hearings. Would that mean Sammy Sosa should be the reigning record holder with his 66 homers in 1998? That would seem disingenuous, for although Sosa has not expressly admitted steroid use, there is plenty of suspicion.

Doing nothing about this dilemma is one option, letting history sort out the truth, but that hardly solves the issues of fairness and historic integrity. Greed was almost certainly the true culprit behind the steroid era as home runs in 1998 brought baseball back from the abyss of fan apathy stemming from the 1994 labor wars. It is likewise probable that baseball dragged its feat on steroid testing in the face of the obvious, done at a time when other sports had no difficulty recognizing, banning, and testing for performance enhancers. The great home run chase and the resurgence of home runs and thus baseball itself was played out on the national stage of television that at first seemed a tribute to the first time that happened in 1961, when Roger Maris and Mickey Mantle captivated the entire nation. But then the truth began to emerge, and those records, and baseball, lost their luster.

But baseball is a prodigal game; it always seems to come back. Even the fast televised action of NFL football or the close-up images of NBA basketball cannot supplant baseball entirely. But baseball could become its own worst enemy if it fails to resolve the burgeoning baseball conflict among history and truth, records and integrity, baseball and posterity. Baseball cannot continue to deny the existence of almost two decades of star power from Roger Clemens to Bonds, Sosa, McGwire, and legions of other players without damaging its own image. Yet the very act of recognizing them and their records inflicts a different kind of injury to the game.

There is one possible solution that lets baseball off the hook without wholly distorting history and truth. When Roger Maris broke Ruth's 60-homer record, the baseball pundits were offended since Maris had an unfair advantage, a 162-game season compared to Ruth's 154 games. Maris was given an implied asterisk for his trouble, tarnishing Maris for no reason other than to preserve the ghost of Ruth as the ultimate baseball icon. Maris never really received an actual asterisk, but he may need one to reconcile the post-steroid records with the players who set them. Whatever else one might conclude about the steroid era and its incumbent dilemmas, it is clear that Roger Maris and Henry Aaron were the last home run record holders in the pre-steroid era. They should be recognized for that achievement, not brushed aside by the dilution of time and tarnished posterity. After all, neither Maris nor Aaron had the advantage of the steroid monster, so to discredit Maris for the 162-game season or to sweep Aaron's lifetime home run achievement under the rug is a distortion of baseball and truth.

But baseball cannot seriously dole out scores of asterisks for those who played in the steroid era, yet it can pay homage to the game and preserve a modicum of integrity by continuing to recognize Maris and Aaron as something other than mere former record holders. For that matter, it might appease one variety of baseball purists if Ruth himself were to be awarded an asterisk as "the last record holder in the 154-game era."

If baseball can rebuild its credibility and put the steroid era in perspective, it has an outstanding opportunity to resurrect itself from the tarnish of its bloated records, many of which could be unbreakable without performance enhancers. The reason is availability through television, radio, the web, and a new wave of mobile tracking devices like Apple's iPhone and even newer generations of "broadcast" devices.

With Wi-Fi streaming and other technology like iPhones, iPods and AT&T's 3G network, baseball can disseminate itself like never before, a process that will produce compounded returns reminiscent of when radio originally billboarded the game and brought a quantum leap of marketing success in the 1920s. One advantage baseball has over other sports is its uniquely quantifiable and comparable statistics known, in the aggregate, as "sabermetrics." Indeed MLB.com will not only stream many games live over the web, but it can exploit new horizons with its legacy of statistics. The MLB "At Bat" offering in 2009 provides real-time scores, pitch-by-pitch game tracking, box scores, and game summaries.[10]

Baseball television broadcasting has progressed radically since the early days of televised sports. As early as 1957, baseball coverage included innovations like the zoom lenses, split-screen pictures, and multiple cameras. Hugh Beach, a producer for the CBS *Game of the Week* baseball telecasts in 1957, saw still further innovation on the distant baseball horizon. Beach believed that "the day is coming when the stay-at-home fan will squint, duck and dodge a fast ball that appears to be coming though the screen into the parlor."[11] Beach had no idea how right he would one day be, even without considering the possibilities of 3-D which is now creeping into modern broadcasting.

In February 2009, the Nielsen Company reported a study conducted during the final three months of 2008 wherein the dean of television rating services found that "Americans are watching more video online, on their cell phones and on television." Called Nielsen's "three screen" report, the findings indicated that the typical American viewer is watching TV more than 151 hours per month, up about six full hours from just one year before and constituting a new all-time high.[12] One reason is the proliferation of niche programming provided by multiple cable channels, where something can be found for everyone. This not only includes history, reality TV, news, vintage television, talk shows, law shows, politics, and movies, but also sports. Hockey fans, for example, can follow games featuring their home teams. This is true of football, NCAA basketball, and non-team sports including the new "X games" contests. But it is particularly true of baseball, which offers, by far, the most games to choose from.

New technology has pervaded the media in many ways beyond just television and hand-held apparatus. The most basic of all baseball broadcasting, radio, has also benefited from the tech explosion. "I feel like a kid again," announced Nathan Olson, a displaced Cubs fan living in Arkansas. Because of satellite radio and web streaming broadcasts, Olson and legions of others can follow their teams at home, wherever that may be. Sometimes that means on the road. One St. Louis truck driver, who makes 600-mile runs, is addicted to satellite radio and the Cardinals games that help pass the time. XM Satellite Radio, before the merger with competitor Sirius, paid major league baseball $650 million for the rights to broadcast games for 11 years.[13]

Long-time broadcast icon Bob Costas, who is sold on the satellite model, harkened his own youth in a *New York Times* interview with reporter Lee Jenkins: "It's exactly what I did when I was 11 or 12, taking the keys to my dad's car, sitting in the driveway and trying to pick up games in different parts of the country." Baseball has always been regarded as the sport best suited to radio, given all its long pauses and blank spaces, noted Jenkins, who poignantly concluded, "For transplanted fans, hearing a game is not unlike telephoning home."[14]

Fans can listen to other sports on satellite radio and web streaming, of course, but nothing is like listening to baseball with its steady pace, "phone home" romance and, just as importantly, its plethora of games. Yes, truck drivers can find their favorite NFL teams on digital radio, but only once a week, 16 times altogether plus a rare playoff game. Baseball provides a daily routine, a glimpse of home and a taste of broadcast voices so familiar that they seem like family not just once a week, but 162 times each season.

Another phenomenon has rejuvenated radio's role in sports entertainment. If talking baseball is a major component of the radio broadcast of games, then why not expand the banter beyond the games? Sports talk radio has surfaced in major markets, devoting the entire broadcast day to discussing, arguing and pontificating about sports with fans themselves who call in to voice opinions, vent anger at team management, or sometimes even be insulted. Mitch Rosen, program director for WSCR (the "Score") sports radio in Chicago, underscored baseball's sentimental value in a July 2009 interview: "Baseball: a summer best friend of the fan." Rosen stresses the relationship that evolves among the team, the announcers, and the listeners.[15] WSCR carries all the Chicago White Sox games in addition to providing relentless sports talk radio.

The listener's entertainment is often someone else's headache, and that means station management. Baseball in the summer is one thing, but baseball in the fall produces its own unique issues: cold weather, rain, sometimes snow, and the occasional religious holiday problem. In particular, the fall Jewish holidays often collide with the playoffs and thus lay claim to their own place in baseball history, by causing famous dilemmas for such players as Hank Greenberg and Sandy Koufax. Sometimes a number of factors come together at once, as they did in the fall of 2008 during a crucial season finale tie-breaker game between the Tigers and White Sox. According to Rosen, although the Sox-Tigers game to determine a playoff spot was a day contest, it still had problems with darkness in more ways than one when a long rain delay pushed the game toward sundown. At that point Sox radio announcer Steve Stone, a former Cy Young Award pitcher who happens to be Jewish, suddenly made a different call with two words guaranteed to invoke terror for station brass. "Gotta leave." The rain had extended the game to the brink of the High Holiday Yom Kippur, causing the abrupt Stone exit (to begin the Yom Kippur observance at sundown) and a quick management decision. The scramble was on, with the day, or dusk, as it happens, saved by Chris Ronge who jumped in to finish the game.[16]

When WSCR is not broadcasting the Sox, it acts as a sounding board for Chicago fans of all local sports including the Blackhawks, Bears, Bulls, and Cubs in addition to the White Sox. In addition to providing a relentless stream of sports consciousness, talk radio provides a way for listeners to vent and the teams to do the listening — sort of sports broadcasting in reverse. But is all this just noise? Do the teams ever really listen? Rosen believes they do. "There are two million people per week listening to Chicago's two sports talk stations [the other being the local ESPN affiliate WMVP]," Rosen notes, "and together they can provide a major factor in team decision making."[17] Whether its voice is always heard by those who count, sports talk radio has flourished throughout the country from coast to coast. Baseball, it seems, has not only rediscovered its radio roots, but those roots are now talking back to team ownership.

What makes for a good baseball announcer? Knowledge of the game, respect for the fans, an ability to relate, a sense of perspective, a nebulous component summed up as talent, and at least one more thing: "teach something," says Rosen.[18] Engage the fans, give them something to think about, relate the intricacies of the game or the history of the game and its players.

The relationship between on-air talent and management is not always rosy, and sometimes the baseball broadcaster "teaches" more than the teams prefer. One of the most celebrated announcers in the history of the game was Red Barber, who did four decades of play-by-play from as early as 1934 for the Reds, followed by the Brooklyn Dodgers and finally a long run with the New York Yankees from 1954 to 1966. Barber's greatest strength may have been his credibility. But one day that same strength caught up to him on that fateful day in September 1966, with a dismal Yankees team mired in last place for the first time since 1912, and as previously noted, Barber could not help but note the paucity of fans at the ballpark where only 413 lost souls turned out for the game that day. Some accounts dispute the connection, but it was only a week later that Barber was told his contract would not be renewed. Red Barber, apparently, had been fired for honesty.

Everything has a price, including candor — especially in the broadcast business — and that includes progress, as well. Armed with corporate resources and satellite technology, Clear Channel took over the baseball broadcast duties for the Pittsburgh Pirates, which meant that the 51-year marriage between KDKA and the Pirates had ended with the close of the 2006 season.[19] Much of the history of baseball broadcasting had begun with Harold Arlin, a wayward engineer who stumbled into the KDKA studios in 1921. With the exodus of the Pirates from KDKA, owned by CBS at the time, baseball broadcasting would continue to move forward, but it would never be quite the same in Pittsburgh.

The most enduring quality of baseball may not lie with its numbers, its stars, or its champions; rather, the game owes much of its longevity to a much more potent attribute, its humanity. On July 4, 2009, a modest story ran locally in San Diego about an unheralded fan with a poignant connection to baseball's profound past. Robert Tierney, 85 years old, had once played catch with a living icon, Lou Gehrig, whose "luckiest man alive" speech had been given to Yankee fans exactly 70 years before. As a teenager in Minnesota, Tierney had a bad leg, no thumb on his throwing hand, and not much future as a ballplayer, even on his Rochester American Legion team.[20] As fate would have it, Tierney's team played near the famed Mayo Clinic where the great Gehrig had gone for treatment for his newly discovered ALS affliction. Gehrig could not resist coming over, and if the boys begged enough he would play catch with them. Although Robert Tierney might very well be the last living person to have played catch with Gehrig, his ties to the Yankee Iron Horse were much greater than a few throws long ago in Rochester, Minnesota. A number of years later, Lou Gehrig's disease — ALS — would claim Tierney's wife, too.

Baseball began somewhere on a grassy field long, long ago. But it became the major league game that we all know when a thunderous hitter named Ruth reinvented the home run spectacle at a time when the spoken-word pictures of radio anointed baseball as the summer friend of our collective youth. Baseball has survived labor wars, gambling, steroids, and the scourge of racism not because it simply is an enduring game, which begs the question, but because it is an indelible part of the American experience, one that grew up with our parents and grandparents during the golden age of broadcasting. Baseball, with its relentless summer games and familiar broadcast voices, is not just an enduring sport, it is family.

> *The other sports are just sports. Baseball is a love.*
> — BRYANT GUMBEL, 1981[21]

Chapter Notes

Introduction

1. Famous Quotes & Authors web site, *http://www.famousquotesandauthors.com/keywords/media_quotes.html* (viewed 04.07.10).
2. Paul Dickson, *Baseball's Greatest Quotations* (New York: Harper Perennial, 1992), 469.
3. "The Wireless Operators, the Distress Call and the Rescue Ship Carpathia," *Titanic* and Other White Star Line Ships, *http://www.titanic-whitestarships.com* (viewed 06.23.10).
4. "KDKA Begins to Broadcast," A Science Odyssey: People and Discoveries, PBS, *http://www.pbs.org/wgbh/aso/databank/entries/dt20ra.html* (viewed 06.26.10).
5. Dickson, *Baseball's Greatest Quotations.*
6. "Play by Play Account of Moonlight Graham's Only Game," Society for American Baseball Research; courtesy of David W. Smith, *http://www.sabr.org/sabr.cfm?a=cms,c,332,34,0* (viewed 04.07.10).
7. Ben Walker, "Hollywood Did Not Invent Moonlight Graham," Associated Press, June 25, 2005.
8. Dickson, *Baseball's Greatest Quotations,* 224.

Chapter 1

1. Malcolm Gladwell, *Outliers: The Story of Success* (New York: Little, Brown, 2008).
2. Dickson, *Baseball's Greatest Quotations,* 137.
3. Sources differ on what really happened, but it seems likely that these broadcasts were actually recreations delivered by written memo and announced over the air.
4. Perhaps WMAQ did not have the equipment necessary to set up live at Wrigley Field, then still known as North Side Park or, more commonly, Cubs Park. At the time, WGN was a leader in technology and live sports programming, already broadcasting auto races and football, which may have explained the initial choice of WGN.
5. The following year, WGN would help change American courtroom history by sending a team to broadcast live from the threshold Scopes monkey trial in Dayton, Tennessee. Quin Ryan was there, reporting the proceedings with engineer Paul Neal, an expensive undertaking that cost $1,000 per day just for the telephone transmission lines back to the Chicago studio. With Clarence Darrow clashing with none other than orator and former presidential candidate William Jennings Bryan over the right to think and teach evolution, it was the trial of the century to that point, and according to some may have been THE trial of the twentieth century. It later inspired the prize-winning play *Inherit the Wind*, which soon became an acclaimed motion picture by the same name. Most of the compelling courtroom testimony featured in the play and the movie was real, taken straight from the trial transcript itself. Careful viewing of the motion picture version will reveal WGN microphones strategically placed in the courtroom.
6. Still sometimes referred to as Weeghman Park at the time, named for the former Cubs owner Charlie Weeghman, who had built the facility in 1914 when he was the owner of the competing Chicago Whales baseball team in the Federal League.
7. A short right field can be inviting for the visitors, too. The first three games at the new Yankee Stadium in 2009 produced 17 home runs, many to right field. In one of those games, on April 17, Cleveland pounded Yankee pitching for 22 runs, including no fewer than four home runs to right and right center.

8. Irving Vaughan, "Cubs Beat Pirates in Opener, 8 to 2," *Chicago Daily Tribune*, April 15, 1925.
9. Jonathan Fraser Light, *The Cultural Encyclopedia of Baseball*, 2nd ed. (Jefferson, NC: McFarland, 2005), 767.
10. "WGN Radio Timeline," *http://wgngold.com/timeline/1920s1930s.htm* (viewed 03.15.06).
11. "Radio Programs for Today," *Chicago Daily Tribune*, April 20, 1925.

Chapter 2

1. Michael J. Haupert, "The Economic History of Major League Baseball," *http://eh.net/encyclopedia/article/haupert.mlb* (viewed 05.27.09).
2. Burt Solomon, *The Baseball Timeline* (New York: Avon, 1997), 244.
3. Ibid.
4. "Harold Arlin," Baseball Library.com, *http://www.baseballlibrary.com/ballplayers/player.php?name=Harold_Arlin* (viewed 05.08.09).
5. "Titanic Facts," *http://www.infoplease.com/spot/titanic.html* (viewed 05.02.09).
6. "Titanic's Wireless Room," The Titanic Radio Page, *http://www.hf.ro/* (viewed 05.09.09 and 05.29.11).
7. Ibid.
8. Ibid.
9. "Guglielmo Marconi," *http://www.nobel-winners.com/physics/guglielmo_marconi.html* (viewed 07.03.10).
10. "Heinrich Hertz," *http://www.inventors.about.com/library/inventors/blradar.htm* (viewed 05.02.09).
11. "Ericsson Buys Most of Marconi for GBP1.2 Billion," *Cellular News*, October 25, 2005, *http://www.cellular-news.com/story/14537.php* (viewed 05.29.11).
12. "Radio Corporation of America," Museum of Broadcast Communication, *http:www.museum.tv/archives/etv/R/htmlR/radiocorpora* (viewed 05.02.09).
13. "The History of Radio," *http://www.inventors.about.com/od/rstartinventions/a/radio_2.htm* (viewed 04.19.09).
14. Ibid.
15. "Who's on First?" *http://www.oldradio.com/archives/general/first.html* (viewed 03.19.06).
16. Ibid.
17. Ibid.
18. "KDKA History." KDKA Radio website, *http://www.kdkaradio.com* (viewed 04.19.09).
19. Ibid.
20. Ibid.
21. Curt Smith, *Voices of Summer* (New York: Carroll & Graff, 2005), 6–7.
22. Dickson, *Baseball's Greatest Quotations*, 358.
23. Ibid, 222.
24. Ralph Kiner quote, *http://baseball-almanac.com/quotes/quokiner.shtml* (viewed 07.05.10).
25. Widely quoted, for example, see *http://baseball-almanac.com/quotes/quokiner.shtml* (viewed 07.05.10).
26. Curt Smith, *Voices of Summer* (New York: Carroll & Graff, 2005), 6.
27. Burt Solomon, *The Baseball Timeline* (New York: Avon, 1997), 247–50.
28. "Grantland Rice," *http://www.britannica.com/EBchecked/topic/502321/Grantland-Rice* (viewed 05.08.09).
29. Ibid.
30. Burt Solomon, *The Baseball Timeline* (New York: Avon, 1997), 268.
31. "Polo Grounds," Ballparks, *http://www.ballparks.com/baseball/national/pologr.htm* (viewed 05.09.09).
32. Ibid.
33. "1921 World Series Sets New Records," *New York Times*.

Chapter 3

1. "Rose Bowl History," *http://www.rosebowlhistory.org* (viewed 05.13.09).
2. J.P. Shanley, "Radio: First Commercial Revisited," *New York Times*, August 31, 1955.
3. "Tribune History," Tribune Company, *http://www.tribune.com/about/history.html* (viewed 05.13.09).
4. "McCormick Foundation — History," *http://www.mccormicktribune.org/mission.aspx*.
5. "McCormick, Joseph Medill." *http://bioguide.congress.gov/scripts/biodisplay.pl?index=m000369.* (viewed 06.21.11).
6. "WGN Radio Timeline," *http://wgngold.com/timeline/1920s1930s.htm* (viewed 07.05.10).
7. Ibid.
8. Ibid.
9. Ibid.
10. Ibid.

11. "Wrigley Field," Ballparks, *http://www.ballparks.com/baseball/national/wrigle.htm* (viewed 05.16.09).

12. Vaughn, "Cubs Beat Pirates."

13. "Famous Trials in American History," *http://www.law.umkc.edu/faculty/projects/ftrials/scopes/scopes.htm* (viewed 05.17.09).

14. Elmer Douglass, "Elmer Spends a Night with Radio Talkers," *Chicago Daily Tribune*, April 15, 1925.

15. "Radio Programs for Today," *Chicago Daily Tribune*, April 20, 1925.

16. "Closeups," *Chicago Daily Tribune*, April 21, 1925.

17. "Radio Programs for Today," *Chicago Daily Tribune*, April 20, 1925.

18. Solomon, *Baseball Timeline*, 254.

19. Solomon, *Baseball Timeline*, 255.

20. Solomon, *Baseball Timeline*, 258.

21. Ibid.

22. Ibid.

23. "Dempsey-Carpentier Fight, July, 1921," *http://www.eht.com/oldradio/arrl/2002-06/Dempsey.htm* (viewed 05.20.09).

24. "Official Site of Jack Dempsey," *http://www.cmgww.com/sports/dempsey/facts.htm* (viewed 05.20.09).

25. "Georges Carpentier," *http://www.britannica.com/EBchecked/topic/96758/Georges-Carpentier* (viewed 05.20.09).

26. "Dempsey-Carpentier Fight, July, 1921," *http://www.eht.com/oldradio/arrl/2002-06/Dempsey.htm* (viewed 05.20.09).

27. "Dempsey vs. Carpentier," *http://www.pophistorydig.com/?tag=the-dempsey-carpentier-fight* (viewed 05.20.09).

28. Ibid.

29. Ibid.

30. Solomon, *Baseball Timeline*, 262.

31. "Fred Lieb," Baseball Library.com, http://www.baseballlibrary.com.

32. Smith, *Voices of Summer*, 8.

33. Ibid.

34. Smith, *Voices of Summer*, 9.

35. Light, *Cultural Encyclopedia of Baseball* (Jefferson, NC: McFarland, 2005), 766.

Chapter 4

1. Light. *Cultural Encyclopedia of Baseball* (Jefferson, NC: McFarland, 2005), 766.

2. Ibid.

3. Ibid., 767.

4. "William Wrigley, Jr.," Answers.com, *http://www.tribune.com/about/history.html*

5. "Al Spalding Stats," Baseball Almanac, *http://www.baseball-almanac.com/players/player.php?p=spaldal Q1* (viewed 07.07.10).

6. "Cap Anson," BaseballHistory.com, *http://www.baseballhistory.com/ballplayers/player.php?name=cap_anson_1852* (viewed 07.07.10).

7. David Fleitz, "Cap Anson," *http://bioproj.sabr.org/bioproj.cfm?a=v&v=l&bIbid=1257&pIbid=305* (viewed 07.07.10).

8. "William Wrigley, Jr."

9. "The Wrigley Building," Wrigley Company, *http://www.thewrigleybuilding.com/* (viewed 05.23.09)

10. "Tribune Tower," Tribune Company, *http://www.tribune.com/about/history.html* (viewed 05.23.09)

11. Bill Veeck with Ed Linn, *Veeck as in Wreck* (Chicago: University of Chicago Press, 2001), 23, 25.

12. Light, *Cultural Encyclopedia*, 767.

13. Robert McG. Thomas, Jr., "Johnny Sylvester, the Inspiration for Babe Ruth Heroics, Is Dead," *New York Times*, January 11, 1990.

14. Solomon, *Baseball Timeline*, 294.

15. Thomas H. White, "Broadcasting Becomes Widespread (1922–1923)," United States Early Radio History, *http://earlyradiohistory.us/sec018.htm* (viewed 04.30.09).

16. Ibid.

17. Ibid.

18. Ibid.

19. "News of the Radiocasts," *Chicago Daily Tribune*, June 29, 1924.

20. "The Automotive Giants in the Early 1920s." Life, Blogger, June 4, 2008. http://life-us.blogspot.com/2008/06/automotive-giants-in-early-1920s.html (viewed 05.31.09).

21. "History and Development of Early Car Radios," Radio Museum, http://www.radiomuseum.org/forum/first_car_radios_history_and_development_of_early_car_radios.html (viewed 05.31.09).

22. "Call Radio Fair Greatest Trade Show in U.S.," *Chicago Daily Tribune*, October 12, 1924.

23. "Cubs Broadcast History," *http://bobsabrwebs.com/index2pho?option=com_content&do_pdf=1&Ibid =119*.

24. Tim Brooks and Earl Marsh, *The Complete Directory of Prime Time Network Television Shows* (New York: Ballentine, 1984), 39.

25. Dickson, *Baseball's Greatest Quotations*, 186.

Chapter 5

1. "Old Hoss Radbourn," Baseball Library.com, *http://www.baseballlibrary.com/ballplayers/player. php?name=Old_Hoss_Radbourn_1854* (viewed 06.06.09).

2. Solomon, *Baseball Timeline*, 285.

3. Doug Myers, *Louisville Slugger Presents Batting Around* (Chicago: Contemporary, 2008), 322.

4. Soloman, *Baseball Timeline*, 285.

5. Gene Smiley, "The U.S. Economy in the 1920s." *http://eh.net/encyclopedia/article/Smiley.1920s.final* (viewed 06.06.09).

6. Ibid.

7. Ibid.

8. Ibid.

9. Edward Larson, *Summer for the Gods* (New York: Basic, 2006), 140, 147.

10. Douglas O. Linder, "State v. John Scopes (The Monkey Trial)," *http://www.law.umkc.edu/faculty/ projects/ftrials/scopes/evolut.htm* (viewed 07.10.10).

11. "W-G-N Will Take Scopes Trial to Record Audience," *Chicago Daily Tribune*, July 12, 1925.

12. "Broadcast of Scopes Trial Unprecedented," *Chicago Daily Tribune*, July 5, 1925.

13. "W-G-N Will Take Scopes Trial."

14. Larson, *Summer for the Gods*, 140, 147.

15. "Has the Baseball Really Been Changed?" *Popular Mechanics*, October 1961.

16. "The Growth of a Service," Early Radio History, *http://earlyradiohistory.us/wwj.htm*.

17. *Federal Base Ball Club of Baltimore, Inc. v. National League*, 259 U.S. 200 (1922).

18. *Hart v. B.F. Keith Vaudeville Exchange*, 262 U.S. 271 (1923).

19. Smith, *Voices of Summer*, 12.

20. "Dempsey Loses on Long Count," History.com, *http://www.history.com/this-day-in-history.do?action= article&id=7028* (viewed 06.24.09).

21. Frank Hinman, "Millions 'See' Fight in Radio Ringside Seats," *Chicago Daily Tribune*, September 23, 1927.

22. Ibid.

23. Bruce Lowitt, "Long Count Allows Tunney to Keep Title," *St. Petersburg Times*, November 30, 1999.

24. Smith, *Voices of Summer*, 12.

25. "1927 World Series," Baseball-Reference.com, *http://www.baseball-reference.com/postseason/1927_ws. shtml* (viewed 06.17.09).

26. "1927 New York Yankees," Baseball-Reference.com, *http://www.baseball-reference.com/bullpen/1927_ Yankees*.

27. "1927 Yankees — Miscellaneous Anecdotes," *http://www.angelfire.com/pa/1927/27anecdotes.html* (viewed 05.27.09).

Chapter 6

1. Dickson, *Baseball's Greatest Quotations*, 425.

2. Hauper, "Economic History."

3. Ibid.

4. "History of the Newsreel," University of San Diego, *http://history.sandiego.edu/gen/filmnotes/news reel.html* (viewed 06.27.09).

5. Ibid.

6. Ibid.

7. "Major League Baseball Attendance from 1890–2006," Baseball Chronology, *http://www.baseballchro nology.com/Baseball/Teams/Background/Attendance/* (viewed 06.27.09).

8. Ibid.

9. Jeff Mullen, "Baseball's New Era of 'Money Ball' Is Expensive Escapism," *Enid News and Eagle*, *http:// www.enidnews.com/opinion/local_story_094233757.html* (viewed 06.27.09).

10. Hauper, "Economic History."

11. "Brief History of the Radio Industry," Duke University Libraries, *http://library.duke.edu/digitalcol lections/adaccess/radio-tv.html* (viewed 06.27.09).

12. "Media in the 1930s," ThinkQuest, *http://library.thinkquest.org/27629/themes/media/md30s.html* (viewed 07.01.09).

13. Elizabeth McLeod, "Old Time Radio Moments of the Century," Old Time Radio, *http://www.old time.com/mcleod/top100.html* (viewed 03.15.06).

14. "Famous Weekly Old Time Radio Shows," Old Time Radio, *http://www.old-time.com/weekly/index. html* (viewed 07.01.09).

15. Ibid.

16. "Media in the 1930s."

17. McLeod, "Old Time Radio Moments."

18. Jennifer Rosenberg, "War of the Worlds Radio Broadcast," About.com, *http://history1900s.about. com/od/1930s/a/warofworld.htm* (viewed 07.01.09).

19. Ibid.

20. McLeod, "Old Time Radio Moments."

21. Light, *Cultural Encyclopedia*, 767.

22. Ibid.

23. Ibid.

24. Charles C. Alexander, *Our Game: An American Baseball History* (New York: MJF, 1991), 155–59.

25. Ibid.

26. Light, *Cultural Encyclopedia*, 767.

27. Myers, *Louisville Slugger*, 324.

28. "Music in Motion: The First Motorola Brand Car Radio," Motorola, Inc., *http://www.motorola.com/ staticfiles/Business/Corporate/US-EN/history/feature-car-radio.html* (viewed 05.31.09).

29. Ibid.

30. Anything About Cars, *http://www.anythingaboutcars.com/1930scars.html* (viewed 05.31.09).

31. Soloman, *Baseball Timeline*, 347.

32. "Cincinnati Reds—1934," Baseball Library.com, *http://www.baseballlibrary.com/teams/byyear.php? team=Cincinnati_Reds* (viewed 07.03.09).

33. Soloman, *Baseball Timeline*, 347.

34. James P. Dawson, "Fight Passed $1,000,000 Mark in Gross Receipts," *New York Times*, September 26, 1935.

35. David Whitely, "Lou Gehrig in 140 Characters? Impossible to Imagine," *http://mlb.fanhouse.com/ 2009/07/03lou-gehrig-in140-characters-impossible/* (viewed 07.05.09).

36. "1939 Radio Interview: Full-length transcript from a radio interview with Lou Gehrig," Rochester, Minnesota (posted March, 2002), *http://moregehrig.tripod.com/id16.html* (viewed 07.04.09).

37. John Helyar, *Lords of the Realm* (New York: Villard, 1994), 41.

38. "A $100,000 Radio Deal Is Completed," *Chicago Daily Tribune*, August 18, 1939.

Chapter 7

1. Smith, *Voices of Summer*, 86.

2. Ibid., 17.

3. Dickson, *Baseball's Greatest Quotations*, 126.

4. "President William Taft Baseball Game Attendance Log," Baseball-Almanac.com, *http://baseball-almanac.com/prz_cwt.shtml* (viewed 07.11.09).

5. "William Howard Taft Quick Facts," MSN Encarta, *http://encarta.msn.com/media* (viewed 07.01.09).

6. Dickson, *Baseball's Greatest Quotations*, 307.

7. "How Did George W. Bush Make His Millions?" Brooks Jackson, posting on CNN, *http://www. cnn.com/allpolitics/stories/1999/05/13/president.2000/jackson.bush/* (viewed 07.11.09).

8. Corey Deitz, "9 Things Your Probably Did Not Know About Ronald Reagan's Radio Career," *Http:// radio.about.com/od/djsandgostqt/a/aa060704a.htm* (viewed 07.11.09).

9. Ibid.

10. Milo Hamilton interview by author, May 10, 2010.

11. "Ford C. Frick Award," National Baseball Hall of Fame and Museum, *http://web.baseballhalloffame. org/hofers/frick.jsp* (viewed 07.18.09).

12. Deitz, "9 Things."

13. Dickson, *Baseball's Greatest Quotations*, 347.

14. "President Ronald Reagan Baseball Game Attendance Log," Baseball-Almanac.com, *http://www.base ball-almanac.com/prz_crr.shtml* (viewed 07.18.09).

15. "Ty Tyson, the World's First Sports Broadcaster," *Detroit News*, February 1, 1996.

16. "Complete Game Broadcasts," Holley Music, *http://www.cooperstownmusic.com/complete.htm* (viewed 05.30.09).

17. Smith, *Voices of Summer*, 17.

18. Solomon, *Baseball Timeline*, 399.

19. Ibid., 401.

20. Ibid., 359.

21. "This Day in History 1935: MLB Holds First Night Game," *http://www.history.com/this-day-in-history.do?action=Article&id=57064* (viewed 07.19.09).

22. Ibid.

23. Ibid.

24. Solomon, *Baseball Timeline*, 417.

25. Ibid., 419.

26. Ibid.

27. Ibid., 420.

28. Ibid.

29. Joseph E. Persico, *Edward R. Murrow: An American Original* (New York: McGraw-Hill, 1988), 153, 155.

30. Ibid., 155.

31. Tom Lewis, "A Godlike Presence: The Impact of Radio on the 1920s and 1930s," Organization of American Historians, *http://www.oah.org/pubs/magazine/communication/lewis.html* (viewed 07.01.09).

32. Ibid.

33. Ibid.

34. Ibid.

35. Ibid.

36. Ibid.

37. "Radio Days — Edward R. Murrow," *http://www.otr.com/murrow.shtml* (viewed 07.19.09).

38. Jeff Zillgitt, "World War II Era of Baseball Now a World Away," *USA Today*, July 19, 2004.

39. Frank Fitzpatrick, "Remembering the Radio Daze of Baseball," *York Daily Record*, *http://ydr.inyork.com/ci_12850538* (viewed 07.22.09).

40. "Major League Baseball Attendance from 1890–2005," Baseball Chronology, *http://www.baseballchronology.com/baseball/Teams/Background/Attendance/* (viewed 06.27.09).

41. Daniel Okrent and Steve Wulf, *Baseball Anecdotes* (New York: Oxford University Press, 1989), 166.

42. "Biography of Dizzy Dean," *http://www.dizzydean.com/biography.htm* (viewed 07.25.09).

43. Smith, *Voices of Summer*, 125.

44. "Dizzy Dean," Baseball Library.com, *http://www.baseballlibrary.com/ballplayers/player.php?name=Dizzy_Dean_1911* (viewed 07.25.09).

45. Official Site of Dizzy Dean, *http://www.dizzydean.com/quotes.htm* (viewed 07.25.09).

46. Soloman, *Baseball Timeline*, 444–46.

47. "One Last Hurrah: Dizzy Dean Pitches for the St. Louis Browns," *http://baseball.suite101.com/article.cfm/hall_of_famer_dizzy_dean#ixzz0M18EeIIm* (viewed 07.25.09).

Chapter 8

1. Dickson, *Baseball's Greatest Quotations*, 107.

2. Doris Kearns Goodwin, *Wait Till Next Year* (New York: Touchstone, 1997), 81.

3. Ibid., 45.

4. Fitzpatrick, "Radio Daze of Baseball."

5. "Baseball Hall of Fame Announcer Red Barber dies at 84," *http://www.history.com/this_day_in_history* (viewed 05.31.09).

6. Fitzpatrick, "Radio Daze of Baseball."

7. John P. Rossi, "Food for Thought: Baseball and American History," The Historical Society of Pennsylvania, *http://www.hsp.org/default.aspx?id=998* (viewed 07.22.09).

8. Gerald Early, "Excerpts from Birdland: Two Observations on the Cultural Significance of Baseball," American Poetry Review, July/August 1996, 9–10.

9. Dickson, *Baseball's Greatest Quotations*, 32.

10. Jim Reisler, *Babe Ruth: Launching the Legend* (New York: McGraw-Hill, 2004), 27.

11. Ibid., 243.

12. *Brown v. Board of Education*, 347 U.S. 483 (1954).

13. "Jackie Robinson Chronology," Baseball Library.com, *http://www.baseballlibrary.com/ballplayers/player.php?name=Jackie_Robinson_1919&page=chronology* (viewed 8-14-10).

14. *Toolson v. New York Yankees*, 346 U.S. 356 (1953).

15. Rossi, "Food for Thought."

16. Official Web Site of Dizzy Dean, *http://www.dizzydean.com/quotes.htm* (viewed 07.25.09).

17. Ibid.

18. Helyar, *Lords of the Realm*, 314.

19. Dickson, *Baseball's Greatest Quotations*, 126.

20. Ibid., 479.

21. Fitzpatrick, "Radio Daze of Baseball."

22. Ibid.

23. Ibid.

24. "Golden Age of Radio 1935–1950," University of San Diego, *http://history.sandiego.edu/GENrecord ing/radio2.html* (viewed 08.02.09).

25. Ibid.

26. Ibid.

27. "Rosey Rowswell," Baseball Library.com, *http://www.baseballlibrary.com/ballplayers/player.php? name=Rosey* (viewed 08.02.09).

28. "Jim Woods Quotes," *http://wapedia.mobi/en/Jim_Woods* (viewed 8.14.10).

29. Dickson, *Baseball's Greatest Quotations*, 187.

30. Ibid., 197.

31. "Liberty Broadcasting System," *http://en.wikipedia.org/wiki/Liberty_Broadcasting_System* (viewed 08.14.10).

32. "The Shot Heard Round the World," *http://baseball.suite101.com/article.cfm/the_shot_heard_round_ the_world* (viewed 08.14.10)

33. Red Smith, "Thomson Authored an Unlikely Ending," ESPN, *http://espn.go.com/classic/s/smith_on_ thomson.html*

34. "John Leonard Quotes," *http://www.brainyquote.com/quotes/qutoes/j/johnleonar115326.html* (viewed 05.08.09).

35. "Casey Stengel Quotes," *http://www.baseball-almanac.com/quotes/quosteng.shtml* (viewed 08.05.09).

36. "Ernie Harwell Quotes," *http://www.baseballalmanac.com/quotes/ernie_harell_quotes.shtml* (viewed 08.02.09).

37. Solomon, *Baseball Timeline*, 569.

38. "Mickey Mantle Quotes." *http://www.brainyquote.com/quotes/authors/m/mickey_mantle.html* (viewed 08.05.09).

39. Dickson, *Baseball's Greatest Quotations*, 191.

40. "100 Memorable Movie Quotes," American Film Institute, *http://connect.afi.com/site/PageServer?page name=100YearsList* (viewed 04.24.09).

Chapter 9

1. Dickson, *Baseball's Greatest Quotations*, 198.

2. 1951 Archives, CBS.com, *http://www.cbs.com/specials/cbs_75/timeline/1950.shtml* (viewed 08.14.10).

3. "Monte Irvin," Baseball Library.com, *http://www.baseballlibrary.com/ballplayers/player/php?name= Monte_Irvin_1919* (viewed 08.14010).

4. Brooks and Marsh, *Prime Time Network TV Shows*, 39, 113, 1030.

5. Ibid., 1030.

6. Ibid., 70.

7. James Walker and Robert V. Bellamy, Jr., *Center Field Shot* (Lincoln: University of Nebraska Press, 2008), 100, 104.

8. Ibid., 101.

9. Ibid.

10. Curt Smith, "Voices of the Game," *http://www.curtsmith.mlbblogs.com/archives/2006/02/dizzy_ dean_easi,html* (viewed 08.14.10).

11. Helyar, *Lords of the Realm*, 98.

12. Alexander, *Our Game*, 228.

13. Helyar, *Lords of the Realm*, 98.

14. Alexander, *Our Game*, 229.

15. Walker and Bellamy, *Center Field Shot*, 103.

16. Ibid.

17. Ibid., 104.

18. "Radio Corporation of America," Museum of Broadcast Communications, *http://www.museum.tv/ eotvsection.php?entrycode=radiocorpora* (viewed 05.02.09).

19. Ibid.

20. "Radio Fans to See and Hear Next Olympics," *Chicago Daily Tribune*, April 8, 1925.

21. Russell B. Porter, "Play Is Broadcast by Voice and Acting in Radio-Television," *New York Times*, September 12, 1928.

22. "Brief History of the Television Industry," Duke University Libraries, *http://library.duke.edu/digital collections/adaccess/radio-tv.html* (viewed 06.27.09).

23. Ibid.

24. Helyar, *Lords of the Realm*, 41.

25. "Edward R. Murrow: A Report on Senator Joseph R. McCarthy," Transcribed by G. Handman from DVD, The McCarthy Years (Edward R. Murrow Collection), *http://www.lib.berkeley.edu/MRC/murrowmc carthy.html* (viewed 09.05.09).

26. Marshall McLuhan, *http://www.marshallmcluhan.com/poster.html* (viewed 04.24.10).

27. "Percentage of Black Players in MLB Rises," *USA Today, http://www.usatoday.com/sports/baseball/ 2009-04-15=mlb-diversity-N.htm* (viewed 04.14.09).

28. Jackie Robinson Quotes, Baseball Almanac, *http://www.baseball-almanac.com/quotes/quojokr.shtml* (viewed 08.14.10).

Chapter 10

1. "Black Famous Baseball Firsts," Baseball Almanac, *http://www.baseball-almanac.com/firsts/first8.shtml* (viewed 04.24.10).

2. Brooks and Marsh, *Prime Time Network TV Shows*, v–xv, 64, 70, 290, 952–53.

3. Ibid., xii.

4. Ibid.

5. Ibid.

6. Ibid., xiii.

7. Ibid., xiv.

8. DuMont Television Network, *http://www.dumonthistory.tv/5.html* (viewed 09.09.10).

9. Ibid.

10. Brooks and Marsh, *Prime Time Network TV Shows*, 1037–38.

11. Ibid., 290.

12. "Roone Arledge Biography," Museum of Broadcast Communications, *http://www.museum.tv/eotv section.php?entrycode=arledgeroon* (viewed 04.24.10).

13. "1936 German Olympics," TV History Online, *http://www.tvhistory.tv/1936%20German%20Olympics %20TV%20Program.htm* (viewed 08.15.10).

14. Walker and Bellamy, *Center Field Shot*, 52, 53, 76, 77, 83, 84, 86, 87.

15. Ibid., 52.

16. "Chicago Cubs Attendance Records," Baseball Almanac, *http://www.baseball-almanac.com/teams/ cubsatte.shtml* (viewed 09.11.09).

17. Ibid.

18. "TV Forecast," *http://www.tvhistory.tv/tv_forecast.htm*.

19. Smith, *Voices of Summer*, 82.

20. Walker and Bellamy, *Center Field Shot*, 77.

21. Ibid.

22. Solomon, *Baseball Timeline*, 501–06.

23. Ibid., 540.

24. Walker and Bellamy, *Center Field Shot*, 83.

25. "History of AT&T Television," *http://www.corp.att.com/history/television/* (viewed 09.12.09).

26. Ibid.

27. "Technical Innovations in Sports Broadcasting," *http://www.ieeeghn.org/wiki/index.php/Technolog- ical_Innovations_in_Sports_Broadcasting* (viewed 09.12.09).

28. Ibid.

29. Ibid.

30. "Leaders of TV Industry Keep Eyes on Chicago," *Chicago Daily Tribune*, July 5, 1952.

31. Ibid.

32. Richard F. Shepard, "N.B.C. to Televise 5 World Series," *New York Times*, July 3, 1956.

33. Ibid.

34. "Sunday Baseball TV Plan Proceeds Despite Minors' Pleas," *New York Times*, December 17, 1957.

35. Helyar, *Lords of the Realm*, 365.

36. Ibid., 51.

37. Dickson, *Baseball's Greatest Quotations*, 106.

Chapter 11

1. Helyar, *Lords of the Realm*, 52.

2. Dickson, *Baseball's Greatest Quotations*, 425.

3. Richard F. Weingroff, "June 29, 1956: A Day in History," Federal Highway Administration, *http:// www.fhwa.dot.gov/interstate/thisday.htm* (viewed 09.19.09).

    4. Ibid.
    5. Helyar, *Lords of the Realm*, 52.
    6. Soloman, *Baseball Timeline*, 563.
    7. "Longest Home Run Ever Hit," Baseball Almanac, *http://www.baseball-almanac.com/feats/art_hr_shtml* (viewed 08.18.10).
    8. "The Story Behind Mickey Mantle's 10 Longest Home Runs," *http://www.themick.com/10homers.html* (viewed 08.18.10).
    9. Soloman, *Baseball Timeline*, 565.
    10. Ibid.
    11. "Vin Scully," Baseball-Reference.com, *http://www.baseball-reference.com/bullpen/Vin_Scully* (viewed 09.20.09).
    12. "Vin Scully," Baseball Library.com, *http://www.baseballlibrary.com/ballplayers/player.php?name=Vin_Scully* (viewed 09.20.09).
    13. "Los Angeles Memorial Coliseum," Ballparks, *http://www.ballparks.com/baseball/national/laxcol.htm* (viewed 09.22.09).
    14. Ibid.
    15. Ibid.
    16. Rick Reilly, "Vin Scully — In 36 Years as Voice of the Dodgers, He's Never Been at a Loss for Words," *Los Angeles Times*, April 8, 1985.
    17. Richard Hoffer, "In Vin Veritas," *Sports Illustrated*, September 8, 2008.
    18. "Los Angeles Dodgers Attendance Records," Baseball Almanac, *http://www.baseball-almanac.com/teams/laatte.shtml* (viewed 09.19.09).
    19. "Dodger Stadium," Ballparks, *http://www.ballparks.com/baseball/national/dodger.htm* (viewed 09.22.09).
    20. "Mel Allen," Baseball-Reference.com, *http://www.baseball-reference.com/bullpen/Mel_Allen* (viewed 09.20.09).
    21. "Mel Allen," Baseball Library.com, *http://www.baseballlibrary.com/ballplayers/player.php?name=Mel_Allen* (viewed 09.20.09).
    22. Soloman, *Baseball Timeline*, 602.
    23. Roger Maris Museum, *http://www.rogermarismuseum.com/statistics/* (viewed 09.26.09).
    24. "Bill Mazeroski Baseball Stats," Baseball Almanac, *http://www.baseball-almanac.com/players/player.php?=mazerbi01* (viewed 09.26.09).
    25. "Roger Maris Baseball Stats," Baseball Almanac, *http://www.baseball-almanac.com/players/player.php?=marisro01* (viewed 09.26.09).
    26. Solomon, *Baseball Timeline*, 619.
    27. "1960: The Road to Camelot," *http://www.kennesaw.edu/pols/3380/pres/1960.html* (viewed 09.28.09).
    28. Liette Gidlow, "The Great Debate: Kennedy, Nixon, and Television in the 1960 Race for the Presidency," History Now, *http://www.historynow.org/09_2004/historian2.html* (viewed 09.28.09).
    29. Ibid.
    30. Solomon, *Baseball Timeline*, 620.
    31. Ibid.
    32. Ibid.
    33. Ibid., 621.
    34. Ibid.
    35. Ibid., 623.
    36. "People: Mar. 30, 1962," *Time*, *http://www.time.com/time/printout/0,8816,895971,00.html* (viewed 09.28.09).
    37. Curt Smith, MLB.com on *Voices of the Game*, *http://curtsmith.mlblogs.com/archives/2007/02/_as_i_was_sayin.html* (viewed 04.28.10).
    38. Solomon, *Baseball Timeline*, 590.
    39. "Radio Chain Sues Baseball for $12,000,000," *Chicago Daily Tribune*, February 22, 1952.
    40. "Communications: End of Liberty," *Time*, *http://www.time.com/time/printout/0,8816,806483,00.html* (viewed 10.01.09).
    41. Haupert, "Economic History."
    42. Ibid.

Chapter 12

    1. Mary Bellis, "Biography of John Bardeen — Transistor Inventor," *http://inventors.about.com/od/bstartinventors/p/John_Bardeen.htm* (viewed 10.07.09).
    2. "Regency TR-1 Transistor Radio History," *http://www.regencytr1.com* (viewed 08.20.10).
    3. Smith, *Voices of Summer*, 110.

4. David Biderman, "Meet Baseball's Chattiest TV Announcers," *Wall Street Journal*, September 3, 2009.

5. Dickson, *Baseball's Greatest Quotations*, 387.

6. Ibid.

7. Ibid.

8. Ibid., 94.

9. Mitch Rosen interview by author on July 17, 2009.

10. "Home Run Calls," Baseball Almanac, *http://www.baseball-almanac.com/quotes/quohomer.shtml* (viewed 08.20.10).

11. "Major League Baseball Attendance from 1890–2005," Baseball Chronology, *http://www.baseball chronology.com/Baseball/Teams/Background/Attendance* (viewed 06.27.09).

12. Helyar, *Lords of the Realm*, 365.

13. Ibid., 364.

14. Gay Talese, "Better Baseball Coverage Promised for New Season," *New York Times*, April 14, 1957.

15. Ibid.

16. Ibid.

17. Helyar, *Lords of the Realm*, 365.

18. Ibid., 366.

19. "Rozelle Made NFL What It Is Today," ESPN Classic, *http://www.espn.go.com/classic/biography/s/rozelle_pete.html* (viewed 08.20.10).

20. "Hale Boggs Biography," *http://www.biographybase.com/biography/Boggs_Hale.html* (viewed 10.21.09).

21. Paul Weiler and Gary Roberts, *Sports and the Law*, 3rd ed. (St. Paul: Thomson-West Publishing, 2004) 641–42, 694.

22. "Pete Rozelle."

23. "Rozelle Made NFL What It Is Today," ESPN Classic, *http://www.espn.go.com/classic/biography/s/rozelle_pete.html* (viewed 08.20.10).

24. Helyar, *Lords of the Realm*, 366.

25. Ibid.

26. Jack Gould, "First Coverage of Games in Color, Like the Dodgers, Is Not a Winner," *New York Times*, September 29, 1955.

27. "Television Timeline," *http://timelines.ws/television.html* (viewed 10.07.09).

28. Ibid.

29. Michael Katz, "TV's Isolated Camera Proves No Substitute for the Umpire," *New York Times*, April 18, 1965.

30. Ibid.

31. "Harvey Kuenn," Baseball Library.com, *http://www.baseballlibrary.com/ballplayers/player.php?name=Harvey_Kuenn* (viewed 10.21.09).

32. "Jim Bunning," Baseball Library.com. *http://www.baseballlibrary.com/ballplayers/player.php?name=Jim_Bunning* (viewed 10.21.09).

33. Solomon, *Baseball Timeline*, 677.

34. Richard Sandomir, "Harry Caray, 78, Colorful Baseball Announcer, Dies," *New York Times*, February 19, 1998.

35. Smith, *Voices of Summer*, 156.

36. "Entire List of 7th Inning Stretch Singers," *http://www.fogpog.com/showthread.php?t=4358* (viewed 10.24.09).

37. Dan Cahill, "Cubs 7th Inning Stretch Jumps the Shark with Richard Dreyfus," *Chicago Sun-Times*, *http://blogs.suntimes.com/sportsprose/2009/09/cubs_7th_inning-stretch* (viewed 10.24.09).

38. Sandomir, "Harry Caray."

39. Light, *Cultural Encyclopedia*, 166.

Chapter 13

1. "Jack Buck," Major League Baseball Online, *http://mlb.mlb.com/mlb/news/tributes/mlb_obit_jack_buck.jsp* (viewed 10.31.09).

2. Smith, *Voices of Summer*, 82.

3. Ibid.

4. "Telstar," *http://www.reference.com/browse/Telstar* (viewed 08.20.10).

5. "Milo Hamilton," Texas Baseball Hall of Fame, *http://www.tbhof.org/bio/2005/biohamilton-toycannon.htm* (viewed 10.28.09).

6. Ibid.

7. Milo Hamilton interview by author on May 10, 2010.

8. Ibid.

9. "1988 World Series: Game 1," Major League Baseball Online, *http://mlb.mlb.com/mlb/baseballs_best/mlb_bb_gamepage.jsp?story_page=bb_88ws_gm1_oakla* (viewed 10.28.09).

10. Ibid.

11. Ibid.

12. "Vin Scully," Baseball Almanac, *http://www.baseball-almanac.com/vin_scully_quotes.shtml* (viewed 08.20.10).

13. "Jack Buck," *http://www. Notablebiographies.com/supp/supplement-a-bu-obituaries/buck-jack.html.*

14. "Jack Buck," Baseball Library.com, *http://www.baseballlibrary.com/ballplayers/player.php?name=Jack_Buck* (viewed 10.21.09).

15. Ibid.

16. "Quotable Mike," *http://arachnerd.wordpress.com/mike-shannon-quotes/* (viewed 10.31.09).

17. Jim Malony, "Players, Colleagues Will Miss Buck," Major League Baseball Online, http://stlouiscardinals.mlb.com/news/article.jspymd=20021619&content_id=56751&vkey=news_stl&text=jsp&c_id=stl (viewed 08.20.10).

18. Steve Kornacki, "Death, Taxes and Buck/McCarver Calling the Series," *Wall Street Journal*, October 30, 2009.

19. Smith, *Voices of Summer*, 360.

20. "Jack Buck," Baseball Library.com.

21. "Biography of Don Drysdale," *http://www.short-biographies.com/biographies/DonDrysdale.html* (viewed 10.31.09).

22. "Don Drysdale," Baseball Library.com, *http://www.baseballlibrary.com/ballplayers/player.php?name=Mike_Shannon* (viewed 10.21.09).

23. "The Language of Al McGuire," *http://espn.com/classic/s/Mcguirisms.html* (viewed 11.01.09).

24. "Humorous Quotes of Al McGuire," *http://www.workinghumor.com/quotes/al_mcguire.shtml* (viewed 11.01.09).

25. Frank Litsky, "Al McGuire, 72, Coach, TV Analyst and Character, Dies," *New York Times*, January 27, 2001.

26. "Bob Uecker," Baseball Library.com, *http://www.baseballlibrary.com/ballplayers/player.php?name=Bob_Uecker* (viewed 10.21.09).

27. "Bob Uecker Biography," Biography Online, *http://www.biography.com/articles/Bob-Eucker-224920* (viewed 11.04.09).

28. "Bob Uecker Quotes," Baseball Almanac, *http://www.baseball-almanac.com/quotes/quouec.shtml* (viewed 11.04.09).

29. Ibid.

30. Ibid.

31. "Tony Kubek," *http://theyplayedthegame.tripod.com/id12.htm* (viewed 11.05.09).

32. Ibid.

33. "NBC's Kubek Wins 2009 Frick Award," National Baseball Hall of Fame Online, *http://web.baseballhalloffame.org/hofers/frick/kubek_tony.jsp* (viewed 11.05.09).

34. Mark Feeney, "Sportscaster Curt Gowdy Dies at 86," *The Boston Globe*, February 21, 2006.

35. Ibid.

36. Ibid.

37. Bruce Lowitt, "Heidi Game Remains Best You Never Saw," *St. Petersburg Times*, September 23, 1999.

38. Feeney, "Curt Gowdy."

39. "Joe Garagiola," Baseball Library.com, *http://www.baseballlibrary.com/ballplayers/player.php?name=Joe_Garagiola* (viewed 11.07.09).

40. "Jackie Robinson Biography," *http://www.biography.com/articles/Jacie-Robinson-9460813* (viewed 11.07.09).

41. Jonathan Eig, "The Real Jackie Robinson Story," *Wall Street Journal*, March 31, 2007.

42. Andy Behrens, "This Old Cub: A Tribute to Ron Santo." ESPN Online, *http://sports.espn.go.com/espn/page3/story?page=behrens/santo/050301* (viewed 11.11.09).

43. Walker and Bellamy, *Center Field Shot*, 268–69.

44. Bob Raisman, "MLB Broadcaster Chip Caray Continues to Drop Ball for TBS," *New York Daily News*, October 10, 2009.

45. Erik Brady, "Baseball Endures Through Changing Times," *USA Today*, *http://www.usatoday.com/sports/baseball/00play/fs095.htm.*

46. James Lincoln Ray, "Game 6 of the 1975 World Series: Pudge Fisk's Homer Ends the Greatest Fall Classic Game Ever Played." *http://baseball.suite101.com/print_article.cfm/game_6_of_the_1975_world_series* (viewed 11.09.09).

47. Ibid.

48. William Leggett, "The Series Was a Prime Time," *Sports Illustrated*, November 3, 1975.

49. "Quotable Mike."

Chapter 14

1. Chic Young (cartoonist), widely quoted.

2. "The Pine Tar Game," Major League Baseball Online, *http://www.mlb.com/mlb/baseballs_best/mlb _bb_gamepage.jsp?story_page=bb_83reg_072483_kernyy* (viewed 08.21.10).

3. Solomon, *Baseball Timeline*, 699–700.

4. Ibid., 699.

5. Ibid., 713–14.

6. Ibid., 724–25.

7. Kenneth Shortgen, Jr., "Why Tall Baseball Pitchers Are Better Than Short Pitchers," *http://www. helium.com/items/220025-why-tall-baseball-pitchers-are-better-than-short-pitchers* (viewed 11.18.09).

8. Ibid.

9. "Steve Stone," Baseball-Reference.com, *http://www.baseball-reference.com/bullpen/Steve_Stone* (viewed 08.21.10).

10. "Mark McGwire's Seventy Home Run Season," *http://www.baseball-almanac.com/feats/feats1.shtml* (viewed 11.22.09).

11. Ibid.

12. Richard Sandomir, "Jack Buck, 77, Measured Voice of Cardinals Baseball," *New York Times*, June 19, 2002.

13. Ibid.

14. Lee Jenkins, "Perfect Season to Perfect Storm: Steroids Taint McGwire Legacy," *New York Times*, March 15, 2005.

15. "Historical Attendance Figures for Major League Baseball," *http://bss.sfsu.edu/tygiel/hist490/mlb attendance.htm* (viewed 11.22.09).

16. "Five Great Moments at Three Rivers Stadium," *The Sporting News*, *http://archive.sportingnews.com/ baseball/ballparks/threerivers.html* (viewed 11.27.09).

17. "World Series Television Ratings Breakdown," *http://www.baseball-almanac.com/ws/wstv.shtml* (viewed 09.12.09).

18. Brooks and Marsh, *Prime Time Network TV Shows*, 1037–40.

19. "World Series Viewership 1973–2008," Nielsen Media Research, Inc., quoted at *TVbythenumbers.com, LLC*, *http://tvbythenumbers.com/2008/11/10/fox-faces-record-low-world-series-tv-ratings* (viewed12.06.09).

20. "Historical Attendance Figures."

21. "World Series Viewership."

22. "History of Television," *http://www.high-techproductions.com/historyoftelevision.htm* (viewed 11.27.09).

23. Ibid.

24. Ibid.

25. Ibid.

26. Ibid.

27. Ibid.

28. Ibid.

29. Ibid.

30. Joyce Leviton, "Skipper Ted Turner Buys the Braves and Promises to Turn Atlanta into Winnersville, U.S.A.," *People* magazine, February 2, 1976.

31. "Ted Turner Biography," *http://www.answers.com/topic/ted-turner* (viewed 11.29.09).

32. Ibid.

33. Ibid.

34. Leviton, "Skipper Ted Turner."

35. "Uniform Names," *http://www.baseball-fever.com/archive/index.php/t-67982.html* (viewed 08.21.10).

36. "Ted Turner Biography."

37. "History of Television."

38. Ibid.

39. "Baseball, a Film by Ken Burns," Public Broadcasting, *http://www.pgs.org/kenburns/baseball/timeline page9.html* (viewed 12.05.09).

40. "History of Television."

41. Ibid.

42. Francie Grace, "Former MVP Ken Caminiti Died of Overdose in New York," CBS News, *http://www. cbsnews.com/stories/2004/10/11/entertainment/main648472.shtml* (viewed 12.05.09).

43. David Hancock, "Jose Canseco: Juiced." *60 Minutes*, CBS News, *http://cbsnews.com/stories/2005/ 08/05/60minutes/main761932.shtml* (viewed 12.05.09).

44. Dave Sheinin, "Baseball Has a Day of Reckoning in Congress," *Washington Post*, March 18, 2005.

45. Mark Fainaru-Wade and Lance Williams, "The Truth About Barry Bonds and Steroids," *Sports Illustrated*, March 6, 2007.

46. George J. Mitchell, *Report to the Commissioner of Baseball of an Independent Investigation into the Illegal Use of Steroids and Other Performance Enhancing Substances by Players in Major League Baseball* (New York: Office of the Commissioner of Baseball, 2007).

47. Ibid.

48. "World Series Viewership."

49. Fainaru-Wade and Williams, "Bonds and Steroids."

50. "World Series Posts Biggest Year-to-Year Growth in History," *http://tvbythenumbers.com/2009/11/05/2009-world-series-posts-biggest-year-to-year-growth-in-history* (viewed 12.06.09).

51. Bill Carter, "Huge Audience for World Series Game, but NFL Still Reigns," *New York Times*, November 2, 2009.

52. Maury Brown, "Inside the Numbers: Final 2009 MLB Regular Season Attendance," *http://www.bizofbaseball.com/index.php?option=com_content&view=article2009-mlb-regular-season-attendance* (viewed 12.06.09).

Chapter 15

1. Danny Goodwin, "Selling Stuff During the Golden Age of Radio," *http://www.old-time.com/commercials/index.html* (viewed 08.02.09).

2. Helyar, *Lords of the Realm*, 365.

3. Ibid.

4. Billy Ingram, "The Goldbergs: The Remarkable Gertrude Berg," *http://www.tvparty.com/vaultgold.html* (viewed 09.05.09).

5. "The Goldbergs," Museum of Broadcast Communications, *http://www.museum.tv/eotvsction.php?entrycode=goodbergsth* (viewed 12.09.09).

6. "History of Television."

7. Ibid.

8. "Technological Innovations in Sports Broadcasting," *http://www.Ieeeghn.org/wiki/index.php/technological_innovations_in_sports_broadcasting* (viewed 08.21.10).

9. Ibid.

10. "Fox Broadcasting Company," Britannica Online, *http://www.britannica.com/ebchecked/topic/215396/fox-broadcasting-company* (viewed 08.21.10).

11. Ibid.

12. Shel Brannan, "How the First-Down Line Works," *http://www.howstuffworks.com/first-down-line.htm* (viewed 12.09.09).

13. Ibid.

14. "PITCHf/x," *http://sportvision.com/main_frames/products/pitchfx.htm* (viewed 12.09.09).

15. Josh Kalk, "A First Look at the 2008 Pitch f/x Data," *The Hardball Times*, April 1, 2008. *http://www.hardballtimes.com* (viewed 12.09.09).

16. "Technological Innovations in Sports Broadcasting."

17. SportsVision Online, *http://www.sportsvision.com* (viewed 12.09.09).

18. Stuart Elliot, "Digital Sleight of Hand Can Put Ads Anywhere," *New York Times*, October 1, 1999.

19. Ibid.

20. Ibid.

21. Ibid.

22. Dickson, *Baseball's Greatest Quotations*, 185.

23. Goodwin, "Selling Stuff."

24. "Tyrus Raymond 'Ty' Cobb," *http://ngeorgia.com/ang/tyrus_raymond_'ty'_cobb* (viewed 12.16.09).

25. "Ty Cobb," Baseball-Reference.com, *http://www.baseball-reference.com/bullpen/Ty_Cobb* (viewed 12.16.09).

26. "Tyrus Raymond 'Ty' Cobb."

27. "Babe Ruth Legends," *http://www.baberuthcentral.com/Legends/* (viewed 12.16.09).

28. "Baby Ruth Candy Bar," *http://hubpages/hub/Baby-Ruth-Candy-Bar* (viewed 12.16.09).

29. "Baseball as America," American Museum of Natural History Online, *http://www.amnh.org/exhibitions/baseball/enterprise/index.html* (viewed 12.16.09).

30. "The Business of Baseball," Library of Congress Online, *http://www.loc.gov/rr/business/BERA/issue3/baseball.html* (viewed 12.16.09).

31. Solomon, *Baseball Timeline*, 507.

32. Ibid., 566.

33. William B. Conklin, "Gillette's $8,500,000 Deal for ABC Shows Includes Football and Baseball," *New York Times*, March 17, 1960.

34. Helyar, *Lords of the Realm*, 16.

35. Ted Hathaway, "From Baseballs to Brassieres: The Use of Baseball in Magazine Advertising, 1890–1960," *NINE: A Journal of Baseball History and Culture* 10, no. 1 (Fall 2001).

36. "Anheuser-Busch — History," *http://www.anheuser-busch.com/History.html* (viewed 08.29.09).

37. "History of Television."

38. "Bob Uecker Biography."

39. "Technology Timeline," *http://www.classicthemes.com/technologytimeline.html* (viewed 11.27.09).

40. Ibid.

41. The Nielsen Company Online, *http://www.nielsen.com* (viewed 11.27.09).

42. Ibid.

43. The concept of neither show was wholly original, but both exploited the modern television medium masterfully.

44. "History of Television."

45. "Interview: Steve Stone," *The Heckler*, September 6, 2004, *http://www.theheckler.com/news/templates/?z=8&a=26* (viewed 11.22.09).

46. *Baltimore Orioles v. Major League Baseball Players Association*, 805 F.2d 663 (1986).

47. "On the Radio: More Advertising Than Baseball," *Hartford Courant*, August 4, 2009.

Chapter 16

1. Pat Doyle, "Baseball Broadcasting from Another Day," *http://www.baseball-almanac.com/minor-league/minor2004a.shtml* (viewed 05.27.09).

2. Jim Kaat, "The Mechanics of a Baseball Broadcast," *Popular Mechanics*, April, 1999.

3. Ibid.

4. Light, *Cultural Encyclopedia*, 767–68.

5. Joshua Harris Prager, "Inside Baseball: Giants' 1951 Comeback," *Wall Street Journal*, January 31, 2001.

6. Ibid.

7. Richard Sandomir, "'Shot Heard Round the World' Echoes, 50 Years Later," *New York Times*, July 8, 2001.

8. Ibid.

9. "Shot Heard Round the World: Giants Win the Pennant," *http://www.baseballchronology.com/baseball/years/1951/shot_heard_round_the_world.asp* (viewed 01.16.10).

10. Ibid.

11. Although bitter at first, Branca later embraced both Thomson and history. The two became close friends in their old age, sometimes touring together and speaking of their 1951 baseball adventure. Even Thomson softened, his denials becoming less emphatic over time.

12. James Robert Walker, "Baseball on Television: The Formative Years 1939–51," *NINE: A Journal of Baseball History and Culture* 11, no. 2 (Spring 2003).

13. "Televise First Night Game — and Results are Amazingly Good," *http://www.tvhistory.tv/1941_June_FIRST_NIGHT_Baseball_Game.JPG* (viewed 10.07.09).

14. "History of Television."

15. Alexander, *Our Game*, 168–69.

16. Solomon, *Baseball Timeline*, 398.

17. Ibid., 498.

18. "Hank Aaron," Baseball-Reference.com, *http://www.baseball-reference.com/bullpen/hank_aaron* (viewed 08.22.10).

19. Walker and Bellamy, *Center Field Shot*, 53.

20. "CBS at 75 — Timeline," *http://www.cbs.com/specials/cbs_75/timeline/1950.shtml* (viewed 08.22.10).

21. "1st World Series Color TV Broadcast," *http://www.brainyhistory.com/events/1955/september_28_1955_117213.html* (viewed 08.22.10).

22. "Syndicate Headed by Two Radio Men," *New York Times*, July 17, 1956.

23. Ibid.

24. "Yankees Timeline," Major League Baseball Online, *http://www.mlb.mlb.com/nyy/history/timeline3.jsp* (viewed 08.22.10).

25. Ibid.

26. Tony Long, "March 11, 1986: FL Adopts Instant Replay," *http://www.wired.com/print/science/discoveries/news/2009/03/dayintech_0311* (viewed 01.23.10).

27. Bill Shaikin, "For World Series, Tradition Still Trumps Instant Replay," *Los Angeles Times*, October 28, 2009.

28. Ibid.

29. Ibid.

30. Ibid.

31. "History of Television."

32. Bill Shaikin, "For World Series, Tradition Still Trumps Instant Replay," *Los Angeles Times*, October 28, 2009.

33. Ibid.

34. "Oakland Athletics: Historical Moments," Sports Encyclopedia Online, *http://www.sportsencyclopedia.com/al/oakland/oak_s.html* (viewed 07.11.09).

35. Helyar, *Lords of the Realm*, 188–89.

36. *Finley v. Kuhn*, 569 F.2d 527 (7th Cir, 1978).

37. Helyar, *Lords of the Realm*, 180–81.

38. "Ted Turner & CNN," *http://www.pophistorydig.com/?p=718* (viewed 05.20.09).

39. Ibid.

40. Ibid.

41. Ibid.

42. Ibid.

43. *Chicago Professional Sports Limited Partnership & WGN v. National Basketball Association*, 95 F.3d 593 (7th Cir, 1996).

44. "All Sports, All the Time," *http://www.pophistorydig.com/?tag=espn-zone* (viewed 05.20.09).

45. Ibid.

46. Solomon, *Baseball Timeline*, 911.

47. "Wrigley Field Gets Lights," CNN/SI, August 8, 1988, *http://sportsillustrated.cnn.com/almanac/video/1988/index.html* (viewed 10.03.09).

48. "World Series Television Ratings Breakdown," Baseball Almanac, *http://www.baseball-almanac.com/ws/wstv.shtml* (viewed 10.07.09).

49. George Vecsey, "A Sport Is Reborn — The Home Run, America's Signature Feat, Invigorates Baseball," *New York Times*, September 4, 1998.

50. Mitchell, *Report to the Commissioner of Baseball*, SR-1, SR-5-7.

51. "Single Season Leaders for Home Runs," *http://www.baseball-almanac.com/hitting/hihr4.shtml* (viewed 02.06.10).

52. Daniel Kaplan, "Tribune's Departure Will Cut Media Owners in MLB to 2," *Street & Smith Sports Business Journal*, April 9–15, 2007.

53. "A Third of U.S. Baseball Teams' Values Decline-Forbes," Reuters, April 23, 2009.

Chapter 17

1. Anthony DiComo, "Waldman Makes World Series History," Major League Baseball Online, October 29, 2009, *http://mlb.mlb.com/news/article.jsp?ymd=20091028&content_id=756* (viewed 10.31.09).

2. "Home Run Derby (2000–2008)," Baseball Almanac, *http://www.baseball-almanac.com/asgbox/hrderby.shtml* (viewed 02.10.10).

3. Rick Kissell, "Fox in TV Ratings Double Play," *Variety, http://www.variety.com/article/VR1118006301.html?categoryid=14&cs=1&query=true+blood+rating* (viewed 02.10.10).

4. Anthony Crupi, "All-Star Game Scores Ratings Home Run," Reuters, *http://www.reuters.com/article/idUSTRE56F15L20090716* (viewed 02.10.10).

5. "All-Star Game Television Ratings," Baseball Almanac, *http://www.baseball-almanac.com/asgbo/asgtv.shtml* (viewed 02.10.10).

6. Kissell, "TV Ratings Double Play."

7. "History of Television."

8. Ibid.

9. Maury Brown, "When Baseball Meets the Largest Cable Television Channel Launch in History," FastCompany.com, *http://www.fastcompany.com/blog/maury-brown/sports-bizness/when-baseball-meets-largest-cable-television-channel-launch-history* (viewed 10.07.09).

10. "MLB.com Streams Baseball to iPhone, iPod, Maybe Sparkling New Business Model," June 17, 2009, *http://mlb.mlb.com/mobile/iphone/* (viewed 09.12.09).

11. Gay Talese, "Better Baseball Coverage Promised for New Season," *New York Times*, April 14, 1957.

12. Taylor Gandossy, "TV Viewing at All-Time High," CNN.com, February 24, 2009, *http://www.cnn.com/2009/showbiz/tv/02/24/us.video/nielson* (viewed 11.27.09).

13. Lee Jenkins, "Baseball Rediscovers Its Radio Days," *New York Times*, July 12, 2005.

14. Ibid.

15. Mitch Rosen interview by author on July 28, 2009.

16. Ibid.

17. Ibid.

18. Ibid.

19. "After 51 Years, Pirates Are Signing Off KDKA Radio," *New York Times*, October 1, 2006.

20. Matthew T. Hall, "A Life Touched by Lou Gehrig — and the Disease Named for Him," *http://www.signonsandiego.com/news/2009/jul/04/life-touched-lou-gehrig-8212-and-disease-named-him/?metro* (viewed 07.04.09).

21. Dickson, *Baseball's Greatest Quotations*, 171.

Bibliography

Books

Alexander, Charles C. *Our Game: An American Baseball History*. New York: MJF, 1991.

Brooks, Tim, and Earl Marsh. *The Complete Directory of Prime Time Network Television Shows*. New York: Ballentine, 1984.

Dickson, Paul. *Baseball's Greatest Quotations*. New York: Harper Perennial, 1992.

Gladwell, Malcolm. *Outliers: The Story of Success*. New York: Little, Brown, 2008.

Goodwin, Doris Kearns. *Wait Till Next Year*. New York: Touchstone, 1997.

Helyar, John. *Lords of the Realm*. New York: Villard, 1994.

Larson, Edward. *Summer for the Gods*. New York: Basic, 2006.

Light, Jonathan Fraser. *The Cultural Encyclopedia of Baseball*. 2nd ed. Jefferson, NC: McFarland, 2005.

Mitchell, George J. *Report to the Commissioner of Baseball of an Independent Investigation into the Illegal Use of Steroids and Other Performance Enhancing Substances by Players in Major League Baseball*. New York: Office of the Commissioner of Baseball, 2007.

Okrent, Daniel, and Steve Wulf. *Baseball Anecdotes*. New York: Oxford University Press, 1989.

Persico, Joseph E. *Edward R. Murrow: An American Original*. New York: McGraw-Hill, 1988.

Reisler, Jim. *Babe Ruth: Launching the Legend*. New York: McGraw-Hill, 2004.

Smith, Curt. *Voices of Summer*. New York: Carroll & Graf, 2005.

Solomon, Burt. *The Baseball Timeline*. New York: Avon, 1997.

Veeck, Bill, with Ed Linn. *Veeck as in Wreck*. Chicago: University of Chicago Press, 2001.

Walker, James, and Robert V. Bellamy, Jr. *Center Field Shot*. Lincoln: University of Nebraska Press, 2008.

Weiler, Paul, and Roberts, Gary. *Sports and the Law*, 3rd ed. St. Paul: Thomson-West Publishing, 2004.

Legal Cases

Baltimore Orioles v. Major League Baseball Players Association, 805 F.2d 663 (1986).

Brown v. Board of Education, 347 U.S. 483 (1954).

Chicago Professional Sports Limited Partnership & WGN v. National Basketball Association, 95 F.3d 593 (7th Cir, 1996).

Federal Base Ball Club of Baltimore, Inc. v. National League, 259 U.S. 200 (1922).

Finley v. Kuhn, 569 F.2d 527 (7th Cir, 1978).

Hart v. B.F. Keith Vaudeville Exchange, 262 U.S. 271 (1923).

Toolson v. New York Yankees, 346 U.S. 356 (1953).

Interviews

Hamilton, Milo. Interview by Eldon Ham, May 10, 2010.

Rosen, Mitch. Interviews by Eldon Ham, July 17 and 28, 2009.

Zimmerman, Rod. Interview by Eldon Ham, May 6, 2010.

Newspaper and Periodical Articles

"After 51 Years, Pirates Are Signing Off KDKA Radio." *New York Times*, October 1, 2006.

Biderman, David. "Meet Baseball's Chattiest TV Announcers." *Wall Street Journal*, September 3, 2009.

"Bob Prince, 68, Broadcaster for the Pittsburgh Pirates." *New York Times*, June 11, 1985.

Braxton, Greg, and Diane Pucin. "Football Broadcaster John Madden Retires." *Los Angeles Times*, April 17, 2009.

"Broadcast of Scopes Trial Unprecedented." *Chicago Daily Tribune*, July 5, 1925.

"Call Radio Fair Greatest Trade Show in U.S." *Chicago Daily Tribune*, October 12, 1924.

"Closeups." *Chicago Daily Tribune*, April 21, 1925.

Conklin, William B. "Gillette's $8,500,000 Deal for ABC Shows Includes Football and Baseball." *New York Times*, March 17, 1960.

Daley, Arthur. "Wait 'Til — *This* Year." *New York Times*, September 7, 1952.

Dawson, James P. "Fight Passed $1,000,000 Mark in Gross Receipts." *New York Times*, September 26, 1935.

Douglass, Elmer. "Elmer Spends a Night with Radio Talkers." *Chicago Tribune*, April 15, 1925.

Early, Gerald. "Excerpts from Birdland: Two Observations on the Cultural Significance of Baseball." *American Poetry Review*, July/August 1996.

Eig, Jonathan. "The Real Jackie Robinson Story." *Wall Street Journal*, March 31, 2007.

Elliot, Stuart. "Digital Sleight of Hand Can Put Ads Anywhere." *New York Times*, October 1, 1999.

Fainaru-Wade, Mark, and Williams, Lance. "The Truth About Barry Bonds and Steroids." *Sports Illustrated*. March 6, 2007.

Feeney, Mark. "Sportscaster Curt Gowdy Dies at 86." *Boston Globe*, February 21, 2006.

"Fight Fans of World Listen in on Title Battle." *Chicago Daily Tribune*, September 24, 1927.

Gould, Jack. "First Coverage of Games in Color, Like the Dodgers, Is Not a Winner." *New York Times*, September 29, 1955.

"Has the Baseball Really Been Changed?" *Popular Mechanics*, October 1961.

Hathaway, Ted. "From Baseballs to Brassieres: The Use of Baseball in Magazine Advertising, 1890–1960." *NINE: A Journal of Baseball History and Culture* 10, no. 1 (Fall 2001): 64–72.

Hinman, Frank. "Millions 'See' Fight in Radio Ringside Seats." *Chicago Daily Tribune*, September 23, 1927.

Hoffer, Richard. "In Vin Veritas." *Sports Illustrated*, September 8, 2008.

Jenkins, Lee. "Baseball Rediscovers Its Radio Days." *New York Times*, July 12, 2005.

_____. "Perfect Season to Perfect Storm: Steroids Taint McGwire Legacy." *New York Times*, March 15, 2005.

Kaat, Jim. "The Mechanics of a Baseball Broadcast." *Popular Mechanics*, April 1999.

Kaempffert, Waldemar. "Who Will Pay for Broadcasting?" *Popular Radio*, December, 1922.

Kaplan, Daniel. "Tribune's Departure Will Cut Media Owners in MLB to 2." *Street & Smith Sports Business Journal*, April 9–15, 2007.

Katz, Michael. "TV's Isolated Camera Proves No Substitute for the Umpire." *New York Times*, April 18, 1965.

Kornacki, Steve. "Death, Taxes and Buck/McCarver Calling the Series." *Wall Street Journal*, October 30, 2009.

"Leaders of TV Industry Keep Eyes on Chicago." *Chicago Daily Tribune*, July 5, 1952.

Leggett, William. "From Mountain to Molehill." *Sports Illustrated*, March 24, 1969.

_____. "The Series was a Prime Time." *Sports Illustrated*, November 3, 1975.

Leviton, Joyce. "Skipper Ted Turner Buys the Braves and Promises to Turn Atlanta into Winnersville, U.S.A." *People* magazine, February 2, 1976.

Lowitt, Bruce. "Heidi Game Remains Best You Never Saw." *St. Petersburg Times*, September 23, 1999.

_____. "Long Count Allows Tunney to Keep Title." *St. Petersburg Times*, November 30, 1999.

Maxwell, Don. "Notes from the Ringside." *Chicago Daily Tribune*, September 23, 1927.

"Mutual Signs 'Game Day' Radio Rights." *Los Angeles Times*, February 25, 1952.

"News of the Radiocasts." *Chicago Daily Tribune*, June 29, 1924.

"On the Radio: More Advertising Than Baseball." *Hartford Courant*, August 4, 2009.

"A $100,000 Radio Deal Is Completed." *Chicago Daily Tribune*, August 18, 1939.

"Planes, Trains Bring Crowd." *Chicago Daily Tribune*, September 23, 1927.

Porter, Russell B. "Play Is Broadcast by Voice and Acting in Radio-Television." *New York Times*, September 12, 1928.

Prager, Joshua Harris. "Inside Baseball: Giants' 1951 Comeback." *Wall Street Journal*, January 31, 2001.

"Radio Chain Sues Baseball for $12,000,000." *Chicago Daily Tribune*, February 22, 1952.

"Radio Fans to See and Hear Next Olympics." *Chicago Daily Tribune*, April 8, 1925.

"Radio Programs for Today." *Chicago Daily Tribune*, April 20, 1925.

Raisman, Bob. "MLB Broadcaster Chip Caray Continues to Drop Ball for TBS." *New York Daily News*, October 10, 2009.

Rick Reilly. "Vin Scully — In 36 Years as Voice of the Dodgers, He's Never Been at a Loss for Words." *Los Angeles Times*, April 8, 1985.

Romano, John. "Tall Pitchers Take Time to Peak." *St. Petersburg Times*, February 22, 2008.

"Roosevelt, in First Presidential Radio Talk, Urges Veterans to Sacrifice Now as in War." *New York Times*, March 6, 1933.

Sandomir, Richard. "Blimps and BaseCams Cause Fans to Lose Sight of Game." *New York Times*, July 14, 1992.

_____. "Caray Family Is Touched by Fans Honoring Harry." *New York Times*, March 3, 1998.

_____. "Harry Caray, 78, Colorful Baseball Announcer, Dies." *New York Times*, February 19, 1998.

_____. "Jack Buck, 77, Measured Voice of Cardinals Baseball." *New York Times*, June 19, 2002.

_____. "'Shot Heard Round the World' Echoes, 50 Years Later." *New York Times*, July 8, 2001.

Shaikin, Bill. "For World Series, Tradition Still Trumps Instant Replay." *Los Angeles Times*, October 28, 2009.

Shanley, J.P. "Radio: First Commercial Revisited." *New York Times*, August 31, 1955.

Sheinin, Dave. "Baseball Has a Day of Reckoning in Congress." *Washington Post*, March 18, 2005.

Shepard, Richard F. "N.B.C. to Televise 5 World Series." *New York Times*, July 3, 1956.

Sullivan, Paul. "Presidential Adviser David Axelrod on Barack Obama as a Sports Fan." *Chicago Tribune*, July 19, 2009.

"Sunday Baseball TV Plan Proceeds Despite Minors' Pleas." *New York Times*, December 17, 1957.

"Syndicate Headed by Two Radio Men." *New York Times*, July 17, 1956.

Talese, Gay. "Better Baseball Coverage Promised for New Season." *New York Times*, April 14, 1957.

"A Third of U.S. Baseball Teams' Values Decline — Forbes." Reuters, April 23, 2009.

Thomas, Robert McG., Jr. "Johnny Sylvester, the Inspiration for Babe Ruth Heroics, Is Dead." *New York Times*, January 11, 1990.

"Ty Tyson, the World's First Sports Broadcaster." *Detroit News*, February 1, 1996.

Vaughn, Irving. "Baseball Season Opens Today for Chicago." *Chicago Daily Tribune*, April 14, 1925.

_____. "Cubs Beat Pirates in Opener, 8 to 2." *Chicago Daily Tribune*, April 15, 1925.

Vecsey, George. "A Sport Is Reborn — The Home Run, America's Signature Feat, Invigorates Baseball." *New York Times*, September 4, 1998.

_____. "Taking a Mental Trip on the Subway to a New York Series." *New York Times*, September 5, 1999.

Walker, Ben. "Hollywood Did Not Invent Moonlight Graham." Associated Press, June 25, 2005.

Walker, James Robert. "Baseball on Television: The Formative Years 1939–51." *NINE: A Journal of Baseball History and Culture* 11, no. 2 (Spring 2003): 1–15.

"Weagant Explains Invention in Radio," *New York Times*, March 6, 1919.

"W-G-N to Give Fight Broadcast from Ringside." *Chicago Daily Tribune*, September 9, 1927.

"W-G-N Will Take Scopes Trial to Record Audience." *Chicago Daily Tribune*, July 12, 1925.

Will, George F. "Radio Was the Politician's Lectern." *Schenectady Gazette*, November 9, 1979.

Zillgitt, Jeff. "World War II Era of Baseball Now a World Away." *USATODAY*, July 19, 2004.

Websites

Adams, Mike. "100 Years of Radio Broadcasting." California Historical Radio Society. *http://www.california historialradio.com/100years.html.*

"Al Spalding Stats." Baseball Almanac. *http://www.baseball-almanac.com/players/player.php?p=spaldalQl.*

"All Sports, All the Time." Pop History Dig. *http://www.pophistorydig.com/?tag=espn-zone.*

"All-Star Game History." Baseball Almanac. *http://www.baseball-almanac.com/asgmenu.shtml.*

"All-Star Game Television Ratings." Baseball Almanac. *http://www.baseball-almanac.com/asgbo/asgtv.shtml.*

"All-Star Games: 1974, 1994." *The Sporting News. http://archive.sportingnews.com/baseball/ballparks/threerivers. html.*

"Anheuser-Busch — History." Anheuser-Busch Companies. *http://www.anheuser-busch.com/History.html.*

"The Automotive Giants in the Early 1920s." Life, Blogger. June 4, 2008. *http://life-us.blogspot.com/2008/ 06/automotive-giants-in-early-1920s.html.*

"Babe Ruth Legends." *http://www.baberuthcentral.com/Legends/.*

"Baby Ruth Candy Bar." *http://hubpages/hub/Baby-Ruth-Candy-Bar.*

"Baseball as America." American Museum of Natural History. *http://www.amnh.org/exhibitions/baseball/enter prise/index.html.*

"Baseball Broadcast Timeline." *http://www.thesoundofbaseball.com/Heritage.html.*

"Baseball Hall of Fame Announcer Red Barber dies at 84." *www.history.com/this_day_in_history.*

"Baseball Radio Broadcasts Bring Back Childhood Memories." Baseball Radio Broadcasts from the Golden Age of Baseball. *http://www.baseball-cards-and-collectibles.com/Baseball-Radio.html.*

Behrens, Andy. "This Old Cub: A Tribute to Ron Santo." ESPNSports. *http://sports.espn.go.com/espn/page3/ story?page=behrens/santo/050301.*

Bellis, Mary. "Biography of John Bardeen — Transistor Inventor." About.com. *http://inventors.about.com/ od/bstartinventors/p/John_Bardeen.htm.*

"Bill Mazeroski Baseball Stats." Baseball Almanac. *http://www.baseball-almanac.com/players/player.php?= mazerbi01.*

"Biography of Dizzy Dean." *http://www.dizzydean.com/biography.htm.*

"Biography of Don Drysdale." Short Biographies. *http://www.short-biographies.com/biographies/DonDrysdale.html.*

"Black Famous Baseball Firsts." Baseball Almanac. *http://www.baseball-almanac.com/firsts/first8.shtml.*

Bloom, Barry M. "Limited Instant Replay Debuts Thursday." Major League Baseball Online. *http://mlb.mlb.com/news/article.jsp?ymd=20080826&content_id=3370519&vkey=news_mlb&fext=.jsp&c_id=mlb.*

"Bob Elson." Baseball-Reference.com. *http://www.baseball-reference.com/bullpen/Bob_Elson.*

"Bob Uecker." Baseball Library.com. *http://www.baseballlibrary.com/ballplayers/player.php?name=Bob_Uecker.*

"Bob Uecker Biography." Biography.com. *http://www.biography.com/articles/Bob-Eucker-224920.*

"Bob Uecker Quotes." Baseball Almanac. *http://www.baseball-almanac.com/quotes/quouec.shtml.*

Brady, Erik. "Baseball Endures Through Changing Times." *USA Today. http://www.usatoday.com/sports/baseball/00play/fs095.htm.*

Brannan, Shel. "How the First-Down Line Works." How Stuff Works. *http://www.howstuffworks.com/first-down-line.htm.*

"Brief History of the Radio Industry." Duke University Libraries. *http://library.duke.edu/digitalcollections/adaccess/radio-tv.html.*

Brown, Maury. "Inside the Numbers: Final 2009 MLB Regular Season Attendance." *http://www.bizofbaseball.com/index.php?option=com_content&view=article2009-mlb-regular-season-attendance.*

_____. "When Baseball Meets the Largest Cable Television Channel Launch in History." FastCompany.com. *http://www.fastcompany.com/blog/maury-brown/sports-bizness/when-baseball-meets-largest-cable-television-channel-launch-history.*

Burns, Ken. "Baseball Timeline." *Baseball.* Public Broadcasting. *http://www.pgs.org/kenburns/baseball/timelinepage9.html.*

"The Business of Baseball." Library of Congress. *http://www.loc.gov/rr/business/BERA/issue3/baseball.html.*

Cahill, Dan. "Cubs 7th Inning Stretch Jumps the Shark with Richard Dreyfus." *Chicago Sun-Times. http://blogs.suntimes.com/sportsprose/2009/09/cubs_7th_inning-stretch.html.*

"Cap Anson." BaseballHistory.com. *http://www.baseballhistory.com/ballplayers/player.php?name=cap_anson_1852.*

"Casey Stengel Quotes." Baseball Almanac. *http://www.baseball-almanac.com/quotes/quosteng.shtml.*

"CBS at 75 — Timeline." CBS Broadcasting. *http://www.cbs.com/specials/cbs_75/timeline/1950.shtml.*

"Chicago Cubs Attendance Records." Baseball Almanac. http://www.baseball-almanac.com/teams/cubsatte.shtml.

"Chicago White Sox Attendance Records." Baseball Almanac. *http://www.baseball-almanac.com/teams/wsoxatte.shtml.*

"Cincinnati Reds—1934." Baseball Library.com. *http://www.baseballlibrary.com/teams/byyear.php?team=Cincinnati_Reds.*

"Classic Baseball Newsreels." Legacy Productions. *http://www.baseballnewsreels.com/1961–1967.*

"Colonel Robert R. McCormick." Cantigny, McCormick Foundation. *http://www.cantigny.org/museums/firstdivision.aspx.*

"Communications: End of Liberty." Time Inc. *http://www.time.com/time/printout/0,8816,806483,00.html.*

"Complete Game Broadcasts." Holley Music. http://www.cooperstownmusic.com/complete.htm.

Covil, Eric C. "Radio and Its Impact on the Sports World." American Sportscasters Online. *http://www.americansportscastersonline.com/radiohistory.html.*

Crupi, Anthony. "All-Star Game Scores Ratings Home Run." Reuters. *http://www.reuters.com/article/idUSTRE56F15L20090716.*

"Cubs All-Time Owners." Major League Baseball Online. http://chicago.cubs.mlb.com/chc/hisory/owners.jsp.

"Cubs Year-by-Year Results." Major League Baseball Online. *http://chicago.cubs.mlb.com/chc/history/year_by_year_results.jsp.*

Deitz, Corey. "9 Things Your Probably Did Not Know About Ronald Reagan's Radio Career." *Http://radio.about.com/od/djsandgostqt/a/aa060704a.htm.*

"Dempsey Loses on Long Count." History.com. *http://www.history.com/this-day-in-history.do?action=article&id=7028.*

"Dempsey-Carpentier Fight, July 1921." The Wireless Age. *http://www.eht.com/oldradio/arrl/2002-06/Dempsey.htm.*

DiComo, Anthony. "Waldman Makes World Series History." Major League Baseball Online. *http://mlb.mlb.com/news/article.jsp?ymd=20091028&content_id=756.*

"Dizzy Dean." Baseball Library.com. *http://www.baseballlibrary.com/ballplayers/player.php?name=Dizzy_Dean_1911.*

"Dodger Stadium." Ballparks.com. *http://www.ballparks.com/baseball/national/dodger.htm.*

"Dodgers Attendance Records." Baseball Almanac. *http://www.baseball-almanac.com/teams/laate.shtml.*

Doyle, Jack. "Dempsey vs. Carpentier, July 1921." Pop History Dig. *http://www.pophistorydig.com/?tag=the-dempsey-carpentier-fight.*

Doyle, Pat. "Baseball Broadcasting from Another Day." Baseball Almanac. *http://www.baseball-almanac. com/minor-league/minor2004a.html.*

"Edward R. Murrow: A Report on Senator Joseph R. McCarthy." Transcribed by G. Handman from DVD, The McCarthy Years (Edward R. Murrow Collection). *http://www.lib.berkeley.edu/MRC/murrowmccarthy. html.*

"Elston Howard Facts." *http://www.thebaseballpage.com/players/howarel01.php.*

"Entire List of 7th Inning Stretch Singers." Fogpog.com. *http://www.fogpog.com/showthread.php?t=4358.*

"Ernie Harwell Quotes." Baseball Almanac. http://www.baseballalmanac.com/quotes/ernie_harell_quotes. html.

"Famous Weekly Old Time Radio Shows." Old Time Radio. *http://www.old-time.com/weekly/index.html.*

"1st World Series Color TV Broadcast." Brainy History Online. *http://www.brainyhistory.com/events/1955/ september_28_1955_117213.html.*

Fitzpatrick, Frank. "Remembering the Radio Daze of Baseball." *York Daily Record. http://ydr.inyork.com/ ci_12850538.*

"Ford C. Frick Award." National Baseball Hall of Fame and Museum. *http://web.baseballhalloffame. org/hofers/frick.jsp.*

"40 Years Ago Today: Harry Caray Let Go as Cardinals Broadcaster." Multimedia, KSDK, Inc. *http://www. ksdk.com/news/local/story.aspx?storyid=187028.*

"Fox Broadcasting Company." Encyclopedia Britannica Online. *http://www.britannica.com/ebchecked/topic/ 215396/fox-broadcasting-company.*

"Fried Lieb." Baseball Library.com. *http://www.baseballlibrary.com.*

Gandossy, Taylor. "TV Viewing at All-Time High." CNN.com. *http://www.cnn.com/2009/showbiz/tv/02/ 24/us.video/nielson.*

Gehrig, Lou. "Full-length transcript from a radio interview with Lou Gehrig." KROC-AM Radio, March, 2002. *http://moregehrig.tripod.com/id16.html.*

"Georges Carpenter (French boxer)." Encyclopedia Britannica Online. *http://www.britannica.com/EB checked/topic/96758/Georges-Carpentier.*

Gidlow, Liette. "The Great Debate: Kennedy, Nixon, and Television in the 1960 Race for the Presidency." History Now. *http://www.historynow.org/09_2004/historian2.html.*

"The Goldbergs." Museum of Broadcast Communications. *http://www.museum.tv/eotvsction.php?entrycode= goodbergsth.*

"Golden Age of Radio 1935–1950." University of San Diego. *http://history.sandiego.edu/GENrecording/ radio2.html.*

Goodwin, Danny. "Selling Stuff During the Golden Age of Radio." *http://www.old-time.com/commercials/ index.html.*

Grace, Francie. "Former MVP Ken Caminiti Died of Overdose in New York." CBS News. *http://www.cbsnews. com/stories/2004/10/11/entertainment/main648472.shtml.*

"Grantland Rice." Encyclopedia Britannica Online. *http://www.britannica.com/EBchecked/topic/502321/Grant land-Rice.*

"Hale Boggs Biography." Biography Base. *http://www.biographybase.com/biography/Boggs_Hale.html.*

Hall, Matthew T. "A Life Touched by Lou Gehrig—and the Disease Named for Him." *http://www.signon sandiego.com/news/2009/jul/04/life-touched-lou-gehrig-8212-and-disease-named-him/?metro.*

Hancock, David. "Jose Canseco: Juiced." *60 Minutes.* CBS News. *http://cbsnews.com/stories/2005/08/05/60 minutes/main761932.shtml.*

"Hank Aaron." Baseball-Reference.com. *http://www.baseball-reference.com/bullpen/hank_aaron.*

"Harold Arlin." Baseball Library.com. *http://www.baseballlibrary.com/ballplayersplayer.php?name=Harold.*

"Harry Caray." Baseball Library.com. *http://www.baseballlibrary.com/baseballlibrary/ballplayers/C/Caray_ Harry.stm.*

"Harry Caray—Moving On and Up." Famous Sports Stars. *http://sports.jrank.org/pages/777/Caray-Harry- Moving-On-Up.html.*

"Harvey Kuenn." Baseball Library.com. *http://www.baseballlibrary.com/ballplayers/player.php?name=Harvey_ Kuenn.*

Haupert, Michael J. "The Economic History of Major League Baseball." Economic History Association. *http://eh.net/encyclopedia/article/haupert.mlb.*

"Henry Grantland Rice." Tennessee Encyclopedia of History and Culture. *http://tennesseeencyclopedia. net/imagegallery.php?EntryID=R031.*

"Historic Baseball: The History of Baseball Game Broadcasting." *http://www.historicbaseball.com/fea/base ballbroadcasts.html.*

"Historical Attendance Figures for Major League Baseball." *http://bss.sfsu.edu/tygiel/hist490/mlbattendance.htm.*

"History and Development of Early Car Radios." RadioMuseum. http://www.radiomuseum.org/forum/ first_car_radios_history_and_development_of_early_car_radios.html.

"History of AT&T Television." AT&T ICDS. *http://www.corp.att.com/history/television/.*

"History of Radar." About.com. *http://inventors.about.com/library/inventors/blradar.htm.*

"History of Television." *http://www.high-techproductions.com/historyoftelevision.htm.*

"History of the Newsreel." University of San Diego. *http://history.sandiego.edu/gen/filmnotes/newsreel.html*

"Home Run Derby (2000–2008)." Baseball Almanac. *http://www.baseball-almanac.com/asgbox/hrderby.shtml.*

"Home Run Records in a Single Season." Baseball Almanac. *http://www.baseball-almanac.com/recbooks/ rb_hr2.shtml.*

"Humorous Quotes of Al McGuire." *http://www.workinghumor.com/quotes/al_mcguire.shtml.*

Ingram, Billy. "The Goldbergs: The Remarkable Gertrude Berg." *http://www.tvparty.com/vaultgold.html.*

Ingram, Clarke. "Appendix Three: News and Sports." DuMont Television Network. *http://www.dumont history.tv/a3.html.*

_____. "Channel Five: Programming." DuMont Television Network. http://www.dumont-history.tv/5.html.

"Jack Buck." Major League Baseball Online. *http://mlb.mlb.com/mlb/news/tributes/mlb_obit_jack_buck.jsp.*

"Jack Buck." http://www.Notablebiographies.com/supp/supplement-a-bu-obituaries/buck-jack.html.

"Jackie Robinson Biography." Biography.com. *http://www.biography.com/articles/Jacie-Robinson-9460813.*

"Jackie Robinson Chronology." Baseball Library.com. http://www.baseballlibrary.com/ballplayers/player.php name=Jackie_Robinson_1919&page=chronology.

Jackson, Brooks. "How Did George W. Bush Make His Millions?" *http://www.cnn.com/ALLPOLITICS/stories/ 1999/05/13/president.2000/jackson.bush/.*

"Jim Bunning." Baseball Library.com. *http://www.baseballlibrary.com/ballplayers/player.php?name=Jim_Bun ning.*

"Jim Woods Quotes." Wapedia. *http://wapedia.mobi/en/Jim_Woods.*

"Joe Garagiola." Baseball Library.com. *http://www.baseballlibrary.com/ballplayers/player.php?name=Joe_ Garagiola.*

"John Leonard Quotes." *http://www.brainyquote.com/quotes/qutoes/j/johnleonar 115326.html.*

Johnson, Eric. "Nightline Classic: Al Campanis." ABC News. *http://abcnews.go.com/Nightline/ESPNSports/ story?id=3034914.*

Kalk, Josh. "A First Look at the 2008 Pitch f/x Data." *The Hardball Times,* April 1, 2008. *http://www.hardball times.com.*

"KDKA Begins to Broadcast." A Science Odyssey: People and Discoveries, PBS. *http://www.pbs.org/wgbh/aso/ databank/entries/dt20ra.html.*

Kissell, Rick. "Fox in TV Ratings Double Play." *Variety. http://www.variety.com/article/VR1118006301.html? categoryid=14&cs=1&query=true+blood+rating.*

Klosterman, Chuck. "Life After Halftime." Esquire. Hearst Communications, Inc. *http://www.esquire.com/ features/chuck-klostermans-america/ESQ0207.*

"The Language of Al McGuire." ESPN Classic. *http://espn.com/classic/s/Mcguirisms.html.*

Lewis, Tom. "A Godlike Presence: The Impact of Radio on the 1920s and 1930s." Organization of American Historians. http://www.oah.org/pubs/magazine/communication/lewis.html.

Linder, Douglas O. "State v. John Scopes (The Monkey Trial)." University of Missouri-Kansas City. *http:// www.law.umkc.edu/faculty/projects/ftrials/scopes/evolut.htm.*

"Longest Home Run Ever Hit." Baseball Almanac. http://www.baseball-almanac.com/feats/art_hr_shtml.

"Los Angeles Dodgers Attendance Records." Baseball Almanac. *http://www.baseball-almanac.com/teams/ laatte.shtml.*

"Los Angeles Memorial Coliseum." Ballparks.com. *http://www.ballparks.com/baseball/national/laxcol.htm.*

"Major League Baseball Attendance — 2009." ESPN.com. *http://espn.go.com/mlb/attendance.*

"Major League Baseball Attendance from 1890–2005." Baseball Chronology. *http://www.baseballchronology. com/Baseball/Teams/Background/Attendance/.*

Matuszewski, Erik. "Baseball Playoffs Help TBS Hit Television Ratings Home Run." Bloomberg. *http://www. bloomberg.com/apps/news?pid=20670001&sid=aYcsezOfSbjg.*

McLeod, Elizabeth. "Old Time Radio Moments of the Century." The Original Old Time Radio. *http://www. old-time.com/mcleod/top100.html.*

McLuhan, Marshall. "If It Works, It's Obsolete." *http://www.marshallmcluhan.com/poster.html.*

"Media in the 1930s." ThinkQuest. *http://library.thinkquest.org/27629/themes/media/md30s.html.*

"Media Quotes." Famous Quotes and Authors.com. *http://www.famousquotesandauthors.com/keywords/media_ quotes.html.*

"Mel Allen." Baseball Library.com. http://www.baseballlibrary.com/ballplayers/player.php?name=Mel_Allen.

"Mel Allen." Baseball-Reference.com. *http://www.baseball-reference.com/bullpen/Mel_Allen.*

"Mickey Mantle Quotes." *http://www.brainyquote.com/quotes/authors/m/mickey_mantle.html.*

"Mike Shannon." Baseball Library.com. *http://www.baseballlibrary.com/ballplayers/player.php?name= Mike_Shannon.*

"Milo Hamilton." Texas Baseball Hall of Fame. *http://www.tbhof.org/bio/2005/biohamilton-toycannon.htm.*

Mishkind, Barry. "Mutual Broadcasting System History." The Broadcast Archive. *http://www.oldradio.com/ archives/prog/mutual.htm.*

"Mission & History." McCormick Foundation. *http://www.mccormicktribune.org/mission.aspx.*

"MLB.com Streams Baseball to iPhone, iPod, Maybe Sparkling New Business Model." Reiter's Mobile TV Report. June 17, 2009. *http://mlb.mlb.com/mobile/iphone/.*

"Monte Irvin." Baseball Library.com. *http://www.baseballlibrary.com/ballplayers/player/php?name=Monte_Irvin_1919.*

Mullen, Jeff. "Baseball's New Era of 'Money Ball' Is Expensive Escapism." *Enid News and Eagle. http://www. enidnews.com/opinion/local_story_094233757.html.*

Murrow, Edward R. "A Report on Senator Joseph R. McCarthy." *See It Now*, CBS Network-TV. *http://www.lib. berkeley.edu/MRC/murrowmccarthy.html.*

"Music in Motion: The First Motorola Brand Car Radio." Motorola, Inc. *http://www.motorola.com/staticfiles/ Business/Corporate/US-EN/history/feature-car-radio.html.*

"Mutual Broadcasting System History." *http://www.oldradio.com/archives/prog/mutual.htm.*

"NBC's Kubek Wins 2009 Frick Award." National Baseball Hall of Fame. http://web.baseballhalloffame.org/ hofers/frick/kubek_tony.jsp.

The Nielsen Company. *http://www.nielsen.com.*

"1927 — Murderers' Row." *http://www.thenewmurderersrow.com/.*

"1927 New York Yankees." Baseball-Refer-ence.com. *http://www.baseball-reference.com/bullpen/1927_ Yankees.*

"1927 World Series." Baseball-Reference.com. *http://www.baseball-reference.com/postseason/1927_ws.shtml.*

"1927 Yankees— Miscellaneous Anecdotes." Angelfire. *http://www.angelfire.com/pa/1927/27anecdotes.html.*

"The 1930s Cars Chugged Along Despite the Great Depression." Anythingaboutcars.com. *http://www.any thingaboutcars.com/1930scars.html.*

"1936 German Olympics." TV History Online. *http://www.tvhistory.tv/1936%20German%20Olympics% 20TV%20Program.htm*

"1951 Archives." CBS Broadcasting Inc. *http://www.cbs.com/specials/cbs_75/timeline/1950.shtml.*

"1960: The Road to Camelot." Kennesaw State University. *http://www.kennesaw.edu/pols/3380/pres/1960.html.*

"1988 World Series: Game 1." Major League Baseball Online. *http://mlb.mlb.com/mlb/baseballs_best/mlb_bb_ gamepage.jsp?story_page=bb_88ws_gm1_oakla.*

"Old Hoss Radbourn." Baseball Library.com. *http://www.baseballlibrary.com/ballplayers/player.php?name= Old_Hoss_Radbourn_1854.*

"100 Memorable Movie Quotes." American Film Institute. *http://connect.afi.com/site/PageServer?page name=100YearsList.*

"One Last Hurrah: Dizzy Dean Pitches for the St. Louis Browns." http://baseball.suite101.com/article.cfm/ hall_of_famer_dizzy_dean#ixzz0M18EeIIm.

"People: Mar. 30, 1962." Time Inc. *http://www.time.com/time/printout/0,8816,895971,00.html.*

"Percentage of Black Players in MLB Rises" USAToday.com. *http://www.usatoday.com/sports/baseball/2009-04-15=mlb-diversity-N.htm.*

"Pete Rozelle." Sports Broadcasting Hall of Fame. *http://www.sportsvideo.org/portal/hof/articles/publish/ Pete_Rozelle.shtml.*

"Pirates All-Time Broadcasters." *http://mlb.mlb.com/pit/history/broadcasters.jsp.*

"PITCHf/x." Sportvision. *http://sportvision.com/main_frames/products/pitchfx.htm.*

"Play by Play Account of Moonlight Graham's Only Game." Society for American Baseball Research; courtesy of David W. Smith. http://www.sabr.org/sabr.cfm?a=cms,c,332,34,0.

"Polo Grounds." Ballparks. *http://www.ballparks.com/baseball/national/pologr.htm.*

"President Ronald Reagan Baseball Game Attendance Log." Baseball Almanac. *http://www.baseball-almanac. com/prz_crr.shtml.*

"President William Taft Baseball Game Attendance Log." Baseball Almanac. http://baseball-almanac.com/ prz_cwt.shtml.

"Quotable Mike." The ArachNerd. *http://arachnerd.wordpress.com/mike-shannon-quotes/.*

"Quotes." *http://www.dizzydean.com/quotes.htm.*

"Radio Corporation of America." Museum of Broadcast Communications. *http://www.museum.tv/eotvsection. php?entrycode=radiocorpora.*

"Radio Days— Edward R. Murrow." Radio News, Old Time Radio. *http://www.otr.com/murrow.shtml.*

Ralph Kiner Quote. Baseball Almanac. *http://baseball-almanac.com/quotes/quokiner.shtml.*

Ray, James Lincoln. "Game 6 of the 1975 World Series: Pudge Fisk's Homer Ends the Greatest Fall Classic Game Ever Played." Suite101.com. *http://baseball.suite101.com/print_article.cfm/game_6_of_the_1975_ world_series.*

"Red Barber." Baseball Library.com. *http://www.baseballlibrary.com/baseballlibrary/ballplayers/B/Barber_Red. stm.*

"Regency TR-1 Transistor Radio History." *http://www.regencytr1.com.*

"Roger Maris Baseball Stats." Baseball Almanac. *http://www.baseball-almanac.com/players/player.php?= marisro01.*

"Roone Arledge Biography." Museum of Broadcast Communications. *http://www.museum.tv/eotvsection.php?entrycode=arledgeroon.*

"Rose Bowl History." *http://www.rosebowlhistory.org/.*

Rosenberg, Jennifer. "War of the Worlds Radio Broadcast." About.com. *http://history1900s.about.com/od/1930s/a/warofworld.htm.*

"Rosey Rowswell." Baseball Library.com. *http://www.baseballlibrary.com/ballplayers/player.phpname=Rosey.*

Rossi, John P. "Food for Thought: Baseball and American History." The Historical Society of Pennsylvania. *http://www.hsp.org/default.aspx?id=998.*

Rowen, Beth. "Titanic Facts." infoplease, Family Education Network. *http://www.infoplease.com/spot/titanic.html.*

Schoneherr, Neil. "African-American Writing Featured in Books Edited by Gerald Early." Washington University in St. Louis. http://news-info.wustl.edu/news/page/normal/13233.html.

Shortgen, Kenneth, Jr. "Why Tall Baseball Pitchers Are Better Than Short Pitchers." *http://www.helium.com/items/220025-why-tall-baseball-pitchers-are-better-than-short-pitchers.*

"The Shot Heard Round the World." *http://baseball.suite101.com/article.cfm/the_shot_heard_round_the_world.*

"Shot Heard Round the World: Giants Win the Pennant." *http://www.baseballchronology.com/baseball/years/1951/shot_heard_round_the_world.asp.*

"Single Season Leaders for Home Runs." Baseball Almanac. *http://www.baseball-almanac.com/hitting/hihr4.shtml.*

Smiley, Gene. "The U.S. Economy in the 1920s." *http://eh.net/encyclopedia/article/Smiley.1920s.final.*

Smith, Curt. "Voices of the Game." *http://www.curttsmith.mlbblogs.com/archives/2006/02/dizzy_dean_easi,html.*

Smith, Red. "Thomson Authored an Unlikely Ending." ESPN. *http://espn.go.com/classic/s/smith_on_thomson.html.*

"Sony TR-63 Transistor Radio Teardown — Introduction." iFixit. *http://www.ifixit.com/Teardown/Sony-TR-63-Transistor-Radio-Teardown/1219/1.*

"Statistics." Roger Maris Museum Online. *http://www.rogermarismuseum.com/statistics/.*

Stephenson, Parks. "The Marconi Wireless Installation in R.M.S. Titanic." *The Oldtimer's Bulletin* 42, no. 4 (2002). *http://marconigraph.com/titanic/wireless/mgy_wireless.html.*

"Steve Stone." Baseball-Reference.com. *http://www.baseball-reference.com/bullpen/Steve_Stone.*

Stone, Steve. "Interview: Steve Stone." *The Heckler*, Sept. 6, 2004. *http://www.theheckler.com/news/templates/?z=8&a=26.*

The Story Behind Mickey Mantle's 10 Longest Home Runs. TheMick.com. http://www.themick.com/10homers.html.

"Super Bowl XVLV Beats M.A.S.H. Finale for U.S. Viewership Record." *http://www.nfl.com/superbowl/story?id=09000d5d8164bc7b&template=with-video-with-comments&confirm=true.*

"Technological Innovations in Sports Broadcasting." IEEE Global History Network. *http://www.Ieeeghn.org/wiki/index.php/technological_innovations_in_sports_broadcasting.*

"Technology Timeline." *http://www.classicthemes.com/technologytimeline.html.*

"Ted Turner Biography." Answers.com. *http://www.answers.com/topic/ted-turner.*

"Ted Turner & CNN." *http://www.pophistorydig.com/?p=718.*

"Televise First Night Game — and Results are Amazingly Good." *http://www.tvhistory.tv/1941_June_FIRST_NIGHT_Baseball_Game.JPG.*

"Television Timeline." *http://timelines.ws/television.html*

"Telstar." Reference.com. *http://www.reference.com/browse/Telstar.*

"This Day in History 1935: MLB Holds First Night Game." History.com. A&E Television Networks. *http://www.history.com/this-day-in-history.do?action=Article&id=57064.*

"Thomas Edison & GE." General Electric Company. *http://www.ge.com/company/history/edison.html.*

"The Titanic Radio Page." *http://www.hf.ro.*

"Tony Kubek." *http://theyplayedthegame.tripod.com/id12.htm.*

"Tony Kubek." Baseball Library.com. *http://www.baseballlibrary.com/ballplayers/player.php?name=Tony_Kubek.*

"Tribune History." Tribune Company. *http://www.tribune.com/about/history.html*

"Tribune Tower." Tribune Company. *http://www.tribune.com/about/history.html.*

"2005: Flat Screen TV's & HDTV are the 'IN' Thing of the Year." History of Television. *http://www.high-techproductions.com/historyoftelevision.htm.*

"Ty Cobb." Baseball-Reference.com. *http://www.baseball-reference.com/bullpen/Ty_Cobb.*

"Vin Scully." Baseball Almanac. http://www.baseball-almanac.com/vin_scully_quotes.shtml.

"Vin Scully." Baseball Library.com. *http://www.baseballlibrary.com/ballplayers/player.php?name=Vin_Scully.*

"Vin Scully." Baseball-Reference.com, Sports Reference LLC. *http://www.baseball-reference.com/bullpen/Vin_Scully.*

"The Visitor in Your Living Room: Radio Advertising in the 1930s." American Studies, University of Virginia. *http://xroads.virginia.edu/~CLASS/am485_98/graham/visitor.html.*

"Weekly Old Time Radio Shows." Old Time Radio. *http://www.old-time.com/weekly/index.html.*

Weingroff, Richard F. "June 29, 1956: A Day in History." Federal Highway Administration, Federal Highway Administration. *http://www.fhwa.dot.gov/interstate/thisday.htm*.

"WGN Radio." *http://www.statemaster.com/encyclopedia/WGN-(AM)*.

"WGN Radio Timeline." *http://wgngold.com/timeline/1920s1930s.htm*.

White, Thomas H. "Broadcasting Becomes Widespread (1922–1923)." United States Early Radio History. *http://earlyradiohistory.us/sec018.htm*.

_____. "The Growth of a Service," *http://earlyradiohistory.us*.

_____. "United States Early Radio History." *http://earlyradiohistory.us/sec017.htm*.

Whitely, David. "Lou Gehrig in 140 Characters? Impossible to Imagine." *http://mlb.fanhouse.com/2009/07/03/lou-gehrig-in-140-characters-impossible/*.

"Who Is Harry Caray?" KnowledgeRush. *http://www.knowledgerush.com/kr/encyclopedia/Harry_Caray/*.

Wilderson, David B. "Baseball and TV: A 'Dysfunctional Marriage.'" MarketWatch, July 16, 2008. *http://www.marketwatch.com/story/the-union-baseball-tv-has*.

"William Howard Taft." Baseball Library.com. *http://www.baseballlibrary.com/ballplayers/player.php?name=William_Howard_Taft*.

"William Howard Taft Quick Facts." MSN Encarta. *http://encarta.msn.com/media*.

"William Wrigley, Jr." Answers.com. *http://www.answers.com/topic/william-wrigley-jr*.

"The Wireless Operators, the Distress Call and the Rescue Ship Carpathia." *Titanic* and Other White Star Line Ships, *http://www.titanic-whitestarships.com*.

"World Series Posts Biggest Year-to-Year Growth in History." *http://tvbythenumbers.com/2009/11/05/2009-world-series-posts-biggest-year-to-year-growth-in-history*.

"World Series Television Ratings Breakdown." Baseball Almanac. *http://www.baseball-almanac.com/ws/wstv.shtml*.

"World Series Viewership 1973–2008." Nielsen Media Research, Inc. Quoted in "Updated World Series TV Ratings 1968–2008," TVbythenumbers.com, LLC. *http://tvbythenumbers.com/2008/11/10/fox-faces-record-low-world-series-tv-ratings*.

"Wrigley Field." Ballparks. http://www.ballparks.com/baseball/national/wrigle.htm.

"Wrigley Field Gets Lights." CNN/SI. *http://sportsillustrated.cnn.com/almanac/video/1988/index.html*.

"Yankee Stadium Dimensions." Ballparks. http://www.ballparks.com/baseball/american/yankee.htm.

"Yankees Timeline." Major League Baseball Online. *http://www.mlb.mlb.com/nyy/history/timeline3.jsp*.

Zimmerman, Andrew. "How Does Doppler Radar Work?" About.com. *http://physics.about.com/od/physicsintherealworld/f/dopplerradar.htm*.

Index

Page numbers in **bold italics** indicate illustrations.

Aaron, Hank 104, 121–23, 142, 147, 158, 186, 188, 198, 219, 220, 230–31, 237
Abbott and Costello 102, 105, 113
ABC *see* American Broadcasting Company
Abrams, Roger 195
A.C. Nielsen Co. 209
Adams, Franklin P. 46
Adams, Henry 104
The Aldrich Family 116
Alexander, Grover Cleveland 16
Ali, Muhammad 9, 69, 134, 150, 166, 191, 227
All in the Family 78, 189–90, 210
All My Children 202
All-Star Game 87, 90, 97, 135–36, 155, 162–63, 208, 210, 220, 225–26, 234, 235
Allen, Dick 165
Allen, Gracie 75, 116
Allen, Fred 64, 75
Allen, Mel 56–57, 65, 90, 99, 106, 112, 142, 146, 150–52, 156–57, 159, 162, 176, 178, 221
Allen, Steve 136
Alou, Moises 210
American Bandstand 162
American Broadcasting Company (ABC) 116–20, 128–31, 161–63, 173, 182, 190, 195, 208, 221, 228
American Football League 160
American Idol 210
American League (MLB) **49**, 54, 71, 80, 150, 186
American Needle v. NFL 160
American Sportscasters Association 143
American Sportsman 177
American Sportswriters Association 112

American Telephone and Telegraph (AT&T) 24, 32, 60–**61**, 134, 237
America's Got Talent 234
Amos 'n' Andy 55–56, 64, 68, 76, 78, 94, 116
Anderson, Dave 170
Andy Griffith 226
Angels *see* California Angels; Los Angeles Angels
Anheuser, Eberhard 208
Anheuser-Busch 118, 141, 171, 208
Ann-Margret 166
Anson, Cap 45–46, 124
antitrust laws 65–66, **86**, 141, 152, 160, 163
AOL Time Warner 228, 231, 235
Apple: iPhone 237; iPod 235; Macintosh 209
Arledge, Roone 130
Arlin, Harold 12, 22, 26, **27**, 28, 31, 32, 65, 72, 85, 90, 109
Armstrong, Neil 121, 223
Army, U.S. 176, 178
Ashburn, Richie 95, 133–34
asterisk, implied 237
Astor, Vincent 40
AT&T *see* American Telephone & Telegraph
Athletics *see* Kansas City Athletics; Oakland Athletics; Philadelphia Athletics
Atlanta Braves 179, 193–95, 226, 226–228, 235; *see also* Milwaukee Braves; Boston Braves
Atlanta Hawks 18, 194
Atlanta Journal-Constitution 30
attendance, major league 17, **47**, 74, 96, 106–07, 137, 158–59, 189–90

Baby Ruth candy bar 206–07
The Baby Ruth Hour 207
Baer, Max 82
Baker, Dusty 188, 211
Baker, Frank "Home Run" 13, 71
BALCO 196–97
Ballpark at Arlington 87
Baltimore Orioles 90, 118, 141, 187, 189, 221
Baltimore Ravens 203
Banks, Ernie 134, 147, 168–69, 219, 231
Barber, Red 72, 81–82, 90–91, 98–**99**, 102, 106, 109, 111–112, 120, 138, 142–43, 146–47, 157, 164, 216, 220–21, 239
Barkley, Charles 174
Bartman, Steve 210–11
Barzun, Jacques 100–101, 104–05
baseball cards 207
Baseball Is a Funny Game 179
Baseball Magazine 40
Baseball Network 195
Baseball Weekly 217
Baseball Writers Association 40
Batman 129
Bauer, Hank 133, 157
BBC *see* British Broadcasting Company
Beach, Hugh 158, 237
The Beach Boys 154
The Beatles 162, 201
Belcher, Tim 170
Bell, Bert 159
Bell Laboratories 134, 154
Belushi, Jim 166
Bench, Johnny 180
Benny, Jack 64, 75, 112, 116, 128, 138
Berenger, Tom 175
Berg, Gertrude 200–01

265

Bergen, Edgar 75–77
Berger, Wally 231
Berle, Milton 111, 128
Berman, Chris 19
Bernie Mac show 166
Bernsen, Corbin 175
Berra, Yogi 104, 112, 133, 147,
150–51, 157, 171, 174, 177, 225
Berry, Chuck 166
Beverly Hillbillies 210
Beverly Hills 90210 202
billboarding games 48, 75, 215,
217, 237
billy goat curse 211
Billy Goat Tavern 225
Bird, Larry 174, 217
Black, Jack 166
Blatz Beer 208
Blockbuster 205
Blue, Vida 226
Bluege, Ossie *113*
Boggs, Hale 160–61
Boggs, Wade 90
Bonds, Barry 27, 195, 197–98,
231, 236
Boone, J.J. *61*
Boston Braves 140–41, 218
Boston Red Sox 41, 95, 118–19,
124, 165, 176–77, 180, 183, 195,
208, 212, 223
boxing, televised 116
Boyer, Ken 164
Bradshaw, Terry 202
The Brady Bunch 173
Branca, Ralph 98, 110–11, 215–17
Braun, Ferdinand 119
Braves *see* Atlanta Braves; Mil-
waukee Braves
Breadon, Sam 80
Brennaman, Marty 181
Brett, George 157, 185
Brickhouse, Jack 19, 56, 84–85,
90, 96, 105–06, 129, 132, 138,
156, 166–67, 168, 179
Briggs Stadium 221
British Broadcasting Company
(BBC) 24
Britt, Jim 106
Brock, Lou 164–65
Brokaw, Tom 108
Brooklyn Dodgers 54, 72, 79,
82–83, 98, *99*, 109–10, 117, 120,
122, 124, 132–33, 135, 137–38,
139–43, 146, 162, 177, 200–01,
216, 218–20, 239
Brosnan, Jim 179
Brown, Bobby 157
Brown, Hubie 174
Brown v. Board of Education 100,
103–04, 122, 124
Bruce, J. E. *49*
Bryan, William Jennings 36
Buck, Jack 18, 43, 44, 84, 90, 156,
166, 168, 170–71, 177, 182, 188
Buck, Joe 19, 172, 177
Bucknor, C.B. 223
Bud Light 208
Budweiser 118, 205, 208

Bull Durham 105
Bumstead, Dagwood 184
Bunning, Jim 144, 163
Burns, George 75, 112, 116
Burns, Ken 100, 195
Busch, Adolphus 208
Busch, August, III 165
Busch, Gussie 118, 208
Busch Beer 208
Busch Stadium 118, 209
Bush, George W. 6, 19, 87
Butkus, Dick 168, 208

Cable News Network (CNN)
190, 192, 194, 227
Caesar, Sid 111, 128
California Angels *see* Los Ange-
les Angels
"called shot" homerun 79
Caminiti, Ken 196
Campanella, Roy 98, 104, 122,
133–34, 140–41, 143, 217
Campanis, Al 153, 228
Campbell's Soup 76
Campeneris, Bert 190
Candid Camera 137
Cannizzaro, Chris 221
Cannon, Jimmy *124*
Canseco, Jose 170, 196–97
Capital Cities Group 228
Captain Midnight 76
Captain Video 129
car radio 53, 80
Caray, Chip 155, 166
Caray, Harry 18, 56, 84, 90, 105–
06, 112, 156, 164–67, 169, 171,
179–80, 185, 187–88, 206, 211,
224
Caray, Skip 179–80
Carbo, Bernie 180
Carew, Rod 186
Carlin, George 104
Carnegie, Andrew 160
Carpentier, Georges 39
Carson, Johnny 56, 128, 175
Carty, Rico 186
Catch 222 175
Catcher in the Wry 175
cathode ray tube 119
Cavalcade of Stars 129
CBS *see* Columbia Broadcasting
System
C.E. Hooper, Inc. 64
Cellar, Emmanuel 145, 161
*Centerfield Shot: A History of
Baseball on Television* 117, 131,
133
Cepeda, Orlando 164
Chance, Frank 46
Chase & Sanborn Hour 76–77
Chase Hotel 85
Chavez Ravine 145
Cheers 192, 210
Chesterfield cigarettes 76
Chicago American 48
Chicago Bears 168, 191
Chicago Board of Trade 34, 37
Chicago Bulls 211

Chicago Colts 45, 68
Chicago Cubs 15, 16, 17, 19, 28,
43, 44–45, *47*, 56, 71, 73, 75,
79–80, 82, 85–86, 88–92, 96–
97, 104, 119, 131–32, 159, 166–
67, 168–69, 185, 187, 200,
210–11, 215, 218, 220, 228–29,
231
Chicago Daily News 67, *76*
Chicago Fire *see* Great Chicago
Fire
Chicago Loop 105
Chicago Tribune 227–29, 231
Chicago Whales 46
Chicago White Sox 15, 21, 54–
56, 68, 85, 87, 90, 116–17, 119,
132, 137, 144, 156, 165, 168, 173,
187, 238
Chicago White Stockings 45
Child, Julia 162
Children's Television Act 192
Childress, Alvin 116
Cincinnati Bengals 203
Cincinnati Reds 79, 81–83, 91–
92, *99*, 120, 136–37, 151, 180,
190, 207, 218–19
Clear Channel 239
Clemens, Roger 235
Clemente, Roberto 27, 116, 141–
42, 147
Cleveland, Grover 206
Cleveland Indians 64, 90, 106,
116–17, 124, 231
Cleveland Naps 46; *see also*
Cleveland Indians
Clydesdale horses 208
CNN *see* Cable News Network
Cobb, Ty 21, 29, 50, 69, 71, 83,
206
Coca-Cola (Coke) 205–06
Cohen, Gary 155
Colavito, Rocky 219
Coleman, Jerry 90
Collins, Doug 174
Collins, Ripper 82
Collins, Tom 175
color commentators 172–74, 180
Columbia Broadcasting System
(CBS) 60, 75, *99*, 113, 116,
118–21, 128, 130, 135, 137, 143,
146–47, 161, 170, 182, 189–91,
196, 201–02, 212, 220–21, 234,
239
Combs, Earl 70
Comcast 235
Comerica Park 209
Comiskey, Charles 54, 212
Comiskey Park 220, 234
commercials, radio and televi-
sion 200–01
*Common Law Origins of the
Infield Fly Rule* 103
Connal, Scotty 182
Conrad, Frank 26
Coogan, Jackie 69
Cook County Hospital 105
Coolidge, Calvin 207
Coor's Field 209

Correll, Charles 55, 94
Cosell, Howard 131, 156, 175, 191
Costas, Bob 19, 176, 238
Court-TV 192
Cousy, Bob 173
Cowan, Tommy 29–30
Cox Communications 235
Coyle, Harry 158, 182
Cronin, Joe 151
Cronkite, Walter 191
Crosby, Bing 76
Crosley Field 218
Crowe, Russell 166
Cuba 100
Cuban, Mark 166
Curtiss Candy Company 206–07
Cusack, John 166
Cuzzi, Phil 223

Dallas 78, 191, 210
Darcy, Pat 180
Dark, Alvin 110
Darrow, Clarence 35–36, 61, 104
Dateline NBC 192
Davis, Mike 170
Dean, Dizzy 18, 80, 84, 95, 97, 106, 108, 111, 117, 119, 130, 138, 171–72
Dean, Paul "Daffy" 96–97
Death Valley Days 89
Dempsey, Jack 38–39, 61, 69–70
Depression *see* Great Depression
Detroit Sports Broadcasters Association 90
Detroit Tigers 90–91, 112–13, 125, 144, 161, 163, 164, 171, 186, 214, 218, 220–21, 231, 238
Dick Van Dyke Show 226
Dictaphone 50
DiMaggio, Joe 82–83, 91, 95, 105, 108, 132–33, 157, 218
DirecTV 235
Disney 129–30, 228, 231
Disneyland 145
Ditka, Mike 166, 168, 191
Doby, Larry 104, 124, 134, 217
Dodger Stadium 145, 209
Dodgers *see* Brooklyn Dodgers; Los Angeles Dodgers
Dominican Republic 100
Donnelley, Thorne 34
Dorsey, Tommy 76
Dragnet 128
Drees, Jack 54
Dressen, Charlie 110
Drysdale, Don 144, 156, 173, 186–87
Dudley, Jimmy 54
DuMont Network 116, 120–21, 127–30, 133, 191
Dunaway, Donald 141
Dunphy, Don 116
DuPont 73
Durocher, Leo 141
Dutton, T.D. **61**
DVD player 235

Early, Gerald L. 100, 104
Ebbets Field 79, 82, 98, 102–103, 137–38, 140, 142, 217, 219
Ebersol, Dick 176
Eckersley, Dennis 170
The Ed Sullivan Show 128, 136, 201
Eddy, William 131–32
Eisenhower, Dwight 85, 105, 107, 140
Electrophone 50
Elson, Bob 18, 54, 72, 83–85, 90, 96, 116, 169
Emancipation Proclamation 115
Emerson, Ralph Waldo 111, 216
Enberg, Dick 155
Ennis, "Big" Del 133
ER 210
ESPN 79, 131, 136, 190, 203–04, 210, 228
ESPN Radio 228
Etten, Nick 157
Evans, Dwight 180
Evening Telegram 40
Evers, Johnny 46
Evian 205

Faraway Hill 127
Farnsworth, Philo 119
Farrell, James 208
Favre, Bret 198–199
The FBI 129
Federal-Aid Highway Act 140
Federal Baseball League 35, 46, 65–66
Federal Baseball v. National League 87, 107, 118, 152
Federal Communications Commission (FCC) 111
Federal Radio Commission 25, 60
Fehr, Donald 196
Feller, Bob 91–92, 95, 133, 144, 187
female broadcasters, baseball 233
Fenway Park 58, 144, 209
Fessenden, Reginald 5, 25
Fetzer, John 161, 221
Fetzer Broadcasting 221
Fibber McGee 76
Field, Marshall 48
Field of Dreams 105
Fingers, Rollie 190, 226
Finley, Charles 85, 165, 212, 225–26
Fisk, Carlton 136, 180–82, 184, 188, 219
Fitzgerald, F. Scott 174
Fitzpatrick, Frank 95, 107
Flanner, Joe 44
Flatbush 145
Flip Wilson Show 190
Flood, Curt 164–65
Florida Marlins 195, 210
Forbes Field *27*, 218
Ford, Gerald 10
Ford, Henry 40, 59, 215

Ford, Whitey 118, 133–34, 147, 157, 171, 209
Ford Motor Co. 220
Foreman, George 69, 150, 166
Foster, George 180
Fox Television Network 135, 172, 191–92, 194, 202, 204, 210–11, 223, 234
FoxTrack 203
Foxx, Jimmy 112, 218, 230–31
Foxx, William 69
Fraley, Oscar 151
Frampton, Peter 166
Franks, Herman 215
Frazee, Harry 21, 40
Frazier, Joe 227
Frick, Ford 43, 79, 90, 149–51, 157
Frick Award 89–90, 112, 142, 146, 169, 175
Friday Night Fights 116, 127, 208
Friedan, Betty 84
Friend, Bob 163
Frisch, Frankie 30
Frost, George 53
Frost, Robert 107
The Fugitive 78

Gaedel, Eddie 48, 166
Galvin, Paul V. 81
Game of Shadows 196–97
Game of the Day 152
Game of the Week 96, 108, 117–19, 130, 138, 158, 161–62, 176–77, 179, 208, 221, 237
Garagioloa, Joe 90, 156–57, 171, 175–78, 181, 185, 221
Gardner, Gayle 233
Gates, Bill 9
Gedeon, Elmore 95
Gee, Johnny 186
Gehrig, Lou 43, 63, 67, 70–71, 72, 78, 81–83, 146, 188, 206, 218, 230, 240
General Electric 24, 39, 76, 92, 127
General Foods 191
General Mills 76, 200
General Motors 81, 192
Gerard, Lou 181–82
Getty Oil 228
Giamatti, Bart 112
Giamatti, Paul 112
Giants *see* New York Giants; San Francisco Giants
Gibson, Bob 155, 164–65, 186–87
Gibson, Josh 103
Gibson, Kirk 170–71, 182
Gibson, Mel 166
Giles, Warren 137, 151, 158
Gillette Cavalcade of Sports 116, 137
Gillette Razor Co. 83, 106, 118, 208, 220
Girardi, Joe 84
Girl Talk 162
Girls Baseball 116

Gladwell, Malcolm 9
Gleason, Jackie 111, 129
Glenn Miller Show 96
Godfrey, Arthur 128, 137
The Goldbergs 200–01
golden age of radio 64, 107
Gone with the Wind 77, 91
Goodbye, Mr. Chips 77
Gooding, Cuba, Jr. 166
Goodwin, Doris Kearns 98, 107
Gordon, Joe 157
Gosden, Freeman 55, 94
Gould, Jack 162
Gowdy, Curt 84, 90, 99, 176, 181
Graham, Archibald "Moonlight" 6–7
Graham, Virginia 162
Grand Ole Opry 65
Grange, Red 10, 15, 36, 49, 73, 168
Grapes of Wrath 80, 91
Great Chicago Fire 45
Great Depression 59–60, 72, 74–76, 78–81, 91, 101, 108, 109, 143, 218
Great Recession 231
Green, Pumpsie 124
Green Bay Packers 198–99
"green light letter" 92
"Green monster" wall 144, 181–82, 184
Greenberg, Hank 72, 91, 125, 218, 230–31, 238
Griffey, Ken 180
Griffith Stadium 133, 141
Grimes, Burleigh 13, 21
Groat, Dick 147
Gulf War 192, 227
Gumbel, Bryant 240

Hagman, Larry 191
Halas, George 10
Haley, Bill 139
Hall of Fame, baseball 31, 113, 116, 148, 162, 236
Hamilton, Milo 19, **88**–90, 169–70, 182
Hamm's Beer 208
Hampton, Dan 191
Harding, Tonya 194
Harding, Warren G. 50
Haron, Merle 175
Harrelson, Ken 56, 155
Hartford Courant 212
Hartman, Harry 57
Harwell, Ernie 90, 111–12, 166, 216
HBO (Home Box Office) 227
HD television 19, 100, 199, 224, 230, 231–32, 235
Hearst, William Randolph 62
Hearst News 73
"Heidi game" 177
Heilman, Harry 21
Helyar, John 159
Hemingway, Earnest 104, 139
Herald Tribune 29
Hermann, August **49**

Hershiser, Orel 170
Hertz, Heinrich 23–24
Higby, Kirby 91
Hindenburg 73
HitZone 203
Hodges, Gil 98, 110, 133, 140, 143–44
Hodges, Russ 90, 109, 112, 116, 216
Hoffman, Solly 52
Holmes, Oliver Wendell, Jr. 46, 67
Hollywood 72
Holtzman, Ken 190
Home Run Derby 219
Honey, Stan 204
The Honeymooners 78, 129
Hood, Raymond M. 47
Hoover, Herbert 68, 93, 109, 111, 120
Hopalong Cassidy 116
Hornsby, Rogers 21, 37, 63, 231
Houk, Ralph 157
Hour Glass 127
Houston Astros 89, 159, 170
Howard, Elston 134, 150–51
Howells, John Mead 47
Hoyt, Waite 31, 113
Hubbell, Carl 82
Hughes, Howard 129
Hughes, Pat 179
Hunter, Jim "Catfish" 190

I Love Lucy 210, 226
Imus, Don 153
instant replay 222–23
Intel 154
International Olympics Committee 196
Irvin, Monford "Monte" 115
Ivory Soap 83

Jackson, Keith 156, 175
Jackson, Reggie 190
Jackson, "Shoeless" Joe 21, 113
Japan 100
Jeffries, James 73
Jenkins, Elliott 34
Jenkins, Lee 238
Johnson, Ban 48–**49**, 54, 71
Johnson, "Big" Ed 117
Johnson, Ervin "Magic" 174, 217
Johnson, Jack 73
Johnson, Randy 186
Johnson, Walter 20
Johnson's Wax 76
Jones, Bobby 30
Jordan, Michael 169, 217, 227
Juiced 196

Kaat, Jim 157, 214
Kalas, Harry 95, 99, 107, 112
Kaney, Sen 35
Kansas City Athletics 144; *see also* Oakland Athletics; Philadelphia Athletics
Kansas City Monarchs 124
Kay, Michael 155

KCBS Radio 25
KDKA Radio 12, 15, 22, 25, 26, **27**, 28–29, 32, 40, 47, **55**, 169, 239
Kennedy, John F. 87, 149, 162
Kentucky Derby 43, 56
Kerrigan, Nancy 194
Killebrew, Harmon 186, 219
Kiner, Ralph 27–28, 133, 174
King, Martin Luther 83, 123
Kinsella, W.P. 6
KMOX Radio 164, 172, 188
Knorr, Fred 221
Knorr Broadcasting Company 221
Kodak 73
Kool Cigarettes 76
Koppel, Ted 228
Korea 95
Korean War 118
Koufax, Sandy 143, 173, 187, 238
KQW Radio 26
Kraft Foods 76
Kraft Television Theater 127
KRIV-TV 202
KROC Radio 83
KTTV-TV 202
Kubek, Tony 90, 142, 156, 175, 177, 181
Kuehn, Harvey 163
Kuhn, Bowie 194, 220, 225, 227
Kuiper, Duane 155
Kupcinet, Irv 168
Kuralt, Charles 149
KWGN-TV 233
KWK Radio 85
KYW Radio 34–35, 37
K-Zone 204–05

LaHood, Ray 84
Lajoie, Nap 46
Lamonica, Daryle 177
Landis, Kenesaw 14, 21, 54, 65, 74, 87, 91, 103, 115, 124–25, 134, 217
Lane Tech High School 53
Lardner, Ring 40, **42**, 44–45, 102
Larsen, Don 107, 143
Lasker, Albert 46, 47
Lasorda, Tommy 170
Law & Order 128
A League of Their Own 97
Leave It to Beaver 226
Leeds, William B., Jr. 69
Lefebvre, Ryan 155
Lemon, Bob 90
Leno, Jay 166
Leonard, John 112
Let's Make a Deal 162
Letterman, David 56, 128
Levitan, Paul 136
Liberty Broadcasting System 74, 109, 152, 215–16
Library of Congress 114
Lieb, Fred 40
Life magazine 201
Lincoln, Abraham 115
Lindbergh, Charles 73, 93–94

"little cat feet" 43
Little League 98, 131
Lockman, Whitey 110
Lolich, Mickey 171
The Lone Ranger 76, 96, 116
Long, Huey 94
Long, Russell 160
Lords of the Realm 159
Los Angeles Angels (of Anaheim)
 173, 223, 231
Los Angeles Dodgers 144–45,
 155, 159, 161, 170, 173, 197,
 199–200, 228, 231
Los Angeles Memorial Coliseum
 144–45, 154
Los Angeles Rams 159
Los Angeles Times 223
Louis, Joe 82, 125
Louis-Dreyfus, Julia 166
Lowry, "Peanuts" 90
Lynch, Stephen 196
Lynn, Fred 180

Macintosh commercial 209
Mack, Connie 212
Mack, Ted 128
MacNider, Hanford 69
MacPhail, Larry 82–83, 157, 200,
 218
Madden, John 173, 202
Madison Square Garden 53
Maglie, Sal 110
Mahoney, John 166
Major League 175
Major League Baseball Advanced
 Media 222
Major League Baseball Players
 Association 121, 163
Mann, Arthur 107
Mann Act 73
Manning, Tom 91
Mantle, Mickey 16, 19, 106, 113,
 141–42, 146–51, 153, 157, 164,
 176, 179, 188, 219–20, 229–31
Manuel, Barry 188
Marconi, Guglielmo 23–24
Marconiphone 53
Marcus Welby, MD 129
Marichal, Juan 221
Marine Corps 95
Maris, Roger 16, 19, 43, 90, 100,
 106, 142, 146–53, 162, 164,
 169–71, 179, 188, 198, 219–20,
 229–31, 236–37
MarketWatch 225
Marlboro Beer 208
Martin, Billy 112, 133, 157, 185,
 209
Martin, Ned 181
Martinez, Dennis 143
Martinez, Pedro 187
Marx, Groucho 64
M*A*S*H 78
Mathews, Gary 227
Mathewson, Christy 30
Mauch, Gene 90
Maverick 129
Mayo Clinic 83, 176, 240

Mays, Carl 21, 30–31
Mays, Willie 95, 104, 115–16, 118,
 122, 123, 131, 134, 162, 188, 219,
 230
Mazeroski, Bill 27, 147–48, 175
McCarthy, Joseph 121, 123, 220
McCarver, Tim 164, 172, 174, 189
McCormick, Robert R. 33–34,
 47
McCormick Foundation 34
McCovey, Willie 186
McDowell, Sam 186
McDuffie, Terris 124
McGeehan, Bill 14, 19, 41
McGraw, John 30
McGuire, Al 173–74
McGwire, Mark 153, 170, 188–
 89, 195–97, 220, 229, 231, 236
McLain, Denny 108, 165, 171, 186
McLendon, Gordon 109–10, 152,
 216
McLuhan, Marshall 123, 180
McMahon, Jim 191
McNally, Dave 193, 226
McNamee, Graham 17, 19, 40–
 41, 42, 43, 44–45, *52,* 54–55,
 65, 72–73, 79, 93
Medill, Joseph 33
Meet the Press 108
Melrose Place 202
Menken, H.L. 36, 40, 62
Meredith, Don 130, 156, 172
Merkle, Fred 30
Merriam, Dwight 83
Messersmith, Andy 193–94,
 226–27
Meusel, Bob 64
Meusel, Emil 38
Michaels, Al 172
Michel, Bob 84
Michelob Beer 208
Midwest Radio Central, Inc. 34
Miller, Marvin 107
Miller, Reggie 174
Miller Beer 209
Miller Brewing 208
Miller Park 209
Milwaukee Braves 139, 142, 144,
 174–75; *see also* Atlanta Braves
Milwaukee Brewers 175, 179, 199
Minneapolis Millers 83
Minnelli, Liza 93, 195
Minnesota Twins 186, 223
Minnesota Vikings 198
Minoso, Minnie 122, 217
Minow, Newton 162
Mississippi River 87
Mr. Belvedere 175
Mr. Smith Goes to Washington
 77, 91
Mitchell, George J. 197, 230
Mitchell Report 197, 230
Mize, Johnny 157
MLB Network 235–36;
 MLB.com 237
Mobile Oil 83, 200
Mod Squad 129
Modell, Art 161

Monday Night Baseball 174
Monday Night Football 127, 129,
 131, 156, 172, 182, 191, 210, 228
Montegna, Joe 166
Morgan, Joe 156, 174, 180, 183
Morgan, Mike 188
Morrison, Herbert 73–74
Morse code 89
Motorola 53, 81
Movie of the Week 129
Movietone News 73
Mrs. Goldberg 138
MTV 192
Mueller, Bill 172
Mueller, Don 110
Murcer, Bobby 157
Murderers Row 60, 63, 67, 70–
 71, 78, 146, 229
Murdoch, Rupert 191–92, 202
Murray, Bill 166
Murrow, Edward R. 93, 108, 121,
 220
Musial, Stan 164–65
Mutual Broadcasting System 83,
 85, 91, 109, 136, 152

Narragansett Beer 208
NASCAR 204
National Baseball Commission
 49
National Basketball Association
 (NBA) 66, 208, 211, 236
National Broadcasting Company
 (NBC) 60, 74, 91, 106, 109,
 116, 119–20, 126, 130, 135–37,
 143, 162, 177–78, 181–82, 190–
 91, 195, 201–02, 216, 218, 222,
 234
National Collegiate Athletic
 Association (NCAA) 66, 203,
 234
National Football League (NFL)
 66, 159, 162, 194, 202–03, 210,
 236
National Hockey League (NHL)
 66, 204
National League (MLB) 59, 65,
 80, 159, 163
National War Fund 97
The Natural 105, 133
Navy, U.S. 24, 26, 50, 85, 92
NBA *see* National Basketball
 Association
NBC *see* National Broadcasting
 Company
NBC Orchestra 94
NCAA *see* National Collegiate
 Athletic Association
Neely, Mark 155
Negro Leagues 64, 80, 124, 134
Nelson, Lindsey 111, 119
Ness, Eliot 48
Nestle 206–07
Nettles, Graig 185
network television, first 127
New Orleans Saints 161
New York Daily News 111, 179
New York Giants 31, 40–*42,* 54,

64, 79, 82, 91, 109–10, 115, 117,
  135, 140–42, 163, 215–16, 219,
  221
New York Jets 161, 177
New York Knicks 173
New York Mets 28, 159, 162–63,
  195, 199, 221, 228–29
New York, New York 195
New York Times 50, 81, 117, 119,
  158, 163, 189, 196, 204, 215,
  229, 238
New York Times Magazine 201
New York Tribune 29
New York Yankees 29, 31, 40–41,
  48, 54, 70–71, 79, 81–82, 91,
  99, 104, 106, 112, 120, 132, 134,
  137, 141, 146–47, 151–53, 157,
  159, 161–62, 172, 175, 179, 188,
  197–99, 201, 212, 214, 218–19,
  221, 223, 231, 239
Newark Eagles 115
Newark Sunday Call 30
Newcombe, Don 98, 103, 110,
  118, 122, 134, 140–43
News Corporation 204, 231
newsreels 73
NFL *see* National Football
  League
NHL *see* National Hockey
  League
Nickelodeon theaters 73
Nielsen, Arthur 209
Nielsen ratings 116, 189–91, 197–
  98, 209–10, 225, 229, 234, 235,
  237
night games 218–20, 229
Nightline 131, 153, 228
Nixon, Richard 87, 105, 123, 149
Nixon-Kennedy debate, televised
  121
Nolan, Gary 180
NY Journal 30

Oakland Athletics 165, 170–71,
  190, 196–97; *see also* Kansas
  City Athletics; Philadelphia
  Athletics
Oakland Raiders 161, 177
Obama, Barack 6, 19, 87, 124
Odom, Johnny "Blue Moon"
  225
O'Hara, Johnny 4, 95
The Old Man and the Sea 105,
  139
Old Style Beer 208
Olympics 130, 134, 159, 194, 210,
  215–16
O'Malley, Peter 228
O'Malley, Walter 103, 124, 137–
  38, 139–42
Omnicom 205
O'Neill, Buck 134
O'Neill, Harry 95
Orange Crush 76
Original Amateur Hour 137
Oswald, Lee Harvey 162
Ott, Mel 82
"out of left field" 104

Ovaltine 76
Owens, Jesse 125

Pabst Blue Ribbon Bouts 116
Packer, Billy 174
Pafco, Andy 110
Paige, Satchel 64, 124–25, 217
Paley, William 60, 121
Palmer, Jim 172, 174
Palmiero, Rafael 196
Pappas, Milt 150
Paramount 128
Parker, Dave 27
Parks, Rosa 123–25
Pathé, Charles 73
Payton, Walter 168, 191
PBS *see* Public Broadcasting
  System
Peabody Award 176
Pearl Harbor 89, 92, 95
Pepsodent 76
Perez, Tony 180, 225
The Perfect Season 189
Perils of Pauline 73
Perry, William "Refrigerator" 191
Petco Park 209
Philadelphia Athletics 73, 116,
  144; *see also* Kansas City Ath-
  letics; Oakland Athletics
Philadelphia Phillies 91, 95, 99,
  107, 117, 133, 137, 159, 163, 169,
  172, 198, 204, 216, 220
Philco 53, 75
Piazza, Mike 195
Piersall, Jimmy 179, 185
Piniella, Lou 112, 174, 185
Pipp, Wally 13, 37, 43, 63
PITCHf/x 203
Pittsburgh Pirates 16, 22, 26, 43,
  44, 54, 64, 79, 92, 97, 109, 119, 141,
  148, 178, 189, 218, 221
Piven, Jeremy 166
play-o-graph *14*
Plessy v. Ferguson 122
Polo Grounds *11*, 13, 20, *22*, 29–
  30, 37, *38*, 40, 82, 144, *147*, 162,
  184
Popular Mechanics 214
Post, Wally 219
Power, Vic 134
Presley, Elvis 136, 139
Pride of the Yankees 93, 105
Prince, Bob 90, 109
Prior, Mark 210
Proctor & Gamble 200
Prohibition 208
Providence Grays 58
Pryor, Richard 84
Public Broadcasting System
  (PBS) 195
Pulliam, Harry **49**

Quality Network 83
Queen Victoria 50
Queens of America 116

"rabbit ball" 113
RACEf/x 204

Radbourn, "Old Hoss" 58
Radio Corporation of America
  (RCA) 24, 32, 40, 60, 75, 93,
  119–20, 127, 130, 193, 218
Radio Hall of Fame 175
Radio Manufacturers Association
  81
Radiola-17 93
Raleigh Cigarettes 76
Ramis, Harold 166
Rat Patrol 129
Raytheon 154
RCA *see* Radio Corporation of
  America
RCA Building 94
Reagan, Ronald 19, 56, 87–**88**,
  90, 96, 105, 124, 131, 185, 213,
  227
recreations (game) **68**, 213–14
Reese, "Pee Wee" 98
Republican National Convention
  136
reserve clause 164
Rexall Drug Stores 76
Reynolds, Allie 157
Rice, Grantland 14, 29–31, **38**,
  90, 102, 121
Rice, Jim 180
Richardson, Bobby 147, 175
Rickard, Tex 39
Rickey, Branch 27–28, 97, 103,
  105, 115, 124–25, 131, 170, 177–
  78, 217
Rivers, Joan 202
Rizzuto, Phil 133, 142, 156–57,
  221
Roberts, Robin 133, 163, 208
Robins, Tim 166
Robinson, Frank 151, 231
Robinson, Jackie 97, 98, 100,
  103–04, 106, 110, 112, 115, 120,
  123–25, 126, 132, 134–35, 142–
  43, 157, 162, 177–78, 217, 219–
  20
Rockefeller, John D., Jr. 40, 65
Rocky King 129
Rogers, Will 104
Rogers Communications 228
Rolling Stones 162
Ronge, Chris 239
The Rookies 129
Roosevelt, Franklin D. 85, 92,
  104, 126
Rose, Pete 113, 180
Rose Bowl 32–33
Roselle, Pete 74, 159, 160–61
Rosen, Mitch 156, 238–39
Rossi, John P. 105
Rowswell, Rosey 56, 72, 109
Royal Pains 235
Ruby, Jack 162
Rudi, Joe 190, 226
Runyon, Damon 40, 102
Ruppert, Jacob 69
Rustun, Scotty 81
Ruth, Babe 6, 9, 12, 20, 21, 27,
  29–31, 37, 42–43, 48–50, 58–
  60, 63, 65, 67, 70, 72, 78–79,

82–83, 106, *113*, 146–*47*, 51, 184, 186, 188, 198, 206–07, 218, 220, 229–30, 236–37
Ryan, Quin 16, 17, 19, 35–37, 43, 44, 54–56, 65, 67, 90

St. Louis Browns 44, 48, 79, 96, 108, 118, 141, 169
St. Louis Cardinals 44, 80, 88, 96, 98, 118, 141, 148, 157, 159, 162, 164–65, 169, 171–72, 177–78, 198, 208, 238
Sam 'n' Henry 55
San Diego Padres 204
San Francisco Chronicle 196
San Francisco Giants 144, 187, 197, 204
Sandburg, Carl 43
Sandburg, Ryne 169
Sanford & Son 78
Santo, Ron 179
Sarnoff, David 39, 119
satellite radio 238
Saturday Night at the Movies 127
Saturday Night Live 166
Sauer, Hank 90
Sawyer, Eddie 133
Schenkel, Chris 116, 129
Schenz, Henry Leonard 215
Scherick, Edgar 116, 119, 130
Schiff, Adam B. 125
Schlitz Beer 118
Schmidt, Mike 231
Schulman, Paul 205
Scopes, John 62
Screen Actors Guild 89, 170
Scully, Vin 18, 19, 56, 64, 90, 99, 105–06, 112, 138, 143, 145, 154–56, 162, 166, 170–71, 179
Seabiscuit 73
Seaver, Tom 157, 186
See It Now 121
Segui, Diego 186
Seinfeld 210
Selig, Bud 196, 223, 230
September 11 195
Seven Days 205
The Shadow 96
Shannon, Mike 171–72, 183
Shea Stadium 93, 162, 195
Sheen, Charlie 175
Sherman Act 160
Shilling, Curt 196
Simmons, Curt 118
Simms, Phil 174
Simpson, Jim 176
Simpson, O.J. 194
The Simpsons 192, 202
Sims Act 73
Singletary, Mike 191
Singleton, Ken 214
Sisler, George 21, 37
60 Minutes 196
Skelly Oil 76
Skelton, Red 116
Skowron, "Moose" 147, 150–51
Smith, Gov. Alfred E. *147*
Smith, Bubba 208

Smith, Curt 70, 84, 96, 100, 143, 152
Smith, John 124
Smith, Red 106, 111
Snider, Duke 140, 143, 144, 219
Snyder, Frank 38
Snyder, Jimmy "the Greek" 153
Soldier Field 52, 69
Sosa, Sammy 153, 185, 188–89, 196–97, 220, 229, 231, 236
Spahn, Warren 95, 116
Spalding, Al 45
Speaker, Tris 54, 71
Spink, Alfred H. 44
spitball 13
The Sporting News 44–45, 79, 206
Sports Broadcasting Act of 1961 74, 145, 153, 160–62
Sports Illustrated 152, 215–16
sports talk radio 238
Sportsman's Park 20, 118, 178
Sportvision 202, 204, 206
spot news reporting 126
Springfield Body Corporation 53
Stagecoach 77
Standard Oil 65, 160
"Star Spangled Banner" 93
Stargell, Willie 27
stealing signs 215–16, 221
Steinbrenner, George 113, 161
Stengel, Casey 38, 72, 98, 112, 133, 139, 147, 152, 158, 174
steroids, steroid era 195–98, 230–32, 236–37
Stewart, Dave 170
Stockton, Dick 181
Stone, Steve 187–88, 211, 239
Storm, Hannah 233
Stram, Hank 172
Street & Smith Sports Business Journal 204
Studebaker 81
Summerall, Pat 202
Sunday Night Baseball 127, 131
Sunday Night Football 128
Super Bowl 209–10, 234
Suppan, Jeff 188
Supreme Court, U.S. 65, *86*, 100, 104, 119, 122–24, 141, 145, 160
surround sound 136
Sylvester, Johnny 49–50

Taft, Charles Phelps 46, 86
Taft, William Howard 19, 46, 66, *86*–87, 105
Taft Broadcasting Company 86
"Take Me Out to the Ball Game" 164, 166
TBS Television 227–28, 235; *see also* Turner Broadcasting System; WTBS Television
telegraph *11*, 20, *22*, *88*
teletype 213–14
televised baseball: color 115; first 120, 220
television: coast-to-coast coverage 134; close-ups 135; color

115, 119, 127, 135, 162, 201, 218; first images 119; graphics 35, 201–03; stereo 202; "super slow mo" 135; *see also* HD television
Telstar Satellite *61*, 134, 162
Texas Baseball Hall of Fame 169
Texas Instruments 154
Texas Rangers 87
Theismann, Joe 174
They Stand Accused 129
This Week in Baseball 151
Thomas, Dave "Showboat" 124
Thome, Jim 84
Thomson, Bobby 30, 110–11, 116, 121, 131, 135, 184, 215–17, 219–20
Thorne, Gary 155
Thursday Night Football 131
Tiant, Luis 180
Tierney, Robert 240
Tiger Stadium 90
Tilden, Bill 49
Time magazine 114, 227
Time Warner *see* AOL Time Warner
Tinker, Joe 46
RMS *Titanic* 5, 23, 24
TK-43 "big tube" camera 201, 218
TNT *see* Turner Network Television
Toast of the Town 128
Today Show 179
Toledo Mud Hens 46
The Tonight Show 128, 175, 202
Toolson v. New York Yankees 104, 123
Toronto Blue Jays 176, 212, 228
Totten, Hal 52, 54–55, 65, 67–68, 70, 72
Trachsel, Steve 189
transistor amplifier 154
transistor radio 145, 154
Transitone TH-1 53
Tribune Tower 47, 54, 136, 225
Trimble, Joe 149
Triple Crown 82, 142
Tropicana Field 209
Truman, Harry 122, 134
Trump, Donald 166
Tunney, Gene 61, 70
Turner, Ted 18, 190–94, 226–27, 231, 235
Turner Advertising Company 193
Turner Broadcasting System (TBS) 179, 210–11; *see also* TBS Television; WTBS Television
Turner Network Television (TNT) 228
TV Guide 190
Two and a Half Men 234
Tyson, Ty 90–91

Uecker, Bob 90, 156, 166, 174–75, 177, 179, 185, 209
UHF (ultra high frequency) 120

Understanding Media: The Extensions of Man 123
United Paramount Theaters 120, 129
United Press International 151
U.S. Army *see* Army, U.S.
U.S. Cellular Field 209
U.S. Navy *see* Navy, U.S.

Vanderbilt, William 40
Vaughn, Vince 166
VCR video player 192
Veeck, Bill, Jr. 48, 64, 97, 104, 124–25, 166, 179, 217, 219
Veeck, Bill, Sr. 48
Verkin, David 204
VHF (very high frequency) 120
Victrola 50
Vietnam War 143, 220
Villante, Tom 138
virtual advertising 204, 206
virtual placements 205
Visser, Lesley 233

Wagner, Honus 27, 83, 85
Waitkus, Eddie 133
Waldman, Suzyn 233
Walker, Moses Fleetwood 46
Wallace, Mike 196
The Walter Compton News 129
War of the Worlds 77–78
Warner Bros. Studios 129
Warren, Earl 122
Warren Commission 161
Washington, Herb 225
Washington Nationals 231
Washington Senators *42*, 54, 64, 113, 117, 119
Watergate 143
WBZ Radio 14
WCBS Radio 157, 233
WCBS-TV 115, 127
WCFL Radio 70, 169
WCOL Radio 171
WDAP Radio 34–35, 48
WDHD-TV 201
WEAF Radio 32–33, *41–42*, 43
WEBH Radio 70
The Wednesday Night Program 127
Weeghman, Charles 35, 46
Weeghman Park 104
Weeks, Sinclair 140
Welles, Orson 77
Wells, H.G. 77
WENR Radio 54
West Side Park 105
Western Union *88*
Westinghouse 24, 26, 32, *42*, 50

WFAN Radio 233
WFLD-TV 202
WFTZ-TV 133
WGES Radio 70
WGN Radio 15, 16, 19, 34–36, 43, 44, 48, 51, 54–56, 61–63, 67, 69, 83
WGN-TV 131–33, 136, 159, 168, 187, 205, 211, 228
WGY Radio 14
WGY-TV 120
WHA Radio 25
Wheaties 83, 120
White, Bill 157
Who Wants to Be a Millionaire? 210
Who's on First? 102, 105, 113–14
Wide World of Sports 130, 162
widescreen format 100, 111, 156
Wi-Fi 237
Wilhelm, Hoyt 95
Will, George 5, 107
Williams, Billy 186
Williams, Fred 49
Williams, Ken 37
Williams, Spencer 116
Williams, Ted 82–83, 92, 95, 112, 118, 133, 142, 177
Wilson, Hack 49
Winchell, Walter 94
WIND Radio 54
Wipeout 235
The Wireless Age 38
Wizard of Oz 77, 91
WJAZ Radio 15, 34–35
WJJD Radio 54
WJRJ-TV 193, 226
WJZ Radio 14, 29–30, *38*, 51
WKRC Radio 86
WLS Radio 37, 64, 70, 73, 83
WLW Radio 83
WMAQ Radio 15, 48, 52, 54, 56, 67–70, 79
WMCA Radio 216
WMGM Radio 111, 216
WMVP Radio 239
WNBC Radio 60
WNBC-TV 127, 220
WNEW-TV 202
WOAW Radio 37
WOC Radio 87, 89
Wolfe, Thomas 91, 107
Wood, George 58
Woods, Jim 109, 171
Woolf, Virginia 105
WOR Radio 83, 200
WOR-TV 133, 201, 228
World Series *11*, *14*, *22*, 29–30, *38*, 40–*41*, *42*, 43, 45, 48–50,

52, 54, 64–65, 68, 70, 73, 82–83, 85, 91, 97, 106, 116, 120, 127, 131–36, 140–42, 144, 146–48, 151–52, 157, 159, 162–64, 168–69, 171–72, 175, 177, 180–83, 184, 188, 190, 195, 198, 208, 210, 215, 217–20, 222–23, 229, 233–35
World Trade Center 121, 195
World War I 24, 33, 39, 44, 73, 91
World War II 79, 85, 91–94, 96–97, 101, 105, 108, 118, 120, 122, 127, 143, 146, 178, 189
World's Fair, Chicago 234
WOSU Radio 171
WPIX-TV 157, 228
WPOP Radio 212
WQJ Radio 37
WRCA Radio 33
WRET-TV 193–94
Wrigley, Philip K. 97, 131–32, 219
Wrigley, William, Jr. 15, 28, 36, 45, *47*–48, 54, 67, 131, 157, 212
Wrigley Building 34, 47, 54
Wrigley Chewing Gum 207
Wrigley Field 35, 43, *52*, 58, 60, 79–80, 92, 104, 132, 153, 166, 166, 168, 179, 184, 187, 205, 209, 211, 215, 229
Wrigley Field, West Coast 219
WSAI Radio 81
WSCR Radio 34, 156, 238–39
WTBS Television 18, 194, 227–28; *see also* TBS Television; Turner Broadcasting System
WTCG-TV 227
WTIC Radio 212
Wuthering Heights 77
WWJ Radio 90–91
WXYX Radio 83

X-Games 238

Yankee Stadium 16, 29, 40, 43, 58, 82, 102, 142, 146–*47*, 164, 184–85, 209
Yastrzemski, Carl 177, 180, 186
YES Network 231, 233
You Bet Your Life 173
Young, Cy 206
Yvars, Sal 215

Zenith Electronics 15, 34–35, 154
Zimmerman, Rod 84
Zworykins, Vladimir 119